MANAGEMENT for ATHLETIC/SPORT ADMINISTRATION:

Theory and Practice
SECOND EDITION

Francis J. Bridges, Ph.D.
Libby L. Roquemore, MBA

ESM BOOKS

MANAGEMENT FOR ATHLETIC/SPORT ADMINISTRATION:
Theory and Practice

Printing History:
ESM Books paperback textbook 2nd edition
First printing, June 1996

For any information about this book, including purchasing, contact:
ESM Books
Educational Services for Management, Inc.
235 E. Ponce deLeon Avenue, Suite 307
Decatur, Georgia 30030-3412
404-373-6386

ISBN 0-9623126-5-7
Library of Congress Catalog Card Number 96-85086

Printed in the United States of America

PREFACE

We are proud to publish the second edition of *Management for Athletic/Sport Administration—Theory and Practice*. The field of sport management continues to grow. Today, over 180 colleges and universities in the United States offer majors in sport management and many more schools offer selected courses in the field.

Since the publication of our first edition in 1992, interest in academic content has expanded, and this new edition reflects those concerns. We have relied on input from professors, reviewers and students as well as our own analysis to add four new chapters of material and to update and revise all the previous chapters. These changes have strengthened the text.

New chapters in this edition include a separate chapter on "Leadership" (Chapter 12); a comprehensive chapter on "Managing Change, Conflict and Stress" (Chapter 14); an informative chapter on "Performance Appraisal and Rewards" (Chapter 16); and the expansion of information technology into a chapter on "Management Information Systems" (Chapter 17).

The text is organized into five sections: "The Professional Perspective" (four chapters); "Planning and Decision Making Functions" (three chapters); "Organizing the Work Force" (three chapters); "The Human Side of Administration" (four chapters); and "The Controlling Process" (three chapters).

Special Features

Each chapter contains a number of special features designed to strengthen a student's understanding of management and his or her ability to apply this knowledge to the job of a sport manager:

1. Presentation of quality-tested subject matter in an *understandable* manner so that students can comprehend the material and maximize the benefit they receive from class lectures and outside study.

2. A comprehensive chapter on the "Legal Aspects of Sport Administration" (Chapter 4). This chapter provides information on how the field of sports law emerged, the issues relative to sports law, and how these issues have an impact on the different factions of the sports industry.

3. Optional pedagogical techniques at the end of each chapter provide flexibility for the instructor. *Critical Incidents* and *Assignments for Personal Development* are features which, when assigned, enhance class discussions and allow students to apply the theory and concepts presented in each chapter to real situations in sport administration.

4. A *Glossary of Key Terms* for each chapter highlights the important management topics students should know and helps students review chapter material.

5. Two *Practical Concepts in Management* are presented at the end of each chapter. These concepts reflect the practical, not theoretical, side of management. Most would agree that invoking good common sense is necessary when making organizational decisions—especially in that huge part of the manager's job when people are part of the situation. Concepts are ideas and not management rules, principles or theories.

6. This text also includes such traditional features as *Learning Objectives* at the beginning of each chapter to focus the student's attention; a concise *Summary* at the end of each chapter, and *Review Questions* to help students assimilate the content of the chapter.

For instructors using the text, there is a comprehensive *Instructor's Resource Manual (IRM)* and a Test Bank which contains two sets of questions (25 questions in each set) for each chapter. The *IRM* contains answers to all the Review Questions plus comments and suggestions about using the Critical Incidents and the Assignments for Personal Development.

Acknowledgments

Special appreciation goes to numerous professional colleagues in the United States who made contributions, reviewed materials, and gave encouragement to the writing of this text. Some of these associations span many years, and all listed have had an impact on the development of this material in either a tangible or inspirational way:

P. Stanley Brassie—Head, Department of Physical Education and Sport Studies, The University of Georgia;

Rex Brumley—retired Athletics Director, Broward Community College;

Nan Carney-Debord—Associate Director of Athletics, Ohio Wesleyan University;

Michael J. Cleary—Executive Director of the National Association of Collegiate Directors of Athletics;

Marygrace Colby—retired Assistant Director of Athletics, Santa Clara University;

Vincent Cullen—Athletics Director, Rhode Island Community College;

Kenneth E. Farris—Associate Director Emeritus of Athletics, University of Oklahoma;

Guy Lewis—Chairman, Department of Sport Administration, University of South Carolina;

Jack Lengyel—Athletics Director, United States Naval Academy;

James E. Murphy, III—Associate Director of Athletics and Chief Financial Officer, Georgia Tech;

Homer Rice—Assistant to the President and Director of Athletics, Georgia Tech;

Francis X. Rienzo—Director of Athletics, Georgetown University;

Thomas P. Rosandich—President, United States Sports Academy;

Joseph Schabacher—Professor Emeritus of Management, Arizona State University;

Helen Smiley—Director of Athletics, Western Illinois University;

Robert E. Smith—Athletic Business Manager, University of Oklahoma;

Don Tencher—Athletics Director, Rhode Island College;

Albert Twitchell—formerly of Rutgers University and St. Thomas University;

Al Van Wie—formerly Athletics Director, The College of Wooster, and Educational Consultant;

John W. Winkin—Baseball Coach, University of Maine (Orono);

Glenn Wong—Department Head, Sport Management Program, University of Massachusetts at Amherst.

Finally, we wish to thank Ms. Mary B. Brown and Mr. Neil Kilgore for their graphic arts and production expertise.

To you who teach this course, we hope you find *Management for Athletic/Sport Administration* (second edition) a useful resource to complement your knowledge, teaching talent and expertise in the field of sport management.

Francis J. Bridges
Libby L. Roquemore

ABOUT THE AUTHORS

Francis J. Bridges is Professor Emeritus of Management at Georgia State University. He received his Ph.D. from the College of Commerce and Business Administration at the University of Alabama. He also holds an M.S. in Industrial Management from Georgia Tech, a B.S. from Georgia Tech and a B.S. from the United States Merchant Marine Academy (Kings Point). In addition, Dr. Bridges did postdoctoral work at the Business School of Harvard University.

Dr. Bridges is the author or co-author of ten textbooks in the field of management. While a full-time professor at Georgia State, he received nineteen awards from alumni and student groups for teaching excellence.

In addition to teaching, Dr. Bridges served as Director of Intercollegiate Athletics for 23 years and was involved in coaching for over thirty years.

Dr. Bridges' special interest is speaking to American managers about the development of professionalism in the science and art of management. Annually he speaks to hundreds of managers throughout the U.S. Dr. Bridges will mark 24 years as a teaching staff member of the Management Institute sponsored each year by the National Association of Collegiate Directors of Athletics (NACDA) in 1996.

Libby L. Roquemore is Vice President and Chief Financial Officer of Educational Services for Management, Inc., a management training and consulting firm located in Atlanta, Georgia. She received her MBA degree in finance and BBA degree in economics from Georgia State University. For eighteen years Ms. Roquemore served on the staff of Georgia State University in intercollegiate athletics. During her career in intercollegiate athletics, she was an administrator of both men's and women's programs. She served as an officer in every level of the Association for Intercollegiate Athletics for Women (AIAW) and was active in the development and growth of women's intercollegiate athletics throughout the U.S. She was a Charter Member of the Council of Collegiate Women Athletics Administrators, a member of NACDA, and served on the Advisory Committee of the Broderick (now Honda-Broderick) Awards when it was formed under the NCAA. In addition, Ms. Roquemore is the author or co-author of four books in management and business and has worked with authors of other textbooks as a resource person and editor for materials developed for college courses.

CONTRIBUTING AUTHORS

Glenn M. Wong is the Department Head of the Sport Management Program at the University of Massachusetts at Amherst, where he is an Associate Professor. He also serves as Adjunct Professor in the University of Massachusetts Labor Relations Program. He holds a B.S. from Brandeis University, where he was captain of the basketball team, and a J.D. from Boston College Law School. A member of the Massachusetts Bar and the Labor Arbitration Panel of the American Arbitration Association, Professor Wong specializes in the area of sports law. He is the author of *Essentials of Amateur Sports Law* (1988, revised in 1994) and co-author of *Law and Business of the Sports Industries*. He has written numerous law review articles and currently authors a monthly column, "The Sports Law Report" for *Athletic Business* magazine. Professor Wong has been an invited speaker at over 50 national and local conferences on sports law and labor relations issues. He is a consultant for various athletic organizations and has served as a salary arbitrator for major league baseball.

Lisa Pike Masteralexis received her B.S. in Sport Management from the University of Massachusetts at Amherst and her J.D. from Suffolk University School of Law. She is an Assistant Professor of Sport Law in the Sport Management Program at the University of Massachusetts-Amherst, where she teaches courses in Amateur and Professional Sport Law as well as Labor Relations in Professional Sport. Professor Masteralexis recently received her college's Outstanding Teaching Award and was awarded a Lilly Teaching Fellowship. She is a member of the state bar of Massachusetts and serves as counsel to Sport Ventures International.

CONTENTS

SECTION II: PLANNING AND DECISION-MAKING FUNCTIONS

SECTION III: ORGANIZING THE WORK FORCE

SECTION IV: THE HUMAN SIDE OF ADMINISTRATION

SECTION V: THE CONTROLLING PROCESS

SECTION I

THE PROFESSIONAL PERSPECTIVE

Chapter 1.   Sport Management

Chapter 2.   Overview of Management

Chapter 3:   The Management Environment and Management's Ethical and Social Responsibilities

Chapter 4:   Legal Aspects of Sport Administration

CHAPTER 1

SPORT MANAGEMENT

After studying this chapter, **you will know:**

- The meaning of the word sport
- The economic impact of the sport industry on the total economy
- Something about academic programs in sport management
- Academic trends in sport management
- Why it is important to become computer literate
- The definition of management
- A major cause of management failure
- Names and contributions of important management pioneers
- How to classify management thought
- The current trend in management thought
- The nature of this book

Introduction

Sport management or the management of sport is not a new activity. Thousands of years ago games and contests were held. Organizers of these events were managers. References to games such as falconry, footracing, bow and sling contests, dancing, gambling and joking are found throughout the *Bible* (see Figure 1-1 for specific citations).

ACTIVITY	CITATION
FALCONRY	JOB: Chapter 41, Verse 5
FOOTRACING	PSALMS: Chapter 19, Verse 5 ECCLESIASTES: Chapter 9, Verse 11
BOW AND SLING CONTESTS	SAMUEL: Chapter 20, Verse 20 JUDGES: Chapter 20, Verse 16
DANCING	MATTHEW: Chapter 11, Verses 16 AND 17
JOKING	PROVERBS: Chapter 26, Verse 19 JEREMIAH: Chapter 15, Verse 17
GAMBLING	MATTHEW: Chapter 27, Verse 35

FIGURE 1-1: BIBLICAL REFERENCES TO GAMES (SPORTS)

Webster's Dictionary defines sport as *"that which amuses; diversion; outdoor game or recreation of athletic nature."*[1] Other definitions refer to sport as a specific diversion involving physical exercise and having a set form and body of rules.[2]

Professor Harold VanderZwaag of the University of Massachusetts at Amherst defines sport as *a competitive physical activity, utilizing specialized equipment and facilities, with unique dimensions of time and space, in which the quest for records is of high significance.*[3] We can add to this definition of sport that it involves mental activity as well as physical activity.

Today, the sport industry in the United States encompasses millions of people who directly participate in recreational activities, are members of teams, purchase sport equipment, and/or enthusiastically follow, in person or via television, various sporting events as spectators (see Figure 1-2).

The interest in sport activities is at an all time high in the United States and growing. The economic impact of the sport industry on the total economy is staggering. If you consider moneys spent for equipment, travel, tickets, injuries, admissions, insurance, supplies, memberships, etc., the sum is enormous. Figures 1-3 and 1-4 show some statistics for selected spectator sports and for sales of sporting goods products.

The sport industry has grown along with the interest in sport activities, creating a need for competent people to fill a wide variety of jobs at every level of all types of sports organizations.

One problem that faces future sport managers is an imbalance in the supply and demand for personnel to fill the available jobs. The number of men and women who wish to enter the sport industry in some capacity exceeds the current number of jobs available. Participants in job fairs frequently find two candidates for every open position, although entry-level jobs offer low pay and long hours to those who are hired. The message to students who desire a career in the sport industry is to get properly prepared so that they will have the needed skills and background to compete for jobs successfully.

ACTIVITY	ALL PERSONS		SEX		AGE							
	Num-ber	Rank	Male	Female	7-11 years	12-17 years	18-24 years	25-34 years	35-44 years	45-54 years	55-64 years	65+ years
Total	230,406	(X)	111,851	118,555	18,561	21,304	25,650	41,808	40,761	28,644	20,922	32,758
Number participated in:												
Aerobic exercising[1]	24,886	9	3,527	21,359	647	1,837	4,852	7,514	4,996	2,610	1,181	1,250
Backpacking[2]	9,229	24	6,196	3,033	779	1,280	1,501	2,477	2,067	850	170	104
Baseball	16,682	16	13,451	3,232	5,422	5,283	1,834	1,7244	1,658	511	87	164
Basketball	29,631	8	21,332	8,299	5,751	9,361	5,305	4,766	3,257	857	146	189
Bicycle riding[1]	47,918	3	24,562	23,357	11,204	8,794	4,551	8,808	6,980	3,441	2,030	2,111
Bowling	41,305	6	20,714	20,591	3,890	5,039	7,222	9,484	7,625	3,919	1,716	2,410
Calisthenics[1]	10,800	21	4,571	6,230	1,132	2,024	1,508	1,824	1,712	1,099	657	844
Camping[3]	42,698	5	23,165	19,533	5,302	5,336	4,767	10,000	8,580	4,135	2,355	2,224
Exercise walking[1]	64,427	1	21,054	43,373	1,848	2,816	5,690	12,525	14,045	10,185	7,782	9,536
Exercising w/ equip.[1]	34,900	7	16,901	17,999	425	3,025	6,595	9,105	7,065	4,257	2,217	2,210
Fishing—fresh water	45,333	4	30,449	14,885	4,623	4,945	4,946	9,913	9,561	5,044	3,156	3,146
Fishing—salt water	12,079	20	8,337	3,743	938	882	1,358	2,276	2,593	1,603	1,251	1,178
Football	14,723	17	12,879	1,843	2,495	5,227	3,410	2,203	1,032	202	94	60
Golf	22,633	10	17,212	5,421	840	1,692	3,074	5,192	4,620	3,180	1,956	2,080
Hiking	19,462	13	10,741	8,721	1,851	2,439	2,224	4,604	4,358	1,873	1,035	1,078
Hunting with firearms	18,455	14	16,303	2,152	540	1,695	2,575	4,658	4,282	2,380	1,311	1,014
Racquetball	5,407	25	4,161	1,246	162	550	1,704	1,590	936	380	71	15
Running/jogging[1]	20,283	12	11,429	8,854	1,727	4,008	4,088	4,393	3,489	1,565	680	331
Skiing—alpine/downhill	10,495	22	6,462	4,033	453	1,549	2,766	2,807	1,698	921	230	70
Skiing—cross country	3,727	26	1,738	1,989	298	469	273	530	1,084	580	314	179
Soccer	10,273	23	6,509	3,764	4,543	3,063	889	839	626	254	51	9
Softball	17.943	15	10,426	7,517	2,886	3,817	3,101	4,446	2,813	532	191	157
Swimming[1]	61,353	2	27,713	33,640	10,507	10,874	7,860	11,293	10,075	4,941	2,756	3,047
Target shooting	12,804	19	10,195	2,609	746	1,640	1,057	3,288	2,723	1,345	546	459
Tannis	14,197	18	8,302	5,896	1,003	2,464	3,375	3,076	2,357	1,091	558	274
Volleyball	20,477	11	9,777	10,700	1,333	5,443	4,402	4,961	3,150	823	252	112

X Not applicable.   [1]Participant engaged in activity at least six times in the year.   [2]Includes wilderness camping.   [3]Vacation/overnight.

FIGURE 1-2: PARTICIPATION IN SELECTED SPORTS ACTIVITIES: 1993.

(in thousands. For persons 7 years of age or older. Except as indiciated, a participant plays a sport more than once in the year. Based on a sampling of 10,000 households)

Source: National Sporting Goods Association, Mt. Prospect, IL, *Sports Participation in 1993: Series I* (copyright).

SPORT	Unit	1985	1987	1988	1989	1990	1991	1992	1993
Baseball, major leagues:[1]									
Attendance	1,000	47,742	53,182	53,800	55,910	55,512	57,820	56,852	71,237
Regular season	1,000	46,824	52,011	52,999	55,173	54,824	56,814	55,873	70,257
National League	1,000	22,292	24,734	24,499	25,324	24,492	24,696	24,113	36,924
American League	1,000	24,532	27,277	28,500	29,849	30,332	32,118	31,760	33,333
Playoffs	1,000	591	784	541	514	479	633	668	636
World Series	1,000	327	387	260	223	209	373	311	344
Players' salaries[2]									
Average	$1,000	371	412	439	497	598	851	1,029	1,076
Basketball: [3] [4]									
NCAA—Men's college:									
Teams	Number	753	760	761	772	767	796	813	831
Attendance	1,000	26,584	26,798	27,453	28,270	28,741	29,250	29,378	28,527
NCAA—Women's college:									
Teams	Number	746	756	754	765	782	806	815	826
Attendance	1,000	2,072	2,156	2,325	2,502	2,777	3,013	3,397	4,193
Pro:[5]									
Teams	Number	23	23	23	24	27	27	27	27
Attendance, total[6]	1,000	11,534	13,190	14,070	16,586	18,586	18,009	18,609	19,120
Regular season	1,000	10,506	12,065	12,654	15,465	17,369	16,876	17,367	17,778
Average per game	Number	11,141	12,795	13,419	15,088	15,690	15,245	15,689	16,060
Playoffs	1,000	985	1,091	1,397	1,077	1,203	1,109	1,228	1,322
Players' salaries:									
Average	$1,000	325	440	510	603	817	989	1,202	1,348
Football:									
NCAA college:[4]									
Teams	Number	509	507	524	524	533	548	552	560
Attendance	1,000	34,952	35,008	34,423	35,116	35,330	35,528	35,225	34,871
National Football League:[7]									
Teams	Number	28	28	28	28	28	28	28	28
Attendance, total[8]	1,000	14,058	[9]15,180	17,024	17,400	17,666	17,752	17,784	14,772
Regular season	1,000	13,345	[9]11,406	13,539	13,626	13,960	13,841	13,829	13,967
Average per game	Number	59,567	[9]54,315	60,446	60,829	62,321	61,792	61,736	62,352
Postseason games[10]	1,000	711	656	658	686	848	813	815	805
Players' salaries:[11]									
Average	$1,000	194	203	239	295	352	415	645	636
Median base salary	$1,000	140	175	180	200	236	250	325	330
National Hockey League:[12]									
Regular season attendance	1,000	11,621	12,118	12,418	12,580	12,344	12,770	14,158	16,106
Playoffs attendance	1,000	1,153	1,337	1,327	1,356	1,442	1,328	1,346	1,440
Horseracing:[13] [14]									
Racing days	Number	13,745	14,208	14,285	14,240	13,841	(NA)	13,644	(NA)
Attendance	1,000	73,346	70,105	69,949	69,551	63,803	(NA)	49,275	(NA)
Pari-mutuel turnover	Mil. dol.	12,222	13,122	13,616	13,867	7,162	14,094	14,078	(NA)
Revenue to government	Mil. dol.	625	608	596	585	611	624	491.3	(NA)
Greyhound:[15]									
Total performances	Number	9,590	11,156	12,904	13,393	14,915	(NA)	17,528	(NA)
Attendance	1,000	23,853	26,215	26,477	33,818	28,660	(NA)	28,003	(NA)
Pari-mutuel turnover	Mil. dol.	2,702	3,193	3,291	3,278	3,422	3,422	3,306	(NA)
Revenue to government	Mil. dol.	201	221	230	239	235	(NA)	204.2	(NA)
Jai alai:[13]									
Total performances	Number	2,736	2,906	3,615	3,835	3,620	3,610	3,288	(NA)
Games played	Number	32,260	38,476	47,716	(NA)	(NA)	(NA)	45,067	(NA)
Attendance	1,000	4,722	6,816	6,414	5,227	5,329	(NA)	4,634	(NA)
Pari-mutuel turnover	Mil. dol.	664.0	707.5	663.6	553.0	545.5	(NA)	425.9	(NA)
Revenue to government	Mil. dol.	50	51	44	39	39	39	30.1	(NA)

FIGURE 1-3: SELECTED SPECTATOR SPORTS: 1985 TO 1993. (continued)

SPORT	Unit	1985	1987	1988	1989	1990	1991	1992	1993
Professional rodeo:[15]									
Rodeos	Number	617	637	707	741	754	798	791	782
Performances	Number	1,887	1,832	2,037	2,128	2,159	2,241	2,269	2,245
Members	Number	5,239	5,342	5,479	5,560	5,693	5,748	5,760	6,415
Permit-holders (rookies)	Number	2,534	2,746	3,310	3,584	3,290	3,006	2,888	3,346

NA Not available. [1]Source: The National League of Professional Baseball Clubs. New York, NY, *National League Green Book*; and American League of Professional Baseball Clubs, New York, NY, *American League Red Book*. [2]Source: Major League Baseball Players Association, New York, NY. [3]Season ending in year shown. [4]Source: National Colegiate Athletic Assn., Overland Park, KS. For women's attendance total, excludes double-headers with men's teams. [5]Source: National Basketball Assn., New York, NY. [6]Includes All-Star gam, not shown separately. [7]Source: National Football League, New York, NY. [8]1987 through 1992 includes preseason attendance, not shown separately. [9]Season was interrupted by a strike. [10]Includes Pro Bowl, a nonchampionship game and Super Bowl. [11]Source: National Football League Players Association, Washington, DC. [12]For season beginning in year shown. Source: National Hockey League, Montreal, Quebec. [13]Source:Association of Racing Commissioners International, Inc. Lexington, KY. [14]Includes throughbred, harness, quarter horse, and fairs. [15]Source: Professional Rodeo Cowboys Association. Colorado Springs, CO., *Official Professional Rodeo Media Guide*, annual, (copyright).

FIGURE 1-3: SELECTED SPECTATOR SPORTS: 1985 TO 1993.

Source: Compiled from sources listed in footnotes.

SELECTED PRODUCT CATEGORY	1980	1985	1987	1988	1989	1990	1991	1992	1993	1994 proj.
Sales, all products	16,691	27,446	33,942	42,093	45,184	44,111	42,943	42,434	44,107	46,150
Annual percent change[1]	-1.4	4.0	10.9	24.0	7.3	-2.4	-2.6	-1.2	3.9	4.6
Percent of retail sales	1.7	2.0	2.2	2.5	2.6	2.4	2.3	2.2	2.1	2.1
Athletic and sport clothing[2]	3,127	3,376	4,645	10,736	11,557	11,382	12,057	10,101	9,643	9,952
Athletic and sport footwear[3]	1,731	2,610	3,524	3,772	5,763	6,263	6,300	6,242	5,919	6,019
Walking shoes	(NA)	263	512	752	1,237	1,509	1,375	1,375	1,367	1,408
Gym shoes, sneakers	465	656	693	783	1,125	1,177	1,181	1,113	936	936
Jogging and running shoes	397	572	475	460	515	519	555	574	574	551
Tennis shoes	359	470	367	353	508	582	597	589	471	462
Aerobic shoes	(NA)	178	401	327	415	389	381	376	318	305
Basketball shoes	86	185	169	226	293	428	449	456	407	407
Golf shoes	68	109	130	128	129	157	173	182	192	202
Athletic and sport equipment[3]	6,487	8,922	9,900	10,705	11,503	11,965	12,063	12,816	13,460	14,449
Firearms and hunting	1,351	1,699	1,804	1,894	2,139	2,202	2,091	2,533	2,565	3,027
Exercise equipment	(NA)	1,216	1,191	1,452	1,748	1,824	2,106	2,050	2,498	2,697
Golf	386	730	946	1,111	1,167	1,219	1,149	1,338	1,255	1,330
Camping	646	724	858	945	996	1,072	1,006	903	908	927
Bicycles (10-12-15-18+ speed)	(NA)	975	930	819	906	1,092	(NA)	(NA)	(NA)	(NA)
Fishing tackle	539	681	830	765	769	776	711	678	708	715
Snow skiing	379	593	661	710	606	606	577	627	629	677
Tennis	237	273	238	264	315	287	295	296	189	191
Archery	149	212	224	235	261	265	270	334	285	294
Baseball and softbell	158	176	173	174	206	217	214	245	303	309
Water skis	123	125	148	160	96	88	63	55	51	51
Bowling accessories	107	106	129	129	143	155	155	164	159	156
Recreational transport	5,345	12,539	15,873	16,880	16,360	14,502	12,524	13,275	15,085	15,730
Pleasure boats	1,718	6,753	8,906	9,637	9,319	7,644	5,862	5,765	6,282	6,722
Recreational vehicles	1,178	3,515	4,507	4,839	4,481	4,113	3,615	4,412	4,775	4,838
Bicycles and supplies	1,233	2,109	2,272	2,131	2,259	2,423	2,686	2,723	3,534	3,640
Snowmobiles	216	162	188	273	301	322	362	376	495	530

NA Not available. [1]Represents change from immediate prior year. [2]Category expanded in 1988; not comparable with earlier years. [3]Includes other products not shown separately.

FIGURE 1-4: SPORTING GOODS SALES, BY PRODUCT CATEGORY: 1980 TO 1994

[In millions of dollars, except percent. Based on a sample survey of consumer purchases of 80,000 households, except recreational transport, which was provided by industry associations. Excludes Alaska and Hawaii]

Source: National Sporting Goods Association, Mt. Prospect, IL. *The Sporting Goods Market in 1994*, and prior issues (copyright).

Academic Programs in Sport Management

Over 180 colleges and universities in the United States offer undergraduate and/or graduate programs in sport management. While program titles vary, the thrust of each program is to prepare students for careers in the world of sport. In just thirty years, academic programs in sport management have grown from one to the present number. Also, such programs already exist in other countries including Canada, Korea, Japan, Taiwan, Australia, France, England, South Africa and more.

Most sport management programs today are housed in the department of physical education and/or recreation, but it is not inconceivable to forecast that programs in the future may be initiated by Colleges of Business or by other units such as Public and Urban Administration. Colleges of Education might decide that sport management majors fit best into their education administration programs. Because of the popularity of sport management programs, the specific location of these programs may produce some real competition between academic departments and colleges on campus.

Sport management programs prepare graduates for entry into many facets of the sport industry: high school and college athletic administration; jobs in professional sports organizations; community recreational programs; amateur sport organizations; private clubs; sport programs in social agencies; arena and coliseum management; sport marketing and consulting firms; public relations and sport news media; fitness centers; and the sporting goods industry. While this is not an all inclusive list, it does indicate the wide range of opportunities within the sport industry. Some graduates may also pursue advanced degrees and return to the field as academic professors, researchers and consultants in sport management.

The world of sport is one of the last major industries in the United States to recognize the need to train people to become management professionals through offering a major in sport management at the collegiate level. Ohio University, in 1966, established a Sport Administration Program that is considered the first. Several other colleges, such as St. Thomas University (formerly Biscayne College) and St. John's University, followed shortly thereafter.

Several professional collegiate athletic organizations saw the need for improvement in athletic administration years ago. The National Association of Collegiate Directors of Athletics (NACDA) began sponsoring an annual three-day Management Institute in 1967. Over 2,000 sport administrators from community colleges to major universities and the top conferences in intercollegiate athletics have participated in these annual offerings. In addition, the College Athletic Business Managers Association (CABMA) sponsored management seminars for their members for many years.

Academic Trends in Sport Management

The major academic trends in sport management that affect programs today are these:

- An ever-increasing number of colleges are offering a major in sport management. Since 1992, approximately forty new collegiate sport management programs have been introduced in the United States alone.

- More full time faculty who teach sport management classes have an academic background in the field of sport management along with experience in the industry.

- A greater number of textbooks are being written specifically for courses in the sport management curriculum.

- There is a surge of scholarly research being published in academic journals. *The Journal of Sport Management*, the official journal of the North American Society for Sport Management, is just such a journal. The editorial policy of this journal states that it publishes articles that focus on the theoretical and applied aspects of management related to sport, exercise, dance and play. Other journals as well publish scholarly research of sport management professionals.

- Select programs in sport management are becoming more international in scope and study. One such program is being developed at Georgia Tech. The essential program components of Georgia Tech's proposed **Center for International Sport Business & Economics** are these:

  - A Master's level certificate specialization in "International Sports Business and Economics";

  - An International Research program on sports business and economics;

  - An annual International Conference on "Sports Business and New Technology"[4]

The program at Georgia Tech will be part of the Ivan Allen College of Management, Policy and International Affairs (see Figure 1-5 for a statement of this program's Mission and Objective). Among other sport management programs with international scope are those at the United States Sports Academy and The University of South Carolina.

STATEMENT OF MISSION

THE IVAN ALLEN COLLEGE OF MANAGEMENT, POLICY AND INTERNATIONAL AFFAIRS SEEKS TO ESTABLISH A PREMIER RESEARCH AND STUDY CENTER ON SPORTS ORGANIZATIONS AND THE SPORTS BUSINESS. ITS RESEARCH AND PROGRAMS WILL COVER THE INTERRELATIONSHIPS BETWEEN SUPPLIERS TO AND SUPPORTERS OF THE GLOBAL SPORTS INDUSTRY, AS WELL AS THE MANAGEMENT OF SPORTS ORGANIZATIONS. THIS CENTER WILL HAVE AN INTERNATIONAL FOCUS SPANNING AMATEUR AND PROFESSIONAL SPORTS ORGANIZATIONS. ITS INTERESTS WILL INCLUDE THE MANAGEMENT AND REGULATION OF LEAGUES AND INTERNATIONAL COMPETITIONS, THE SPONSORSHIP AND MANAGEMENT OF EVENTS AND FACILITIES, AND THE IMPACT OF SPONSORSHIP AND PROMOTION IN THE INDUSTRY AND BROADER SOCIETAL VARIABLES.

STATEMENT OF OBJECTIVE

TO BECOME AN INTERNATIONALLY RECOGNIZED AND SUPPORTED EDUCATIONAL AND RESEARCH ORGANIZATION WHOSE PROGRAMS WILL IMPROVE THE EXECUTIVE LEADERSHIP AND VALUE-ADDED EFFECTIVENESS THROUGHOUT THE WORLDWIDE SPORT INDUSTRY.

FIGURE 1-5: STATEMENTS OF MISSION AND OBJECTIVE OF GEORGIA TECH'S CENTER FOR INTERNATIONAL SPORTS BUSINESS & ECONOMICS

Source: Bulletin of the Georgia Tech Center for International Sports Business & Economics, 1996.

- More collegiate sport management programs are becoming involved in the accreditation process established by a Joint Task Force composed of members from NASPE (National Association for Sport and Physical Education) and NASSM (North American Society for Sport Management). Standards for voluntary Accreditation were approved by a NASPE Delegate Assembly in 1992. According to Dr. P. Stanley Brassie, former Co-chair of the Joint Task Force and currently Head of Sport Studies at the University of Georgia, 35 sport management programs are in varying stages of preparing folios required as part of the accreditation process. Dr. Brassie also reports that, as of early 1996, three undergraduate, five masters programs and two doctoral programs have been approved for accreditation. Students should understand that accreditation requirements relate primarily to curriculum standards and to the need to have qualified, full-time faculty working with the sport management programs.

Much change has occurred in the sport industry over the last decade and more is to come. Sport management programs, by necessity, have changed as well. This change involves staying abreast on new issues, new products, new legal decisions, changing legislation, new governance organizations, mergers and more. Sport management programs adapt to change by offering new courses, engaging in research projects, reviewing current case studies and reading expert opinions on timely topics.

Of particular concern in the future is the preparation of students for the electronic age of communications (see Chapter 17). Most organizations today desire managers and staff personnel that are computer literate and well versed on Information Technology (IT). *Information Technology is computer and communications technology and its applications.* The sport industry, like all major industries, will rely heavily on electronic communications in conducting its business. Sport management programs will have to prepare their students by offering a curriculum which includes courses that meet this challenge.

The Study of Sport Management

The study of management as applied in the sports world is the same as the study of management as applied to running IBM. There are many myths or misunderstandings about the meaning of management. For example, we read about sport management jobs such as facilities manager, marketing (ticket) manager, equipment manager, spa manager, recreation manager, business manager, etc. These are misleading job titles because the only thing one manages is **people**. Managers often have *responsibility* for the control and use of facilities, moneys, equipment and other resources, but you manage people. The most challenging job in any organization is that of a manager who is held totally responsible for results as he or she tries to use human and other resources effectively and efficiently.

Management is defined as the achievement of predetermined objectives working through others (employees). This is a hint that just being a knowledgeable specialist in any given field, such as a certified public accountant, does not directly correlate with being an effective manager.

The subject of management is broad and includes hundreds of topics. Not everyone succeeds in management and not everyone should be a manager. But if you are willing to study and prepare; you enjoy a challenge and excitement; and you want to be different, perhaps a career in sport management is for you.

The Need for Professionals in Management

Historically over ninety-eight percent of all first time managers are placed in their first supervisory jobs without being trained to manage first. This "sink or swim" approach is inexcusable and happens in organizations throughout the world everyday. Can you imagine hiring a head football coach who has no knowledge of the game? Also, about eighty percent of all first time managers are promoted upward from the ranks of nonmanagement employees. The best of nonmanagement employees tend to be selected for new management jobs, often leaving the organization shy one excellent employee and not happy with the new manager's performance. The failure to train people to be professional managers is the number one cause of management failure in the United States. This practice is common in the world of sport as well as in business and government. It behooves students to learn all they can about the subject of management. Knowing the subject does not guarantee success when one graduates and goes into a sport management position, but it gives one a distinct "edge" over those recently hired or promoted who lack management knowledge.

There is a shortage of competent professional managers in every type of organization at every management level. Managers, men and women, who really know the subject of management and know how to use resources effectively and produce timely and efficient results in a quality-oriented way are always at a premium. Professional managers pride themselves on the results they achieve and on the full development of the personnel they manage, just as head coaches are judged on their won-loss records and on how well they develop the potential of their student-athletes. Professional managers accept total responsibility for outcomes, good and bad, and look forward to the challenge of each new day. Do you think all managers have this attitude?

The Management Movement

Management as a practice has existed since the creation of formal organizations. Thousands of years ago mankind decided that more could be accomplished through organized group effort than through individual effort. People in charge of group effort, no matter what the title given to them, were managers. These managers had the power to direct and control human activity. While the evolution of management as a formal discipline spans centuries, the emergence of general theories of management is relatively recent.

As previously mentioned, the first academic programs in sport management in the United States did not originate until the 1960s. Management did not emerge as a recognized discipline until the Twentieth Century, and it was not taught as an academic subject in colleges in the United States until the 1920s. In the beginning, the stress was on industrial management rather than on general management. This is understandable since this country's growth and dominance as a world power was based on its newly realized industrial might.

By the 1940s, collegiate schools of business were in vogue and management became a major field of study. By the 1950s, colleges offered courses in general management and stressed that management is a *basic process*. In effect, this means that *managers in any type of organization, located anywhere, engage in the basic process of management as they work through people to achieve objectives. This basic process involves the functions of planning, organizing, implementing and controlling activity.*

Pioneers in Management

The modern management movement began over 100 years ago. Between 1880 and 1920 about twenty individuals who pioneered management theories and techniques routinely practiced today started their work. Prior to that time, all the way back to the beginning of recorded history, groups and individuals made contributions to the development of management. Figure 1-8, entitled "Selected Highlights of American Management Development," shows some of the major contributions to the development of management from 1900 to the mid-1980s.

From this listing of pioneers the most important individuals, in a modern sense, are Frederick W. Taylor, Frank Gilbreth, Lillian Gilbreth, Henri Fayol, Henry L. Gantt and Elton Mayo. These management pioneers were well known in their own time and made a lasting impact on the practice of management today.

Frederick W. Taylor (1856-1915) is considered the "Father of Scientific Management." He was born in Germantown, Pennsylvania, and received a graduate degree in mechanical engineering from Stevens Institute in 1883. As a side point, Taylor won the United States Amateur Doubles Tennis Championship in 1881.

Taylor's management training was gained from his own observations and the experiments he performed to discover better ways to manage while employed as Chief Engineer at Midvale Steel Company in Philadelphia. After leaving Midvale, he worked as a consulting engineer to management seeking to use time and motion studies to determine how long a worker should take to perform any given task; to develop uniform standards for work; to find a method for matching workers to jobs (allowing for differences in skill); and to learn better ways to supervise and motivate workers.

Taylor wrote extensively on his "Taylor System" of management, and he defended it before dubious critics on many occasions. When Taylor went into a company to work, he attempted to accomplish these four things:

1. Increase physical output.

2. Decrease unit production costs.

3. Lessen employee fatigue

4. Increase wages through increased profits.

Taylor stressed cooperation between labor and management, and he advocated individual rewards for productivity above the standard. It was Taylor's goal to focus attention on increasing the size of the surplus rather than on the division of it between management and workers.[5] Taylor's principles of management are stated simply in Figure 1-6.

1. Develop a science for each element of a man's work, which replaces the old rule-of-thumb method.

2. Scientifically select and then train, teach, and develop the workman, whereas in the past he chose his own work and trained himself as best he could.

3. Heartily cooperate with the men so as to insure all of the work being done in accordance with the principles of the science which has been developed.

4. There is an almost equal division of the work and the responsibility between the management and the workmen. The management take over all work for which they are better fitted than the workmen, while in the past almost all of the work and the greater part of the responsibility were thrown upon the men.

FIGURE 1-6: TAYLOR'S PRINCIPLES OF SCIENTIFIC MANAGEMENT

Source: Frederick W. Taylor, *Principles of Scientific Management* (New York: Harper & Bros., 1991), pp. 36-37.

Taylor developed an incentive plan, called Taylor's Differential Piece Rate Incentive Plan, which was widely accepted by industry. Today this plan is viewed as an example of traditional motivation theory where pay is directly related to job performance or productivity.

Taylor defined "scientific management" as the combination of his four principles (see Figure 1-6). Taylor's system of scientific management was more philosophical and conceptual than mechanical; and the significance of his contribution to management was that he not only assimilated theories, but implemented them and proved them workable.

Frederick W. Taylor's major legacy to management was the mental revolution his system spawned. His system required research to establish standards for all elements of work. It required planning and control to make the system function properly, and it brought about a new cooperation between management and labor to achieve greater benefits for both.

Contemporaries of Taylor, **Frank Gilbreth** (1868–1924) and **Lillian Gilbreth** (1878–1972) were an extraordinary couple, well matched in interests and complementary in abilities. Lillian assisted Frank with his work on motion study, work which paved the way for modern applications of job simplification, meaningful work standards and incentive wage plans.

Frank Gilbreth used film and timing devices to eliminate wasted motion from any and every job. It was his lifelong quest to find the best way to do any task. In finding this, he felt he could eliminate wasted motion and lessen worker fatigue while simultaneously increasing output and improving workers' pay. He coined the term "therblig" for each of the seventeen basic motions ("therblig" is Gilbreth spelled backwards with the "th" transposed). Frank Gilbreth is considered the "Father of Motion Study," but his fame did not come until after he died in 1924.

Lillian Gilbreth, considered the "First Lady of Management," worked with her husband during his many experiments, but she had unique talents in psychology and management herself. After his death, she pursued a career as a management consultant and college professor. Lillian was highly educated and interested in the human side of management. Her training in psychology led her to work on fatigue in the workplace and to help retrain crippled soldiers who returned from World Wars I and II. She was a pioneer in adapting jobs and findings jobs for handicapped people.

Among the techniques the Gilbreths developed in their work were process charts and flow diagrams; a card system on personnel that predates merit-rating systems; many technical devices for measuring motion in timed, sequential steps; and using written instructions to lessen confusion and misunderstanding. But the contributions of the Gilbreths to scientific management go beyond motion study. Both of the Gilbreths were concerned with the development of workers to their fullest potential through better, more effective training; improved work methods; better work environments and tools; and a healthy psychological viewpoint.

Lillian outlived Frank Gilbreth by 48 years and worked throughout the remainder of her life to benefit both the physical and mental health of workers. When she died in 1972 at the age of 94, she had an earned doctorate in psychology from Brown University plus twenty-six honorary doctorates. Her doctoral dissertation, *The Psychology of Management*, was published as a book. Lillian had a full life as a psychologist, lecturer, teacher, poet, industrial engineer, management consultant, college professor and the mother of twelve children.

The "Father of Modern Management Theory" was a Frenchman, **Henri Fayol** (1841–1925). In 1916, Fayol wrote (in French) a classic book called *General and Industrial Management*. Had this book been translated into English before the late 1940s, Fayol might have been more important to the development of management thought than Taylor.

Fayol was an executive in a French mining company and all his work dealt with the executive managerial role (as opposed to Taylor's work which dealt with the operative level of management). Fayol began at the top and worked downward; Taylor worked from the lowest level of management upward.

Fayol used the word "administration" throughout his work. He defines *administration as observing the general principles of planning, organizing, commanding, coordinating and controlling*, which are his functions of management.

Fayol provided the first complete theory of management. He defined the functions of management clearly and completely and called them "universal," meaning applicable, to all forms of group activity (a concept known as the Universality of Management). Fayol established fourteen management principles (see Figure 1-7) necessary for the effective practice of management. Finally, Fayol believed that management should be taught in the schools to everyone from elementary school on up. This belief in management education led him to develop his management theory.

1. **Division of Work:** This means "Specialization." The object of division of work is produce more and better work with the same effort.

2. **Authority and Responsibility:** Authority is the right to give orders and the power to exact obedience. Responsibility is a corollary of authority: Authority is not to be conceived separately from responsibility.

3. **Discipline:** This is essentially obedience, application, energy behavior and outward marks of respect. The best means of establishing and maintaining discipline: good superior (supervisors or managers) at all levels; agreements as clear and fair as possible, and penalties judiciously applied.

4. **Unity of Command:** An employee should receive orders from one superior only. Dual commands are a constant source of conflict.

5. **Unity of Direction:** All effort of everyone in the organization should be focused on the same objective.

6. **Subordination of Individual Interest to General Interest:** The interest of one employee or a group of employees must not prevail over the interest of the concern as a whole.

7. **Remuneration of Personnel:** The price of services rendered: time rate, job rates, or piece rates. All rewarding of effort (remuneration) should be fair and reasonable.

8. **Centralization:** The individual industry should find the optimum degree of centralization or decentralization. Increasing the importance of the subordinate's role is to decentralize, to reduce it is to centralize.

9. **Scalar Chain:** Fayol treats the line of authority as links in a chain. Here he suggested a bridge between two levels of subordinates allowing them to communicate (known as Fayol's "gang plank").

10. **Order:** Social order—there must be an appointed place for every employee and every employee be in his appointed place.

11. **Equity:** Fairness that results from a combination of kindliness and justice that leads to loyalty.

12. **Stability of Tenure of Personnel:** Instability of tenure is both a cause and effect of bad management. Successful firms have stability of personnel.

13. **Initiative:** The power of thinking out and executing plans and ideas is initiative. A superior manager allows subordinates to do this. It brings great satisfaction to employees and is a source of strength for business.

14. **Esprit de Corps:** There is strength in unity and harmony. Real management talent is needed to coordinate effort, encourage initiative, use each man's abilities, and reward each employee's merit without causing jealousy or disrupting harmonious relations.

FIGURE 1-7: HENRI FAYOL'S FOURTEEN UNIVERSAL PRINCIPLES OF MANAGEMENT

Source: Condensed from Henri Fayol, *General and Industrial Management*, trans. Constance Storrs (London: Isaac Pitman and Sons, 1949).

Henry L. Gantt (1861–1919) was a contemporary and protégé of Taylor who added a dimension of humanism to scientific management. In his later years, Gantt pleaded for wider recognition of the human factor in management and for recognizing that factors other than money served as incentives to influence employee behavior.[6]

Gantt's contributions to management development were not original ideas, but rather refinements that added greatly to the progress and meaning of scientific management. His first of four major contributions was the Gantt Chart, still used today to compare actual to planned performance (see Chapter 5 for a complete discussion of the Gantt Chart).

Gantt's second major contribution was a wage incentive system known as a task-bonus system. It guaranteed the worker a day wage for output less than a standard, offered a bonus in addition to the day wage for reaching the standard, and further rewarded the worker for exceeding the standard.[7]

Gantt's other two significant management contributions are both based on humanism: insisting that people be taught, trained and led to work rather than driven to do so, and placing emphasis on service rather than on profits. Gantt believed the latter was essential for our business system to survive, and he did more to advance the theory of industrial responsibility than any of his predecessors.

Harvard professor **G. Elton Mayo** added knowledge of social factors gained from experiments to management theory. Between 1927 and 1947, Mayo conducted experiments at the Department of Industrial Research at Harvard. The program began as a result of the famous Hawthorne Studies that Mayo conducted at Western Electric's Hawthorne Works near Chicago. The Hawthorne Studies were the first full-scale research studies which were scientifically constructed, carefully and completely documented, conducted by trained professional researchers, and which received the full cooperation of management and labor. Financing was provided by the Rockefeller Foundation.[8]

The impact of Mayo's work on the development of management was astonishing. Within ten years, personnel and human relations managers cited Mayo's work to support the belief that each individual's problems were so important to the efficient operation of an organization that every manager should be concerned with personnel and human relations.[9] The studies were established to test the effect of working conditions on productivity. Mayo's finding was that something other than working conditions affected the workers' behavior—a "something else" called social factors such as self-esteem, morale, status and good working relationships. The end product of the Hawthorne Studies was the growth of a whole profession of behavioral scientists: personnel counselors, industrial chaplains, sensitivity trainers, group dynamicists, sociogram analysts, nondirective interviewers, role-playing instructors, critical incident teachers, industrial psychologists and sports psychologists. All these behavior specialists initiated the ongoing effort to satisfy management's need to create work environments conducive to maximum long-term productivity.[10]

This brief look at some of the forerunners of modern management should help students appreciate techniques and practices still used today. Gilbreth's studies of human activity on film led the way for analysis of athletic endeavors on film, which is a whole industry today. Gantt's visual control chart is used by organizations now when scheduling facilities, activities or events. Recognizing the importance of departmental and team morale has its roots in the work of Mayo, Lillian Gilbreth and others. Mrs. Gilbreth's pioneering work in adapting jobs for handicapped people was a factor in creating athletic competition for these people. The stress on organizations of all types to accept social responsibility, develop acceptable ethical behavior, and provide service as a primary objective can be traced to the work of Henry L. Gantt. Taylor's application of his scientific method to operational activities and his determination to establish fair performance standards have widespread use in the sport industry today. Fayol's universal principles of management include many that have become associated with sport teams and the sport industry: such as specialization (football players and teams as well as coaches specialize in defense, offense, kicking, etc.); harmonizing individual goals with organizational (team) goals; equity of opportunity across gender and ethnic lines; and *esprit de corps*, that spirit of unity and harmony that is often the difference in athletic competition.

Approx. Time	Individual or Group	Significant Management Contribution(s)
1900	Frederick W. Taylor	Scientific management; systems applications; need for cooperation between labor and management; high wages; equal division of work between labor and management; functional organization; cost system; methods study; time study; work standards
	Frank B. and Lillian M. Gilbreth	Science of motion study; therbligs; human relations; psychology; reducing fatigue; retraining handicapped for new jobs
1901	Henry L. Gantt	Task and bonus system; humanistic approach to labor; Gantt chart; management's responsibility for training workers
1910	Hugo Munsterberg	Application of psychology to management and workers
	Harrington Emerson	Efficiency engineering; twelve principles of efficiency
1911	Harlow S. Person	Initiated first scientific management conference in U.S.; gave academic recognition to scientific management
	J. C. Duncan	First college text in management
1915	H. B. Drury	Criticism of scientific management reaffirmed initial ideas
	R. F. Hoxie	Criticism of scientific management reaffirmed initial ideas
	F. W. Harris	Economic lot size model
	Thomas A. Edison	Devised war game to evade and destroy submarines

FIGURE 1-8: SELECTED HIGHLIGHTS OF AMERICAN MANAGEMENT DEVELOPMENT

Approx. Time	Individual or Group	Significant Management Contribution(s)
1916	Henri Fayol	First complete theory of management; functions of management; principles of management; universality of management concept; basic process school of management thought; recognized need for management to be taught in schools
1923	Oliver Sheldon	Developed a philosophy of management; principles of management
1924	H. F. Dodge H. G. Romig W. A. Shewhart	Use of statistical inference and probability theory in sampling inspection and in quality control by statistical means
1927	G. Elton Mayo	Sociological concept of group behavior; Hawthorne Effect; concept of morale
1930	Mary P. Follett	Managerial philosophy based on individual motivations. Group process approach to solving managerial problems
1931	James D. Mooney	Principles of organization recognized as universal; named scalar principle
1938	Chester Barnard	Theory of organization; emphasis on systems; sociological aspects of management; need for communication
	P. M. S. Blackett, et al/British	Operations research
1943	Lyndall Urwick	Collection, consolidation and correlation of principles of management
	Abraham Maslow	Hierarchy of needs motivation theory
1947	Max Weber	Organizational theory called bureaucracy
1951	Ralph C. Davis	Three categories of objectives; primary objective is service
1954	Peter F. Drucker	Management is a practice and should focus on results; humans are greatest resource, technology just a tool
1950s	Frederick Herzberg	Motivation theory based on hygiene and motivator factors; job enrichment
1957	Northcotte Parkinson	Humorous look at administration; Parkinson's Law: Work expands to fill the time allowed for it

FIGURE 1-8: SELECTED HIGHLIGHTS OF AMERICAN MANAGEMENT DEVELOPMENT

Approx. Time	Individual or Group	Significant Management Contribution(s)
1960	Douglas McGregor	Theory X and Theory Y views of workers and managers
1961	Rensis Likert	Participative management
1962	Chris Argyris	Sensitivity training for managers
1964	Victor H. Vroom	Expectancy theory of motivation
1971	Ernest Dale	Empirical school of management theory
1981	William Ouchi	Theory Z system of management
1985	Gifford Pinchot, III	Coined term "intrapreneurs" for new type of corporate manager who runs own business within framework of large corporation

FIGURE 1-8: SELECTED HIGHLIGHTS OF AMERICAN MANAGEMENT DEVELOPMENT

Source: Based on Claude S. George, Jr., *The History of Management Thought*, (Englewood Cliffs, NJ: Prentice-Hall, Inc., 1968).

Classifying Management Thought

The chronological evolution of management has not ended, but instead has given way to a combination of ideas, principles and guidelines. These are integrated into different approaches to the study and practice of management, usually called "Schools of Management Thought."

In 1961, management scholar Harold Koontz termed the existing six different approaches to the study of management "The Management Theory Jungle".[11] In 1980, he revised the number upward to these eleven:

1. Empirical or case study approach
2. Interpersonal behavior approach
3. Group behavior approach
4. Cooperative social system approach
5. Sociotechnical systems approach
6. Decision theory approach
7. Systems approach
8. Mathematical or "management science" approach
9. Contingency or situation approach
10. Managerial roles approach
11. Operational theory approach[12]

The best summation of this surplus of theories is that **there is no one best way to manage**. In order to assimilate the evolution of management theory and see the direction of its future, this text considers these five schools of thought:

1. Traditional or "scientific management" approach

2. Behavioral approach

3. Basic process approach

4. Quantitative or management science approach

5. Synergistic systems approach

Traditional or "Scientific Management" Approach. This is the production or shop management orientation dedicated to reducing waste and improving efficiency. Taylor, the Gilbreths, Gantt and their followers were the instigators of this approach. Now more of a systematic management approach than a scientific one (due to the technical prowess and advances in the 1990s), it is especially necessary to management today to stem any fall in the productivity rates of American manufacturers to keep them competitive with foreign producers. The shortcoming of this approach is its assumption that people are mostly interested in earning more money; but the advantages still pertain to today's economy: reduce waste and promote production efficiency.

Behavioral Approach. Historically, Gantt led the trend toward humanism in management. People as individuals are the center of any cooperative effort (managers manage people). Managers in the behavioral school concentrate on the workers and their interpersonal relationships. Behaviorists study motivation; group dynamics; morale; individual needs, wants and desires of employees; communication, and leadership techniques. This approach uses all the social sciences: psychology, sociology, social psychology and anthropology. These theorists view the business environment as a social organization where effort can be maximized through better human relations. Proponents include Munsterberg, Gantt, Mayo, Mary Parker Follett, Oliver Sheldon, Chester Barnard and the motivation theorists like Maslow and Herzberg.

Basic Process Approach. Based on Henri Fayol's writing and work, this school of management thought is fundamental to all others. Management is a basic process. All managers, anywhere in the world, in any kind of organization (profit seeking and nonprofit; capitalist or socialist) engage in working through people to accomplish predetermined goals and objectives using the same functions of management (the basic process). Theorists differ on the names of these functions, and they have been increased over time to divide those dealing directly with personnel (such as staffing and directing for the general term implementing); but the theory is that the process or functions of a manager are universal: planning, organizing, implementing and controlling.

Quantitative or Management Science Approach. This school of management thought is often called the mathematical or operations research approach because of its emphasis on the development of mathematical models to simulate management situations and test management hypotheses. It began in Britain in 1938 as operations research for use in fighting World War II, but has grown tremendously since the war because of computers which facilitate computations and the testing of models. The quantitative approach stresses logic and objectivity in making decisions and is of help to management in resolving technical problems. Since many management problems involve people, however, there are limitations to the use of mathematical models.

Synergistic Systems Approach. The real mission of today's managers is to combine the resources under their direction so effectively and efficiently that, over time, the value of the end result is greater than the sum of the values of the resources used. This is "management synergy." Proponents of the synergistic system school study management by combining the parts of the system under the assumption that the whole is greater than the sum of its parts. The other schools of thought we have discussed work the opposite way: They study management by dividing the whole into its parts, assuming the whole is just equal to the sum of its parts.

Synergistic managers deal with all the internal and external variables an organization faces; identify all the relevant factors needed to achieve preset objectives; and discover the maximum way to synthesize (combine) these parts into a greater whole.

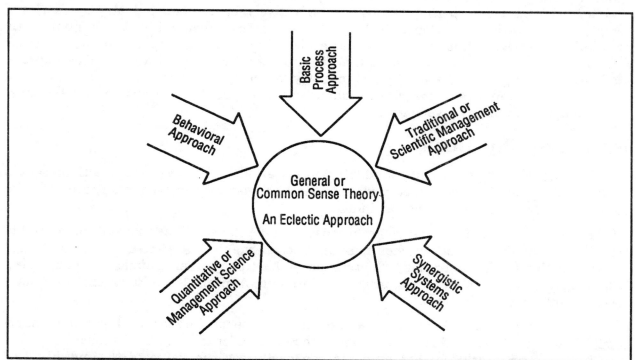

FIGURE 1-9: THE CONVERGING APPROACHES TO MANAGEMENT

The Emerging Current Trend in Management Thought

The latest school of management thought has been called *eclectic, situational, a contingency approach, or a general theory of management.* It is a compilation of relevant methods, techniques and theories drawn from all the existing schools of thought and approaches to management applied with a liberal use of common sense (see Figure 1-9). This "common sense approach" to management uses mathematical techniques to solve quantifiable problems and relies on motivation and leadership techniques to gain workers' respect and cooperation. It depends more on the **art** of management than on the **science** in applying experience and learned principles and concepts.

This trend of management thought makes having a personal philosophy of management a necessary tool to achieve managerial success. Guided by convictions based on theories and methods tested over time, today's managers can be consistent in dealing with employees (something both employees and government regulations require). They will pick and choose the parts of management history and management thought they feel comfortable applying (their personal art of management). Stress and stress-related problems encountered by many modern managers can be reduced by not trying to imitate a style of management that does not suit one's personality and/or philosophy.

The contingency approach to management recognizes that not every person or every situation responds to the same management style. Managers manage individuals and must tailor a management approach to the needs, wants and desires of each individual under their supervision. This is perhaps shown most effectively for the sport industry by a series of commercials showing notoriously volatile head coaches musing about the humanistic approach they must assume to reach a star athlete. In summary, the trend in management is to use the approach that best suits the situation and the people involved. This requires students of management for any type of industry to know as much about management and the various techniques and theories in management as possible in order to find the most effective approach in any given situation.

Nature of This Book

By reviewing the "Contents," students will get an idea of the major subjects presented in this book. All subjects discussed pertain to the management of people in any kind of organization, including those in the sport industry.

The primary jobs of managers are discussed in depth as well as the continuous activities of problem-solving and decision-making. Special chapters are included on the "Legal Aspects of Sport Administration;" "Motivation and Employee Performance;" "Leadership;" "Managing Change, Conflict and Stress;" "Performance Appraisal and Rewards;" and "Management Information Systems."

Every effort has been made to present to students the most important topics in management. In addition, every effort has been made to relate major management subjects to examples in the sport world so that students can easily see the value of the material. All "Incidents" and "Assignments for Personal Development" at the end of each chapter are designed so that students will have to apply the management material in the chapter to settings and subjects in the sport industry.

Keep in mind that management as an activity is universal in nature. The basic jobs of managers are the same whether one manages in the sport industry, at General Motors or in any type of government. All managers must plan, organize, implement and control as they work through people to attain objectives. All managers confront problems and make decisions. All managers tend to be judged on performance and must take full responsibility for the results of their actions. And, as previously stated, management is not a career for everyone.

The approach in this book is **general**, not specialized. Some students will graduate and move on to jobs as recreation directors, fitness center directors, coaches, directors of athletics, teachers, managers of private clubs and so forth. Whether you begin your career in management in promotions/public relations; fundraising; facilities operations; sports information; as a high school, college or professional sports administrator; or in some area of the consumer sports industry, you can learn from studying the information in this book. The greatest value of this information will apply when you become a supervisor of other people, but the techniques and tools you gain will assist you in any area of sport management.

The information in this book will help you focus on your responsibilities as a manager. Management, because it deals with people, is not an exact science. There are no rules, laws or one-to-one relationships in management. There are principles, concepts and research findings which can influence a manager's actions. But any manager acts alone and often will not know if action taken today is good or bad until time has passed. The more you know about the subject of management itself, the more confident you should be when you take management action.

No manager is perfect, however; all managers make mistakes dealing with people, planning, controlling activities, making decisions, analyzing problems and implementing solutions. The **great** managers simply perform their management duties more effectively and make fewer mistakes than the average ones. A .300 hitter in baseball is one hit out of ten at-bats better than a .200 hitter; but the .300 hitter probably makes two or more times as much money, has a longer term contract, is known everywhere and revered by fans. A great manager has that same type of track record: consistently just a bit better than others at the same job. Studying this text should add to your knowledge about management and give you the opportunity to become one of the **great** managers in the future.

Summary

Over 180 colleges and universities in the United States offer undergraduate and/or graduate programs in Sport Management. Titles of these programs vary considerably; however, all programs are aimed at preparing students for careers in the world of sport administration.

Interest in sport activities is at an all time high. It is estimated that sport is a multi-billion dollar industry in the United States and still growing. The growing participation in sports along with the expanding industry has generated a need for competent people to manage at every level in all types of sport organizations. This demand has directly affected the growth of programs in sport management/administration at academic institutions.

Sport management programs do not have a standardized academic core curriculum This problem is being addressed by an official accrediting body established by representatives of collegiate sport management programs.

The study of management as applied to the sport industry is the same as the study of management applied to running General Motors or an agency of government. Management is the activity of achieving predetermined objectives by working through people; it is not an activity of managing moneys, equipment, facilities, tickets or other "things."

The real world of management is not the ideal environment for many people. Management is for special people who can accept responsibility, deal with problems, make sound decisions and work through people to achieve effective and efficient end results.

There is a tremendous need for professionals in sport management. Most new managers in any kind of organization are placed in their jobs without any prior training in management.

Contributions to the development of management have been made by individuals and ethnic groups since the beginning of recorded history. Since 1900, these individuals emerge as influential pioneers of management as it is taught and practiced today: Frederick W. Taylor, Frank and Lillian Gilbreth, Henri Fayol, Henry L. Gantt and G. Elton Mayo. Among the different approaches to the study and practice of management are the Scientific Management Approach, the Behavioral Approach, the Basic Process Approach, the Management Science Approach, and the Synergistic Systems Approach. The emerging current trend in management thought is called the Contingency Approach which is a compilation of relevant methods, techniques and theories drawn from all the existing schools of thought and approaches to management applied with a liberal use of common sense to fit an existing situation.

This book approaches management as a general, not specialized, subject. Management is a universal activity, i.e., all managers, located anywhere in any type of organization or industry, perform the same jobs or functions—planning, organizing, implementing and controlling—as they work through other people toward achieving preset objectives.

Review Questions

1. Why do you think so many men and women desire a career in sport management/administration?

2. What is the value of studying management prior to working as a sport manager/administrator?

3. What is your definition of management?

4. Are there aspects about the role of a manager and the world of management that do not appeal to you?

5. What are some of the trends in sport management education?

6. List the major contributions of each modern management pioneer.

7. Discuss the emerging current trend in management thought.

Assignments for Personal Development

1. Interview two or three veteran sport managers and ask them to tell you what kind of management training they had before they assumed their first supervisory job. Exchange responses with other students in class and evaluate the types of preparation/ training these managers had.

2. Review some of the major contributions of the pioneers in management. Find some specific activity or practice used today in the sport world that relates to one of these contributions.

Incident

SHOULD HE OR NOT?

Charlie George is an enthusiastic young sports reporter on the staff of the local daily newspaper. In a university town of 60,000 people, he covered all sporting events from amateur leagues to high school and college competition.

While a journalism major in college, Charlie participated in student government, was a basketball cheerleader and maintained a solid "B" average.

Over the past few months he has thought about making a career change. He loves the sports world, but does not like the sixty to seventy hours a week he spends covering all the town's sporting events. One possible career change is moving into a job in Sports Information at some college or university. A second option is to return to school in the graduate program in Sport Administration at the local university. If he were to follow this second course, he figures he could get a part-time job and survive for a year or two.

Charlie's main concern is whether a degree in Sport Administration and a loss of income for two years is really worth it. After all, he already has one degree in journalism and two years of excellent and varied work experience.

Questions:

1. What are the advantages and disadvantages of each of Charlie George's career options?

2. Recommend a course of action for Charlie George to follow with a complete justification of your recommendation.

Glossary of Key Terms

CABMA: The College Athletic Business Managers Association.

Information Technology (IT): Computer and communications technology and its applications.

Journal of Sport Management: The official publication of the North American Society for Sport Management.

Management: Achieving predetermined objectives working through other people (employees).

NACDA: The National Association of Collegiate Directors of Athletics.

NASPE: The National Association for Sport and Physical Education.

NASSM: The North American Society for Sport Management.

Pioneers in Management: Individuals who, through their contributions, began the modern management movement in America in the early 1900s and had lasting influence on the practice of management today. Some of them are F. W. Taylor, Frank and Lillian Gilbreth, Henri Fayol, Henry L. Gantt and G. Elton Mayo.

Sport: A competitive physical (and mental) activity, utilizing specialized equipment and facilities, with unique dimensions of time and space, in which the quest for records is of high significance [one of many definitions].

Practical Concepts in Management
MANAGERS TEND TO BE UNDERPAID

Normally when you get promoted to management, you get an increase in pay. This is one of the incentives that attracts people to the field. The increase in pay is exciting, but it alone is hardly reason enough to accept a manager's job.

When you review the demands on managers, the risks, the total responsibility, being judged on results, the long hours, the pressure, the deadlines, and the problems with employees, then pay (and increases in pay) fade as a reason for a career in management.

Many top level managers earn spectacular salaries on the surface, but the risks of their jobs are so great and the longevity in the position so brief on average that annual income may not be as high as it appears.

The point to keep in mind is that management is a performance oriented world. Adequate compensation for a job done well follows performance. Do not expect to be overcompensated in advance of your contribution to the organization. For this reason, managers tend to run behind others on pay schedules.

Be careful of managers who have the attitude that "when they pay me more, I'll do more." These people are "losers" and are likely only temporary employees in management.

MANAGERS ARE TOTALLY RESPONSIBLE

Of all the points a new manager should learn, the Total Responsibility Concept is the most vital. This concept states that a manager is absolutely, totally responsible for everything that happens, good or bad, from his or her position in the organization downward. This responsibility begins the first day you are in the job.

A manager is employed to work on behalf of another manager above him or her (the boss). In the manager's area of supervision, often referred to as the scope of responsibility, no matter what problems occur, no matter how much success is achieved, and no matter the nature of the activity, that immediate manager is responsible.

The Total Responsibility Concept wipes out excuses. If you are the person in charge, the manager, then you are the one responsible for **everything** from your position downward. You cannot shift the blame nor fault to those below you for the failure to attain results. Some management prospects shrink from this kind of responsibility, and they refuse to be promoted into management positions because of it.

Being a manager is not for everyone. Not all employees, no matter how good an employee they are, want the additional responsibility that accompanies supervising people and directing the use of organizational resources.

References and Chapter Notes

[1] Webster's *Dictionary* (U.S.A.: Ottenheimer Publishers, Inc., 1970), p. 361.

[2] *The American Heritage Dictionary* (New York: Dell Publishing Co., Inc., 1983), p. 660.

[3] Harold J. VanderZwaag, *Policy Development in Sport Management* (Indianapolis, Ind.: Benchmark Press, Inc., 1988), p. 3.

[4] Information provided by Dr. Malcolm J. MacKenzie, Administrative Director, Center for International Sports Business & Economics, Georgia Tech.

[5] Lyndall Urwick, ed., *The Golden Book of Management* (London: Millbrook Press, 1963), p. 74.

[6] Urwick, ed., *Golden Book*, pp. 89-91.

[7] Henry L. Gantt, "A Bonus System for Rewarding Labor," *Transactions of the American Society of Mechanical Engineers*, Vol. 23 (1901), p. 373.

[8] A complete discussion of the Hawthorne Studies is presented in Chapter 11.

[9] "Workers Can Be a Team, Too," *Business Week*, May 25, 1963, pp. 49-50.

[10] Claude S. George, Jr., *The History of Management Thought* (Englewood Cliffs, N.J.: Prentice-Hall, Inc., 1968), p. 130.

[11] Harold Koontz, "The Management Theory Jungle," *Academy of Management Journal 4* (December, 1961), pp. 174-188.

[12] Harold Koontz, "The Management Theory Jungle Revisited," *Academy of Management Review 5* (April, 1980), p. 176.

CHAPTER 2

OVERVIEW OF MANAGEMENT

After studying this chapter, **you will know**:

- The general nature of management
- The real meaning of management
- Major management functions and understand the basic management process
- Levels of management
- General skills needed by managers at each level
- What the science and art of management means
- The definition of an entrepreneur and the role of women in management
- That management as a career can be exciting and challenging
- How to test your sincerity about a career in management

Introduction

From Chapter 1 we know that the sport management movement is ongoing and growing. The popularity of sport in the United States is at an unprecedented high: thousands of people would love to swap their present jobs for ones in some part of the sport industry. For students majoring in the field of sport management/administration, the message is to prepare yourselves to perform competently and professionally as a manager once you enter the field. Competition for sport management jobs is keen; only the best will survive in the long-run.

Chapter 2 provides a broad overview of the world of management. This chapter stresses the real meaning of management and describes some general skills needed by all managers. The specific functions of managers are discussed along with a distinction between the science and the art of management. Students should grasp the fundamentals of management and build upon them just as any coach would stress fundamentals to players when developing high skill performers. Included in this chapter is "The Management Sincerity Test" (see Figure 2-11). This exercise will help students determine whether they are likely to enjoy the world of management.

The activity of managing has been around thousands of years. As a formal field of study, however, management is a relatively new discipline. Sport management programs, likewise, are relatively new although the management of sport has been around thousands of years. It is important to understand that management is a universal activity; i.e., all of the principles, concepts and theories in the field of management are applicable to managers in any kind of organization, located anywhere, regardless of the nature of the organization's activity.

The Nature of Management

In order for management as a function to exist, three conditions must be met:

1. There must be a *formal* organization.

2. The organization must have a clearly defined goal or purpose for existing.

3. The organization must have a hierarchical structure in which some people are in charge of others.

Clearly, **managers** are those people who are in charge of others in a formal organization. To be a manager, one is either appointed or elected to the position, or one starts an organization and decides to be the owner-manager.

In the United States, there are approximately 125 million people in the labor force.[1] Of this number, 10.8 per cent (about 13 million of the gainfully employed) are classified as managers. What do these people manage? They manage **people**. The titles which these managers have on their jobs, however, may lead to some confusion about just what they manage. For example, there are Office Managers, Production Managers, Inventory Managers, Traffic Managers and many other misnomers. In the sport world, we have Coaches, Commissioners, General Managers, Athletics Directors, Facilities Managers, Owners, Directors of Recreation Services, and Club Managers just to mention a few management titles. To clarify, **managers** have responsibility for and control over many resources, such as money, equipment, inventory, supplies, etc. as well as people; but, for this text, we stress that the only resource they **manage** is people.

The activity of management focuses attention on the proper coordination and utilization of all organizational resources whether they are human, financial, physical or informational. The purpose of *management* is to achieve desired organizational objectives.

In addition, managers must focus their attention on environmental changes that can affect plans and decisions. The environment of society today changes rapidly and is more complex than it has ever been. Managers must be aware of social and technological changes as well as governmental laws and regulations which can impact their actions. Also, there are the increased scarcity and rising costs of natural resources, plus a trend toward the internationalization of virtually all business, and including the sport industry.

How can managers properly coordinate and use organizational resources within the framework of their particular environmental constraints? In order to do this best and make progress on achieving goals and objectives, managers employ sound planning, organizing, implementing and controlling activities along with timely decision-making. These activities are the main functions (jobs) of managers and will be discussed in more depth throughout this book.

Management Defined

Different scholars and practitioners have many different definitions of management. While the definitions have significant differences, they also have similarities. The key similarity is that *management is a process of coordinating the utilization of organizational resources toward the achievement of predetermined objectives*. The activity of managing is a process because all managers have major jobs or functions to perform as they work with employees and other resources to achieve the objectives. Although the traditional definition of a **process** is *a logical sequence of steps or jobs arranged in a particular manner to achieve the desired result*, students should not expect management to fit this description of a process. Management is not an activity that can be programmed in a logical, sequential way. There is no chronology of steps arranged in a one, two, three, etc. order leading to the ultimate end result.

The definition of management used in this text emphasizes the importance of the human element as the one factor of production that can grow and become more valuable for the benefit of the person, their boss (manager) and the company. Other resources are important too, but none are as valuable as the employees who use their mental and physical skills to achieve desired results under the direction of managers. Thus, the definition of management used throughout this text is *the process of optimally utilizing human resources to achieve predetermined goals and objectives in the most efficient and effective way possible*. (See Figure 2-1 for a graphic demonstration.)

A distinction should be made between efficiency and effectiveness. **Efficiency** refers to producing a desired result at the lowest cost or combining resources in the best possible way. **Effectiveness** refers to achieving the desired end result in the most timely manner.

Managing is a complex activity that defies conformity to a single definition. The management world is filled with problems, uncertainties, risks and challenges, but provides unlimited opportunity to those who are willing to accept the responsibilities.

Functions of Management

Functions of management refer to the main activities that managers perform when doing their jobs. Figure 2-2 lists typical daily activities that managers perform and more could be added to this list. Clearly, managers stay busy!

The **main** functions of management, however, can be reduced to four, five or six depending on your source. Historically, from the time of management pioneer Frederick W. Taylor in the late 19th Century to today, management experts have identified what they believe to be the main jobs or functions of managers. Taylor, called the "Father of Scientific Management," said the main job of managers is "planning" and that of the workers is "doing."[2] Henri Fayol, a noted French management pioneer and executive, stated in his book, *Industrial and General Administration*, that the five functions of management are planning, organizing, commanding, coordinating and controlling.[3]

In much of today's management literature, the main functions of a manager are identified as planning, organizing, staffing, leading and controlling. While some discrepancy exists between authors, scholars and practitioners on all the functions or jobs of managers, there is agreement that these three are essential: planning, organizing and controlling.

In this text, we will identify four functions of management considered to be the main activities of all managers. When managers are involved in these four functions, they are said to be engaged in the **basic process of managing**. These four functions are **planning, organizing, implementing and controlling**.

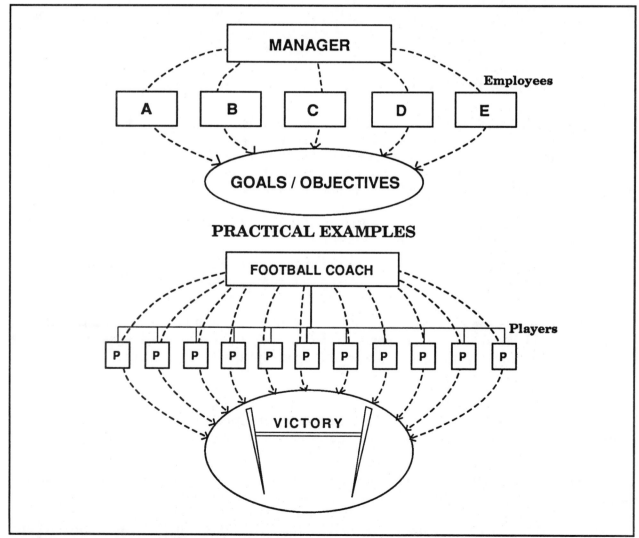

FIGURE 2-1: MANAGEMENT—Working Through Employees to Achieve Objectives

Planning	Timing
Hiring	Relaying
Firing	Implementing
Evaluating	Executing
Controlling	Budgeting
Deciding	Repairing
Coordinating	Communicating
Reviewing	Motivating
Creating	Instructing
Problem Solving	Correcting
Organizing	Interpreting
Disciplining	Staffing
Appraising	Promoting
Originating	Leading
Directing	Delegating
Scheduling	Auditing

FIGURE 2-2: TYPICAL DAILY ACTIVITIES
OF MANAGERS

If you check the list of activities in Figure 2-2, all identified jobs of managers can be grouped under one of these functions. For example, coordination is part of the organizing function; scheduling is part of the job of planning; appraising is part of controlling; motivating is part of implementing. The exceptions to this are problem-solving and decision-making which are activities that permeate all of the management functions.

How many of the daily activities of a manager listed in Figure 2-2 would be the responsibility of a general manager of a professional sports team or an athletics director at any size college or university? The answer is all of them!

By identifying the major activities of managers and studying each one separately, one is able to combine them and understand more clearly the management process of planning, organizing, implementing and controlling. It will become evident how managers use this process as they work through people to achieve predetermined goals and objectives.

Future chapters are devoted to in-depth study of each of these functions. For now, we will define and describe in general each function along with comments about the importance of decision-making and problem-solving.

Planning

Planning, as a management activity, is setting goals and objectives and then developing a detailed method of achieving them in a specified time period, with a minimum of problems, in the most efficient and effective way possible.

Planning may cover a long-run or short-run time period, may be for an entire organization or for a department, group or individual. In sport management, planning can cover one year (such as a sport's season) or it can cover many years (such as the planning of major facilities construction or the span of time required for funding an endowment program). The significant point to remember about planning is that all planning activities are **futuristic**. While top management executives of a large organization are planning five to twenty years ahead, a first level supervisor may be planning a two-week or a quarterly production schedule. Regardless of the time period or the management level involved, the planning activity deals with the **future**.

Good planning is designed to minimize problems in the effort of going from point A to point Z. Good planning leads to a more efficient effort and a more effective end result. Efficiency and effectiveness mean greater productivity. Good planning becomes the standard which can be reviewed as the plan proceeds to help control performance.

Poor planning, on the other hand, is generally considered to be the number one reason why individuals and organizations fail to achieve their desired end results. Poor managerial planning is the leading cause of organizational failure in the United States.

Organizing

Managers have a responsibility to organize the efforts of employees to reach the objectives successfully. This means putting the right person with the correct skills into the right spot. The sole purpose of sound organization is to create an efficiency of effort. This requires a manager to coordinate effectively the use of employees and all other resources.

Various organizational structures are used to provide a sound framework for the activities of any organization. The type of organizational structure will depend on the nature of the work activities being performed.

A formal organization is a group of people working together toward common objectives with clearly established lines of authority, responsibility, accountability and communication.

The manager's job is to make certain that employees do work together harmoniously and that common goals and objectives are achieved working within the established hierarchy.

Implementing

Implementing is putting the plans and programs of management into action working through the employees. Implementing can be called *executing, actuating or directing.* Any standard dictionary defines the verb **implement** literally as "to put into practice."

Without question, sound planning and organizing are essential to successful management; but without effective implementation, the planning and organizing efforts are wasted.

This function of management involves working directly with employees to achieve the objectives effectively and efficiently. Managers who are sound implementers understand people. They tend to be good leaders and knowledgeable managers who understand the subjects of motivation, incentives, job satisfaction and all other people-oriented skills.

Successful implementers strive to work through people to achieve the desired end result and, simultaneously, bring positive benefits to the employee, the organization and the immediate manager. The quality here that sets the outstanding managers and implementers apart from the rest is that their employees not only perform what they ask but want to do these tasks as well as possible.

Controlling

The control function is designed primarily to insure that performance is on schedule according to a plan. Sound planners include control techniques so that once plans are implemented, there is an automatic way of measuring performance against the plan. If discrepancies between the plan and performance appear, then corrective action is taken.

All control programs have these three essential steps:

1. Establish a standard (plan).

2. Appraise conformance to the standard (inspection).

3. Take corrective or remedial action when the standard is exceeded.

Theoretically, if planning, organizing and implementing are done perfectly, the control function is not needed. Since people are not perfect managers and cannot perfectly regulate all conditions around them, we need the control function.

The need for control programs varies greatly depending on such things as the precision necessary in the work, the type of activity, and the skill and ability of the employees; but all control programs should be introduced carefully to do a particular job and then disbanded when the need disappears. The value of the control program in saved costs, fewer problems and better quality output and so forth must outweigh the cost of implementing the program for it to be efficient and effective. If these benefits do not more than cover the costs of the control program, then the program should not be introduced.

The Basic Management Process

Planning, organizing, implementing and controlling are the functions which form the cornerstone of managerial activity in any type of organization. The functions interrelate and overlap. Rarely does a manager just plan or just organize. Several activities within each function may be occurring at the same time. A manager can review and isolate what he or she is doing at a particular point in time, however, and can readily classify the activity into one of the four functions of the basic process of management. Figure 2-3 illustrates common managerial activities under each function.

```
SELECTED RESPONSIBILITIES
Planning                          Implementing
• Set organizational goals        • Provide leadership
• Prepare budgets                 • Direct efforts
• Schedule work                   • Execute plans and programs
• Forecast demand                 • Reward performance
• Research                        • Expedite work-in-progress


Organizing                        Controlling
• Coordinate resources            • Formalize standards
• Staff open positions            • Review work activities
• Develop job descriptions        • Take corrective action
• Delegate work                   • Evaluate personnel
• Formalize communications        • Audit finances
```

FIGURE 2-3: FUNCTIONS OF MANAGEMENT

This approach to the study of management is called the *process approach*. When managers plan, organize, implement and control as they work through people to achieve objectives, they are said to be performing the *basic process of management*.

Decision-making is not normally listed as a separate management function. But decision-making permeates every management activity. You make decisions when you plan, organize, implement and control. The importance of decision-making cannot be stressed too much.

Decision-making stands alone as the single most important daily activity of a manager. Every manager in the world deals with problems, issues, and people; and makes decisions. The majority of these managers are judged on the results of their decisions. If decisions did not have to be made and all the input factors weighed and judged in this process, there would be no need for managers!

Management Titles

Management job titles may be confusing to a new student in management. Figure 2-4 shows some of the more common job titles in the military, in business, in government and in education.

Regardless of classification, all of these titles and many more show that the individuals holding these job titles are in management positions. They hold positions of authority (power); they are responsible for results; and their job is to achieve predetermined goals and objectives working through others.

MILITARY TITLES:	General Major Lieutenant Sergeant Chief Petty Officer
BUSINESS TITLES:	Chief Executive Officer Owner Superintendent Department Head Supervisor Foreman
GOVERNMENT TITLES:	President Governor Director Commissioner Mayor Chief of Police
EDUCATION TITLES:	Academic Dean Director of Athletics Department Chair Head Coach Provost Chancellor

FIGURE 2-4: SELECTED MANAGEMENT TITLES

Levels of Management

Managers are generally classified as either part of top management, middle management or first-level management as shown in Figure 2-5.

Top Management. The top management of any type of organization generally includes the organization's executives: the Chief Executive Officer (CEO), President, Executive Vice President and Vice Presidents. Some typical titles in the sport world would be Executive Director, Owner, Conference Commissioner, Athletics Director or Director of Parks and Recreation. These positions provide overall direction to the entire organization. They formulate objectives and policies; plan for the long-term; and make decisions that affect every facet of the organization.

Middle Management. Middle managers such as Branch Managers, Superintendents, Human Resource Managers, and similar titles are identified as managing through other managers. In sport management/administration, they may be called General Managers of pro teams, Directors of Player Personnel or Head Coaches. The middle manager's primary job is to implement programs of action within the framework of the policies set by top level management. They do this by working through first-level managers who are their immediate employees (subordinates). Normally this task requires good leadership ability, effectiveness as a communicator, control skills, and some comprehension of the technical aspects of the work that is to be done.

First-Level Management. First-level managers are often called first-line managers. Their job titles are usually Supervisor, Foreman or Department Head. In the sports industry, they may be the manager of a pro baseball team, the supervisor of maintenance for facilities, or the supervisor of a county's swimming pools. These managers deal directly with nonmanagement or operating employees. Because they represent the organization to these personnel, first-level managers are vital to any organization. No organization is as effective and efficient as it might be without highly competent first-level managers. First-level managers have the tasks of delegating work to nonmanagement employees, instructing them in proper work methods, correcting them, and controlling activity. The manager must know what is to be done, how it is to be done, when it is to be done, and must make certain that it is done.

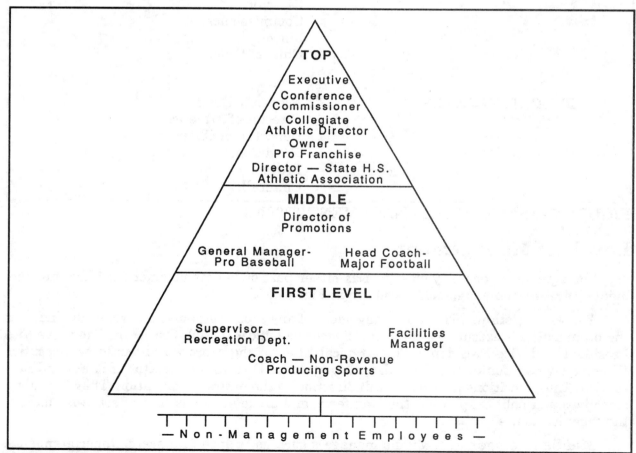

FIGURE 2-5: THE LEVELS OF MANAGEMENT

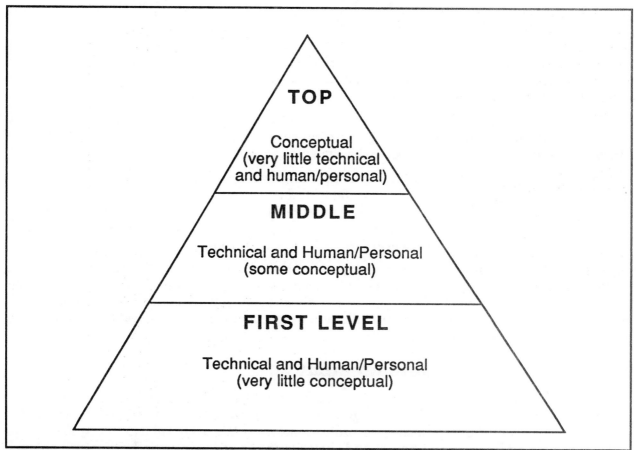

FIGURE 2-6: LEVELS OF MANAGEMENT AND GENERAL SKILLS NEEDED BY
EACH IN LARGE ORGANIZATIONS

General Skills Needed by Managers

The basic process of management emphasizes that planning, organizing, implementing and controlling along with timely decision-making are the most important jobs of management. To be effective in fulfilling these management functions, Robert L. Katz suggests that managers need three general skills:

Technical Skills. These skills involve knowledge of operations, activities, processes, inventory and the mechanics of performing particular job tasks.

Human/Personal Skills. These are the people skills: working well with people, providing good leadership, communicating effectively, and empathizing with employees

Conceptual Skills. This is the rarest of all skills: the ability to relate and understand all aspects of the organization as a whole; to see the importance of each part as it interacts with every other part; "the big picture." Strategic planning, decision-making and coordinating are the major management activities which require conceptual skills.[4]

Figure 2-6 shows the relative importance of each general skill to managers at each level in large organizations. In small organizations, upper-level managers will need all three skills.

First-level managers who directly manage operating (nonmanagement) employees need good human/personal skills and strong technical skills since they delegate work, control performance, and often train employees to become skilled performers.

Middle managers who work through other managers continue to need good human/personal skills and generally need less specific technical knowledge than first-line supervisors. The need for technical skill can change, however, depending on the nature of the work involved and the type of organization. At this level they must have some conceptual skill since they are often involved in overall organizational planning.

Top-level managers in large organizations are viewed as the "conceptualizers," i.e., those who have a responsibility to lead and direct the organization as a whole toward the successful accomplishment of its objectives—short-term and long-term. These individuals may have excellent human/personal skills and much technical knowledge, but the primary skill they need is good conceptual ability.

Science and Art of Management

Management theorists and practitioners generally agree that management is both a science and an art. Little about management qualifies it as a pure science; however, the application of scientific approaches to problem-solving, the accumulation of systematized data from past and ongoing research, and the origination of theories and principles do qualify management as a social science.

The principles of management are basic truths not the fundamental, largely inflexible laws of the physical sciences. A management principle usually evolves historically from ideas, beliefs or observations of organizational activity, eventually becoming standards of conduct for managers who wish to apply them. Management principles tend to have validity, but they are not absolutes which must be adhered to strictly when managing.

Literature abounds in collegiate libraries on every imaginable management subject. Management is considered an academic discipline, and many students in business schools in the United States select this subject as their major field of study. Sport management scholars also are conducting and publishing many studies in select journals throughout the United States. Literature in this field is growing rapidly. Of particular interest to students are articles published in the *Journal of Sport Management* that focus on the theoretical and applied aspects of management related to sport, exercise, dance and play.

Management is also an art. Managers rely on their experience and acquired knowledge to influence their courses of action when dealing with people, implementing decisions and solving problems. The **art** of managing refers primarily to how a manager performs his or her duties or the way a particular manager does things. Managers are "performers" just as artists are in the field of music and drama. The art of managing is individualistic, with each manager having his or her own management style. There is an old saying that "managers should be nonconformists who know when to conform," which means that there is a certain amount of latitude allowed managers in performing their duties. But all management activity must fall within the framework of acceptable organizational behavior.

Principles, theories and the use of scientific approaches may provide managers a rational approach to dealing with organizational problems and decisions; but all decisions and programs of action must be implemented effectively by individuals to achieve desired results. Management is both a science and an art.

Entrepreneurship and Women in Management

An entrepreneur is not necessarily a professional manager and vice versa. An entrepreneur is a person who undertakes the task of starting an organization to produce a product or service based on his or her own ideas. Entrepreneurs tend to be creative and motivated people who build an organization to the point where professional management is needed. The entrepreneur may make the transition to professional manager and plan, organize, implement and control effectively. Otherwise, a professional manager who can perform these tasks well may be employed to run the organization which the entrepreneur has created.

Even entrepreneurs must perform basic management functions when starting a new organization; but after the organization grows to a certain size, they need more professional management. Many of America's best known, successful large organizations were started by two or three entrepreneurs who also made the transition to professional management. Some examples are Microsoft, Compaq, Apple Computer and Scientific Atlanta.

Women as well as men have the entrepreneurial spirit. According to the Small Business Administration in 1992, American women own an estimated 6.5 million of the 15 million small businesses. Women-owned businesses employ about 11 million workers which is more than the *Fortune* 500 companies. The National Association of Women Business Owners reports that in the early 1990s, women started businesses 1-1/2 times more frequently than men did. Figure 2-7 provides data about women-owned businesses in the United States.

One of the factors leading women to start their own businesses faster than men is their educational achievement. As shown in Figure 2-8, more women than men graduated with bachelor's and master's degrees from United States colleges in 1990. Since women are paid less than men for comparable work, many educated women choose to form their own businesses and take advantage of the independence and opportunity business ownership provides.

Overall the number of women in managerial/professional jobs increased 35.34% from 1985 to 1990. Today, approximately 48% of all managerial/professional jobs in the United States are held by women (see Figure 2-9). This category includes doctors, lawyers and other professional jobs.

Other significant indications of the strength the lure of entrepreneurship has on Americans are the addition of collegiate courses in entrepreneurship at many top colleges and universities and the effort by large organizations to make management positions within the organization seem like business ownership for the job holders. This effort is now known as "intrapreneurs," a word coined by a manager at the 3M company who wrote a book about that company's program. *Intrapreneurs are managers who function within the structure of a formal organization, but have the challenge and responsibility of performing their jobs like entrepreneurs or business owners.* It has become a way to keep top management talent from leaving organizations to start their own businesses.[5]

Entrepreneurs on the move

Businesses owned by women have been increasing in unprecedented numbers, according to a study by the National Foundation of Women Business Owners:

➤ **There are 5.4 million** women-owned U.S. business.
➤ **Some 11.7 million** people work for women-owned businesses, the same number as for Fortune 500 companies.
➤ **Women-owned** firms will add 350,000 workers and will create more jobs than Fortune 500 companies will during 1992.
➤ **9 percent** of them have annual sales of more than $1 million.
➤ **Top 10 states** where women-owned businesses are booming: California, New York, Texas, Illinois, florida, Pennsylvania, Michigan, Ohio, New Jersey and Washington.

Source: National Foundation for Women Business Owners

FIGURE 2-7: *Atlanta Journal*, July 20, 1992.

Women lead the way on BAs, MAs

In 20 years, American women have overtaken men as the dominant college-educated gender, both on the bachelor's and master's levels.

BACHELOR'S DEGREES	1970	1980	1990
Women	341,276	455,806	558,169
Men	451,380	473,611	491,488
Percent Women	**43%**	**49%**	**53%**
MASTER'S DEGREES	1970	1980	1990
Women	82,667	147,332	170,201
Men	125,624	150,749	153,643
Percent Women	**40%**	**49%**	**53%**
LAW	1970	1980	1990
Women	801	10,754	15,378
Men	14,115	24,893	21,059
Percent Women	**5%**	**30%**	**42%**
MEDICINE	1970	1980	1990
Women	699	3,486	5,138
Men	7,615	11,416	9,977
Percent Women	**8%**	**23%**	**34%**

Source: National Center for Education Statistics

FIGURE 2-8: COLLEGE GRADUATION RATES BY GENDER

Women in Sport Management

No accurate data is available to denote how many women hold **management positions** in the sport industry. The industry is large and difficult to define and includes jobs in retailing, manufacturing and marketing of sporting goods as well as the traditional jobs in various athletic and professional sports administration. It include positions in public relations, advertising and communicating relating to sport products, events and contests. The industry includes sports activities in organized form such as those sponsored in recreational leagues and those in high schools, colleges and professional leagues. The industry is vast in size and continually growing.

The number of women in sport management positions may equate with the overall national figure of 28 percent (see a larger discussion of women and minorities in management in Chapter 3). Figure 2-9 reflects the percentage growth of women in management/professional jobs in the United States between 1985 and 1990.

A specific example to support the generalization that women in sport management jobs today is increasing is found in Figure 2-10. Campus leadership positions held by females increased significantly from 1987-88 to 1992-93. Campus leadership positions are identified as senior athletics administrators, athletics directors and faculty athletics representatives at NCAA member schools. Out of 832 member institutions in the study, 649 females are employed as senior women athletics administrators. Of these, 92 females are athletics directors and 116 are faculty athletics representatives. Each category increased in numbers over a five year period, with increases varying between four percent and sixteen percent.[6]

Management As a Career

Students today have the opportunity to select a major from hundreds of choices. One of the most exciting to select is **management**. The study of management does not guarantee one a job nor does it mean success as a manager once a job is found. Being a manager does guarantee excitement, risks and a sense of power and responsibility. The opportunity for advancement in management is unlimited if one demonstrates competency in his or her first management position.

Should everyone study management and make it a career? The answer is, "No." Not even the best employees already working in the labor force are necessarily suited for management careers.

The factors that make people good managers are diverse and numerous, but one fact remains constant. If you wish to make management a career, you should get prepared. Preparation will not guarantee successful job performance, but the lack of proper preparation is a major cause of management failure. Studying management and learning the time-tested principles that have been developed over the years is one of the best ways to prepare for a career in management. In addition, a manager must realize there are conditions peculiar to the field of management which make a management career a challenge. Managers work long hours, accept total responsibility for the work of employees below them, and operate in a world of stress. These are just some of the peculiar conditions facing managers which are addressed in Figure 2-11, a questionnaire concerning your sincerity about a management career.

	Number of Jobs*	% Male	% Female	% Black	% Hispanic
Growth in employment	9,727	6.18	12.74	12.97	27.74
Growth in managerial/ professional jobs	5,161	8.48	35.34	9.24	19.96

* In thousands.

FIGURE 2-9: PERCENTAGE GROWTH IN EMPLOYMENT AND MANAGERIAL/ PROFESSIONAL JOBS (1985-1990)

Source: *Statistical Abstract of the United States* (Washington D.C.: U.S. Department of Labor, 1992), pp. 392-93.

Beyond academic preparation, managers learn to manage from experience on the job. Experience is a great teacher if those in management can relate what is happening to what they have learned. Many organizations provide in-house management training programs; send personnel to off-site management seminars to improve their management skills; and have ongoing programs devoted to the review and discussion of management literature. These are ways to keep managers aware of modern trends and continue their management education. Mixing experience with acquired knowledge is the foundation for growth and development in management.

Many new managers in organizations are promoted from the ranks of nonmanagement employees. Existing employees who demonstrate competency in their work and exhibit management potential (in the view of higher managers) are often picked for first-level management jobs . While these employees have good to excellent technical knowledge, they may need special management training to prepare them for supervisory activities. Then, their management skills are learned from experience and periodic training sessions if such are provided by the organization.

	1987-88 $N = 785$*		1992-93 $N = 832$*		% Change
	N	%	*N*	%	
Senior woman athletics administrator	487	62	649	78	16
Female athletics director					
One department	55	7	92	11	4
Two departments				33	4
Female athletics representative	71	9	116	14	5

Note: *Total number of schools in the NCAA.

FIGURE 2-10: CAMPUS LEADERSHIP POSITIONS HELD BY FEMALES IN THE NCAA

Source: Dorothy J. Lovett and Carla D. Lowry, "Is Liberal Feminism Working in the NCAA?" *Journal of Sport Management*, Vol. 9, No. 3, September, 1995, p. 267.

Students will enjoy taking the "Management Sincerity Test" (Figure 2-11). Answering some questions with a "no" does not mean you cannot be a good manager. It simply means that there are some aspects of management and the job of a manager that you do not particularly like.

Are You Sincere About a Career in Management?

If you think you are ready for the challenge of a career in management, answer the following questions. If your answers are positive, you are sincere about pursuing a career in management, and you have recognized some of the conditions which make management a challenge. It is a new world for those who have been in non-management positions, and to accept the conditions is not always easy. It takes a special type of person to succeed and be outstanding in the field of management, the most demanding of professional careers.

Make this list of questions your starting point as you check your sincerity about that management career:

1. Do you like being in charge of other people?
2. Do you like to have the responsibility for the actions of others?
3. Do you think you could take satisfaction in seeing employees under your supervision succeed?
4. Would you like being judged on results—good or bad?
5. Would you like a job where your bosses have little appreciation for excuses?
6. Do you enjoy being a "team" player?
7. Do you like visibility?
8. Do you think you can lead others positively toward objectives and do so consistently?
9. Would you enjoy setting the model for employee conduct on the job?
10. Could you accept working 50 - 60 hours per week routinely when nonmanagement employees work 40?
11. Are you confident you know the subject of management and know what managers are supposed to do?
12. Do you thrive under a certain amount of stress caused by unusual demands, deadlines, schedules, and dealing with a multitude of different personalities?
13. Do you enjoy problem-solving and decision-making and the risks that accompany implementing your decisions?
14. Can you put aside personal interests and preferences and do what is best for the organization?
15. Can you handle pressure from your peers, your bosses, and your subordinates?

FIGURE 2-11: THE MANAGEMENT SINCERITY TEST

Source: Francis J. Bridges, *So You Want To Be A Manager?* (Decatur, Georgia: ESM Books, 1984), pp. 7-8.

Chapter Summary

Approximately 10.8 per cent of people in the United States labor force are classified as managers. Management is an activity that focuses attention on the proper coordination and utilization of organizational resources. The purpose is to achieve desired organizational objectives.

While there are many definitions of management, the one used in this text states: Management is defined as the process of optimally utilizing human resources to achieve predetermined goals and objectives in the most efficient and effective way possible.

Managers have major activities they engage in when performing their jobs. These activities are called "functions of management." The main functions of management are planning, organizing, implementing and controlling. Decision-making is another major function; but because it is part of each other function, it is not listed separately.

Management is referred to as a "basic process" because all managers plan, organize, implement and control as they work through people to achieve organizational objectives.

There are many different management job titles in the world of business, government and education. All titles indicate managers are in positions of authority (power) with direct responsibility for the performance of employees below them. Typical titles would be Mayor, General, Governor, Chief Executive Officer, Deans, Coaches, Chancellor and others.

There are three levels of management in large organizations: top management, middle management and first-level management. Managers at these three levels need certain general skills to plan, organize, implement and control effectively. These three general skills are technical, human or personal, and conceptual. The size and nature of the organization dictate the degree of skills needed by managers at each of the management levels.

There seems to be agreement that management is both a science and an art. Little about management qualifies it as a pure science, but the application of scientific approaches to problem-solving along with ongoing research and the accumulation of a vast amount of literature on management subjects qualifies it as a social science. The art of management refers to the way and how managers work with people and implement plans and programs. Managers develop their own style of managing based on their acquired knowledge of the subject and skills learned from their experiences. Managers are performers just as musicians and actors are and often their effectiveness, when working with people, depends on they way and how they do things.

An entrepreneur is not necessarily a professional manager and vice versa. An entrepreneur is a person who undertakes the task of starting an organization to produce a product or service based on ideas which he or she has. When a startup organization becomes a certain size, professional management will be needed to run the organization. Entrepreneurs may or may not have the skills of a professional manager. Intrapreneurs are managers who function within large, formal organizations but have the freedom and responsibility of an entrepreneur.

Today, many women have the entrepreneurial spirit. According to the Small Business Administration in 1992, an estimated 6.5 million of the 15 million small businesses in the United States were owned by women. Overall the number of women in managerial/professional jobs in the United States is approximately 48%. The percentage of women in sport management jobs is increasing yearly.

Management as a major field of study is an option for students. The study of management does not guarantee one a job nor does it mean success as a manager once employed. Being a manager does guarantee excitement, risks, and a sense of power and responsibility. The opportunity for advancement in management is unlimited if one demonstrates competency in their first management position.

Review Questions

1. What are the three conditions that must be met for management as a function to exist?

2. Define management.

3. List and explain the major management functions.

4. Why is decision-making considered to be the single-most important daily activity of a manager?

5. What are three general skills needed by managers?

6. Explain the difference between management as a science and as an art.

7. Distinguish between an entrepreneur and a professional manager.

8. What are the most important tips you could give someone who has decided on a career in management?

Assignments for Personal Development

1. Interview two different managers who are in athletics administration. Ask them to list or tell you their most difficult management problem(s). Then, have each of them list the factors about being a manager which they enjoy the most. In a class discussion of the various responses, you will begin to a get a more realistic perspective of the job of a manager.

2. Executive managers are often referred to as "uncommon" or "non-normal" people. This means they are unique, one of a kind individuals, or they might be called "originals." Historical examples of such individuals are Napoleon, Vince Lombardi, John Wooden and Ronald Reagan. Locate or research two outstanding executives, in any field, who by their records are considered exceptional! Identify five or six personality traits of each of your choices and explain to your colleagues why these people are unique.

Incident

PROMOTION OF A PEER

Majorie Atkins is one of the most experienced people in the Public Relations and Promotions Department of a major league baseball franchise. The veteran manager of the department became seriously ill, rather suddenly; and without much notice, Majorie was named to replace him. Majorie had never thought about being the boss nor had she shown any interest in the job. But, she knows she is as qualified as any of the other eight full time employees, and she knows she has more seniority than most.

The prospect of being the boss, however, bothers her a bit. The main problem, as she sees it, is that about half of the employees are doing about seventy percent of the work with the other half "floating" -- out sick a lot, complaining behind the backs of higher management, and not doing a full share of the work. If the person appointed to the manager's job were to take the work seriously, this new boss has to correct this situation. Correcting it could mean firing friends and making enemies.

One week after being in the new position, Majorie noticed that work performance of the entire group is slipping some and several of the employees seem to resent her as the new boss.

She decided it was time to call her first meeting and get a few things straightened out.

Questions:

1. Do you think Majorie is properly prepared to handle managerial problems such as the ones she faces? Discuss your answer.

2. What style of management would you recommend Majorie adopt when conducting her first meeting with employees? Explain.

Glossary of Key Terms

Art of Management: When managers rely on their experiences and acquired knowledge to influence their course of action in dealing with people and problems. The art of managing refers primarily to the how and way managers do things -- a personal management style.

Basic Management Process: Refers to the process of implementing the functions of management as you work through employees to achieve predetermined objectives.

Controlling: An activity designed primarily to insure that performance is on schedule according to a plan or standard.

Entrepreneur: A person who undertakes the task of starting an organization to produce a product or service based on ideas which he or she has.

Formal Organization: A group of people working together toward common objectives with clearly established lines of authority, responsibility, accountability and communication.

General Skills Needed by Managers: It is widely accepted that managers need three general skills to perform their management duties: technical skill, human/personal skill, and conceptual skill.

Implementing: Putting the plans and programs of management into action working through the employees.

Management: The process of optimally utilizing human resources to achieve predetermined goals and objectives in the most efficient and effective way possible.

Management Functions: The main jobs, duties or activities of managers (functions) are planning, organizing, implementing and controlling.

Planning: As a management activity, it is setting goals and objectives; then, developing a detailed method of achieving them in a specified time period, with a minimum of problems, in the most efficient and effective way possible.

Principles of Management: Basic truths, but not fundamental laws such as are found in the physical sciences; they apply generally to management situations.

Science of Management: The application of scientific approaches to problem-solving, the accumulation of systematized data, ongoing research, and the origination of theories and principles.

Practical Concepts in Management

THE UNIVERSALITY OF MANAGEMENT CONCEPT

Henri Fayol, a Frenchman, pioneered study and research in the field of general administration in the 1920s. He originated the "universality of management" concept. The theory is that any manager in any kind of organization, located anywhere, will engage in the basic process of management (planning, organizing, implementing and controlling) as he or she works through people to achieve objectives.

The fundamental concepts of management do have universal application. Managers around the world do have the same major responsibilities. The difference in management, one company to another or one nation to another, rests in the styles and techniques used by individual managers as they plan, organize, implement and control; and in the different attitudes, cultural disparities, values about work, etc. that employees bring to the workplace.

MANAGERS ARE UNCOMMON PEOPLE

Once you go into management, you become different! You are no longer "one of the gang," and you may even lose some of your friends if you have been promoted from within. Becoming a manager requires an adjustment in your behavior and your thinking. Management is full of responsibility, high expectations and **pressure**.

All your thoughts as a manager must be centered on what is best for the organization. You, the manager, are the "company" to nonmanagement employees. And don't think that every statement you make and every action you take is not being observed by your employees! They won't miss anything!

These changes from nonmanagement to management make you "different." You have new, greater responsibilities; you have authority (power); your perspective is different; indeed, your **world** is different. This makes you a vastly different type of person from the ordinary employee. You are now part of a group called the "uncommon."

As you move upward in the management ranks, you become even more different, more uncommon, than the nonmanagement employee. You may advance high enough to be considered (humorously) **abnormal**! This means you have achieved managerial success, but people like you are few in number

References and Chapter Notes

[1] Bureau of Labor Statistics, "Employment and Earnings," January, 1992.

[2] Frederick W. Taylor, *Principles of Scientific Management* (New York: Harper and Brothers, 1911).

[3] Henri Fayol, *Industrial and General Administration*, trans. J. A. Courbrough (Geneva: International Management Institute, 1930).

[4] Robert L. Katz, "Skills of an Effective Administrator," *Harvard Business Review*, 52, No. 5 (September-October, 1974), pp. 90-102.

[5] Gifford Pinchot, III, *Intrapreneuring* (New York: Harper and Row, 1985).

[6] Dorothy J. Lovett and Carla D. Lowry, "Is Liberal Feminism Working in the NCAA?," *Journal of Sport Management*, Vol. 9, No. 3, September, 1995, p. 267.

CHAPTER 3

THE MANAGEMENT ENVIRONMENT
AND MANAGEMENT'S ETHICAL
AND SOCIAL RESPONSIBILITIES

After studying this chapter, **you will know:**

- The definition of the term "environment"
- The internal and external constraints that affect management
- The main contemporary trends that affect management
- The economic responsibilities of managers
- The meaning of "ethics" and ethical management behavior
- A model for making ethical decisions
- The meaning of "social responsibility"
- What society expects of management
- Critical problems facing management at the year 2000
- How management can adapt to changes in the environment

Introduction

Chapter 3 provides an overall view of the social and economic environment in the United States as we approach the year 2000. Major legislation, trends and movements are discussed. Managers in the sport industry must be aware of the total environment and not narrow their focus to the trends and problems in their unique organization world. Issues in society in general affect the actions and concerns of managers in every industry, including all segments of the sport industry. Those who manage or direct recreation programs, high school, college and professional sports programs; those who manufacture and sell equipment for the sport industry; consultants for marketing and fundraising; operators of fitness centers and all those who manage some aspect of the sport industry must be current and aware of trends in society

To function within the society we have in the United States in a professional and acceptable manner, management must observe certain ethical and socially responsible guidelines. In the sport industry, which often involves working with young people, this is especially important. A section of this chapter deals with the ethical and social responsibilities of sport managers. Of particular interest to students hoping to become sport managers is a model for making ethical decisions which can guide their decision-making process.

The purpose of this chapter is to give students and individual managers an opportunity to learn the components of the environment in general and to see those factors of the environment that affect their jobs in particular. It is essential that managers in every industry relate events and contemporary issues to their own situations. The problems that confront professional sports leagues differ from those that face college, high school or recreation programs; but all must function within the same general environment. The strength of action management may take in any controversial situation is tempered by the legal, social and ethical aspects of the environment.

The Management Environment

The environment of management in any industry is the sum of all the social, cultural, economic and physical factors that influence the lifestyle of an individual, organization or community. No person or organization can function separately from these surroundings which always present constraints on behavior. Managers may exercise power or authority, but they must adjust to their environment. Management's authority (the ability to act or react) is limited by the internal and external constraints imposed by the environment.

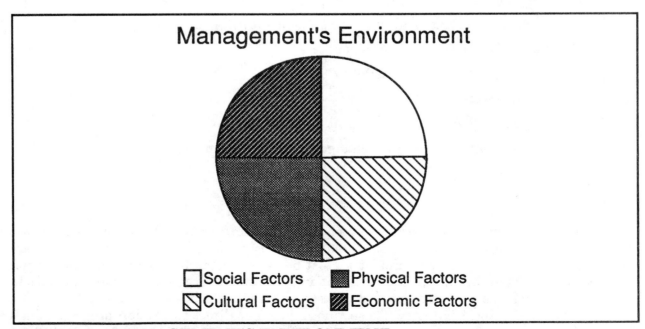

FIGURE 3-1: MANAGEMENT'S ENVIRONMENT

Internal Constraints

Among the large number of environmental constraints that affect managers are those that originate within the organization. These are called *internal constraints*, of which the following are principle examples:

Constraints imposed by organizational documents. Many corporations, government agencies and nonprofit organizations have organizational documents which specify what that organization can and cannot do. These documents may be corporate charters, constitutions, bylaws and their amendments. Many collegiate athletic programs have incorporated athletic associations with corporate charters and bylaws. Any professional team or facility such as a country club, health club, fitness center or spa would also be guided by these types of documents. Other internal constraints that affect sport management include employment contracts, job descriptions, and the regulations in the employer's personnel handbook. The purpose of each of these is to define what the organization is, tell how it is expected to function, and set the limits on its actions. Management's actions in these organizations are restricted by the language of such documents.

Constraints imposed by limited resources. An organization has capital resources, personnel and physical facilities. None of these is unlimited. Once an organization has reached the limit of any of these resources, its management actions are restricted. Eastern Airlines, for instance, had lost money for many years; and finally faced bankruptcy unless it could be bought by another organization. This forced the management of Eastern into the action that led to its being acquired by Texas Air Corporation, which ultimately led to Eastern's demise. Both operative and management personnel can place limits on management's actions, also. If the expansion of production cannot be supported by employees in the right numbers with the right skills, an expansion may have to be postponed. If the current management team is stretched already and new management talent is not readily available, a new product line or new territory may have to wait. Physical plant facilities can also limit production or expansion. The types of constraints created by limited resources in the sport industry are not that different. Professional sports teams often trade a highly paid player because their payroll costs are too great, or they may bypass signing an available (and needed) player because of salary caps and a lack of revenues to justify the investment. Many high schools and colleges lack the desired physical plant facilities to conduct their athletic programs at the level they desire. Limited resources of every type have an effect on all managerial decisions.

Constraints imposed by organizational guidelines. Organizational guidelines are anything that management introduces to influence the behavior of employees. Organizational guidelines include policies, procedures, rules and many other specific plans. All organizational guidelines place limits on what the organization and its managers may do. For example, a policy that the company will not be undersold places pricing limits on managers. If the organization has a rule against employing family members in the same department, personnel hiring and placement is affected. And if there is a set procedure or series of steps to take in purchasing new equipment, a manager's flexibility in purchasing is limited. In many colleges, a central purchasing office handles the procurement of all equipment and supplies that cost more than a minimal amount. This could affect a coach's ability to get exactly the equipment he or she wants for a team and usually adds time to the delivery. In many national chains of fitness centers and spas, there are certain brands of products that must be used, leaving local managers out of the decision-making. Organizational guidelines are developed by top management who also set the broad long-range plans called strategies to achieve goals and objectives. Within these strategies are guidelines that also restrict the actions of lower-level managers. In the sports industry, for example, if a conference commissioner's office negotiates a promotional arrangement with a particular airline for publicity and financial incentives in exchange for teams' using that airline for all travel, the athletics directors and coaches at the member schools have little or no flexibility in making travel arrangements.

Constraints imposed by custom or long-established practice. A custom is a practice which has been carried on for so long with mutual consent that it becomes unwritten law. Customs are often associated with employees in a particular area. It is the custom in some areas of the U.S. to observe Columbus Day as a holiday; in other areas, the Friday before Easter is traditionally a work holiday. If management tries to change these customs, it could cause morale problems and would be difficult to achieve. If it has been the custom in an organization to be lenient with sick leave or not to expect a doctor's excuse for absence due to illness, the manager who attempts to reinstate the requirement for a doctor's note will face limits and may be unable to make the change. Custom can be a strong limiting force on management's action, especially concerning management-employee relations and management-community relations. In sport management, many communities will not condone scheduling athletic contests on religious holidays. It has been only recently, and then because of television revenue and pressure, that collegiate contests have been played on Sundays. It is an established practice in most colleges not to schedule athletic events during students' final exams.

External Constraints

External constraints are those environmental constraints imposed on an organization from outside the organization. External constraints are generally beyond the direct control of an organization. Some major external constraints that can restrict management's action are the following:

Constraints imposed by legal and political consideration. Legal-political constraints include laws and regulations, taxes and political stability. Laws originate usually from some type of management abuse of power. When the best interests of society are served by restricting the power of an organization, an industry or its management to act, laws are passed. For example, when air pollution became a national tragedy, laws were passed to force businesses to end their pollution practices. The Wall Street scandal of the mid-1980s involving violations of insider-trading rules led to harsher rules and stricter enforcement. Managers face laws that limit their power to act in such areas as fair hiring practices, minimum wages, working conditions and the safety of workers, competitive practices, pricing, product safety, the sale of stock, the acquisition of other companies or mergers with other companies, business locations, and many other factors.

The location of a business is particularly influenced by legal and political constraints. Within the U.S., local zoning laws, free port exemption laws, state tax laws, and right-to-work laws (laws that say a person may not be required to join a union in order to keep a job and which vary by state) concern management in making decisions and limit management's action. Internationally, political stability may be the most important factor in restricting management's action.

An organization has no control over the action of a foreign government. Organizations which operate abroad are subject to special taxes, requirements that they employ a certain percent of native workers, and even nationalization of property. The stability of the government is of utmost concern to management of multinational organizations. The ability to continue operating in some foreign countries is affected by political decisions, not action taken by the organization's management. For example, when the U.S. escalated its hostility with Libya, several oil companies were required to cease operations there by the U.S. government. The sport industry has not been immune to political constraints. Several Olympic Games have been disrupted by political activities: the 1972 Games in Munich at which terrorists kidnapped and killed participants and which forever placed all Olympic Games organizers on guard for a repeat of that type of activity; and boycotts at Olympic Games based solely on political stances, such as the U.S.'s own boycott of the 1980 Games in Moscow and Russia's boycott of the 1984 Games in Los Angeles in rebuttal. Political activity around the world has a lasting effect on such international athletic competition as the Olympic Games, and restricts the actions of the Games' planners and organizers.

Any organization that operates internationally always has management action restricted by the foreign nation's customs and mores (moral attitudes and habits). Today, this includes the U.S. sports industry. Many college and professional teams travel abroad to participate in exhibition games to demonstrate a sport new to that country or to compete against international teams. American athletes, and their coaches and team managers, participate in baseball, football and basketball throughout the world. Sport managers may find jobs in international games such as the Olympics or World Games, and they can use their expertise to get interesting jobs with leagues in foreign countries. But traveling teams and individuals must understand in advance the customs, laws and cultures of the countries they visit. They should prepare carefully before encountering a problem that could prove politically as well as personally embarrassing. It could be something as dangerous as illegal drugs found in their possession or something purely cultural like the type and color of a team's uniforms. Sport managers who are involved with international competition must be aware of every aspect involved in this work.

Management does have avenues to affect government action in the U.S. at the local, state and national levels. Managers often testify before governmental committees and commissions, present evidence, or lobby to influence the action of government. An organization cannot usually control what any government body does, however, and its efforts to do so may bring it more unfavorable publicity and cause more harm than the ultimate governmental action. Even the sports industry is not exempt from government investigation and action: Congress has conducted hearings on the effectiveness of sport governance organizations for collegiate athletics to determine whether they should have their authority limited and professional sports leagues have been specifically excluded from antitrust legislation.

Constraints imposed by the public. As consumers, the public holds tremendous power over the practices of any organization. The production decisions of any organization's managers depend on public acceptance of their products. If the public cannot be convinced to buy a particular product, this is a constraint imposed by the consuming public on management actions. If a company gains bad publicity or is exposed as practicing poor quality control, the public can place a constraint on management action through boycotts or by seeking greater publicity for its point of view. For example, when several hundred consumers had problems with the Audi 5000 automobile and got no positive action from the manufacturer, they took their case to the public (through television's *60 Minutes*) and were finally successful in forcing Audi to recall the cars and make an effort to correct the problem. A classic example of how a public event—the tampering with a product in its capsule form—affected management decisions is found in Tylenol. The makers of Tylenol, after suffering and recovering from one episode of product tampering, experienced a second wave of its capsules' being poisoned. This second episode led them to discontinue manufacturing all their products in capsule form (although it was the most popular form of the product) and to develop new forms which were tamper-proof as well as new tamper-resistant packaging. Management's action was constrained by public demand for a safe product and by the public's demand for a product similar to the best-selling capsule form. In the sport industry, the most recent example of how the public affects management actions may be found in the major league baseball strike of 1994-95. How important was public pressure on the major league players association and on the owners to end the strike and get the 1995 season started? Suffice it to say, both sides agreed to play the season, starting a little late, even though the dispute that had ended the 1994 season months early was not yet settled. The public responded to their actions by staying away from games in droves, leaving a lasting impression on both the owners and management of the teams and the management of the players association.

Over the last several years, the public has reacted with concern to the national problem of substance abuse. The publicity associated with this problem in the sport industry alone has been tremendous. Athletes have been fined, banned from competition and stripped of titles for using mind-altering and/or performance-enhancement substances. Many teams have been forced to set up special programs within their organizations to deal with these problems among team members. Public pressure has been a major force in causing the introduction of drug testing of athletes at periodic intervals. This type of additional responsibility puts a new burden on sport managers to balance the interests of the public with the rights of the athletes involved.

Perhaps no issue will affect sport management more in the coming years than AIDS. Professional athletes in several sports have come forward in recent years and admitted being HIV positive, i.e., carrying the virus that causes AIDS. Because of the risks associated with sports activities and the implication that AIDS could be spread through contact with an injured victim, it is clearly foreseeable that all collegiate and professional athletes may soon be routinely tested for the virus that causes AIDS. The Centers for Disease Control and Prevention in Atlanta, Georgia announced in March of 1992 that one million Americans are now believed to be infected with the AIDS-causing virus. This equates to one in every 250 citizens of the U.S. being a carrier of this deadly disease. It is reasonable to assume that sport managers will have to determine what action is necessary to protect all those in contact sports and/or those who use equipment that is openly available. Every sport organization will need to have a plan for dealing with an HIV-infected athlete as well as a program in place for testing, protecting the rights of the athletes, and determining the status of those affected. The rights of the individuals will have to be carefully balanced against the needs and concerns of fellow teammates and the general public. It is a crucial issue to be faced and there is an urgent need to prepare for such action.

The public has affected sport management/administration at the high school and collegiate level in another way. Disturbed by reports of the academic standards (or lack of them) for student-athletes, the public's demand for accountability led to the passage of state laws in many areas dictating "no pass, no play" for students participating in extracurricular activities, primarily athletics. At the collegiate level, dismal graduation rates at many prominent schools fostered an investigation and renewed emphasis on "normal progress" toward degrees for student-athletes as well as annual analysis of their graduation rates compared to the general student population. Scrutiny such as this on the academic side of student-athletes limits the actions of sport managers/administrators and coaches at both levels.

Constraints imposed by the actions of competitors. To continue the Tylenol example, other producers of over-the-counter painkillers were forced to follow Tylenol's lead and eliminate capsule-form products from their product lines until they could make them tamper proof. This represents a constraint imposed by the competition in this case because these other manufacturers were trying not to appear careless in the wake of Tylenol's consumer-oriented action. The so-called air fare war that began with airline industry deregulation in the 1980s is another example of a constraint imposed on management action by competition. Airlines must match competitors' prices in common markets in order not to be beaten. This shows how competition can affect (and impose a constraint on) management's action in pricing and marketing. If a firm holds an important patent, the action of its competition may be restricted. In the case of Polaroid and Kodak, Kodak was forced to leave the instant camera market due to Polaroid's exclusive patent on the camera and process. Few organizations can act without being restricted by the actions of their competitors. In the sport industry, sports equipment companies are always affected by competition and their competitors actions because it is a highly lucrative and crowded field.

Constraints imposed by labor unions. Management action is limited by the contracts it negotiates with labor unions. These contracts affect management decisions about wages, vacation policy, retirement plans, working conditions, grievance procedures, and employment (including termination) policies. Although labor unions represent only about 15.8 percent of employees in the U.S. (in 1993) and they no longer appear to wield the power they once did in negotiating contracts for their members, unions remain a strong force in those industries in which they do exist. The manufacturing industry, especially automobile, textile and steel; the transportation industry; coal mining; all professional sports leagues, and many communications and media industries (such as telephone companies, newspapers, and the television and motion picture industries) remain union strongholds. In all professional sports leagues, player associations and associations of various officials (such as baseball umpires) significantly influence management practices and affect the conduct of the sport.

Constraints imposed by society. Through its elected officials, society ultimately sets the legal and social climate in which organizations operate. If any segment of society is concerned with product safety, pollution, protection of the environment and natural resources, energy conservation, unfair employment practices, etc., that concern will eventually appear in the form of laws and regulations restricting management's actions. Some of the current laws affecting organizational behavior and the social responsibility and ethics of business and its management are discussed later in this chapter.

If an organization or an industry needs particular skills in its work force, it must look to society for the education and skills it needs. If these skills are not available, the decisions of management are affected.

One of the most significant ways that society in general affects management is through the sociological attitudes toward work, profit seeking and change. Management's actions are restricted by these attitudes and are constrained by how eager people are to work and be supervised.

Constraints imposed by the economy. Economic factors that affect management's actions include the availability of capital, the interest rate, the inflation rate, and other monetary and fiscal policies within government. The Federal Reserve System holds virtual control over interest rates and the money supply. Action by the Fed restricts management's ability to get the amount of money it wants, when it wants it, and at a favorable rate of interest. This can mean management decisions regarding expansion, research and development of new products and techniques, and pricing are affected. The timing of management's decisions and implementation of those decisions can also be affected by the ready source of attractively-priced capital. Management can be forced to fund projects through internal financing if the economic environment is not right for borrowing; and this can be an expensive way to meet financial needs. The price that any organization must pay for needed capital is not within its control, and this lack of control over the cost of capital influences and restricts management's actions.

Obviously poor economic conditions nationally or regionally affect the sport industry. Lack of available capital has forced many sporting goods firms out of business. When several million workers are out of jobs during a recession, fitness centers suffer a loss of revenue and members. Season ticket sales to collegiate and professional athletic contests, usually a major source of revenue for the sponsors, fall sharply in difficult economic times. These are examples of constraints imposed by the economy that influence a sport manager's actions and generate reactions

Constraints exclusive to sport management. No external constraints are more familiar to sport managers than those associated with athletic governance associations. The National Collegiate Athletic Association (NCAA) and the National Association of Intercollegiate Athletics (NAIA) as well as counterparts for junior colleges, high school athletic associations, and the league offices of professional sports groups have elaborate rules and regulations to guide and direct the athletics directors, coaches and all personnel involved, including such external groups as alumni and booster clubs. These rigid restrictions influence and control the behavior of coaches when they recruit student-athletes; of managers and owners when they negotiate with prospective players; of all personnel who support and participate in sports with regard to gambling, public personal conduct and more. The handbooks which contain these guidelines are required learning for sport managers.

Significant Contemporary Trends that Affect Management

One of the few constants in society today is change. Managers must remain flexible and be able to adapt to changing attitudes about work and authority, about increasing government intervention, about the expansion of markets internationally, about the demands of better-educated and more aware consumers, and about changes in the population that impact the labor force. In addition, managers must cope with the movement of the economy in the U.S. away from manufacturing to a service-oriented economy.

One of the reasons that management is such a challenging career is that managers must be prepared to deal with this constantly changing environment. Students in sport administration programs should realize that the sport industry is predominantly service-oriented. This means that the success or failure of any aspect of the sport industry is directly related to the satisfaction of its customers. To satisfy customers, who are the users or purchasers of a product or service, requires managers to stay abreast of changes in society as well as changes in technology which affect their operations. Well designed academic programs in sport administration should prepare students to follow contemporary trends in society and adapt to them. For example, the average age of the population in the U.S. by the year 2010 will be significantly higher than it is today. By 2010, more than 65 million citizens will be over age 65; and these people will be healthier, more active and wealthier than any senior citizens before them. Will sport managers be prepared to offer the services and products needed and desired by such a large segment of the population? The following sections detail some of the pertinent trends affecting management in all types of organizations.

Changing ideas about work and authority. No one has defined work as fun, but today's generation takes such a dim view of work that new terms have been coined to describe it. The old puritan work ethic that work is good and necessary for moral well-being has been replaced by the "new work ethic" and the "new breed" workers, as described in Figure 3-2.

The social revolution among young people in the 1960s and 1970s has generated a whole new set of values for American society. Alfred L. Seelye has described the aims of this generation as follows: "Advocates express desire for 'a better quality of life,' defined as a cleaner environment, consumerism, rights of minority groups including women, egalitarianism with emphasis on redressing all economic and social inequities, and more participatory decision making."[1] This can also be described as a revised American dream.

The revision of the American dream may be an outgrowth of the "me generation." It replaces working hard to achieve greater material success with emphasis on mental and physical well-being, balance between work and leisure, greater personal satisfaction, and dissatisfaction with dull, unchallenging jobs.[2] The obvious emphasis is on self-fulfillment and achieving personal happiness.

Some observers attribute the decline in the work ethic to the turn toward a welfare society. Because of welfare programs, food stamps, unemployment insurance, social security and similar programs, it is now possible to survive economically without working. This makes people less willing to work at any job they dislike. A second reason for the decline in the work ethic may be that the advances in technology which have produced such strides have made many jobs boring for workers, particularly people who are better educated. It is a fact that the labor force as a whole is better educated now than it was 20 years ago (see Figure 3-2). Further, younger workers do not value pride in work and craftsmanship as highly as older workers; they do not wish to become as involved in company and community affairs; and they are less loyal to a single organization.[3] Couple these factors with an increasing challenge to authority in general, and it is apparent that managers face tremendous challenges in dealing with employees.

The challenges to authority have evolved since the 1960s when draftees challenged the authority of the federal government and refused to serve in the armed forces. The challenge extended to business where the authority to discharge employees has been questioned in various court actions. The old-time manager who was a virtual dictator is being replaced by one who must gain acceptance of his authority before exercising it.

Statistics on the New Breed Work Force

- Women: 45% of the labor force in 1988; expected to be 47% by 2005.

- African-Americans: 11% of the labor force in 1990; expected to be 12% by 2005.

- Hispanics: 8% of the labor force in 1990; expected to be 11% by 2005.

- Asian and other: 3% of the labor force in 1990; expected to be 4% by 2005.

- White, non-Hispanic: 79% of the labor force in 1990; expected to be 73% by 2005.

- Age: Median age = 36.6 years in 1990; expected to be 40.6 years by 2005.

- Education: Those with 1-3 years of college up from 15% in 1975 to 21% in 1990; 4 or more years of college, up from 18% in 1975 to 25% in 1990; 4 years of high school or less, down from 67% in 1975 to 53% in 1990.

- Jobs Profile: Service-producing jobs are up from 70% in 1975 to 77.1% in 1990 and are expected to be 81% by 2005. Goods-producing jobs are down from 29.5% (1975) to 22.9% (1990) and projected to be 19% by 2005.

- More Affluent: Median family incomes are up from $20,800 in 1980 to $34,788 in 1991 with half of all families depending on two or more wage earners.

- Cost to Employers: The Employment Cost Index (ECI) for civilian workers is up from 100 in June, 1989 to 112.2 in 1991.

- Employed Fewer Hours Per Week: 39 in 1991 vs. 39.3 in 1989 with more paid benefits and more paid holidays.

FIGURE 3-2: CHANGES IN THE WORK FORCE

Sources: Bureau of Labor Statistics, *Occupational Outlook Handbook*, 1992-93 edition, pp. 9-10 and *Statistical Abstract of the United States* 1992, pp. 389, 413-414.

The reasons that authority has been challenged are many. Abuse of power by managers is the most important one. When managers abuse their authority and extend it beyond common sense, such as imposing unreasonable conditions on employees, the power will be challenged. Permissiveness in society in general is a second reason that employees challenge authority. Many people who have authority now decline to use it, and authority not backed with action soon becomes weaker. Finally, scandals in business and government, such as Watergate in the 1970s and the insider-trading scandal of the 1980s, have left people disillusioned with those in power. Followers want their leaders and authority figures to set a proper example and to lead by action not words.

These changes in the attitudes of American workers have brought management many problems. Excessive absenteeism, poor workmanship, high personnel turnover, working at minimal capacity, and other symptoms present distinct problems for management. The overall result of these changes has been the decline of American productivity and America's loss of status in world markets. The challenge to managers today is what can they do to reverse the effects of the new work ethic and how can they restore respect for authority among American workers.

Competent professional managers who are people-oriented can overcome all of the negative trends and attitudes in society. Managers have a challenge to become as professional as managers as the top professionals are in any other field of endeavor, such as medicine.

Those who follow the new work ethic want challenging and meaningful work in addition to good monetary pay and generous fringe benefits. They also need nonmonetary rewards such as recognition and respect from their peers. One measure which managers can take to make work more interesting is to use job rotation (moving a worker from one task to another). Another device management can use is job enlargement (the worker performs a greater variety of tasks). Both of these can help with the boredom of routine jobs.

Managers must remember that they manage individuals, not groups of people; and they must know their personnel so well that they can align personal goals with organizational goals. This will aid in motivating workers, which is one of management's biggest challenges.

The demand for a different quality of work life leads organizations to offer employees more flexibility in work schedules and to attempt to change the work place to increase worker productivity and satisfaction. The broad concept of quality of work life refers to the way in which work "provides an opportunity for an individual to satisfy a wide variety of personal needs—from the need to survive with some security to the need to interact with others, to have a sense of personal usefulness, to be recognized for achievement, and to have an opportunity to improve one's skills and knowledge."[4]

In addition to placing emphasis on the factors stressed in the quality of work life concept, managers must face other challenges in dealing with the new breed of workers to achieve greater acceptance of managerial authority and to increase worker productivity. Specifically, the new breed of worker expects management to address the social philosophy of **egalitarianism** with direct action. *Egalitarianism advocates social, political, and economic equality.* Women will enter the work force in increasing numbers, and the gap between the earnings of men and women as well as that between whites and minorities must be addressed and narrowed. More women in the work force (see Figure 3-3) will also spur management to erase the inequalities in status and increase both the number of women in management in general as well as the number of women in higher-level management jobs. Equal Employment Opportunity laws which already exist will be more closely obeyed by management because of the continual efforts of women and African-Americans and other minorities.

Intervention in business by government. Equal Employment Opportunity laws are just one of the many current laws affecting business. Despite an attempt in the late 1970s and early 1980s to deregulate the transportation, banking, petroleum and other industries, the overall effect of government regulation of business increased. And the signs are that it will continue to increase as society grows more complex and the rights of individuals need protection.

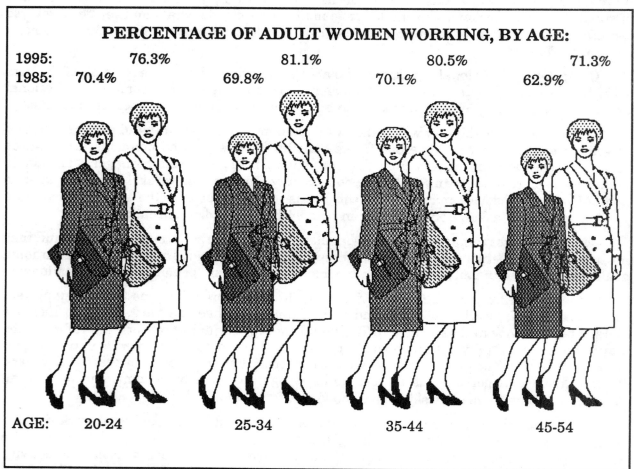

PERCENTAGE OF ADULT WOMEN WORKING, BY AGE:

1995: 76.3%	81.1%	80.5%	71.3%
1985: 70.4%	69.8%	70.1%	62.9%

| AGE: 20-24 | 25-34 | 35-44 | 45-54 |

FIGURE 3-3: WORKING WOMEN ON THE RISE
Estimates for 1995 predict 59% of all women will be working, compared with 55.4% in 1986.
Source: U.S. Bureau of Labor Statistics

In 1993 there were more women and minorities in key managerial roles including the sport industry. While the numbers are not large, the trend has been established. Numerous colleges in the U.S. have women as the top athletics administrator, and more African-Americans have been named as head coaches, managers and executives than ever before. Other minorities are seeing more opportunity in management positions as well although the numbers are small. Being properly prepared for job openings in management is the best way for anyone to gain an advantage in the job market. Preparation begins with education and knowledge of the field of sport administration.

Forty years ago an employer could advertise a job opening and specify what race, sex and age range the applicant must be. The employer could also pay one worker less than another doing the same job for no certifiable reason. Promotion into management positions for women and minorities was rare. Today, it is illegal to discriminate in hiring on any of the above bases and workers doing the same job are entitled to equal pay. Government regulations, in response to such social movements as the Civil Rights Movement of the 1960s, have on paper eliminated much of this discrimination. The Equal Employment Opportunity Commission, which reports directly to the president, enforces equal employment rights for women and minorities. Under Title VII of the Civil Rights Act of 1964, organizations are required to take **affirmative action** (make special effort, often by establishing special programs, to increase the proportion of women and minority-group members in management positions) to eliminate inequities in the status of women and minorities. While these programs have brought about much change and much paperwork for businesses to comply with them, progress is slow in correcting all the inequities (see Figures 3-4 and 3-5). In 1995 many of these affirmative action programs were questioned seriously both by business and at several levels of government, including court rulings that effectively weakened the mandate for such programs based on quotas.

By 1992, the U.S. Bureau of Labor Statistics reports that women comprise 45.4 percent of the total labor force and 40.6 percent of the jobs classified as "Managers/Executives/Administrators (*Employment and Earnings*, January 1992). The most reliable estimates of women in pure management positions by 1992 is that approximately 28 percent of all managers are women.

FIGURE 3-4: INEQUALITIES IN PAY AND STATUS (Weekly Salary)

Source: U.S. Bureau of Labor Statistics, *"Employment and Earnings."* Jan., 1992, Table 56, p. 223.

All organizations are influenced by federal, state, and local governments. Reporting requirements for such activities as payroll (federal, state and local income taxes withheld; social security taxes withheld, and other deductions from paychecks); sales taxes; specifications for safety of work environments; and even starting and ending a business place demands on all American organizations. For an employer, the federal government requires a quarterly report of income and social security taxes withheld from employees' salaries—even if the business is small and has only one (perhaps even part-time) employee. As long as a taxable income is paid, the organization (profit-seeking and nonprofit as well) must file this report. And this does not include reports to the state and/or local government, the state labor department for unemployment tax which every employer must report and pay, and possibly reports to the EEOC on changes in employees' status.

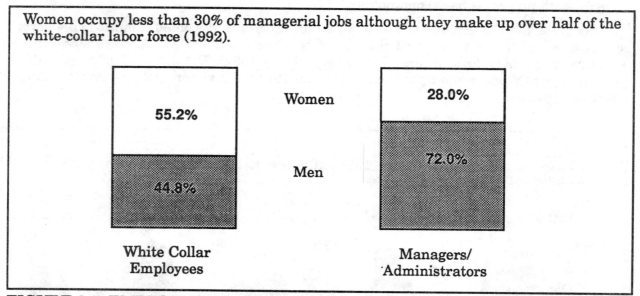

FIGURE 3-5: EMPLOYMENT AND EARNINGS
Source: Bureau of Labor Statistics, Jan., 1992, pp. 223-225.

Other government regulatory agencies which have had a major influence on American management's actions in the last 15-20 years are the Occupational Safety and Health Administration (OSHA) and the Environmental Protection Agency (EPA). OSHA was established in 1970 to ensure that a safe and comfortable work environment could be guaranteed every worker. While managers agree that the purpose is sound, not all believe the regulations and requirements themselves are good. OSHA's section in the Code of Federal Regulations is almost 1,500 pages, and managers must be constantly aware of the requirements these regulations place on them and the work environment. The EPA, established in 1970, is supposed to guard the environment against contamination and pollution. It has not been popular when a plant shut down and jobs were lost because the company could not meet the EPA specifications for pollution; but the problem the EPA addresses is a serious one which American managers will have to continue working to correct in partnership with the government.

How does the continued involvement of government in business affect today's managers? Management action is restricted by some government regulations, but primarily it makes the job of a manager more complex and involves the manager in keeping detailed records on hiring, firing and promotions; safety of the workplace and accidents; quotas of women and minorities in various levels of management, and many other facets of day-to-day work.

No one suggests that the government intervention is not necessary, but many managers will agree that compliance with increasing government regulation is an added burden.

Expansion of markets internationally. International competition is not a thing of the future, it is a fact of today's economy. American productivity diminished and the quality of American output slipped so much that many consumers turned to goods produced in foreign countries for satisfaction. An example is the highly popular videocassette recorder (VCR). It is believed that between 75% and 90% of all homes will own at least one VCR in the near future, and none is manufactured in America. American consumers have bought foreign-made products in record amounts in the last ten years, and America's trade deficit has grown dramatically as a result.

The effect of increased international competition on American managers is to force them to become more productive, more efficient, and more creative. America's strength in the international market lies in high technology industries and services.

Factors which have opened international markets include better and faster communication and easier travel to all parts of the earth. Many higher-level American managers will have their jobs complicated by international trade. They must know different languages, the laws of trading nations, customs and traditions of other countries, what the foreign political climate is and other facets of each country with which their organizations trade. In addition, they must remain current on any American tariffs and/or trade agreements affecting each of these countries. Further, many managers will be travelling abroad as part of their duties. Perhaps a middle-level manager in a textile firm has production contracts with foreign manufacturers. He or she will be travelling there to confirm deals, sign formal agreements, and to monitor compliance with the contract specifications. As recent news events have shown us, travel to some areas is not always safe for Americans. This adds a further complication to the manager's job which some "new breed" workers (who are also in management) may decline to accept. So, management can be affected by having difficulty filling jobs for personnel who must communicate and travel internationally.

An excellent example of taking American knowledge and professionalism in athletics administration and specialized subjects within sport management to international markets involves the United States Sports Academy located in Daphne, Alabama. The Academy has negotiated many contracts with foreign governments to provide trained personnel to coach and teach subjects in sport: coaching, sport behavior, sports medicine and fitness, sport research and sport management/administration.

The rise of consumerism. Today's American consumer is better educated and less willing to accept defective and inferior products than in years past. Since Ralph Nader inaugurated the current trend toward consumer protection in the 1960s, American consumers have demanded better and safer products and have gained a consumer "bill of rights," as published by the Consumer Advisory Council established by President John F. Kennedy in 1962.

Among the rights now advocated by consumers are the following:

The right to safety. Consumers have the right to be protected from dangerous products or those which could become dangerous if misused. Laws require warnings and explicit use instructions.

The right to be informed. Information directed at consumers must not be fraudulent, deceitful, or misleading. The Federal Trade Commission polices advertising to protect consumers from false information. And, the Truth-in-Lending Act of 1969 requires that consumers are clearly informed about the interest rates and terms of loans they make. Care labeling laws give consumers information on the proper care (washing, dry cleaning, etc.) of garments to protect them and maintain any properties of the fabric (such as fire-retardant children's clothes).

The right to choose. Consumers are guaranteed through several trade and antitrust laws that competition will not be unlawfully restrained.

The right to be heard. The Consumer Protection Act of 1975 and the Agency for Consumer Advocacy that it established work to provide consumers a voice in legislative matters affecting them.

Management must clearly take the interest and concerns of consumers seriously when manufacturing products and providing services. Managers will have to focus on increasing product quality to meet the demand of consumers and on providing goods and services desired by consumers. Service-producing industries are not exempt from consumer scrutiny.

Changes in population and demographics. Changes in the growth of the population are important to an economy, but of even more importance to management in the future is the demographic makeup of that population. Demography is the statistical study of human populations with emphasis on size and density, distribution, and vital statistics. A demographic fact about the U.S. population is that it is growing at record slow rates. This, coupled with lower death rates in the U.S., changes the composition of the population: fewer young people, more older ones. Some have dubbed this change in the population the "graying of America," and it has significant implications for management.

These changes in the composition of the U.S. labor force will produce interesting results. Because the baby boom generation will reach middle age in the 1990s, there will be more competition for middle-level management jobs. The low birth rate will shrink the supply of entry-level workers, which could cause labor shortages and raise pay rates in an effort to compete effectively for the best available workers. The retirement age has already been raised from 65 to 70, so managers must be prepared to have older employees who will work longer than ever before. Each of these factors will have to be met with management adjustments.

These population changes also affect the demand for goods and services which management will have to project. It is estimated that the median age in the U.S. will reach 35 by the year 2000,[5] and this means a shift in consumer goods from those aimed at the under-25 generation to the larger middle-age group. Older Americans, both those working and those retired, will comprise a larger market than in previous history, giving rise to new products designed for senior citizens and putting emphasis on products used by them. Gerber Products Company of Freemont, Michigan, a leading producer of baby foods, has seen enough of a trend to diversify into insurance, apparel and trucking. It is also interested in marketing food for seniors, according to spokesman Leonard Griehs.[6] The political clout of the older segment of the population will also grow and have more influence on laws and government.

Figure 3-6 shows the anticipated changes in the population through 1990 for people of working age.

Shift to a service economy. According to the Bureau of Labor Statistics, the service field will lead all others in job growth into the 1990s. Specifically, jobs in the medical services and business services areas will expand. Many service industries are dominated by small, private companies. This limits the need for many levels of management but opens the door to whole industries which provide management services.[7]

Such a trend can lead to more entrepreneurs among the managers of tomorrow. It may be the right match for the personality of the new breed of worker: great satisfaction and no one to blame or answer to except oneself; set one's own work/leisure mix; achieve just as much material success as one desires, etc. It is also a fact that more inventions per firm are produced by small businesses, emphasizing the innovative quality of management and employees.

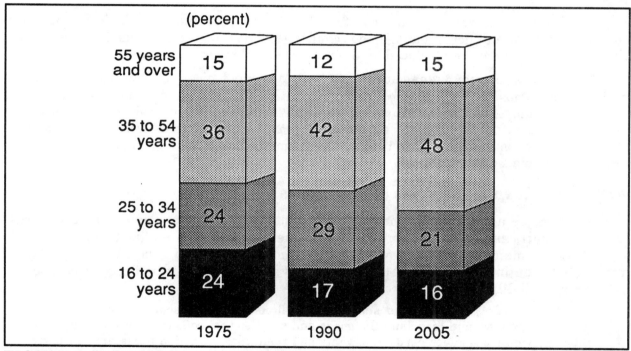

FIGURE 3-6: THE AGE DISTRIBUTION OF THE LABOR FORCE IS CHANGING.
Source: Bureau of Labor Statistics, *Occupational Outlook Handbook, 1992-1993 Edition*, p.9.

In the May, 1987 issue of *Inc.*, a list of the 100 fastest growing small public companies was published. It is dominated by service firms, with the leaders long-distance phone companies, broadcasters, medical research firms, and computers. Of the 100 fastest growing small public companies, 55 are service companies.[8]

Managing in the service industry involves the same functions as managing in the manufacturing sector, but there are differences. Managers of service organizations will work more closely with the consumers. There will be fewer middle-level management jobs, since many of these service organizations are small firms; therefore, more emphasis will be placed on first level managers. In some service industries, it is common for employees to work outside a central office, at home for instance. This makes these employees more difficult to monitor and increases the complexity of the manager's job.

The continued importance of technology. Technology has been the dominant factor in the workplace for many years, and the future shows no sign of its diminishing. Managers do not manage technological forces such as machines, but technology has a significant effect on management. Those managers who work in high technology industries are concerned with research and development and innovation of new machines, new features for existing machines, and other devices. They must also market their inventions. Those managers in industries not directly involved with creating technological advances must be concerned with whether to use and how to use the new technology. People will be affected in either case, as managers will have to determine how much to invest in machinery that replaces people.

Manufacturing managers may soon find their "employees" include robots. Robots themselves will not pose difficult management challenges, but integrating them with people and retraining people who are displaced by them will be challenges for management.

The implications for management involved in technological change are to create and maintain an atmosphere which encourages innovation so that technological advances can be developed. Management must also hone human relations skills to deal with the problems people will encounter when high technology becomes a part of their work environment or displaces them, specifically how to prepare them to accept change and how to retrain employees displaced by machines.

Economic Responsibilities of Managers

Most people agree that the primary responsibilities of management are economic: to provide products and services, to provide employment, and to earn profits. Even in nonprofit organizations, managers must provide services, employment, and generate enough capital resources to continue operating. Managers in any kind of organization cannot escape economic responsibilities.

To provide products and services. The first economic responsibility of management is to produce and distribute the goods and services that consumers want. Managers must determine consumer needs and wants and then take the action necessary to satisfy them. Since American consumers have great freedom to choose between alternatives, management decisions about production and providing services are complex. Managers must always be alert to changes in consumer preferences and must take quick action to accommodate such changes.

To provide employment. If the private sector of the American economy did not provide adequate jobs for those who can and want to work, the government would have to intercede. In America, private enterprise provides approximately 85 percent of all jobs, with various levels of government providing most of the rest.

The level of employment is a key economic factor. Most economists concur that the maximum level of employment at any given time is 96 percent. When 96 percent of the work force is employed, the economy is at **full employment**. An economic recession occurs when the employment rate is between 90 percent and 96 percent, with the lower percentage indicating the severity of the recession. If employment falls to 90 percent or below, we are experiencing an economic depression. The **labor force** is defined as those people ready and able to work.

Management has a responsibility to make jobs interesting and challenging as well as available. For most people, time spent at work represents one of life's most important facets; so, society expects management to make work psychologically rewarding. It is a challenge to managers to keep jobs interesting and to create new jobs for people displaced by technology.

To earn profits. Profit-seeking organizations cannot survive for long without earning profits. In addition, profits are necessary in the capitalistic economic system to pay taxes; finance growth and modernization; and to fund research and development that leads to new products and improvements in existing ones. Stockholders and creditors pay close attention to profits earned in deciding whether to invest capital or fund projects. Management's first purpose is always to survive, and earning profits is a necessity to achieve this.

In accomplishing these economic responsibilities, management must contend with the current problem of declining productivity. Inflation and limited energy resources, which had been problems for management in the recent past, are not as prominent in the 1990s.

Management's Ethical and Social Responsibilities

Ethics and social responsibility are two pertinent topics in the field of management for business, education and government. Every day a new item appears detailing the devious, unethical or illegal practice of some organization or its management. The problem is also a truly equal opportunity vice: It affects government and other nonprofits equally as often as profit-seeking businesses; and there is no discrimination on the basis of race, sex or national origin. Former executive directors of both the United Way and the NAACP have stood accused of misappropriating funds; and the founder/president of a huge drugstore chain as well as the long-term president of a small church-related college have allegedly embezzled funds from their respective organizations.

The sport industry has not been bypassed. Collegiate sports programs frequently spend time on "probation" as ordered by various governance authorities for violating rules and regulations. This problem became so widespread several years ago that the NCAA developed a "death penalty" for those programs who had been punished repeatedly, a probation/punishment so severe that it threatens the continued existence of the collegiate program. And the "death penalty" has been applied to some programs. Both professional and collegiate sports programs have been shocked with gambling investigations and big name stars, owners and whole programs have been punished. Drug use, both illegal street drugs and steroids, have caused turmoil in all levels of the sport industry and have forced the formulation of detection and enforcement programs that are controversial for their "ethical" correctness and invasion of privacy.

Colleges and universities have responded to the challenge to be more ethical by revamping curricula to require courses on ethics, social responsibility and social issues affecting modern people. It behooves managers at any level of any type of industry to become familiar with ethical considerations and develop a code of ethical behavior. If managers do not behave ethically, some governance authority will develop and enforce its own ethical behavior system over them eventually. The demand for ethical action has never been greater.

Laws have been passed and continually updated to block the attempts of organizations to act in a way contrary to the best interests of the environment, consumers' rights and fair competition. Such regulations may be considered an attempt to legislate social responsibility.

Some issues in ethics are clear for those in sport management/administration: Use of drugs to enhance performance is illegal; gambling on one's own team where they can and do affect the outcome is improper for any player or coach/manager; falsifying a student-athlete's academic record to gain and/or maintain eligibility for participation is outlawed. But other issues that involve ethics are less well defined: Is it unethical for fitness clubs to pressure people to join with tactics used successfully (and regularly) by those who sell other products? How "ethical" are the hiring practices of organizations if minorities and women are underrepresented in management positions? Such issues as these raise the fundamental debate about the definition of ethics.

Ethics

One of the categories that the philosophers of ancient Greece named as a major pursuit of man is the ethical/moral, which they defined as the pursuit of goodness and virtue.[9] In business, ethics is more often focused on the justification of a person's actions and the search for a coherent set of values or ideals that can guide the actions of an individual or an organization when their actions may cause conflicts with others or with society in general.[10]

Descriptively, "ethical" behavior has grown to mean "legal," "virtuous," or highly "moral" behavior. Ethical behavior is the object of much attention today in all types of industry. Officials at every level of government have been caught in illegal and unethical behavior, leaving the people of the U.S. with doubts about the actions government takes. Business has been racked by scandals that involve total industries, such as the insider trading and savings and loan failures (which were linked) in the 1980s and various reports of product manipulations and price fixing. Consumers have been left wary of nearly all business practices. Religion has suffered its own scandals involving everything from fraud in fundraising to sexual indiscretions. Within organizations themselves, employees are becoming disillusioned with their managers. A study conducted by Donald L. Kanter of Boston University's School of Management and Philip H. Mirvis of the University's Center for Applied Social Science found these startling facts: In the opinion of their employees these facts about bosses emerged: (1) 5-15 percent exhibit deviant behavior during working hours; (2) 10-20 percent of drug abusers are managers, business owners and professionals; and (3) 78 percent of the workers distrust their supervisors.[11] If nearly four out of every five employees in the U.S. distrust the management of their organizations, clearly there is a problem with ethics in American management.

Ethics is generally considered to be a set of moral values or principles. It deals with what is good or bad and with the moral duty and obligations of individuals or societies. A professional organization may have a "Code of Ethics" to govern the conduct of its members or subscribers. Often ethical and legal conduct are confused. Ethical behavior goes beyond what is legally correct and adds to the behavior a degree of social acceptability. Ethics can change with the fluctuating attitudes of society. For example, owning a mink or other luxury fur coat was once the ultimate symbol of success for most women; today, many of those women consider the raising of such animals for that purpose obscene and demonstrate vigorously against such displays. Once alligators were an endangered species which could not be legally killed; but now they are caught and used for shoes, belts and purses because the moratorium led to overpopulation. Changes in the sports industry also reflect this; for example, the change in participation in the Olympics: For many years, the U.S. would now allow any Olympic athlete to be defined as a "professional" in his or her sport; now, professional athletes can and do compete under the U.S.'s banner. In ethical behavior situations, sometimes the morally correct action depends on many factors.

The difference between morality and ethics is often one of semantics. Morality defines a value structure that limits behavior. Ethics concerns the justification and application of moral standards. Most dictionaries indicate these two words are synonyms.

Management's Ethical Responsibilities

The most widely known and practiced theories of ethics are based either on *deontology (the theory of moral obligation)* or *teleology (the doctrine that ends or results are the true reality in nature)*. The focus of deontology is on the basic moral good of the action; while teleological ethical theories, primarily utilitarianism, focus on end results or consequences—simply put, maximizing the best effect for the greatest number.

When a sport manager/administrator or a manager in any industry makes a decision, he or she must weigh the ethical implications of both the end results of the decision and the decision-making process. Laws, governance organizations and the demands of the public may even add the dimension of intention of the decision to these factors.

Managers are involved with ethics on a daily basis. Every decision made in operating any organization has to encompass three essential core activities: (1) achieving the objectives, (2) maintaining the internal system, and (3) adapting to the demands of the external environment.[12] Ethics concerns the interrelationships between people and their institutions. A manager makes a decision based on his or her ethical code; then, he or she initiates action which is right or wrong, in the best public interest or not, fair or unfair, or legal or questionable. The answer to some of the questions may lie in developing a model for ethical decision-making.

Making Ethical Decisions

Managerial decision-making is not an exact science because managerial decisions involve value judgments based on the individual's ethical beliefs. The difficulty of making decisions is compounded by the vagueness of the future relating to the decision. Once you add elements of the specific environment and its factors to the decision-making process, the manager has a difficult job weighing all the facts, values, concerns and possibilities to arrive at an ethically proper decision. The decision-making process must begin, however, with the clear knowledge that the desired action and its end result are legal.

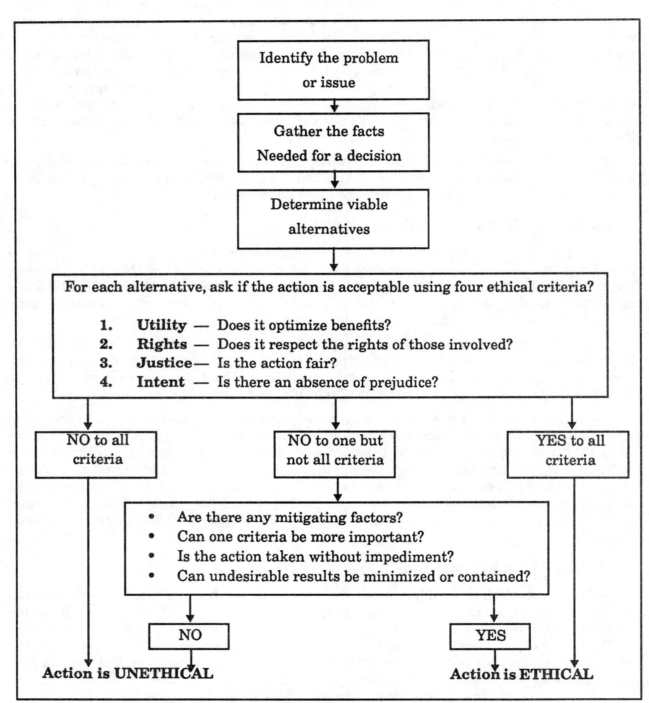

FIGURE 3-7: A MODEL FOR ETHICAL DECISION-MAKING

Based on Cavanaugh, G., *American Business Values*, 2nd Ed., Englewood Cliffs, N.J.: Prentice Hall, 1984.

Once the legality of the situation and question is firmly established, a model that can be followed in making decisions based on ethical considerations is shown in Figure 3-7. In this model, four criteria are used to evaluate the ethical quality of a decision: utility, rights, justice and intent. If there is some confusion or uncertainty among these four criteria, more in-depth analysis must be made on the weighted importance of each factor, the freedom with which the action is taken, and the prospect of undesirable results. In each instance of judgment, the ethics of the person making the decision and his or her personal ethical beliefs are the basis for any consideration of facts and information. After a decision is reached using this model, the decision-maker should always follow-up to determine how closely the actual consequences or effects of the decision came to those that were desired or expected.

Professional Ethics

Controversy surrounds the concept of professional organizations who develop a self-regulating Code of Ethics for their members. But most would agree that such a statement of professional conduct and expectation would be a step in the right direction.

In the sport management industry, such a single Code of Ethics is difficult to develop because of the wide spectrum encompassed by the field. One effort has been made, however, to formulate such a code. The North American Society for Sport Management (NASSM) has approved an ethical creed for sport managers and has a committee working on an ethical code for its members (see Figure 3-8 for the creed).

PROFESSIONAL MEMBERS OF THE NORTH AMERICAN SOCIETY FOR SPORT MANAGEMENT, LIVING IN A FREE, DEMOCRATIC SOCIETY, HAVE RESPECT FOR THE WORTH AND DIGNITY OF ALL PEOPLE IN OUR SOCIETY. AS PROFESSIONALS WE HONOR THE PRESERVATION AND PROTECTION OF FUNDAMENTAL HUMAN RIGHTS. WE ARE COMMITTED TO A HIGH LEVEL OF PROFESSIONAL PRACTICE AND SERVICE, PROFESSIONAL CONDUCT THAT IS BASED ON THE APPLICATION OF SOUND MANAGEMENT THEORY DEVELOPED THROUGH A SCIENTIFIC BODY OF KNOWLEDGE ABOUT SPORT AND DEVELOPMENTAL PHYSICAL ACTIVITY'S ROLE IN THE LIVES OF ALL PEOPLE. SUCH PROFESSIONAL SERVICE SHALL BE MADE AVAILABLE TO CLIENTS OF ALL AGES AND CONDITIONS, WHETHER SUCH PEOPLE ARE CLASSIFIED AS ACCELERATED, NORMAL OR SPECIAL INSOFAR AS THEIR STATUS OR CONDITION IS CONCERNED.

AS NASSM MEMBERS PURSUING OUR PROFESSIONAL SERVICE, WE WILL MAKE EVERY EFFORT TO PROTECT THE WELFARE OF THOSE WHO SEEK OUR ASSISTANCE. WE WILL USE OUR PROFESSIONAL SKILLS ONLY FOR PURPOSES WHICH ARE CONSISTENT WITH THE VALUES, NORMS, AND LAWS OF OUR SOCIETY. ALTHOUGH WE, AS PROFESSIONAL PRACTITIONERS, DEMAND FOR OURSELVES MAXIMUM FREEDOM OF INQUIRY AND COMMUNICATION CONSISTENT WITH SOCIETAL VALUES, WE FULLY UNDERSTAND THAT SUCH FREEDOM REQUIRES US TO BE RESPONSIBLE, COMPETENT, AND OBJECTIVE IN THE APPLICATION OF OUR SKILLS. WE SHOULD ALWAYS SHOW CONCERN FOR THE BEST INTERESTS OF OUR CLIENTS, OUR COLLEAGUES AND THE PUBLIC-AT-LARGE.

FIGURE 3-8: NASSM ETHICAL CREED (approved 1989)

Source: E. Zeigler. Proposed creed and code of professional ethics for the NASSM, *Journal of Sport Management*, 3,2-4.

Such a creed or code is another step toward professionalism. Many factors that affect segments of industries are controlled by legal regulations, but much behavior and conduct depends on the personal ethics of the practitioners. Individuals must consider how strong their own personal ethical values are; their personal integrity and the courage they have in following their conscience; the degree to which ethical behavior is demanded or encouraged in their work environment; and the various role models and mentors that have influenced their attitude and work environment. The professional ethics of any group is merely the sum total of the individual members or practitioner's personal ethics. In the sport industry many personnel, such as head coaches, who have shown a disregard for the rules and regulations of their respective segments of the industry find jobs hard to get. This is an example of self-regulation of another type.

Social Responsibility

There is no one clear, widely accepted definition of the social responsibility of management. One authority defines it as: "the moral and ethical content of managerial and corporate decisions over and above the pragmatic requirements imposed by legal principle and the market economy."[13] Another source says that it is simply "the duty of business to promote (or at least not damage) the welfare of society."[14] As people consider the concept of social responsibility and ethical behavior in every industry, they should see the complicated factors and issues that arise. *For use in this text, however, we will condense the social responsibility of management into acting in the best interests of society in general.*

The concept of social responsibility originated with Henry Gantt (refer to management history in Chapter 1) whose humanistic approach to management included industry's responsibility for training workers. Gantt did more to encourage industrial responsibility than anyone before him. Increasingly in recent years, the public has demanded accountability from all types of institutions.

Management's failure to perform in the best interests of the public had led to bad publicity that eroded confidence and trust in that organization and in business in general. When the public outrage becomes great, the government usually steps in with some type of regulation or punishment.

The most important social responsibilities of organizations, and thus of the managers who make and carry out decisions, are these:

To provide safe products. As we have seen with Tylenol and several automobile examples, organization are expected to improve the safety of their products or remove the unsafe ones from the marketplace. The public holds the producer accountable if its product injures consumers.

To provide a safe and healthy work environment. When accidents and injuries on the job reached high levels, the public demanded action. It came in the form of the government regulations (OSHA). Now, the concern management faces about the workplace involves eyestrain from video terminals and other health effects of high technology. In addition, many companies are responding to the social pressure to provide substance abuse counseling and physical fitness programs as part of a healthy work environment.

To protect the physical environment. Since the early 1960s, great emphasis has been placed on conserving resources and eliminating pollution from our environment. Management decisions have been affected by the public pressure and ultimate government regulation which resulted. Many socially responsible businesses have taken this even farther by landscaping plant sites into parklike facilities and doing more than meet the government requirements for pollution control. These actions cost money and must be allocated in plans for construction of facilities.

To provide equal opportunities for women and minorities. We have discussed this elsewhere in this chapter, but many organizations have responded to the public interest in equal opportunity by deliberately filling management openings with women or minorities. Organizations which have well-developed affirmative action programs make them public to gain the favorable reaction. One effect of going beyond government requirements has been a growing number of lawsuits charging reverse discrimination by predominately white males who were bypassed without any other reason. Management must proceed with care to achieve equal opportunity without encountering legal challenges to its actions.

To obey both the spirit and letter of laws—be ethical. The public is demanding that organizations and their managers not only obey laws but also respect the intent of the regulation. If a company chooses to ignore pollution-control requirements that would be more expensive than paying the fine associated with noncompliance, its critics will not be satisfied. The intent of the regulation is to control pollution, not to collect fines; and public pressure will continue to swell until managers are held personally accountable for such decisions. Organizations have the resources to maneuver within the law, but the public now expects more ethical behavior. Ethical behavior is defined as taking the action that is right and just and that conforms to accepted standards for behavior. Increasingly, the public is demanding not only legally correct behavior of managers, but highly ethical conduct as well.

To provide public-service programs. Society demands that organizations give back to the community some of the profits they take. In Georgia, the electric utility, Georgia Power Company, has increased rates dramatically to pay for a nuclear power plant. Public pressure forced them to initiate a program to aid those who have difficulty paying the higher rates. Many companies recycle waste products; others sponsor scholarship programs for their employees' children; and some donate organizational time and talent to the United Way and other charities. Managers who favor these actions believe it advances the long-term best interests of their organizations as well as provides a social good deed.

The Social Responsibility Controversy

Not everyone believes that organizations have social responsibility. Economist Milton Friedman, who has repeatedly advocated that the only responsibility business has is to maximize profits and obey the law, says this:

> The only entities who can have responsibilities are individuals; a business cannot have responsibilities. So the question is, do corporate executives, provided they stay within the law, have responsibilities in their business activities other than to make as much money for their stockholders as possible? My answer to that is, no, they do not. Take the corporate executive who says, "I have responsibilities over and above that of making profits." If he feels he has such responsibilities, he is going to spend money in a way that is not in the interest of the shareholders.[15]

Professor Friedman is the leading proponent of this view, but he is not alone. Others view the primary goal of management, maximizing profits, with some modification.

In the article, "The Ethical Roots of the Business System," Douglas S. Sherwin defines an interdependent system within each enterprise where each of three groups—owners, employees and customers—is essential for survival. Sherwin maintains that profit is not the only purpose of business; rather, the proper focus should be on equitable distribution of benefits and rewards to all parts of the system. If any one segment is disenchanted or failed by management's actions, they will reduce their contribution to the system. Economic performance will suffer as a result of this reduction, and the purpose of the business institution in society will be compromised. Sherwin's idea of the underlying ethical/social responsibility of management is that, in conjunction with the other segments in the system, they will "make public policy affecting business more reflective of the needs and desires of American society."[16]

H. Mintzberg calls Professor Friedman's view wrong, but adds that socially responsible behavior by business is not the solution to all society's problems. He believes that management, along with public policy, should stress behavior that contributes and adds something useful to society, rather than being destructive. In this view, committment and personal ethics are the keys to true social responsibility of business because such attitudes are reflected by the employees who are the most critical group.[17]

John Dobson says that the goals of profit maximization and social responsibility are not mutually exclusive. Managers can reconcile the two motives through their desire to develop and maintain the organization's reputation and public image. Dobson calls an organization's reputation an implied contract with four key characteristics:

1. A firm can have several reputations for different attributes.

2. A firm builds a reputation by demonstrating a consistent mode of behavior to its stakeholders (e.g., customers, creditors, shareholders, etc.).

3. The building or maintaining of a reputation can require net expenditures in the short-run, presumably in the expectation of net revenues in the long-run. Thus the decision whether to build or maintain a reputation at any time can essentially be viewed as a capital budgeting decision.

4. A firm's reputation can act as an implicit contractual enforcement mechanism: individuals may reject short-term opportunistic behavior in favor of actions which, although costly in the short-run, will be perceived as maximizing long-run wealth through maintenance of their reputations.[18]

Corporate philanthropy reflects the views of Dobson. Organizations seek to improve and maintain their reputations in the long-run by developing and publicizing their participation in short-run social programs and projects. Many sport industry organizations participate in community programs and sponsor various types of corporate philanthropy efforts to enhance their reputations.

Despite the debate over just what social responsibility is and whether organizations have such responsibilities, the general consensus is that managers will have to face greater social responsibilities in the future.

Laws Affecting Management's Social and Ethical Behavior

As mentioned earlier, when public outrage or demand reaches a certain point, government and other governing organizations take steps to insure that management acts in a socially and ethically proper way. This takes the form of laws, regulations and rules. There are hundreds of such laws, regulations, rules and enforcement agencies. Many of these federal laws and regulations are discussed as applied to the sport industry in Chapter 4, "Legal Aspects of Sport Administration." Those federal laws which apply to employment are discussed in Chapter 10, "Staffing." Figure 3-9 shows those federal regulatory agencies that are concerned with social responsibility and ethics issues that affect the actions of sport managers as well as all other managers. There are specific federal laws that address product safety and environmental issues as well that may be of concern to sport managers, especially those products such as guns which have strict labeling requirements to protect children.

REGULATORY AGENCY	ORIGIN	ACTIVITY OR FUNCTION
Federal Trade Commission (FTC)	Federal Trade Commission Act (1914)	Enforces antitrust violations with the Justice Department; sets standards on unfair methods of competition and deceptive consumer practices including false advertising
Equal Employment Opportunity Commission Agency (EEDC)	Title VII, Civil Rights Act (1964)	Investigates complaints and issues rulings on employment discrimination based on sex, age, race, color, religion, or national origin
Environmental Protection Agency (EPA)	National Environmental Policy Act (1969)	Sets standards and enforces federal laws on pollution control
Occupational Safety and Health Administration (OSHA)	Occupational Safety and Health Act (1970)	Responsible for regulating safety and health working condition of employees
National Highway Traffic Safety Administration (NHTSA) (created in 1970)	Motor Vehicle Safety Standards Act (1966); Highway Safety Act (1966)	Regulates automobiles and other vehicle safety standards
Consumer Product Safety Commission (CPSC)	Consumer Product Safety Act (1972)	Sets safety standards in the production of consumer products
Federal Election Commission (FEC)	Campaign Finance Act (1974)	Supervises funding national election campaigns, including business contributions and political action

FIGURE 3-9: MAJOR FEDERAL REGULATORY AGENCIES DEALING WITH SOCIAL RESPONSIBILITY AND ETHICS ISSUES

Environmental and Ethical Problems Facing Managers in the Future

Planning and keeping informed. Managers must be aware of the changes in the environment and remain flexible in responding to them. One key to doing this is to plan effectively and to make contingency plans. In Chapter 5, we will discuss planning in detail, including when and how to allow for contingencies.

Managers can accommodate changes in the environment by gathering and using information well. Internal sources of information are readily available: absenteeism reports, sales data, equipment repair records, quality control reports and such provide managers with valuable information for making new plans and altering existing ones. For collegiate sport managers, it has become advisable to have coaches file forms detailing trips for recruiting and scouting to ascertain their conformance to rules and regulations. Students' records are sources of most academic information needed by athletics administrators at every level to determine eligibility and progress toward graduation.

Managers in any industry can read newsletters, professional journals, popular magazines, attend professional meetings and conventions, join professional groups, attend clinics and use other external sources for information about trends and developments in the economy and in their respective industries, including those involved in sport management/administration.

Ethics Officers. Approximately 20 percent of the 1,000 largest American industrial and service organizations have *ethics officers.* W. Michael Hoffman, director of the Center for Business Ethics at Bentley College in Waltham, Massachusetts, calls this one of the newest and fastest growing professions in American business. The idea of establishing positions to enforce codes of ethics arose after the mid-1980s when scandals focusing on improper and illegal business practices made news regularly. Federal sentencing guidelines passed in 1991 that mitigated penalties against organizations which had ethics programs in place added momentum to the trend. Ethics officers form the moral conscience of an organization, making certain that the mission and statement of corporate values and accepted conduct are followed. One concern about their position has been raised: They must have the authority to effect change in an organization's operations to bring them in line ethically. Ethics consultant Barbara Ley Toffler emphasizes that it is important not to place people in the position of having to choose between acting ethically or boosting productivity, which might lead to cutting corners or breaking rules. These two goals should be complementary, not mutually exclusive. Acting ethically should increase the public's trust and confidence in an organization and its products, leading to improvement in its profitability.[19] In the sport industry, many collegiate athletics programs have added personnel to fill this type of role. Titles vary from compliance officer to academic advisor, but the purpose is the same: see that all effort is made to perform and operate ethically within the rules.

Ethics and Strategy. In philosophy, there is a concept known as common morality. *Common morality is that group of general rules that apply to most situations in which one must make an ethical judgment.* Most people live by a set of common morality rules most of the time. Once we define a set of common morality principles, we can derive some principles of business and management ethics. Students of sport management/administration will see how well these basic common morality rules can be applied to activities in the sport industry:

> **The Principle of Promise Keeping** states that most people should keep their promises most of the time.

> **The Principle of Avoiding Harm** states that most people should not inflict physical or mental harm on others most of the time.

> **The Principle of Mutual Aid** states that people should help others in need if the cost is not greater than they can afford.

The Principle of Respect for Persons states that most persons most of the time should treat each other as ends in themselves not as means to the ends of others.

The Principle of Respect for Property states that most people most of the time should use other people's property only after gaining their consent.

From these simple principles of common moral behavior, we can derive some general principles for guiding management ethics. There are seven principles stated by Freeman and Gilbert to guide decision-making toward better business ethics:

1. Always tell the truth to customers in your advertising.
2. Act to maximize the well-being of stockholders within the bounds of the law.
3. Balance the interests of all stakeholders.
4. Achieve the most social good that you can.
5. Follow standard business practices most of the time.
6. Keep your contractual and promissory obligations.
7. Treat employees with dignity and respect.[20]

Ethics applies to strategy because it guides the course of any organization through each decision made. Business ethics must prepare managers to face new situations in which there are often conflicting purposes or goals and which need new means for making decisions.

Moral Managers. As the year 2000 approaches, managers face becoming more involved in value issues, using publicly acceptable personal ethics in making organizational decisions. Public organizations can no longer afford the scandals that unethical and immoral as well as illegal management behavior have brought upon them. Government restrictions will be tightened in response to public demands if organizations do not meet the acceptable standard for moral management.

In the book *Managers for the Year 2000*, Harold F. Smiddy, a former President of the Academy of Management and an outstanding executive management educator, suggests six ways to prepare managers for the future while retaining them in useful and challenging jobs:

1. Monitor leadership development using new standards for ethics in management in evaluating candidates.
2. Make change normal using continuing education.
3. Reward "internal entrepreneurs" by encouraging innovation.
4. Have managers participate in social planning to meet the organization's social responsibility to all stakeholders in the community.
5. Provide training in diplomacy or political processes so that managers know how to influence outcomes in confrontation situations.
6. Make explicit use of different management styles by helping managers select the management style best suited to the particular activity being managed.[21]

Managers make decisions concerning resources and stakeholders (everyone who has an interest or stake in the outcome of a situation or a decision). The most convenient method of measuring the success of the manager's efforts has been profit maximization or, in the case of sport industry managers, victories or championships. But this goal is now not satisfactory and acceptable to the public alone. Managers must also be concerned with social values and with balancing the desires of its resource contributors and stakeholders. This requires understanding of the political process and how to use it to maximize priorities. Part of the continuing education of today's managers, through educational institutions and organizational development programs, must be to prepare them as "diplomats" in the business world. The new measure of the manager's success will include how well he or she evaluates value issues and how skillfully the manager achieves highest priorities.[22]

Summary

The environment of management is the sum of all the social, cultural, economic and physical factors that influence management action. Management authority is limited by various internal and external constraints in the environment. Some of the primary internal constraints are organization documents, limited resources, organization guidelines and customs. External constraints include those imposed by legal and political considerations, the public, competitors, labor unions, society and the economy.

The practice of management is affected by many current trends. Among the most important trends are changing ideas about work and authority, increased intervention in business by government, the expansion of markets internationally, the rise of consumerism, changes in the size and demographics of the population, the shift away from a manufacturing-based economy to a service-based one, and the continued growth and importance of high technology.

Management's economic responsibilities are to provide products and services, to provide employment, and to earn profits (or generate the funding required to continue operations if a nonprofit enterprise).

In order to cope with a rapidly changing environment, managers must remain flexible and must master the function of planning, including allowing for contingencies. Above all, managers in every industry in the U.S. must become more professional in carrying out the duties and functions of their jobs.

Ethics and social responsibility are two pertinent topics in the field of business and management. In addition, the problem of ethical and socially responsible behavior affects nonprofit and governmental organizations as well.

Laws have been enacted to block the attempts of organizations to act in a way contrary to the best interests of the public on issues involving the environment, consumers' rights and fair competition. Such regulations may be considered an attempt to legislate social responsibility.

Ethics is generally considered to be a set of moral values or principles. Descriptively, "ethical" behavior has come to mean "legal," "virtuous" or highly "moral" behavior. The most widely known and practiced theories of ethics are based on either deontology (the theory of moral obligation) or teleology (the doctrine that ends or results are the true reality in nature). Deontology stresses the basic moral good of the action while teleology focuses on the end results, namely to maximize the best effect for the greatest number. Ethics concerns the interrelationships between people and their institutions. Some professional organizations have developed a self-regulating Code of Ethics for their members.

There is no one clear, widely accepted definition of the social responsibility of management. In this text, the social responsibility of management is acting in the best interests of society in general. The most important social responsibilities of organizations and their managers are to provide safe products; to provide a safe work environment; to protect the physical environment; to provide equal opportunities for women and minorities; to obey the laws, and to provide public service programs.

There are conflicting views about social responsibility. The renowned economist Milton Friedman leads the faction that believes business has only one responsibility: to maximize profits while obeying the law.

The federal government has passed many laws relating to managerial ethics and social responsibility. Most of these laws were enacted in response to unethical practices and abuses. The general categories of these regulations are competitive behavior and trade; consumer protection; product safety, and environmental protection. There are many regulatory agencies set up to enforce the various laws and acts in this area. Government becomes involved in social responsibility legislation when business has failed to respond to issues that affect the needs of society.

One trend in the field of management and business is the creation of ethics officers in large organizations. Approximately 20 percent of the largest American organizations have such positions.

Managers in the future will need to be trained in political processes or diplomacy to handle all the duties required of them skillfully.

Review Questions

1. Define the environment of management.

2. List and discuss the internal constraints to management action.

3. List and discuss the external constraints to management action and explain their significance.

4. Discuss the "new breed" worker and the decline in the work ethic.

5. How has government regulation affected management?

6. How do changes in the size and composition of the population affect management?

7. What are management's economic responsibilities?

8. Discuss the distinction between ethics and morality.

9. Define social responsibility and explain what society expects of management.

10. What is the importance of a group of professional colleagues in one industry having a "code" or "creed?"

Assignments for Personal Development

1. Suppose a Head Football Coach at First University is under investigation for governance rules violations in his program by his staff, boosters, players and himself. Second University offers him a better job as its Head Football Coach and he accepts, moving into the new job immediately. Second University administrators know nothing about the pending investigation, and he discloses nothing to them in a thorough round of interviews. What are the ethical responsibilities of the coach? Of the Athletics Director at First University? Of the Administration of Second University? Of the investigators?

2. Controversial issues have dominated the news concerning sport administration in recent years. Set up debates with your classmates to discuss the social responsibility/ethical issues in the following situations: "Bait and Switch" advertising by health clubs and spas; discrimination by private athletic clubs; the presence of female reporters in the locker rooms of professional sports teams (or male reporters in all-female team's locker rooms); and the abuse of recreation and little league players by overzealous parent/fans.

Incident

CROSSING THE LINE

Janett Swinson answered the phone as she walked into the house from the part time job. "Come over to the school and meet with me and Coach Jackson as soon as you possibly can," said Harold Russell. Coach Russell is the girls' basketball coach at the local high school where Janett's daughter, Ellen, is a senior, all-state player. Fearing that Ellen had been injured at practice, Janett hurried to the school.

When she opened the door to Athletics Director Jackson's office, Janett saw both coaches seated around a desk with Ellen slumped in a chair, pale and somewhat disoriented.

Coach Jackson spoke first, "She got sick at practice, Janett, and we discovered she is drunk. I am afraid this is too serious a problem to ignore."

"I have decided to suspend her from the team for the rest of the season," added Coach Russell, who himself had been shaken by Ellen's actions. He had helped her seek a college scholarship and was responsible for the five full scholarship offers she had received from top name schools.

Janett guided Ellen to the car to go home. "The season is only half over and you are through. I hope you realize what you have done to your future and our family," Janett said through her own tears.

Questions:

1. How involved should a coach and/or athletics director become in a student-athlete's personal problems?

2. Was this action by the school athletics administrators justified? How far should local school personnel go to police the actions of students and student-athletes?

Glossary of Key Terms

Affirmative Action Plan: Special program to eliminate inequities in the status of women and minorities.

Code of Ethics: When professional organizations develop a self-regulating statement of professional conduct and expectations.

Common morality: A group of general rules that apply to most situations in which one must make an ethical judgment.

Demography: The statistical study of human population with emphasis on size and density, distribution and vital statistics.

Deontology: The ethics theory of moral obligation.

Egalitarianism: A social philosophy that advocates social, political and economic equality.

Environment of Management: The sum of all the social, cultural, economic and physical factors that influence the lifestyle of an individual, organization or community.

Ethical behavior: Has grown to mean "legal," "virtuous" or highly "moral" behavior.

Ethics: A set of moral values or principles.

Ethics Officers: Positions established in large organizations to ensure that the mission and statement of corporate values and accepted conduct are followed.

External Constraints: The environmental limits that affect managerial actions and originate outside the framework of the organization.

Federal Trade Commission: A federal agency which has broad authority in consumer protection as well as in enforcing antitrust legislation.

Food and Drug Administration: A federal agency with the authority to act in protecting the public from unsafe foods and medicines and from products that are mislabeled.

Foreign Corrupt Practices Act of 1978: A federal law forbidding organizations in the U.S. from making any type of payments (bribes) to acquire foreign contracts.

Internal Constraints: Those environmental limits that affect managerial actions and originate within the organization.

The National Environment Policy Act of 1969: Federal law which created the Environmental Protection Agency; was passed to preserve, protect and improve the environment.

Occupational Safety and Health Act of 1970 (OSHA): Federal law which established specific safety guidelines that affect most U.S. organizations; designed to reduce work-related injuries and deaths, protect employees on the job and improve job conditions.

Proactive management: Business and management responding to social and economic problems before they are forced to do so; taking an active approach to social and economic issues affecting the public.

Quality of Work Life: Refers to the way in which work provides an opportunity for an individual to satisfy a wide variety of personal needs.

Social responsibility of management: Acting in the best interests of society in general.

Teleology: The ethics doctrine that ends or results are the true reality in nature; e.g., utilitarianism.

Practical Concepts in Management

MANAGERS SET THE TONE AND EXAMPLE

An often overlooked responsibility of new managers is that of setting the tone and example for the employees you manage. Setting the tone refers to the "spirit" of the work group. Establishing a positive attitude toward work, generating an air of enthusiasm, and creating a sense of importance about the work being done are examples of positive "spirit."

Setting the example for other employees to follow relates to absenteeism, work habits, being on time, having a positive attitude toward higher management and the company, and actions that demonstrate company loyalty.

It is unlikely that your employees will be the ideal types of workers in attitude and behavior unless you set the example and lead the way.

Further, managers have a responsibility to demonstrate fairness and ethical standards of conduct when dealing with customers, clients and employees. This also influences the attitudes and behavior patterns of employees.

MANAGERS MUST WEAR THE MANAGEMENT HAT

Whether you begin your career with a position in management or are promoted into management from a nonmanagement job, you will have to adjust your attitude. You will have to think and act like a manager.

You, as a manger, are the "company" to your employees. What you say, do, don't say is the company to them. One of your major responsibilities is to act and speak in the best interest of the organization. For this reason, you should associate with managers, think like a manager, act like a manager, and in every way be a manager.

This does not imply that you can have no friends among nonmanagement employees. It simply means that they should know and you should know that every decision you make as a manager is going to be in the best interest of the organization. Sometimes such decisions may override friendships.

One test of a manager's integrity and character is whether he or she can consistently respect the feelings and rights of employees and customers while doing what is right for the organization.

References and Chapter Notes

[1] Alfred L. Seelye, "Societal Change and Business-Government Relationships," *MSU Business Topics* 23 (Autumn 1975): 7.

[2] Daniel Yankelovich and Bernard Lefkowitz, "The New American Dream," *The Futurist* 14 (August, 1980): 14-15 and Daniel Yankelovich, "New Rules in American Life: Searching for Self-fulfillment in a World Turned Upside Down," *Psychology Today* 15 (April, 1981): 35-91

[3] David Cherrington, "The Values of Younger Workers," *Business Horizons* 20 (December 1977): 18-30.

[4] G. Lippitt and J. Rumley, "Living with Work--The Search for Quality in Work Life," *Optimum* 8 (January, 1977): 38.

[5] "The Graying of America," *Newsweek* 89, February 28, 1977, p. 50.

[6] William Dunn, New age for the aged," *USA Today*, August 20, 1986, pp. 1A, 8A.

[7] Charley Blaine, "Services field leads job growth," *USA Today*, February 24, 1986, p. 1E.

[8] Harriet C. Johnson, "Future belongs to services, 'Inc.' says," *USA Today*, April 30, 1987, p. 1B.

[9] Russell L. Ackoff, *The Art of Problem Solving* (New York: John Wiley & Sons, 1978), p. 14.

[10] R. Edward Freeman and Daniel R. Gilbert, Jr., *Corporate Strategy and the Search for Ethics* (Englewood Cliffs, NJ: Prentice Hall, Inc., 1988), pp. 44-45.

[11] Lisa Crowe, "What does your staff really think of you?," *Atlanta Journal/Constitution*, March 2, 1987, pp. 1C, 11C.

[12] Chris Argyris, *Integrating the Individual and the Organization* (New York: John Wiley & Sons, Inc., 1964), p. 120.

[13] Robert H. Bork, "Modern Values and Social Responsibility," *MSU Business Topics*, Spring, 1980, p.7.

[14] Ferdinand F. Mauser and David J. Schwartz, *American Business*, 6th ed. (San Diego, CA: Harcourt Brace Jovanovich, 1986), p. 94.

[15] Quoted in Robert A. Dahl, "A Prelude to Corporate Reform," *Business and Society Review*, Spring, 1972, pp. 17-18.

[16] Douglas S. Sherwin, "The Ethical Roots of the Business System," in Contemporary Moral Controversaries in Business, ed. A. P. Iannone (New York: Oxford University Press, 1989), pp. 35-43.

[17] Henry Mintzberg, "The Case for Social Responsibility," in *Contemporary Moral Controversaries in Business*, ed. A. P. Iannone, p. 174.

[18] John Dobson, "Management Reputation: An Economic Solution to the Ethics Dilemma," *Business and Society* (Spring 1991), pp. 13-20.

[19] "More businesses recruit ethics officers," Associated Press, August 24, 1993 as reprinted in *The Atlanta Journal/Constitution*, p. F3.

[20] Freeman and Gilbert, *Corporate Strategy and The Search for Ethics*, pp. 55-60.

[21] Harold F. Smiddy, "The Indispensability of Voluntary Teamwork," in *Managers for the Year 2000*, ed. by William H. Newman (Englewood Cliffs, NJ: Prentice-Hall, Inc., 1978), pp. 116-118.

[22] William H. Newman, "Irrepressible Opportunities," in *Managers for the Year 2000*, pp. 119-129.

CHAPTER 4

LEGAL ASPECTS OF SPORT ADMINISTRATION

Glenn M. Wong
Lisa Pike Masteralexis*

In this chapter, you will become familiar with the following terms:

Sports law	Libel	Programmatic approach
Collective bargaining agreements	Slander	Institutional approach
Federal court system	Agency law	Equal Rights Amendment
Trial system	Independent contractor	Equal Pay Act
Contract law	Constitutional law	Title VII of the Civil Rights Act of 1964
Tort liability	Due Process	Antitrust law
Intentional tort	Equal protection	Sherman Antitrust Act
Unintentional tort	Unreasonable search and seizure	Clayton Act
Assault and battery	Invasion of privacy	Labor law
Reckless misconduct	Sex discrimination	Employment discrimination
Negligence	Title IX of the Education	Americans with Disabilities Act
Defamation	Amendments of 1972	Age Discrimination in Employment Act

Overview

Sports law is a growing component of the sports industry, thus those involved in this industry must be knowledgeable about sports law.

This chapter provides information on how the field of sports law emerged, the issues relative to sports law, and how these issues have an impact on the different factions of the

---

* This chapter was contributed by Glenn M. Wong, Professor and Department Head and Lisa Pike Masteralexis, Assistant Professor of the Sport Management Program at the University of Massachusetts at Amherst. The authors would like to acknowledge the contributions in the first edition of the chapter of Carol Barr, Assistant Professor, Sport Management Program, University of Massachusetts for her research and writing assistance and Maureen Kocot for her help in preparation of the manuscript.

sports industry, such as administrators, coaches, officials, and participants. Key areas of the law and their relationship to the sports industry are identified and defined in this chapter. These key areas are contract law, tort liability, agency law, constitutional law, sex discrimination, criminal law, antitrust law, and labor law.

This chapter also delineates how the different areas of the law affect the sports industry, of what the sport manager should be aware regarding these issues, and how the sport person can better deal with potential litigation.

The study of **sports law** is a relatively new field. The first sports law course was offered in 1972 by Professor Robert C. Berry at Boston College Law School. Titled "Regulation of Professional Athletics," the course reflected the fact that most of the sports law issues in 1972 dealt with professional sports. By the end of the 1980s, amateur sports law issues and cases had become as prevalent as professional sports law issues. In the time since Berry's initial sports law course, many law schools and sport management programs have integrated sports law into their curricula. This trend will probably continue into the 1990s, because the increased monetary stakes in the sport industry have propelled all facets of athletics toward a businesslike approach.

What is sports law? It is the application of various areas of the law to a specific industry—the sports industry. The application of the law to sports has in many instances created new and difficult legal issues for judges, lawyers, and athletic administrators. These legal issues have created the need for and—in some instances—produced federal and state legislation specific to athletics. In addition, these unique issues have required the promulgation of rules, regulations, and legal documents pertaining specifically to athletics. An example of federal legislation is Title IX of the Education Amendments of 1972, which governs sex discrimination issues in elementary and secondary schools, colleges, and universities, and is applicable to athletic programs at institutions that receive federal funding. Another example of federal legislation is the Amateur Sports Act, passed in 1978, which governs Olympic sports in the United States. An example of state legislation promulgated for sports is agent legislation, passed in 24 states, which governs the conduct of individuals who represent athletes in contract negotiations with professional teams. In addition, many states have laws pertaining to athletic trainers and/or doctors, requiring their presence at certain high school athletic events. Several states have legislation dealing with fan behavior toward referees and officials, and a number of states have legislation dealing with fitness and exercise facilities. In addition to legislation, some specific rules and regulations governing athletics are listed in the *NCAA Manual*, which is published by the National Collegiate Athletic Association (NCAA). The *NCAA Manual* was first printed in its current format in 1965, although the NCAA bylaws have been printed in earlier forms since 1913.

Contracts have also become an important part of the business side of athletics. There are now standard contracts for professional team athletes. Further, the professional team sport leagues have negotiated **collective bargaining agreements** governing the terms and conditions of employment for players in their respective leagues. Individually-negotiated contracts are the norm for coaches at the college level, for teams that lease facilities and/or broadcast games on television and radio, and for individuals who join health clubs.

Sports law has become increasingly important for sport management personnel. This is evident in that many important leadership positions in athletics are held by lawyers. For example, three current commissioners of professional team sports are attorneys: David Stern in the National Basketball Association, Gary Bettman in the National Hockey league, and Paul Tagliabue in the National Football League. Several general managers of professional sports franchises, college conference commissioners, and athletic directors are also attorneys.

Although many attorneys hold these leadership positions, a law degree is not necessarily a prerequisite to obtaining a key leadership position. Overall, there are certainly more people in key administrative positions in athletics who are not attorneys. However, it certainly helps if the nonattorney is able to recognize and deal with legal issues, simply because legal issues are occurring on a more frequent basis than in previous years. The athletic administrator who has an appreciation and understanding of sport law issues will find it easier to make appropriate administrative decisions to avoid legal difficulties; he or she will also be able to communicate, understand, and question more effectively, as well as instruct the organization's attorney when difficulties do arise.

This chapter provides a starting point for the sport manager who desires to be versed adequately in sports law. The topics for discussion include a review of the court system, contract law, tort law, agency law, constitutional law, sex discrimination law, criminal law, antitrust law, and labor law.

The Court System

The sports manager needs a fundamental understanding of the U.S. legal system to deal effectively with the wide variety of legal matters faced today. There are two basic legal systems in the United States: the federal system and the state system.

Federal Court System

The **federal court system** in the United States consists of the Supreme Court, 13 courts of appeals, 94 district courts, certain specialized courts, and administrative agencies (Figure 4-1). Federal cases are usually first heard in a district court, although a limited number of cases may be initiated in the higher courts of appeals or in the Supreme Court. Cases that are appealed after being heard in the district courts usually go to a court of appeals—or, in rare cases—will go directly to be heard in the Supreme Court.

The Supreme Court is the highest court in the United States and the ultimate authority on all legal issues. Once the Supreme Court decides an issue, all other federal courts must interpret the law by its lead. Nine justices sit on the U.S. Supreme Court, including a chief justice and eight associate justices. The Supreme Court justices are appointed by the President of the United States and confirmed by the U.S. Senate. Justices serve lifetime tenures.

Supreme Court decisions are made after the justices have heard the oral presentations and reviewed the *briefs*, or written arguments, from both parties. Each justice renders an opinion on why a certain decision should be made, and then the justices vote in order of seniority. After a decision has been reached by majority vote, the justices choose one of their members to write the *opinion of the court*. A justice who disagrees with the opinion and did not vote with the majority may write a *dissenting opinion*. A justice who agrees with the majority opinion but not with the reasons it was reached may write a *concurring opinion*.

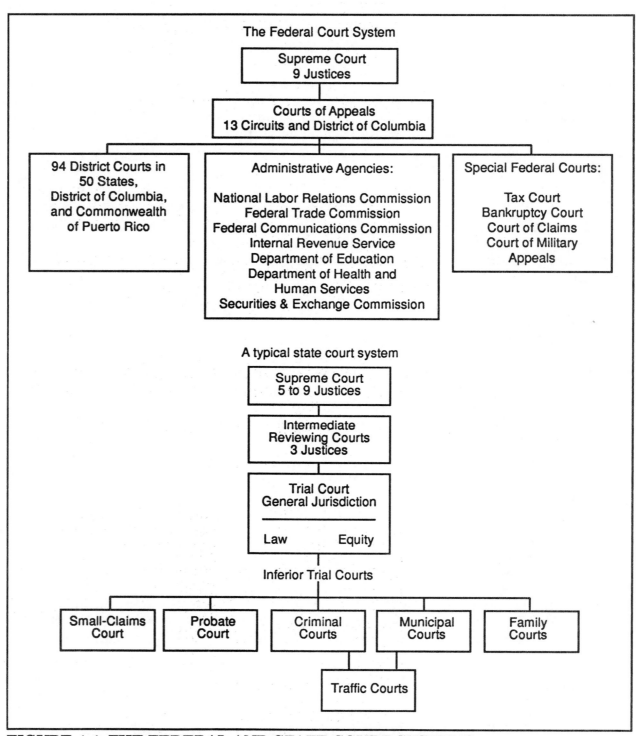

FIGURE 4-1: THE FEDERAL AND STATE COURT SYSTEMS

Source: Wong, G. (1994). *Essentials of Amateur Sports Law, Second Ed.*, Westport, CT: Praeger Publishers.

The United States is divided into 13 judicial districts and the District of Columbia. Each of these districts, called *circuits*, has a U.S. Court of Appeals. These 13 appeals courts have only *appellate jurisdiction*, which means that they review cases tried in the federal district courts and cases heard and decided by the federal administrative agencies (for example, the Internal Revenue Service and the National Labor Relations Board).

The *district courts* are the trial courts of the federal court system. Each state has at least one district court: a total of 94 district courts cover the 50 states, the District of Columbia, and the Commonwealth of Puerto Rico.

Rulings made by such federal agencies as the Federal Trade Commission, the Internal Revenue Service, and the National Labor Relations Board fall into the category of *administrative law*. These agencies are allowed to formulate rules for the administrative area they regulate, to enforce the rules, to hold hearings on any violations, and to issue decisions, including penalties.

State Court System

In general, each of the 50 states has a three-tiered court system, with a trial court level, appellate court level, and supreme court level of review (see Figure 4-1). Each state judicial system hears cases and reviews the law based on its state constitution, state statutes, and previous court decisions. In addition, a state court must often interpret the federal constitution and/or federal statutes, based on how they affect state criminal or civil laws that are reviewed under its jurisdiction.

The Trial System

For many nonattorneys, a group which includes most athletic administrators, the threat of litigation is a very upsetting proposition. However, with some basic information about how the trial system works, the athletic administrator will realize that dealing with the trial system is not as complicated as it first may seem. The trial system can be broken down into the following ten parts:

1. The *complaint* is the initial pleading in a trial, filed by the plaintiff in a civil case and the prosecutor in a criminal case.

2. The *summons* is the actual serving of notice to the defendant, notifying the defendant of the legal action being instituted and ordering the defendant to "answer" the charge by a certain date.

3. The *answer* is the defendant's initial pleading filed in response to the complaint.

4. Two types of *jurisdiction* must be satisfied before a court can hear a case: personal and subject matter. *Personal jurisdiction* requires a court to have sufficient contact with the defendant to bring the defendant into its jurisdiction. *Subject matter jurisdiction* requires a court to have authority to hear the subject matter that is being tried.

5. *Discovery* is a pretrial procedure by which each party to a lawsuit obtains facts and information about the case from the other parties in the case to

assist all parties with trial preparation.

6. The *parties* are the participants in a legal action. The *plaintiff* is a person or party who initiates a legal action by bringing a lawsuit. The *defendant* is the person or party against whom legal action is taken and against whom relief or recovery is sought.

7. The two types of courts in the trial system are the *trial court* and *appeals court*. The *trial court* is the court of original jurisdiction in which all issues are brought forth, argued, and decided on by either a judge or jury. The *appeals court* is the court of review in which issues decided at trial are reexamined for error. No new evidence or issues may be presented in appeals courts.

8. A *jury* comprises a certain number of individuals selected according to the law, who are sworn to inquire of certain matters of fact and declare the truth on evidence to be laid before them. Whether a trial will be a jury or a nonjury trial depends on the nature of the trial. The judge oversees the trial but has limited supervision over the decision determined in a jury trial.

9. The *judgment* is the decision given after the closing statements. The judge either instructs the members of the jury on their options in reaching a decision, or the judge—in a trial without a jury—renders the decision.

10. A judgment by a trial court may be *appealed* when a party (appellant) requests that the trial proceedings be reviewed by a higher court claiming that an error was made at the trial. An appeals court may reverse (disagree with) a lower court's ruling either totally or in part, it may *remand* (return) the case back to the lower court for further proceeding, or it may *affirm* (agree with) the lower court's decision.

Case Citations

Cases throughout this chapter are listed according to their case citation. A case law citation consists of a case title and case citation, which includes the court reporter in which the decision can be found, the volume, the court which made the decision, and the page number. For example, *Shelton v. National Collegiate Athletic Association*, 539 F.2d 1179 (9th Cir. 1976) was a case decided in the federal court of appeals (denoted by F.2d, which is the *Federal Reporter*, Second Series, volume 539, page 1179). The case was heard in the Ninth Circuit Court of Appeals and was decided in 1976. A state court case is listed in a state reporter and/or regional reporter.

A citation's case name will reflect the type of case it is—that is, whether it is a civil or a criminal trial. For example, *Jones v. Smith* is a civil case involving one individual suing another, *State v. Smith* is a state criminal law case, and *U.S. v. Jones* is a federal criminal law case.

Judicial Review

Athletic administrators make decisions regarding athletic rules and regulations daily. As decision makers, athletic administrators must realize that they do not possess complete control over student-athletes as their decisions may be reviewed by courts. Historically, courts have declined to intervene in the internal affairs of voluntary organizations that govern athletic programs, except where *one* of the following conditions is met:

1. The rule violates public policy because it is considered fraudulent or unreasonable.

2. The rule exceeds the scope of the athletic association's authority.

3. The athletic association breaks one of its own rules.

4. The rule is applied in an arbitrary and/or capricious manner.

5. The rule violates an individual's constitutional rights.

The harshness of a rule is not by itself grounds for judicial review. Relief is granted only where one of the above conditions is met. For example, in one case, the court upheld an NCAA rule declaring ineligible collegiate athletes who sign professional contracts against an athlete who claimed he was fraudulently induced into signing a contract with an American Basketball Association team. While the court admitted that the application of the eligibility rule may produce an unreasonable result, the rule did not violate the athlete's equal protection rights [See *Shelton v. NCAA*, 539 F.2d 1179 (9th Cir. 1976)]. On the other hand, the court struck down a good conduct rule regulating an athlete's off-season behavior on the grounds that it exceeded the scope of the athletic association's authority [*Bunger v. Iowa High School Athletic Ass'n*, 197 N.W.2d 555 (Sup. Ct. 1972)]. In another case, the court granted a preliminary injunction to restrain the defendant athletic association from barring the plaintiff's girls' basketball team from postseason play because the association had not followed its own rules when it barred the team from participation [*Christ the King Reg. High School v. Catholic High Schools Athletic Ass'n*, 624 N.Y.S. 2d 755 (Sup. 1995)].

Even where a rule is subject to review, the court's role is limited. A court will not review the merits of the rule, but simply decide whether the rule is invalid on the basis of meeting one of the conditions listed above.

Standing

Standing concerns a plaintiff's right to bring a complaint in court. In order to establish standing the plaintiff must meet three criteria:

1. The plaintiff bringing the action sustained an injury in fact.

2. The interest which the plaintiff seeks to be protected is one for which the court possesses the power to grant a remedy.

3. The plaintiff has an interest in the outcome of the case.

The question of standing is generally one raised by the defense seeking to dismiss a case and not one which the court will raise on its own. In other words, as an initial matter, the plaintiff does not possess a burden of proof with regard to standing, but may be forced to show standing when the issue is raised by the defendant in a case.

Injunctive Relief

When a plaintiff seeks judicial review of an athletic association decision, the plaintiff will also request some form of injunctive relief to bar the rule from being applied. Injunctive relief is designed to prevent future wrongs, rather than to punish past actions. It is only used to prevent an irreparable injury which is suffered when monetary damages will not provide adequate compensation to the injured party. An injury is considered irreparable when it involves the risk of physical harm or death, the loss of a special opportunity, or the deprivation of unique, irreplaceable property. For example a high school senior student-athlete may be granted an injunction to compete in a championship game because he/she may never have that opportunity again.

There are three types of injunctive relief: the temporary restraining order, the preliminary injunction, and the permanent injunction. The *temporary restraining order* is generally issued to a plaintiff in an emergency situation, without notice to the defendant, and is usually effective for a maximum of ten days. Before a court will grant the temporary restraining order, a plaintiff must prove that he/she will face irreparable harm and that money damages would be an inadequate remedy. The *preliminary injunction* is granted to a plaintiff prior to a full hearing and lasts throughout the case. The defendant is given notice and may argue against the preliminary injunction. To be awarded a preliminary injunction the plaintiff must prove:

1. The plaintiff will face irreparable harm without the preliminary injunction.

2. Money damages are an inadequate remedy.

3. The plaintiff can prove that the balance of the hardships favor the plaintiff.

4. The plaintiff possesses a likelihood of success on the merits of the pending case.

A *permanent injunction* requires the same four elements, but is awarded as a remedy following a full hearing on the merits of the case.

An excellent example of the use of injunctive relief is found in *Christ the King Reg. High School v. Catholic High Schools Athletic Ass'n*, 624 N.Y.S. 2d 755 (Sup. 1995). The plaintiff high school girl's basketball team travelled to Pennsylvania and Ohio within the month of December to participate in games. Pursuant to association bylaws, teams of member schools are restricted to one trip outside of the metropolitan area each year. Also pursuant to association rules sanctions are recommended by the Eligibility and Infractions Committee and are later ratified by the Principals' Committee. The Eligibility and Infractions Committee determined that immediate suspension was not required and that a sufficient sanction would be to restrict the plaintiff's tournament play for 1995-96. Rather than ratify the finding, the Principals' Committee informed the plaintiff that the team would be suspended for the rest of the 1995 season and at least one additional season. The plaintiff sought a preliminary injunction to allow the team to play the upcoming game and a permanent injunction to bar enforcement of the suspension. The court granted both motions on the grounds that the defendant athletic association violated its own bylaws in handing out a sanction different than that recommended by the Eligibility and Infractions Committee.

Contract Law

Contract law forms the basis for many of the daily activities of an athletic organization. Athletic administrators who have regular dealings with contract law handle contracts in the following areas: games, officiating, personnel, television and radio, membership, facility lease agreements, vendors, suppliers, and scholarships in collegiate athletics. A *contract* is an agreement between two or more parties that **creates a legal obligation to fulfill the promises made in accordance with the agreement.** A contract can be either written or oral.

Legal Concepts

The legal requirements to the formation of a valid contract are offer, acceptance, consideration, legality, and capacity.

1. An *offer* is a conditional promise made by the offeror to the offeree. An offer usually includes the following essential terms: (1) the parties involved, (2) the subject matter, (3) the time (and place) for the subject matter to be performed, and (4) the price to be paid.

2. An *acceptance* can be made only by the party to whom the offer was made.

3. *Consideration* involves an exchange of value wherein one party agrees through a bargaining process to give up or do something in return for another party's doing the same. Consideration is often viewed as the essential term needed in a contract to make it legally enforceable. Without consideration, there may be a promise to do an act, but it may not be legally enforceable as a contract.

4. *Legality* means that the underlying bargain of the contract must be legal for the contract to be considered valid by the courts. The courts will not enforce illegal contracts, such as gambling contracts, contracts with unlicensed professionals, contracts with "loan sharks," and so forth.

5. *Capacity* is defined as the ability to understand the nature and effects of one's acts. In regard to contracts, the general rule is that anyone who has reached the age of majority (18 in most states) has the capacity to enter into a contract. A minor may enter into a contract, but the minor retains the option to disaffirm the contract at any time. If the minor disaffirms the contract (s)he must return anything of value which has not been earned or paid for under the contract. In addition, those individuals who are deemed mentally incompetent are treated in the same manner as minors when entering into contracts. In other words, mentally incompetent individuals have the capacity to enter into and fulfill contracts, but may disaffirm the contract at any time and return any value which (s)he has received from the contract.

Checklist of information to consider when developing contracts

1. If there have been prior dealings between the parties, the lawyer drafting the new contract should be informed of the nature of these dealings in order to decide whether they have any bearing on the new contract.

2. If the contract can only be performed by the original parties to the contract, the lawyer should be informed so as to state in the contract that it will not be assignable.

3. If any party is to be required to furnish a bond or to make a deposit, this information needs to be incorporated into the agreement.

4. If the parties have agreed to any special conditions, the lawyer drafting the contract must know of the conditions in order to include them in the agreement.

5. The consideration for the contract needs to be identified.

6. A description of the subject matter of the contracts should be provided. If property is the subject matter, then a description of the property should be furnished.

7. If there are any circumstances that would excuse either party from performing the contract, these circumstances should be explained in detail and included in the agreement.

8. The lawyer must be informed whether the parties to the agreement need to view each other's books and records.

9. The attorney should know the means of payment agreed to between the parties for the subject matter of the contract, any agreement as to the payment of attorney's fees should a breach occur, and any agreement as to the payment of any resulting taxes.

10. The attorney should have the name, capacity, and residence of each party to the agreement, as well as information about their ability to sign the contract and bind themselves or the organization they represent.

11. The effective date of the contract, the duration of the contract, and how the contract can be terminated before it runs its stated length all need to be incorporated into the agreement.

12. The attorney must be informed of the liabilities of both parties to the agreement and whether the liability of either party is to be limited under the agreement.

From Wong, G. (1994). *Essentials of Amateur Sports Law, Second Ed.*, Westport, CT: Praeger Publishers.

Breach of Contract

Once it has been demonstrated that a contract is formed by establishing these five criteria, another legal issue that is often raised is whether there has been a breach of contract. A breach of contract is a failure to perform a duty imposed under the contract. Numerous breach of contract cases have arisen in the sports industry. Examples include a lawsuit brought by a coach who argues that a breach of contract occurred when he did not receive compensation for the perquisites that he received as coach when his employment was terminated [see *Rodgers v. Georgia Tech Athletic Association*, 303 S.E.2d 467 (Ga. Ct. App. 1993)], by a professional athlete for a team's breach of contract in not fulfilling the terms of a contract [see *Hennigan v. Chargers Football Co.*, 431 F.2d 308 (5th Cir. 1970)], by stadium authorities against teams which are attempting moves to other cities without fulfilling lease obligations [see *City of Cleveland v. Cleveland Browns* (1995) and *King County v. Seattle Seahawks* (1996)], by a student-athlete who established a breach of contract for a university's failure to grant him reasonable access to their educational programs [see *Ross v. Creighton University*, 957 F.2d 410 (7th Cir. 1992)], and by student-athletes who argued their university's president and athletic administrators breached a contract to them by eliminating their wrestling team [see *Cooper v. Peterson*, 626 N.Y.S. 2d 432 (Sup. Ct. 1995)].

Remedies For a Breach of Contract

Remedies for a breach of contract usually entail monetary damages awarded by the court to the aggrieved party. The philosophy of monetary damages is to compensate the injured party for economic losses. The aggrieved party must justify to the court the damages he or she is requesting.

Contract law is an important area of sports law, and the guidelines in the box on the preceding page are offered to assist organizations in reviewing and developing contracts. In addition, the box below includes a general checklist of typical clauses that are included in most sports contracts.

Checklist of typical clauses in sports contracts

1. Opening. Identifies the parties to the agreement and also the date of the contract and its effective date.

2. Representations and warranties. Contains information about the rights and qualifications of the parties to enter into an agreement and also any express or implied warranties about the subject matter of the contract.

3. Operational language. Contains the subject matter of the contract. The precise rights and duties of the parties under the contract are explained.

4. Other clauses. Certain other clauses may be included, depending on the nature of the contract. Compensation, rights to arbitration for any disagreements, and the right to assign the contract are typical examples of other clauses.

5. Termination. Discusses the length of the contract and the means of ending the agreement.

6. Entire agreement and amendments. Details the comprehensiveness of the contract and its relation to other agreements and also the methods by which the contract can be amended.

7. Closing. Contains the signatures of the parties to the contract, any acknowledgments, and the signatures of any witnesses.

From Wong, G. (1988). *Essentials of Amateur Sports Law.* Second Ed. Westport, CT: Praeger Publishers.

Waivers and Releases of Liability

Waivers and *releases of liability* are contracts whereby a party agrees to give up his/her right to sue under tort law. A waiver is signed before the event or activity in which one who may possibly be injured by participation. It is a contract in which the participant relinquishes any right to sue for the negligence of the event management or organization providing the opportunity in exchange for the opportunity to participate in the event or activity. Under a waiver participants can only waive their right to sue for negligence, not gross negligence or intentional torts. A release of liability is similar to a waiver, but is a contract which a party signs after an injury occurs, whereby the injured party gives up the right to sue at a later date usually in exchange for a financial settlement.

In using waivers sport managers should be concerned with drafting them in a manner in which they are most likely to be upheld. Jurisdictions vary as to whether waivers will be upheld in court. Many courts will invalidate a waiver where there is a flaw in the language such as that the court finds the individual signing the waiver did not knowingly and voluntarily agree to waive his/her right to sue. Thus, a waiver should be drafted with clear, unambiguous and precise language. Some courts have ruled waivers invalid as a matter of public policy. To determine whether a waiver violates public policy, the court will examine a six factor test [*Tunkl v. Regents of the University of California*, 383 P.2d 441 (1963)]. In accordance with the test, the court examines the following six factors to determine if the waiver is enforceable: (1) whether the business involved is of the type generally regulated; (2) whether the party relying on the waiver to limit negligence relief is one which performs services of great importance to the public; (3) whether the party seeking relief from negligence liability offers to serve any member of the public who seeks it; (4) whether the essential nature of the service provided gives the party seeking relief from negligence liability a decisive advantage in bargaining power; (5) whether this bargaining power results in the public being forced to "take or leave" a standardized contract, with no provision for paying reasonable additional fees to obtain protection against negligence; (6) whether as a result of the contract the public using the service is under the control and thus subject to the risk of the carelessness of the party seeking to avoid negligence liability. At least one case has adopted this standard to invalidate the mandatory use of waivers for high school athletes on public policy grounds [*Wagenblast v. Odessa School District*, 758 P.2d 968 (1988)].

Another important issue with regard to waivers is the use of waivers by minors. Since waivers are contracts and minors may disaffirm contracts, it is advisable to have parents also sign the waiver. At least one court has upheld the waiver against the signing parent's claims, while letting the child disaffirm the contract and bring the negligence action along with the non-signing parent [*Childress by Childress v. Madison County*, 777 S.W.2d 1 (Tenn. Ct. App. 1989)].

Tort Liability

A *tort* is a private (or civil) wrong or injury suffered by an individual as the result of another person's conduct. Civil law provides injured individuals with a cause of action by which they may be compensated, or "made whole," through the recovery of damages. In a tort action the injured party institutes the action as an individual in an effort to recover damages as compensation for the injury received. The law of torts covers the following areas:

1. Intentional harm to the person

2. Intentional harm to tangible property

3. Negligence

4. Nuisance

5. Strict liability

6. Harm to tangible personal interests

7. Harm to tangible property interests

Discussed next are the most common torts arising in an athletic setting.

Intentional Vs. Unintentional Torts

Tort law is divided into intentional torts and nonintentional torts. An **intentional tort**— for example, assault and battery—consists of an intent to commit the act and an intent to harm the plaintiff. An **unintentional tort**, or negligence, involves no intent to commit the act and no intent to harm the plaintiff but a failure to exercise reasonable care. **Reckless misconduct, or gross negligence,** falls somewhere between an intentional and unintentional tort and consists of intent to commit the act but no intent to harm the plaintiff.

Assault and Battery

The torts of **assault** and **battery** are intentional torts, meaning there was an intent to commit the act and an intent to harm the plaintiff. Such intentional torts as assault and battery are actions characterized by focusing on the defendant's state of mind. Actual injury is not required to recover for the wrong done.

Assault is the apprehension of imminent harmful contact or battery. For an action to constitute assault, three elements must be present: intent to cause harm by the defendant, apprehension of immediate harm by the plaintiff, and lack of consent by the plaintiff. For example, in a baseball game the pitcher throws a pitch that unintentionally gets away from him and passes dangerously close to the batter. The batter gets angry, charges the mound, and throws his bat in the direction of the pitcher. The pitcher dives out of the way and the bat misses him. The pitcher could bring suit against the batter for assault, because being hit by a bat in that manner is not something the pitcher would consent to in the course of the game and the pitcher's action in diving out of the way of the bat is evidence of his apprehension of being hit by the bat. The bat misses the pitcher, but because of the action, the pitcher could bring suit against the batter for assault.

Battery consists of an unpermitted touching of another person. For an action to constitute battery, three elements must be present: intent to touch by the defendant, actual touching, and lack of consent to the contact by the plaintiff. For example, during a basketball game, Player A intentionally pushes Player B from behind and punches him in the back of the head. As Player B is falling, Player A hits him again, rendering Player B unconscious. Player B can bring suit against Player A for battery because there was an intent to harm, actual touching, and this is not the type of contact to which a basketball player consents.

Reckless Misconduct

Reckless misconduct, a tort, falls between the unintentional tort of negligence and the intentional torts of assault and battery. Reckless misconduct is characterized by intent on the part of the defendant to commit the act but no intent to harm the plaintiff by the act. The act may be defined as willful, wanton, or reckless.

In sport, this theory of liability is often relied on in cases involving co-participants. Courts have found that many sports have created safety rules to help define the often vague line between acceptable and inappropriate conduct between participants. The 1976 case, *Nabozny v. Barnhill*, 335 N.E. 2d 258 (Ill. Ct. App. 1975), established that participants owe a legal duty to other participants to refrain from willful, wanton and reckless misconduct. Nabozny established that where a player violates a safety rule, courts have held that a player may be liable for a tort action where that rule violation is deemed willful, wanton, and reckless. However, in *Gauvin v. Clark*, 537 N.E. 2d 64 (Mass. Sup. Jud. Ct. 1989), the Supreme Court of Massachusetts held that while *Nabozny's* language implies that a violation of a safety rule is all that is needed to establish an actionable tort, *Nabozny* actually established the standard of conduct to be a reckless disregard of safety. In *Gauvin v. Clark*, the defendant caused the plaintiff severe abdominal injuries when he butt-ended him with a hockey stick during a collegiate hockey game. The jury found that while Clark violated a safety rule, he did not act in a willful, wanton, or reckless manner and thus, was released from liability to Gauvin. The Massachusetts Court adopted this standard for two reasons: (1) allowing the imposition of liability in cases of reckless disregard for safety diminishes the need for players to retaliate, and (2) precluding the imposition of liability in negligence cases without reckless misconduct furthers the policy that litigation should not threaten vigorous participation in sport.

Negligence

The most common tort actions in athletics result from negligence. **Negligence** is an unintentional tort that focuses on an individual's conduct or actions. The ability of the injured party to sue and to recover damages for negligence is based on the idea that one who acts should anticipate the consequences that might involve unreasonable danger to others. The courts "measure" the conduct in each negligence case against the "reasonable person" standard—that is, how a person of ordinary sense using ordinary care and skill would react under similar circumstances. For an action to constitute negligence, four elements must be established by the plaintiff: (1) a special relationship exists between the plaintiff and defendant such that the defendant owed the plaintiff a duty of care; (2) the defendant breached the duty of care owed to the plaintiff; (3) actual and proximate cause of the injury to the plaintiff; (4) damages were incurred by the plaintiff.

Defamation

Defamation law is concerned with the protection of personal reputation. *The Restatement (Second) of Torts*, section 559, defines a defamatory communication as one that "tends to harm the reputation of another as to lower him in the estimation of the community or to deter third persons from associating or dealing with him." **Defamation** is an intentional tort in that the defendant need only intend to make the publication of the statement or material. It does not matter whether the defendant did not intend to harm the reputation of the plaintiff, the defendant will still be accountable if he or she intended to make the defamatory statement.

Defamation is divided into libel and slander. Libel is the publication of defamatory matter by writing, whereas slander is the publication of defamatory matter by spoken words. There must be a publication, and the plaintiff must be held up to scorn and ridicule as a result of the defamatory statement.

A public figure—a person who engages in a profession that is of public interest or who assumes a role of special prominence in the affairs of society—**has a more difficult time winning a defamation case** for he/she must **also** prove that the defendant made a written or verbal published statement with actual **malice**, that is, with the knowledge that the material was false or with reckless disregard, whether is was false or not. Proving actual malice is very difficult. And since most athletes, coaches, and many administrators would probably be considered public figures, they will not successfully argue a defamation case unless they can demonstrate actual malice.

Agency Law

Agency Law establishes the legal parameters in the relationships between a principal and an agent who acts for, or represents the interests of, the principal. One purpose of agency law is to hold the principal responsible (to third parties) for the actions of the agent, providing the agent is acting under the authority of the principal. A second purpose is to establish the duties that the principal and agent owe to each other. Under agency law the principal owes the agent three duties which are financial in nature: to compensate, to reimburse, and to indemnify the agent. The agent owes the principal five fiduciary duties. The first is to obey the wishes of the principal. The second is to remain loyal and to avoid conflicts of interest. Since conflicts of interest arise so frequently, the court will allow an agent to continue representing a principal when a conflict of interest is present, provided the agent discloses the conflict to the principal and gives the principal the option to seek representation elsewhere. Third, the agent owes a fiduciary duty to exercise reasonable care in all actions undertaken on behalf of the principal. Fourth, the agent has a duty to notify the principal of all information important to the principal. Finally, the agent owes the principal the duty to account to the principal on a reasonable basis.

In athletics, agency law is raised in employment situations, for example, in tort liability cases in which either or both the supervisor and the company/business/educational institution are sued for the alleged negligence of an employee. A tort liability case involves responsibility for a civil wrong that was committed. In many cases the plaintiff will be able to establish that an agency—not the individual—was responsible when a teacher, coach, trainer, or a full-time fitness club employee is alleged to be negligent. This theory is also called vicarious liability and allows a plaintiff to sue the employer for the employee's negligence. Under vicarious liability the employer need not be negligent. If, however, the employer is negligent and hires an unqualified individual, or does not provide the proper training, the employer's negligence may also provide the basis for an additional claim against the employer. However, many unique situations arise in the sports industry in which the judicial system has to determine whether the principal is responsible or whether, in fact, the individual is an independent contractor.

Independent Contractor

An **independent contractor** is a person who, although in some way connected to the employer, is not under the employer's control. Thus, the employer is not held responsible or liable for the individual's work. The following situations are some in which the issue of whether the person is an independent contractor might be raised.

1. *Physicians hired on a part-time basis by a university athletic department.* As a general rule, a physician provided by a school that is hosting an athletic activity is considered an independent contractor. Although paid by the university, the physician is not in any way under the control of the school when making medical decisions.

2. *Referees.* Some courts have decided that it is the referee's responsibility to ensure that the rules are followed, and an injury that occurs as a result of a violation of these rules should be considered negligent conduct on the part of the referee.
   The courts also need to decide whether there is an employer-employee relationship between the school district and the referee—causing the school district to be responsible for the referee's negligence—or whether the referee is an independent contractor. The current trend is for the courts to find the referee to be an independent contractor.

3. *Part-time instructors at health and fitness clubs.* The court may be asked to decide whether the instructor is an authorized representative of the health and fitness club, thus forming an employer-employee relationship. A key determination for the courts will be whether the club exercised control over the instructor.

Intentional Torts

It should be emphasized that where an agency relationship exists, an employer may not be responsible for all the actions of an employee. The employer is responsible for only those actions which are within the scope of the duties and responsibilities of the position. The general rule in agency law cases is that an employer is not responsible for the intentional torts of an employee. An intentional tort involves an intent to commit the act and an intent to harm the plaintiff. So, for example, when a truck driver gets into a fight with another driver and the other driver suffers severe injuries, the company employing the truck driver is not held responsible when sued under agency theory, since fighting is not within the scope of responsibilities for a truck driver.

The sports setting has created some interesting dilemmas for the judicial system. In *Averill v. Luttress*, 311 S.W. 2d 812 (Tenn. Ct. App. 1957), a pitcher throws a brushback pitch at a batter, and the batter starts toward the mound. The catcher comes up from behind the batter and hits the batter, causing serious injuries. Is the team responsible under an agency theory, since it is the employer of the catcher? Is it within the scope of responsibilities of a catcher to protect a pitcher? In this particular case, the court held that the catcher was liable, but the team was not, since fighting is not within the scope of responsibilities. In a case involving basketball, *Tomjanovich v. California Sports, Inc.*, No. H-78-243 (S.D. Tex. 1979), the team was held responsible. In a game between the Los Angeles Lakers and the Houston Rockets, a fight broke out, and a Laker player hit and injured a Houston Rocket player. The Lakers were sued, because the Laker player was seen as an "enforcer" in the league and known for "dangerous tendencies." Although fighting is usually seen as outside the scope of responsibility in an employer-employee relationship, this case was decided in favor of the plaintiff, and the Lakers were held responsible as the player's employer. The Lakers were sued on the theory that, as the employer of the player, they were responsible for curbing his "dangerous tendencies" and that they had failed to do so.

Player Representation

Agency law is also important when athletes are represented in contract negotiations and/or financial management by agents (also known as player agents or player representatives). A **player agent** is a person authorized by an athlete to act in his or her name, and the agent is entrusted with that athlete's business. The promise of compensation is not required to establish the relationship, although compensation, reimbursement and indemnifications are usually presumed.

Some athletes have brought litigation against agents for an alleged breach of a fiduciary relationship [see *Brown v. Woolf*, 554 F. Supp. 1206 (S.D. Ind. 1983); *Detroit Lions, Inc. v. Argovitz*, 580 F. Supp. 542 (E.D. Mich. 1984)]. Lawsuits may include the alleged improper negotiation of a contract, or more commonly, the alleged mismanagement of the athlete's money. Unfortunately, the number of cases involving athletes who have been taken advantage of by unscrupulous agents is on the rise.

Constitutional Law

The **Constitution** is the basic law of the United States of America, drawn up by the Constitutional Convention in Philadelphia in 1787. The Constitution contains statutory provisions and judicial interpretations concerning important social, economic, and political issues.

As a general rule the U.S. Constitution does not apply to private entities such as professional teams, athletic associations, and private high schools and colleges. However, where it can be argued that the private entity is so enmeshed with the public entity, the court may find state action and apply the Constitution to the private entity [see *Ludtke v. Kuhn*, 461 F.Supp. 86 (S.D.N.Y. 1978)].

Due Process

Due process is an elusive concept. One definition for the term **due process** is "a course of legal proceedings which have been established in our system of jurisprudence for the protection and enforcement of private right" [*Pennoyer v. Neff*, 95 U.S. 714 (18)]. The concept of due process may vary, depending on three basic considerations: (1) the seriousness of the infraction, (2) the possible consequences to the institution or individual in question, and (3) the degree of sanction or penalty imposed.

The constitutional guarantee of due process is found in both the Fifth and Fourteenth Amendments. The Fifth Amendment, enacted in 1791, is applicable to the federal government. It states that "no person...shall be deprived of life, liberty, or property without due process of law." Liberty interests include those fundamental freedoms explicitly guaranteed by the language of the U.S. Constitution. There is no language guaranteeing the right to an education or the right to participate in athletics. On the federal level both are considered privileges. In addition to those freedoms explicitly guaranteed, some courts have protected the right to pursue one's livelihood, the right to be free from stigma or damage to one's reputation as protected interest. In *Tarkanian v. NCAA*, UNLV coach Jerry Tarkanian based his due process claim on these liberty interests as well as the property interest in his position as coach of the Running Rebels. The Nevada Supreme Court found that the NCAA's suspension of Tarkanian would infringe upon his liberty interests because he would be stigmatized by the loss of his position and status as UNLV's basketball coach. The U.S. Supreme Court, however, never considered this argument as the NCAA was deemed a private actor, and thus, had no obligation to provide due process to Tarkanian. In 1886 the Fourteenth Amendment was ratified, reading, "Nor shall any state deprive any person of life, liberty, or property without due process of law...." This amendment extended the applicability of the due process doctrine to the states. In addition, a coach or teacher employed by a state actor will possess a property interest in that position provided (s)he is entitled to the position. Both amendments apply only to federal or state governmental action and not to the conduct of purely private entities.

Although the Constitution extends these liberties to all persons, it is also limiting in that a person must demonstrate deprivation of life, liberty, or property to claim a violation of due process guarantees. Since athletic associations and conferences rarely deprive a person of life, the major interests that trigger the application of a due process clause in the athletic context are deprivations of liberty and property. In collegiate athletics the scholarship has been considered a property right. Unless an athlete or other party can establish that he or she has been deprived of liberty or property, he or she will not be able to establish a deprivation of due process.

Equal Protection

Equal protection is the constitutional method of checking on the fairness of the application of law. Through the equal protection clause of the Fourteenth Amendment, student-athletes and coaches are provided with the means to challenge certain rules and regulations that are of a discriminatory nature. The equal protection guarantee of the Fourteenth Amendment reads, "No state shall...deny to any person within its jurisdiction the equal protection of the laws." Equal protection requires that no person be singled out from similarly situated people, or have different benefits bestowed or burdens imposed, unless a Constitutionally permissible reason exists for doing so.

Different standards of review are used under equal protection analysis. The highest standard of review is that of strict scrutiny. When a rule abridges a fundamental right or makes a distinction based on suspect criteria, the defendant has the burden of proof. The Supreme Court has found three suspect classes: alienage, race, and national origin. Any time a rule has a direct or indirect impact on any of these suspect classifications, or infringes on a fundamental right guaranteed by the Constitution, the strict scrutiny standard will be applied. Under strict scrutiny, for the rule to stand, the defendant must prove to the court that there is an important governmental interest for infringing on fundamental rights or classifying on the basis of race, religion, or national origin. This is a very difficult burden, so plaintiffs generally win. The second standard of review under the equal protection guarantee is that of rational basis. This standard requires only that the rule have some rational relationship to a legitimate organizational purpose. The third standard of review imposes an intermediate test, which falls between the strict scrutiny and rational basis tests. It requires that rules classifying certain groups satisfy an "important" but not necessarily a "compelling" interest.

A student-athlete may argue a violation of equal protection because of the existence of two types of classification—student-athletes vs. non-student athletes—in a drug-testing program. Only student-athletes are tested, whereas non-student athletes do not have to participate in the school's drug-testing program. In all probability the court would apply a rational basis standard in which the plaintiff has the burden of establishing that no rational basis exists for classification. If a drug-testing program called for athletes to be tested on the basis of alienage, race, or national origin, a strict scrutiny standard would be employed by the courts. The drug-testing program would be invalidated unless the defendant could demonstrate that the program was supported by a compelling state interest.

Unreasonable Search and Seizure

The Fourth Amendment provides "[the] right of the people to be secure in their persons, houses, papers, and effects against unreasonable searches and seizures." Applying this protection to a drug-testing program, the act of taking an athlete's urine (or blood) can constitute a **search** within the meaning of the Fourth Amendment. Searches may be deemed reasonable by the courts, however, through the defendant's showing a compelling state interest for the search to occur. Determining whether a drug test is a reasonable search requires a balancing of the state actor's interest in the search against the privacy rights of the person being searched. While a student-athlete may consent to a search, thus waiving the Fourth Amendment protection, there are limitations on the extent to which a state actor may force consent to the search.

Invasion of Privacy

An action for **invasion of privacy** is designed to protect a person's mental peace and/or comfort. The laws prohibiting invasion of privacy are intended to protect the purely private matters of a person. In an action for invasion of privacy, the intrusion must be substantial and must be into an area for which there is an expectation of privacy. Challenges to drug-testing programs have involved invasion of privacy arguments. The major concern in terms of the protection of a student-athlete's privacy rights involves the degree of intrusiveness with which the drug-testing program obtains the necessary urine sample. The courts have noted many times that there is a substantial expectation of privacy in connection with the act of urination. This expectation is balanced, however, against the compelling state interest in testing an individual, obtaining the necessary urine sample, and ensuring that the sample obtained is definitely that individual's. In *Vernonia School District 47J v. Acton*, 115 S.Ct. 2386 (1995), the U.S. Supreme Court upheld the constitutionality of the school district's mandatory and random, suspicionless drug-testing program which targeted student-athletes. The grounds for the decision were (1) student-athletes on the high school level have a lower expectation of privacy; (2) the scope of the search was relatively unobtrusive considering the monitoring procedures employed by the school system; and (3) the drug-testing program served an important governmental interest by attacking a school drug use problem. In the *Vernonia* case, the Oregon Constitution mirrored the Fourth Amendment's search and seizure language. In a state where the Constitution provides for greater privacy to its citizens in that state, a testing program such as Vernonia's may fail. For example, in *University of Colorado v. Derdeyn*, 863 P.2d 929 (Colo. Sup. Ct 1993), the Colorado Supreme Court affirmed lower court rulings which found the University of Colorado's drug-testing program to be violative of the Fourth Amendment's protection against unreasonable searches and seizure.

Sex Discrimination

Sex discrimination in interscholastic and intercollegiate athletics has been challenged using a variety of legal arguments, including Title IX of the Education Amendments of 1972, equal protection laws, state equal rights amendments, and the Equal Pay Act, which was passed in 1963 and became effective in 1964. Most challenges have been based on the equal protection laws and/or Title IX, although several claims based on state equal rights amendments have been brought recently. In a sex discrimination case, the plaintiff usually contends that there is a fundamental inequality, regardless of whether a plaintiff employs an equal protection law, equal rights amendment, or a Title IX approach. In attempting to deal with these claims, the court considers three factors. The first is whether the sport from which women are excluded is one involving physical contact. Total exclusion from all sports or from any noncontact sport is usually considered a violation of equal educational opportunity. The second factor is the quality and quantity of opportunities available to each sex. The courts compare the number of athletic opportunities available to each sex, as well as the amount of money spent on equipment, the type of coaches provided, and the access to school-owned facilities. The third factor the courts consider is age and level of competition involved in the dispute. The younger the athletes involved, the fewer the actual physiological differences that exist. Without evident physiological differences, there is little justification for the exclusion of one sex from athletic participation due to biological differences.

The growth of women's sports and the dramatic increase in women's overall participation in athletics have been impressive. Since 1972 the number of women participating in athletics has more than doubled. Athletic budgets for women's athletics have also increased. These indicators, along with the increases in spectators at women's events and local and national media coverage, point to the growth in women's athletics.

Title IX

The development of athletic opportunities for women may, to a large extent, be attributed to Title IX. Title IX of the Education Amendments of 1972 is a federal statute that prohibits sex discrimination. Section 901(a) of Title IX contains the following language: "No person in the United States shall, on the basis of sex, be excluded from participation in, be denied the benefits of, or be subjected to discrimination under any education program or activity receiving Federal financial assistance." Athletics and athletic programs were not specifically mentioned in Title IX when it first became law in 1972. Congress was generally opposed to placing athletic programs under the realm of Title IX. However, the Department of Health, Education, and Welfare (HEW) took the position that sports and physical education are an integral part of education and specifically included athletics in Title IX in 1974.

The key to the Title IX language lies in the last four words: "receiving Federal financial assistance." Only institutions receiving federal financial assistance are required to be in compliance with Title IX. The legal question revolving around this concept was whether Title IX applies to an entire institution or only to those programs within that institution which receive direct federal assistance. This was an important issue for athletic programs, because most do not receive direct federal funding; however, most institutions receive some form of federal financial assistance.

Scope and applicability of Title IX. *Grove City College v. Bell*, 465 U.S. 555 (1984), dealt with the scope and applicability of Title IX. In this case, the Supreme Court ruled that only those programs within an institution which receive direct financial assistance from the federal government would be subject to Title IX legislation. This interpretation, referred to as the **"programmatic approach,"** virtually negated the impact of Title IX on athletic programs. It was not until the Civil Rights Restoration Act of 1987, passed by Congress in 1988, that the strength of Title IX and its applicability to athletic programs was restored. The passage of this act restored the **"institutional approach"** of the applicability of title IX, and as such, athletic departments within institutions receiving federal financial assistance are now subject to the Title IX legislation.

Title IX compliance. Compliance with the dictates of Title IX is monitored by the Office for Civil Rights (OCR), in the Department of Education. The OCR makes random compliance reviews and also investigates complaints submitted by individuals. The OCR conducts a preliminary review to determine an institution's attempted compliance with Title IX. If the OCR determines that a full hearing should be conducted, the OCR becomes the complaintant and pursues the claim. In this situation the individual who initially submitted the complaint does not have the financial burden that a court case would entail.

The policy interpretation developed by the OCR contains some strict guidelines for assessing Title IX compliance, including the following:

1. The men's program as a whole must be compared with the women's program as a whole. Comparisons are not made sport by sport.
2. In evaluating overall compliance, there is no exemption from Title IX for revenue-producing sports, as well as football.
3. In evaluating athletic participation opportunities, three factors must be considered: the determination of athletic interests and abilities, the selection of sports, and the levels of competition.

4. Schools must provide "equivalent" (but not necessarily identical) athletic benefits, opportunities, and treatment to female and male athletes. That is, overall athletic programs must be "equal or equal in effect" and the overall effect of any differences must be negligible. Important factors in determining equivalency are availability, quality, types of benefits, opportunities, and treatment.

The policy interpretation of Title IX focuses on three areas which the OCR evaluates to determine whether an institution is in compliance with Title IX regulations with regard to athletics. First, the OCR assesses whether an institution's athletic scholarships are awarded on a "substantially proportional" basis. To determine this, the total amount of scholarship money available for each gender is divided by the number of male or female participants in the athletic program. The OCR will find compliance if the results, when compared, are substantially equal amounts of scholarship money spent per athlete (male vs. female). In addition, where a disparity exists which can be explained by legitimate, nondiscriminatory factors the OCR will find compliance.

Second, the OCR assesses the degree to which the institution provides equal treatment, benefits, and opportunities in specific program areas. When determining equality of treatment, the OCR compares such program areas as equipment and supplies, coaching, tutoring, facilities, scheduling, travel, and publicity.

Finally, the OCR assesses the extent to which an educational institution has equally and effectively accommodated the athletic interests and abilities of the male and female students. The effective accommodation of interests and abilities has become a primary focus of Title IX challenges during the 1990s. This determination requires an examination of the institution's assessment of its student body's athletic interests and abilities, the selection of sports offered, and the competitive opportunities available.

In *Cohen v. Brown University*, 879 F.Supp. 185 (D.R.I. 1995), the Federal District Court for the District of Rhode Island discussed the OCR standard for measuring effective accommodation. It stated that the OCR measures compliance first by applying a three-part test and second by applying a two-part test. The three-part test assesses compliance by determining:

1. Whether intercollegiate level participation opportunities for male and female students are provided in numbers substantially proportionate to their respective enrollments;

2. Where the members of one sex have been and are underrepresented in intercollegiate athletics, whether the institution can show a history and continuing practice of program expansion which is demonstrably responsive to the developing interest and abilities of the members of that sex;

3. Where the members of one sex are underrepresented in intercollegiate athletics, and the institution cannot show a continuing practice of program expansion such as that shown above, whether it can be demonstrated that the interest and abilities of the members of that sex have been fully and effectively accommodated by the present program.

The two-part test assesses compliance by examining:

1. Whether the competitive schedules for men's and women's teams, on a program-wide basis, afford proportionally similar numbers of male and female athletes equivalently advanced competitive opportunities; or

2. Whether the institution can demonstrate a history and continuing practice of upgrading the competitive opportunities available to the historically disadvantaged sex as warranted by developing abilities among the athletes of that sex.

Effective accommodation compliance also provides that a school need not establish an intercollegiate team where there is no reasonable expectation of competition in that sport within the institution's normal geographic area of competition. Finally, the section provides that the following factors should be considered in an overall determination of compliance:

(a) Whether the policies of an institution are discriminatory in language or effect; or

(b) Whether disparities of a substantial and unjustified nature in the benefits, treatment, services, and opportunities afforded male and female athletes exist in the institution's program as a whole; or

(c) Whether disparities in individual segments of the program with respect to benefits, treatment, services, or opportunities are substantial enough in and of themselves to deny equality of athletic opportunity.

Equal Protection

Equal protection is the constitutional method of checking on the fairness of the application of any law. Equal protection requires that no person be singled out from similarly situated people, or have different benefits bestowed or burdens imposed, unless a constitutionally permissible reason exists for doing so.

Equal protection is only available to a plaintiff where the defendant is a state actor. Refer to the Equal Protection section on page 102 for a more detailed discussion on the concept in general. For purposes of this discussion the focus here will be on the concept as it applies to sex discrimination.

The U.S. Supreme Court has applied the intermediate level of scrutiny to sex discrimination. The intermediate test, between rational basis and strict scrutiny, requires gender-based classifications be "reasonable, not arbitrary, and must rest upon some ground of difference having a fair and substantial relation to the object of the legislation, so that all persons similarly circumstanced shall be treated alike." *Reed v. Reed*, 404 U.S. 71 (1971). Two years later in *Frontiero v. Richardson*, 411 U.S. 677 (1973), the Supreme Court stated, "what differentiates sex from such nonsuspect statuses as intelligence or physical disability...is that the sex characteristic frequently bears no relation to ability to perform or contribute to society." The Supreme Court has since established the standard that a gender classification will fail unless it is substantially related to a sufficiently important governmental interest.

A factual basis for any gender classification must exist. Mere preferences or assumptions concerning the ability of one sex to perform adequately are not acceptable bases for a discriminatory classification. The intermediate standard requires more than an easily achieved rational relationship, but less than a strict scrutiny standard requires. The class must bear a substantial relationship to an important, but not compelling governmental interest. The relationship between a law or rule's purpose must also be founded on fact, not a general legislative view of the relative strengths or abilities of the two sexes.

Three key factors are considered in an equal protection analysis of athletic discrimination. The first is state action. Before any equal protection claim can be successfully litigated, the defendant must be deemed a state actor. Refer to the previous Constitutional Law section on page 101 for a general discussion of state action.

The second factor is whether the sport involves physical contact. The courts have allowed separate men's and women's teams in contact sports. Unlike race-based classifications, when gender is the determining factor, the "separate, but equal" stance may be acceptable. This "separate, but equal" stance is based on concerns for the participants' health and safety. Where separate teams do not exist, such as in football, a complete ban on the participation of one sex will not be upheld if it is based on generalizations about characteristics of an entire sex rather than on a reasonable consideration of individual characteristics. For example, in *Force v. Pierce City R-VI School District*, 570 F. Supp. 1020 (W.D. Mo. 1983) the district court for the Western District of Missouri struck down a blanket prohibition against female participation in interscholastic football because the court found no relationship between it and the stated governmental interest in maintaining safe athletic programs. A complete ban may, however, be upheld where the ban is shown to be necessary to promote equal opportunity for athletes in one sex and to redress the effects of past discrimination. [see *Clark v. Arizona Interscholastic Association*, 695 F. 2d 1126 (9th Cir. 1982), cert. denied, 104 S.Ct. 79 (1983)]. When the justification is based on promoting equal opportunity and redressing the effects of past discrimination, the court will examine the total number of participants and opportunities to participate in sport available to students of the plaintiff's gender, as opposed to focusing on the particular plaintiff's opportunity to participate in the particular sport at issue.

The third factor is whether both sexes have equal opportunities to participate. "Equal opportunity" usually requires the existence of completely separate teams or an opportunity to try out for the one available team. If there are separate teams, however, it is permissible for the governing organization to prohibit co-ed participation. In challenges to this separate, but equal stance the issue often becomes whether the teams are indeed equal.

Historically, challenging sex discrimination on equal protection grounds has not been very effective for plaintiffs. First, for equal protection to apply the defendant must be a state actor. Second, the intermediate level of scrutiny does provide the defendant with a defense. A defense is available provided the defendant can establish an important governmental reason for the gender-based discrimination. Finally, equal protection provides a private remedy, requiring the plaintiff to absorb the costs of litigation.

Equal Rights Amendment

Although passed in both Houses of Congress in 1972, the federal **Equal Rights Amendment (ERA)** did not receive the necessary 38 votes from the state legislatures by the required ratification date of July 1, 1972. Although a federal ERA has not been ratified, 19 individual states have passed their own equal rights amendments. Thus equal rights amendments have had an impact on athletics at the state level but not at the federal level.

Equal rights amendments at the state level can be very effective and extend greater protection against sex-based classifications than that available under federal equal protection of the Fourteenth Amendment. The state courts, under an equal rights amendment, hold a stricter standard of review regarding the sex-based classification than the lower standard employed by the federal courts under the federal equal protection clause. For example, in *Darrin v. Gould*, 540 P.2d 882 (1975), the lower court considered the equal protection argument and ruled in favor of the defendant. The Washington Supreme Court, however, reversed the decision in favor of the plaintiffs, based on the state's equal rights argument. As such, the court's decision may be effectively downgraded with the subsequent passage of limiting legislation to the state ERA. Regardless of the precarious position in which protection against gender discrimination exists, as evident in *Darrin v. Gould*, the existence of a state ERA may be vital to the success of a gender discrimination case.

Professional Sports

There have not been many sex discrimination complaints or cases in the professional sports arena, because relatively few women participate in professional sports. An area in which litigation has occurred involves the barring of media from locker rooms. In *Ludtke v. Kuhn*, 461 F.Supp. 86 (S.D. N.Y. 1978), the plaintiff, a female sports reporter, was excluded from the locker room of the Yankee clubhouse in Yankee Stadium because of a policy instituted by Baseball Commissioner Bowie Kuhn. Ludtke alleged a violation of equal protection under the Fourteenth Amendment, because male members of the news media were not similarly restricted. The court ruled in favor of the plaintiff Ludtke, thus allowing her access to the Yankee Stadium locker room.

The issue of access to locker rooms for female reporters has been raised in several instances in the 1990s, with the most celebrated case involving Lisa Olson of the *Boston Herald* and the New England Patriots professional football team.

Sex Discrimination in Athletic Employment

The past decade has seen a significant increase in the number of lawsuits brought by coaches in athletic employment. A large number of the lawsuits have involved disparity in coaching salaries and have relied upon three theories: Title IX of the Educational Amendments of 1972, Title VII of the Civil Rights Act of 1964, and the Equal Pay Act of 1963.

Title IX. As discussed on page 105, Title IX prohibits gender-based discrimination in educational institutions receiving federal financial assistance. In 1982 the U.S. Supreme Court upheld the use of Title IX in employment discrimination cases in educational institutions [see *New Haven Board of Education v. Bell*, 456 U.S. 512 (1982)]. In addition, *Franklin v. Gwinnett County School District*, 112 S.Ct. 1028 (1992), upheld a damage award to a plaintiff-victim of intentional discrimination under Title IX. The Supreme Court found nothing in Title IX to prohibit a private cause of action for compensatory damages and attorneys' fees. Since *Franklin*, two widely publicized cases have been brought under Title IX and the Equal Pay Act [see *Tyler v. Howard University*, Civ. Action No. 91-11239 (Sup. Ct. D.C. 1993) and *Stanley v. University of Southern California*, 13 F. 3d 1313 (9th Cir. 1994)].

Equal Pay Act. The Equal Pay Act of 1963, 29 U.S.C. §206 (d)(1), provides that an employer must pay equal salaries to men and women who hold positions that require equal skill, effort, and responsibility and that are performed under similar working conditions.

The courts apply a "substantially equal test" when determining the equality of positions. Differences in salaries are permissible where they are based on a bonafide seniority system, a merit system, quantity/quality system, or a differential based on a factor other than sex. An employer will have the burden of proving these permissible differences where a gender-based salary differential is established by the plaintiff.

In *Stanley v. University of Southern California*, 13 F. 3d 1313 (9th Cir. 1994), the plaintiff former women's basketball coach argued that the University of Southern California discriminated against her by failing to meet her demand of a salary that matched the men's basketball coach, George Raveling. Stanley was denied her claim on the basis that she was not deserving of the same salary because the men's basketball team brought in more revenues and thus, Coach Raveling was subject to greater demands, pressures, and responsibilities. According to the court, these additional pressures and responsibilities, not gender, were the basis for the disparity in salary. Coach Stanley has also pursued a Title IX claim.

Title VII. Title VII focuses on discriminatory hiring, firing, and employment practices within organizations. It forbids discrimination on the basis of race, color, religion, gender, or national origin by employers of more than 15 persons and specifically covers almost all state and local government employees, including employees of most educational institutions. For a successful employment discrimination case a plaintiff coach must first establish that she is a member of a class protected by Title VII (female). Second, if an applicant, she must show that she was qualified for the position and not hired; or, if an employee, that she was performing her position in a satisfactory manner. Third, the coach must prove that she was not hired or if employed, was adversely affected by a change in her working conditions or firing, and that the employer hired a male, treated a similarly situated male employee better, or attempted to replace her with a male who did not possess better qualifications. Once a plaintiff has established this *prima facie* case, the burden shifts to the employer to show credible evidence of a legitimate, nondiscriminatory reason for not hiring her, or if she's employed, for the different treatment. If the employer is able to demonstrate a nondiscriminatory reason for the action, the burden then shifts back to the plaintiff to rebut that evidence. The plaintiff then is given the opportunity to prove by a preponderance of the evidence that the employer's legitimate, nondiscriminatory reason is actually pretext and that gender more likely motivated the employer. In *Deli v. University of Minnesota*, 863 F. Supp. 958 (D. Minn. 1994), the plaintiff women's gymnastics coach, Katalin Deli was unsuccessful in proving a Title VII violation when she argued that her salary disparity was a result of the gender of the athletes whom she coached. The language of the statute provides for protection for discrimination in salary based upon the gender of the employee, not the gender of those the employee coaches. However, in *Pitts v. Oklahoma State University* (unpublished opinion), the court found a Title VII violation when women's golf coach Anne Pitts argued that she was paid less than her male counterpart. A jury awarded Coach Pitts $30,000 in compensatory damages and $6,000 for emotional distress. Coach Pitts was successful because her arguments focused on a comparison of her situation with her male counterpart, as opposed to Coach Deli's focus on the fact she was coaching athletes in a protected class.

The Antitrust Laws

Antitrust laws are designed to promote competition in the business sector through regulation "designed to control the exercise of private economic power" (Gellhorn, 1976). In athletics, antitrust law concerns have primarily involved professional sports leagues, which are composed of private economic entities operated as a business to make a profit. Increasingly, however, amateur athletic organizations have come under the scope of antitrust laws, partly due to the transformation of many areas of amateur athletics into "big business." This situation is particularly true in intercollegiate athletics, primarily football and men's basketball. For example, the NCAA's Football Television Plan for 1982 to 1985 was declared to be in violation of antitrust laws, because it prevented the free flow of the market for televised intercollegiate football. The decision, upheld by the U.S. Supreme Court in 1984, disrupted the entire sports telecasting industry by allowing a glut of televised intercollegiate football to flood the market. The decision caused the financial rights fees for these televised games to drop significantly, and in turn, many institutions experienced a shortfall in their annual budgets.

The two major antitrust laws that form the underlying basis for court decisions are the Sherman Antitrust Act and the Clayton Act.

The Sherman Antitrust Act

The **Sherman Antitrust Act** was passed in 1890 during a period of U.S. history in which business had gained domination over the delivery of goods and services to the detriment of the average citizen. The law was passed to encourage free and open competition in business. The ultimate beneficiary was the consumer, who would not have to pay above-market prices for goods and services. Federal antitrust laws seek to regulate competitive conduct involving interstate commerce. The Sherman Antitrust Act specifically covers transactions in goods, land, or services. Section 1 of the Sherman Act concerns agreements that restrain trade, such as a group of businesses attempting to fix prices among themselves. Section 2 of the Sherman Act seeks to prevent monopolistic action by a business or businesses: an example of such an action is the attempt to control all televised football to prevent another school's or league's games from being telecast. It is permissible for a monopoly to exist for natural reasons, as long as the monopoly then does not attempt to drive out competition through illegal means.

The Clayton Act

The **Clayton Act** was enacted in 1914 to tighten up some of the generalities of the Sherman Act. It was specifically designed to prevent certain practices in the sale of goods in interstate commerce. Specific sections of the Clayton Act deal with corporate mergers, price discrimination, and the operation of labor unions. The Clayton Act provides that nothing contained in the antitrust laws shall be construed to forbid the existence and operation of labor unions; therefore, under the provisions set forth in this act, player associations in sports leagues can be viewed as labor unions formed to keep the interest of the players in mind when they are negotiating collective bargaining agreements within the league.

Professional Sports Applications

Baseball is unique in that it is exempt from the antitrust laws as a result of a 1922 Supreme Court decision, *Federal Baseball Club of Baltimore, Inc. v. National League of Professional Baseball Clubs, et. al.*, 259 U.S. 200 (1922). In *Federal Baseball* the Supreme Court granted the exemption from antitrust because it was not a business engaged in interstate commerce. The Court viewed baseball as a business engaged in presenting local exhibitions deemed purely state affairs. It found that the travel of players across state lines was purely incidental and not a fundamental part of the business of baseball. Over time this exemption has faced attack, but the *Federal Baseball* decision is still viewed as controlling. In 1972, baseball's exemption was attacked in *Flood v. Kuhn*, 407 U.S. 258 (1972). The *Flood* decision was important for two reasons. First, it reaffirmed baseball's exemption by stating that it could only be challenged by Congress and that baseball players should use labor relations to resolve their disputes over the reserve clause. Second, it reiterated that the antitrust exemption only extended to baseball, as the court reiterated that all other team and individual sports were (and are) subject to antitrust laws. Congress has time and again revisited the question of whether baseball should continue to remain exempt from antitrust, but has yet to wage any serious threats to the league's protected status.

In professional football the key antitrust decision was *Mackey v. National Football League*, 407 F. Supp. 1000 (D. Minn. 1975); in hockey it was *McCourt v. California Sports, Inc.*, 600 P. 2d 1193 (1979); and in basketball, *Robertson v. National Basketball Association*, 556 F.2d 682 (2nd Cir. 1977). All three of these cases were filed by the respective player unions on behalf of the individual players to challenge the restraints that the players felt were in violation of the Sherman and Clayton Acts. These restraints included the college player drafts, the reserve clause, the option clause, and other restrictive terms and conditions of employment. The professional team leagues argued that these player restraints were necessary because of the unique nature of professional team sports. As opposed to a regular business environment, in which one business would like to put a competitor out of business, professional team sports need other teams to have games and a league and therefore survive. Consequently, the argument goes, the teams in a league must cooperate off the field be trying to balance the talent among the various teams so as to ensure interesting and close games during a season. In short, in trying to balance these two arguments, the court has applied a standard called the "Rule of Reason." Under the Rule of Reason, the court will allow a defendant to raise as a defense an argument that the restraint is a reasonable one because the defendant has a legitimate business interest in the restraint and it is the least restrictive means of accomplishing that business interest. For instance, the concept of a draft in professional sports may be considered a restraint of trade because when a player is drafted, the player is usually restricted to negotiating with the drafting team for one year which may restrict the athlete's bargaining power with that team. However, a league may argue that it has a legitimate business interest in the draft as it creates competitive balance amongst the teams. Yet, if the league involved is a basketball league and the draft consists of 20 rounds and the league rosters are set at 15 players, the league may have a difficult time arguing that it has developed its draft in the least restrictive means of accomplishing competitive balance. If the draft were, however, limited to two rounds, the Rule of Reason may in fact stand as a valid defense.

What transpired after the court decisions in football, hockey, and basketball was that the Players' Associations for each of the sports negotiated collective bargaining agreements with the leagues in which the Players' Association allowed certain restrictive practices to continue (for example, the player draft), in exchange for which the players received concessions and benefits from management. After having become the subject matter of a labor agreement between management and the players, the restrictive practices of management became insulated from antitrust scrutiny by the nonstatutory labor exemption. By conceding benefits to players, leagues are able to preserve restraints that they believe are necessary to remain economically viable.

Major League Baseball, as previously indicated, has a unique legal situation as a result of the *Federal Baseball* decision. Baseball players have been able to obtain tremendous financial rewards and other benefits through their collective bargaining agreement, even though the Players' Association does not have the benefit of the antitrust laws to sue management. The key decision for the players in Major League Baseball was the arbitration case of *Messersmith and McNally v. Major League Baseball*, decided in 1975. This arbitration decision was affirmed in the court case of *Kansas City Royals Baseball Corporation v. Major League Baseball Player's Association*, 409 F. Supp. 233 (W.D. Missouri, 1976). The players challenged the reserve clause and successfully argued that the clause could only be renewed once, rather than perpetually as management argued. Players would therefore become free agents after the expiration of this one-year renewal. Since this was the period in baseball before the advent of the multi-year contract, this decision resulted in most players in major league baseball becoming potentially free agents in either one or two years. As a result of this arbitration decision, along with the potential for chaos (that is, every player in the league being a free agent), management agreed to a collective bargaining agreement that greatly increased the salaries and benefits for baseball players. The basis of that agreement has become the framework for the subsequent collective bargaining agreements in baseball.

It has been well established that during the term of a collective bargaining agreement, those terms negotiated between labor and management, which outside a collective agreement would be deemed subject to antitrust law, are in fact exempt from antitrust scrutiny. However, a number of recent cases have raised the issue of whether the labor exemption to antitrust continues to protect the leagues from antitrust scrutiny after a collective bargaining agreement between the players association and league has expired. Where the rule or practice which the players contend violates antitrust law was negotiated into the expired collective bargaining agreement and the employer is maintaining the status quo, the decisions in *Bridgeman v. NBA*, 675 F. Supp. 960 (D.N.J. 1987), *Powell v. NFL*, 930 F.2d 1293 (8th Cir. 1989) and *NBA v. Williams*, 43 F.3d 684 (2d Cir. 1995) have extended the exemption past impasse provided that a collective bargaining relationship exists for the players and management. The only means, then, for the players to be successful in an antitrust challenge is where the union has decertified their bargaining unit.

In *McNeil v. NFL*, 790 F.Supp. 871 (D.Minn. 1992), several players challenged the "Plan B" free agency system unilaterally imposed by the owners after the players and owners had reached an impasse in their negotiations (as represented by the players' 1987 strike), and after the decertification of the NFL Players Association as the exclusive bargaining representative of the players. The players prevailed as the Plan B system did not qualify for the labor exemption to antitrust since a bargaining relationship no longer existed between NFL owners and their players.

The law in this area is not, however, well settled. For instance, *Brown v. Pro-Football, Inc.*, 50 F. 3d 1041 (D.C. Cir. 1991), is currently before the U.S. Supreme Court. *Brown* involves the question of whether the nonstatutory labor exemption offers the employer protection from antitrust liability even where a rule or practice is unilaterally imposed by management after impasse is reached. The plaintiff, Antony Brown, is a developmental squad player arguing that the NFL's unilateral imposition of weekly salaries without negotiating with the players constitutes a restraint of trade violative of antitrust. The appellate court in *Brown* found that the labor exemption completely immunized employers from antitrust liability where they impose industry-wide terms and conditions of employment provided that the two had previously engaged in collective bargaining. The events leading to the Brown case also took place while the NFL Players Association was decertified as the player's exclusive bargaining representative.

Antitrust Disputes: Between Teams, Team Owners and the League

Another area in which the antitrust laws have been relied upon is in litigation involving disputes between owners and the league. Until recently, the most celebrated case, *Los Angeles Memorial Coliseum and the Los Angeles Raiders v. NFL*, 726 F.2d 1381 (9th Cir. 1984) involved the Raiders' successful antitrust challenge to league restraints on franchise relocation. A new breed of owners who have made large investments in purchasing and operating teams have been more willing to challenge league rules or policies on antitrust grounds. Part of the reason for the increased challenges comes from the philosophy that the new owners view team ownership as an investment opportunity and they believe that they should be able to control the profits of their teams. The challenges vary from rules restricting the number of games telecast nationally on a superstation [*Chicago Bulls and WGN v. NBA*, 961 F.2d 667 (7th Cir. 1992]; ownership policies [*Sullivan v. NFL (pending) and Kiam v. NFL* (pending)]; marketing and revenue sharing [*Jones v. NFL* (pending)]; and potential owners attempting to purchase and relocate a baseball franchise [*Piazza v. MLB*, 831 F. Supp 420 (E.D.Pa. 1993)].

Antitrust Cases: Individual Athletes Against the League

There have also been antitrust cases brought by individual athletes against the league. Most of these cases have been based on a collective bargaining agreement, which contains the terms and conditions of employment agreed on between the employees (union) and the employer (management). These cases have resulted because the agreement implemented restrictions on individuals who were not part of the bargaining unit. For example, Leon Wood challenged the National Basketball Association because he believed that the salary cap in the National Basketball Association reduced his market value when he was drafted out of college.

The antitrust laws have also been relied on by athletes who were underclassmen and were not eligible for the professional league drafts. In one celebrated case, *Haywood v. National Basketball Association*, 401 U.S. 1204 (1971), Spencer Haywood was successful in arguing that the rule preventing him from being drafted and entering the National Basketball Association restricted his ability to earn a living and was a violation of the antitrust laws. As a result of this case the National Basketball Association, beginning in 1971, has allowed underclass athletes to declare eligibility for NBA draft.

One additional area in which the antitrust laws have been used is where a disciplined player challenges the league. For example, in *Molinas v. NBA*, 190 F. Supp. 241 (S.D.N.Y. 1961), the plaintiff NBA player had been suspended for wagering on games in which he was participating. Molinas application for reinstatement with the league was rejected and Molinas argued that the expulsion from the league restrained trade because he had no economic alternative to playing basketball in the NBA. The court upheld the suspension, finding that the restraint was a reasonable one as the NBA had a legitimate interest in banning gambling and in restoring the public confidence by keeping admitted gamblers out of the NBA.

Amateur Athletic Organizations

In the past, amateur athletic organizations have not been subject to the antitrust litigation faced by the professional sports industry. However, with the increased prominence of amateur athletics and the money now involved, organizations such as the NCAA are increasingly becoming targets for antitrust attack.

Historically, amateur athletic associations, as defendants in antitrust actions, have been successful in arguing that the antitrust laws were inapplicable to them since amateur athletics did not fall into the categories of "trade" or "commerce" as defined by the Sherman Act. Amateur organizations have traditionally argued that since the amateur athletic associations are nonprofit organizations, the primary purpose of which is either educational and/or noncommercial in nature, they are not involved with trade or commerce and are therefore not subject to the antitrust laws. However, in some recent cases the courts are viewing amateur athletics differently, especially the NCAA. The finding by the courts of the requisite involvement in "trade" or "commerce" thereby subjects certain amateur organizations to the antitrust laws. The most celebrated case in this area has been *NCAA v. Board of Regents of the University of Oklahoma*, 468 U.S. 85 (1984), which went to the U.S. Supreme Court. The Supreme Court decided the lawsuit in favor of the University of Oklahoma and the University of Georgia, in which the schools challenged that the NCAA's national television contract was in violation of the federal antitrust laws. This lawsuit has created an open and free market for college football telecasts, allowing many games—several at the same time—to be on television. Another recent case involves an antitrust challenge to an NCAA rule which set limits of $12,000 for academic year and $4,000 for summer salaries for entry-level college coaches in Division I. In *Law v. NCAA*, 902 F. Supp. 1394 (D. Kan. 1995), the Federal District Court for the District of Kansas found that the NCAA's Restricted Earnings Coach Rule was an unreasonable restraint of trade because it specifically prohibited the free operation of a market responsive to the demand for Division I college coaches. In fact, in *Law*, the NCAA acknowledged that prior to the rule's implementation some of the restricted earnings coaches had been paid $60,000 to $70,000. The NCAA defended the rule by declaring it reasonable because it was intended to level the playing field to obtain competitive equity for schools, to provide for an entry-level coaching position, and to cut athletic employment costs of its Division I institutions. The court rejected this argument because the NCAA provided no evidence that the effect of the restricted earnings rule was to level the competitive field for schools, particularly where no limits were set for the three senior coaches on staff; provided no evidence that the restricted earnings positions would be filled by young or inexperienced coaches; and provided no evidence that the restricted earnings rule achieved an overall reduction in athletic department costs.

Despite the *NCAA v. Board of Regents of the University of Oklahoma* and *Law v. NCAA* cases subjecting the NCAA to antitrust scrutiny, the cases are limited to situations where the plaintiff can establish the NCAA's anti-competitive effect on a relevant market. In the *Board of Regents of the University of Oklahoma* the relevant market was the television market and in *Law* it was the market for college coaches. When an eligibility rule is challenged as being anti-competitive and thus violative of the Sherman Act, the plaintiff student-athlete has had difficulty establishing the relevant market impacted by the anti-competitive rule. For instance in *Banks v. NCAA*, 977 F.2d 1081 (7th Cir. 1992) and *Gaines v. NCAA*, 746 F.Supp.738 (M.D. Tenn. 1990), the plaintiffs, student-athletes, challenged the NCAA's restriction on an undrafted football player's returning to school for their senior year of eligibility when they have entered the NFL draft as juniors. Both courts dismissed the cases because the plaintiffs failed to state a claim for which relief could be granted because they could not establish how the no-draft rule restrained trade in the college football labor market. In addition, the court noted that the no-draft rule had no more anti-competitive effect on student-athletes than any other NCAA eligibility requirements such as grades, credit requirements, or possession of a high school diploma.

Antitrust law is a very complex area of the law and, when applied to athletics, has resulted in decisions unique to the field of athletics, since the business relationship of professional teams and amateur sports is unlike any others. Successful antitrust litigation has also resulted in some of the most significant structural changes in professional team sports and college athletics.

Labor Law

Labor law dictates the rules and regulations that govern the relationship between labor and management, defining the rights, privileges, duties, and responsibilities of each. A main component of labor law pertinent to professional sports is the area specifically relating to collective bargaining agreements. The National Labor Relations Act of 1935 (NLRA) was the first step that gave government the power to protect the collective bargaining rights of employees. The NLRA also created an independent agency, the National Labor Relations Board (NLRB) to provide the machinery for enforcing the provisions under the NLRA. The NLRB has jurisdiction over labor law issues.

Professional Sports

As indicated in the antitrust section of this chapter, labor law is extremely important today in professional team sports. All of the professional leagues have significant labor law issues involved in operating those particular industries. The labor relations of all the major team sports are governed now by collective bargaining agreements that are long (up to 200 pages) and sometimes complex (see the salary cap in the NBA, NHL, and NFL), defining the terms and conditions of employment between the employer, the league and the teams and the union and its members—the players. The collective bargaining agreements might, for example, address some of the following issues:

1. Minimum salaries
2. Player freedoms, such as the right to be a free agent
3. Salary arbitration (in major league baseball and national hockey league)
4. A grievance arbitration system to decide disputes between players and clubs
5. Pension benefits
6. Health and medical benefits

7. Training camp compensation
8. Meal money
9. Means of transportation and level of transportation (for example, first-class travel and airflights if the trip is longer than x number of hours)
10. Moving expenses
11. Working conditions
12. Scheduling of games

Team management personnel may also deal with the labor laws with respect to other non-player employees. For example, unionized employees such as the ushers, ticket-takers, carpenters, and other trades groups that run many stadiums and arenas.

The Professional Golf Association (PGA) and the Association of Tennis Professionals (ATP) are the governing bodies for individual player sports. Each runs its own tours for its players, and each has its own set of rules and regulations to govern memberships, tournaments, and play. The PGA and ATP differ from the professional team sports in that they are more akin to trade associations, and there are no player collective bargaining agreements.

Amateur Athletics

None of the athletes involved in amateur athletics are unionized at this point. although some have argued that they should be. Some of the personnel working in an amateur organization such as a college or university may belong to a union and are therefore governed by the union's labor laws and collective bargaining agreements. For example, the faculty at some institutions are unionized, and some of the coaches may be members of that union. Another likely area is the employees on campus, such as the clerical staff or maintenance staff, who may be unionized and governed by a collective bargaining agreement.

Facility Management

Many spectator facilities employ various unionized employees, who may belong to as many as 10 to 15 different union groups, all with different collective bargaining agreements. The facility manager must have a working knowledge of all the agreements. While employees of health clubs are for the most part not unionized, the club manager does not need to be familiar with labor laws.

Employment Discrimination

Sport managers must also be familiar with laws which prohibit employment discrimination. There are both state and federal employment discrimination laws. Since state laws will vary by jurisdiction, the students should become familiar with the following federal laws: the Equal Pay Act of 1963, Title VII of the Civil Rights Act of 1964, the Age Discrimination in Employment Act, and the Americans with Disabilities Act (see Chapter 10, "Staffing" for discussion).

Summary

1. Sports law is a relatively new field. The first ports law course was offered in 1972 by Professor Robert C. Berry at Boston College Law School.

2. Sports law has become an integral part of the curriculum offered by sport management programs in colleges and universities.

3. There are two basic legal systems in the United States: the federal system and the state system

4. The major legal requirements to form of a valid contract are offer, acceptance, consideration, legality, and capacity.

5. A tort is a private (or civil) wrong or injury, suffered by an individual as the result of another person's conduct.

6. Assault and battery are intentional torts that involve an intent to commit the act and an intent to harm the plaintiff.

7. Reckless misconduct is a tort action characterized by a defendants possessing an intent to commit an act and no intent to harm the plaintiff. This standard is most often relied on in tort actions between participants in sport and cases tend to focus on a defendant's violation of a safety rule to establish a willful, wanton, and reckless disregard for the plaintiff's safety.

8. The most common tort actions in athletics result from negligence. Negligence is an unintentional tort that involves no intent to commit the act and no intent to harm the plaintiff but a failure to exercise reasonable care.

9. Agency Law establishes the legal parameters in the relationships between a principal and an agent who acts or represents the interests of the principal. One purpose of agency law is to hold the principal responsible (to third parties) for the actions of the agent, providing the agent is acting under the authority of the principal. A second purpose is to establish the duties that the principal and agent owe to each other.

10. Under agency law the principal owes the agent three duties which are financial in nature: to compensate, to reimburse, and to indemnify the agent. The agent owes the principal five fiduciary duties: obedience, loyalty, reasonable care, notification, and the duty to account.

11. An independent contractor is one who contracts to perform work according to his or her own methods and without being subject to the control of the employer. Thus, an employer will not be held responsible for the negligence of an independent contractor.

12. An employer is not held responsible for intentional torts committed by the employee. An intentional tort involves an intent to commit the act and an intent to harm the plaintiff, and this type of tort is seen as outside the scope of the duties and responsibilities of the position.

13. The constitutional law arguments that are raised in sports include freedom of expres-

sion, due process, equal protection, illegal search and seizure, and invasion of privacy.

14. Sex discrimination in high school and intercollegiate athletics has been challenged using a variety of legal arguments, including Title IX of the Education Amendments of 1972, equal protection laws, state equal rights amendments, and the Equal Pay Act.

15. The Office of Civil Rights monitors compliance with Title IX.

16. Challenging sex discrimination on equal protection grounds has not been very effective for plaintiffs. First, for equal protection to apply the defendant must be a state actor. Second, the intermediate level of scrutiny does provide the defendant with a defense if it can establish an important governmental reason for the gender-based discrimination. Finally, equal protection is a private remedy, requiring the plaintiff to absorb the costs of litigation.

17. Gender discrimination litigation in coaching employment has occurred under the following statutes: the Equal Pay Act of 1963, Title VII of the Civil Rights Act of 1964, and Title IX of the Educational Amendments of 1972.

18. Antitrust law concerns have primarily involved professional sports, although amateur sports have increasingly come under the scrutiny of antitrust laws partly because of the transformation of many areas of amateur athletics into "big business."

19. The professional team sports of basketball, football, and hockey are governed by and subject to the antitrust laws. Baseball is unique and has a special exemption from the antitrust laws.

20. The most celebrated case involving an amateur athletic association and antitrust laws has been the NCAA v. Board of Regents of the University of Oklahoma. The supreme Court ruled that the NCAA's national television contract was a violation of federal antitrust laws. The result of this lawsuit has invoked an open and free market for college football telecasts.

21. Labor law can be defined as the aspect of the law that deals with the rights and privileges due to a laborer.

22. Sport managers must be familiar with the following federal employment discrimination laws: the Equal Pay Act of 1963, Title VII of the Civil Rights Act of 1964, the Age Discrimination in Employment Act, and the Americans with Disabilities Act.

Review Questions and Issues

1. List and give a description of the ten parts to a trial system.

2. List and define the major legal concepts involved in the formation of a contract.

3. Define and give an example of both an assault and a battery.

4. What are the four factors the courts use to determine whether a defendant's action constitutes negligence?

5. List three situations in which an employee may be identified by the courts as an independent contractor, thus resulting in the employer not being held liable for the employee's actions.

6. Define intentional tort. Give an example of a situation in which an intentional tort occurred, and explain why the employer would or would not be held responsible for the intentional tort.

7. Define due process and explain how this concept is used in athletic cases.

8. What three factors are used by the courts in considering a sex discrimination case?

9. What aspect of the Title IX statute initially posed a problem for athletic departments and how has this recently changed?

10. Why hasn't challenging sex discrimination based on the equal protection laws been very successful?

11. How does the Office of Civil Rights (OCR) determine compliance with Title IX?

12. What has historically been the argument regarding amateur athletic associations and their applicability or nonapplicability to the antitrust laws? How has this changed recently.

Glossary of Key Terms

Age Discrimination in Employment Act of 1967 (amended 1978 and 1986): This Act prohibits employers from discriminating in employment against individuals on the basis of age.

Agency Law: Deals with the relationship in which one person, the agent, acts for or represents another, the principal, by the principal's authority.

Americans with Disabilities Act of 1992: Protects disabled applicants and employees from employment discrimination but provides that applicants/employees must be able to perform all essential functions of the position.

Antitrust Laws: The primary laws are the Sherman Antitrust Act (1890) and the Clayton Act (1914). These are laws that were passed to encourage free and open competition in business.

Assault and Battery: Intentional torts designed to commit the act and harm the plaintiff.

Breach of Contract: A failure to perform a duty imposed under a contract.

Collective Bargaining Agreements: Applicable primarily to the professional team sports leagues, such agreements include the governing terms and conditions of employment for players in their respective leagues.

Constitutional Law: The Constitution contains statutory provisions and judicial interpretations concerning important social, economic and political issues.

Contract Law: That body of laws that pertain to contracts which are agreements between two or more parties that are enforceable under the law. Contracts can be written or oral.

Defamation: May be libel (in writing) or slander (spoken words) that tend to harm the reputation of another as to lower him or her in the estimation of the community or to deter third persons from associating or dealing with him or her.

Due Process: A course of legal proceedings which have been established in our system of jurisprudence for the protection and enforcement of private rights.

Equal Pay Act of 1963 (amended 1972): Prohibits wage discrimination on the basis of gender when the jobs require equal skills, effort and responsibility and are performed under similar working conditions.

Equal Protection: The constitutional method of checking on the fairness of the application of law.

Equal Rights Amendment (ERA): A proposed amendment to the Constitution guaranteeing equal rights for all citizens which was never ratified by the required 38 states; however, 19 states have their own such laws. The ERA has an impact on athletics at the state level but not at the federal level. ERA extends greater protection against sex or gender-based classifications.

Federal Court System: Consists of the Supreme Court, 13 Courts of Appeals, 94 District Courts, certain specialized courts and administrative agencies.

Intentional Tort: Consists of an intent to commit the act and an intent to harm the plaintiff (for example, assault and battery).

Independent Contractor: A person who is in some way connected to the employer but not under the employer's control.

Institutional Approach: Refers to the application of Title IX to programs such as athletic departments within institutions which receive federal financial assistance.

Invasion of Privacy: Designed to protect a person's mental peace and/or comfort

Labor Law: Dictates the rules and regulations that govern the relationship between labor and management, defining the rights, privileges, duties and responsibilities of each.

Libel: The publication of defamatory matter by writing.

Negligence: An unintentional tort that focuses on an individual's conduct or actions.

Programmatic Approach: Refers to the scope and applicability of Title IX to only programs which receive direct financial assistance from the federal government.

Reckless Misconduct: A tort action that is characterized by intent on the part of the defendant to commit the act but no intent to harm the plaintiff by the act.

Sex Discrimination: Regards cases where the plaintiff contends there is a fundamental inequality.

Slander: The publication of defamatory matter by spoken words.

Sports Law: The application of various areas of the law to the sports industry.

Title VII of the Civil Rights Act of 1964: Specifically prohibits employment discrimination against individuals on the basis of race, color, religion, gender or national origin.

Title IX of the Education Amendments of 1972: A federal statute that mandates: "No person in the U.S. shall, on the basis of sex, be excluded from participation in, be denied the benefits of, or be subjected to discrimination under any educational program or activity receiving Federal financial assistance." Opened opportunities for women in the sports industry.

Tort Liability: A private (or civil) wrong or injury, other than a breach of contract, suffered by an individual as the result of another person's conduct.

Trial System: Composed of parts involved when a complaint is filed by the plaintiff in a civil case or by the prosecutor in a criminal case.

Unintentional Tort: Involves no intent to commit the act and no intent to harm the plaintiff but does involve a failure to exercise reasonable care (negligence).

Unreasonable Search and Seizure: The Fourth Amendment to the Constitution guarantees the right of people to be secure in their persons, houses, papers and effects against unreasonable searches and seizures.

Case Studies

Constitutional Law

Constitutional law is federal and state statutes written to protect the constitutional rights of the individual. The constitution's guarantees of due process—including equal protection, freedom from illegal search and seizure, and freedom from invasion of privacy—have been argued in athletic situations. These include cases in which the athlete has been forced to do something that he or she does not want to do (such as submit to drug testing) or when the athlete is denied something (such as eligibility). The constitutional safeguards of the Fifth and Fourteenth Amendments apply only when state action is present. The plaintiff in constitutional law claims must first demonstrate that state action is involved before the claim can go to court. An action by any public school, state college, state university, or their officials is construed as state action. State action is present because the state or federal government provides aid to that institution. Once state action is proved, the plaintiff must show that the defendant has infringed on a constitutional right, using either federal or state constitutional law or both.

CASE: *Vernonia School District 47J v. Acton*, 115 U.S. 2386 (1995)

ISSUE: Whether drug testing of high school athletes violates the student-athletes' constitutional privacy rights, right to be free from unreasonable searches and seizures, and equal protection rights?

In *Vernonia School District 47J v. Acton*, the school district observed a sharp increase in drug use. Student athletes were drug users and often were the leaders of the drug culture. This caused administrators particular concern since drug use increases the risk of sports-related injury. The football and wrestling coach witnessed a severe injury suffered by a wrestler and various mis-executions by football players, attributable in his belief to drug use.

Initially, the district responded to the problem by offering classes, speakers and presentations to deter drug use. It even brought in a specially trained dog to detect drugs, but the problem persisted. District officials then held a parent "input night" to discuss the proposed Student Athlete Drug Policy (policy), and the parents in attendance gave unanimous approval. Its expressed purpose was to prevent student athletes from using drugs, to protect their health and safety, and to assistance to drug users.

The policy applied to all students participating in interscholastic athletics. Students wishing to play sports signed a form consenting to the testing and obtained their parents written consent. Athletes were tested at the beginning of the season of their sport. In addition, once each week of the season the names of the athletes are place in a "pool" from which a student, with the supervision of two adults, blindly draws the names of 10% of the athletes for random testing. Those selected are notified and tested the same day, if possible.

The student to be tested completed a specimen control form with an assigned number. Prescription medications that the student was taking were identified by providing a copy of the prescription or a doctor's authorization. The student then entered an empty locker room accompanied by an adult monitor of the same sex. Each boy selected produced a sample at the urinal, remaining fully clothed with his back to the monitor, who stands approximately 12 to 15 feet behind the student. Monitors could watch the student while he produced the sample and listened for normal sounds of urination. Girls produced samples in an enclosed stall, so they were heard, but not observed. After the sample is produced, it is given to the monitor, who checked it for temperature and tampering and then transfers it to a vial.

The samples were sent to an independent laboratory, which tested them for amphetamines, cocaine, and marijuana. Other drugs, such as LSD, may be screened at the request of the district, but the student's identity did not determine which drugs were tested. The laboratory's procedures are 99.94% accurate. The district followed strict procedures regarding the chain of custody and access to test results. The laboratory did not know the identity of the students whose samples it tested. It was authorized to mail written test reports only to the superintendent and to give test results to district personnel over the telephone only after the requesting official recited a private code. Only the superintendent, principals, vice-principals, and athletic directors had access to test results. The results are not kept for more than one year.

If the sample tested positive, a second test was administered as soon as possible. If the second test was negative, no further action was taken. It the second test was positive, the athlete's parents were notified, and the school principal convened a meeting of the student and parents, at which the student was given the option of (1) participation in a six-week assistance program including weekly urinalysis, or (2) suspension from athletics for the remainder of that season and the next athletic season. The student was then retested prior to the start of the next athletic season for which he was eligible. A second offense results in the imposition of option (2); a third offense in suspension for the remainder of that season and the next two seasons.

In the fall of 1991, seventh-grader James Acton signed up to play football at one of the district's grade schools. He was denied participation because he and his parents refused to sign the testing consent forms.

The Fourth Amendment to the United States constitution provides that the federal Government shall not violate "the right of the people to be secure in their persons, houses, papers, and effects, against unreasonable searches and seizures...." The Fourteenth Amendment extends this constitutional guarantee to searches and seizures by state officers, including public school officials. As the Fourth Amendment indicates, the ultimate measure of the constitutionality of a governmental search is "reasonableness." At least in a case such as this, where there was no clear practice, either approving or disapproving the type of search at issue at the time the constitutional provision was enacted, whether a particular search meets the reasonableness standard is judged by balancing its intrusion on the individual's Fourth Amendment interests against its promotion of legitimate governmental interests.

We have found special needs exist in the public school context such that the warrant requirement would unduly interfere with the maintenance of swift and informal disciplinary procedures and strict adherence to the requirement that searches be based upon probable cause would undercut the substantial need of school teachers and administrators to maintain order.

The first factor considered was the nature of the privacy interest upon which the Vernonia search intrudes. The Fourth Amendment does not protect all subjective expectations of privacy, but only those that society recognizes as legitimate. Central to the case was the fact that the subjects were children committed to the temporary custody of the State as schoolmaster.

Fourth Amendment rights are different in public schools than elsewhere and the reasonableness inquiry cannot disregard the schools' custodial and tutelary responsibility for children. For their own good and that of their classmates, public school children are routinely required to submit to various physical examinations and to be vaccinated against various diseases. Therefore, students in the school environment have a lesser expectation of privacy than members of the population generally. Legitimate privacy expectations are even less with regard to student athletes. School sports are not for the bashful. They require "suiting up," and showering and changing. Public school locker rooms, the usual sites for these activities, are not noted for privacy. The locker rooms in Vernonia are typical; no individual dressing rooms are provided; shower heads are lined up along a wall, unseparated by any sort of partition or curtain; not even all the toilet stalls have doors. As the United States Court of Appeals for the Seventh Circuit noted, there is "an element of 'communal undress' inherent in athletic participation." *Schaill v. Tippecanoe County School Corp.*, 864 F. 2d 1309, 1318 (1988).

Athletes have a more greatly reduced expectation of privacy because by choosing to "go out for the team," they voluntarily subject themselves to regulation even higher than that imposed on other students. In Vernonia's public schools, they submit to a preseason physical (including a urine sample), acquire adequate insurance coverage or sign an insurance waiver, maintain a minimum grade point average, and comply with any rules of conduct, dress, training hours and related matters as may be established for each sport by the head coach and athletic director with the principal's approval.

The Supreme Court has recognized that collecting the samples for urinalysis intrudes upon an excretory function traditionally shielded by great privacy. However, the degree of intrusion depends upon the manner in which production of the sample is monitored. Under this policy male students produce samples at a urinal along a wall. They remain fully clothed and only are observed from behind, if at all. Female students produce samples in an enclosed stall, with a female monitor standing outside listening only for sounds of tampering. These conditions are nearly identical to those typically encountered in public restrooms. Privacy interests compromised by this process are negligible. The other privacy-invasive aspect of urinalysis is the information it discloses concerning the state of the subject's body and the materials he has ingested. It is significant that the tests at issue here look only for drugs, and not for whether the student is, for example, epileptic, diabetic, or pregnant. Moreover, the drugs screened for are standard and do not vary by the identity of the student. Finally, test results are disclosed only to a limited class of school personnel who need to know. They are not given to law enforcement or used for school discipline.

Acton argued, however, that the policy was more intrusive than this suggests, because it requires the students, if they are to avoid sanctions for a falsely positive test, to identify in advance prescription medications they are taking. The Court agreed that this raises concern, but did not indicate that requiring advance disclosure of medications is per se unreasonable. While the practice seems to have been to have a school official take medication information from the student at the time of the test, that practice is one set forth in, or required by, the policy. It may well be that the district would have permitted a student to provide the requested information in a confidential manner—for example, in a sealed envelope delivered to the testing lab. Nothing in the policy contradicts that, and when respondents challenged the policy on its face the Court refused to assume the worst.

Finally, the Court considered the nature and immediacy of the governmental concern at issue, and efficacy of this means for meeting it. The District Court held that because the policy also called for drug testing in the absence of individualized suspicion, the district must demonstrate a 'compelling need' for the program. The Court of Appeals appears to have agreed with this view. The Supreme Court stated that was a mistake, however, to think that the phrase "compelling state interest," in the Fourth Amendment context, described a fixed minimum quantum of governmental concern, so as to dispose of the case by answering in isolation the question: Is there a compelling state interest here? Rather, the phrase describes an interest which appears important enough to justify the particular search at hand, in light of other factors which show the search to be relatively intrusive upon a genuine expectation of privacy. Regardless of whether that relatively high degree of government concern was necessary not, it was met in this case.

That the nature of the concern was important—indeed, perhaps compelling—can hardly be doubted. Deterring drug use by schoolchildren is at least as important as enhancing efficient enforcement of laws against the importation of drugs. School years are the time when the physical, psychological, and addictive effects of drugs are most severe. And of course, the effects of a drug-infested school are visited not just upon the users, but upon the entire student body and faculty, as the educational process is disrupted. The necessity for the State to act was magnified by the fact that the evil was being visited not just upon individuals at large, but upon children whom it has undertaken a special responsibility of care and direction. Finally, this program was directed more narrowly to drug use by school athletes, where the risk of immediate harm to the user or those with whom he is playing sport is particularly high. Apart from psychological effects, which include impaired judgment, slowed reaction, and a lessened perception of pain, the particular drugs screened by the district's policy have been demonstrated to pose substantial physical risks to athletes. Amphetamines produce an artificially induced heart rate increase, peripheral vasoconstriction, blood pressure increase, and a masking of the normal fatigue response. Marijuana causes irregular blood pressure responses during changes in body position, reduction in the oxygen-carrying capacity of the blood, and inhibition of the normal sweating responses resulting in increased body temperature. Cocaine produces vasoconstriction, elevated blood pressure, and possible coronary artery spasms and myocardial infarction.

As for the efficiency of this means for addressing the problem: It seems self-evident that a drug problem largely fueled by "role model" effect of athletes' drug use, and of particular danger to athletes, is effectively addressed by making sure athletes do not use drugs. Acton argued that a less intrusive means to the same end was available, namely, drug testing on suspicion of drug use. The Court refused to declare that only the least intrusive search practicable can be reasonable and the Fourth Amendment. Acton's alternative entails substantial difficulties--if it is indeed practicable at all. It may be impracticable, for one thing, simply because parents who are willing to accept random drug tests for athletes are not willing to accept accusatory drug testing for all students. Acton's proposal also risk that teachers will impose testing arbitrarily on troublesome but not drug-likely students. It generates the expense of defending lawsuits over arbitrary imposition or that simply demand a greater process before accusatory drug testing is imposed. And it will add to the ever-expanding diversionary duties of schoolteachers the new function of spotting and bringing to account drug abuse, a task for which they are ill-prepared.

Thus, the Supreme Court found the Vernonia drug testing policy to be reasonable and constitutional.

Sex Discrimination

Sex discrimination complaints have been made in athletic settings, when a plaintiff contends that treatment is fundamentally unequal. Sex discrimination litigation has been brought over females being prohibited from joining a male team, lack of a female team while a male team is offered, inequality of employment of coaches and athletic personnel, inequality in the amount of money made available to females and males in team budgets and scholarships, use and maintenance of facilities, and amount of publicity given to female and male sports and athletes. Males also have filed sex discrimination suits, contending they should be allowed to participate on female teams when no team is offered for males. Sex discrimination complaints have been argued under federal equal protection laws, Title IX, and state equal rights amendments. The plaintiff must prove that the alleged sex discrimination action is a violation of individual rights under federal and/or state law.

CASE: *Cohen v. Brown University*, 879 F.Supp. 185 (D.R.I. 1995)

ISSUE: How is an educational institution's effective accommodation of students' interests and abilities properly measured under Title IX?

The plaintiffs, call present and future Brown University women students and potential students who participate or seek to participate in intercollegiate athletics funded by Brown, contended that Brown discriminated against women when it demoted the women's gymnastics and volleyball teams from full varsity to club varsity status in May of 1991. At the same time, and apparently to comply with Title IX, Brown demoted two men's varsity teams, water polo and golf, to club varsity status. All four teams lost university funding and most varsity privileges.

Brown is an NCAA Division I institution which offers an extensive athletic program—funding 13 sports for women and 12 for men. It also recognizes several sports as "donor-funded" varsities (four men's and three women's teams). Although the number of varsity sports offered to men and women are equal, the selection of sports offered to each gender generates far more individual positions for male athletes than female athletes. Brown provides the financial resources for university-funded varsities and requires donor-funded teams to raise their own funds through private donations. Brown provides services and privileges to the university-funded, but not the donor-funded varsities. A consequence of this two-tiered system is that most donor-funded varsities have found it difficult to maintain a level of competitiveness as high as their ability would otherwise permit. This is due to the reluctance of some schools to play donor-funded teams and the inability of teams to obtain varsity-level coaching and recruits, or to funds for travel, post-season competition, and equipment.

Several donor-funded teams have the interest and ability to compete at the top level [gymnastics, fencing, and skiing] and would benefit from university-funded status. Additionally, women's water polo, a club team, has demonstrated the interest and ability to compete at the highest level. While all four teams would benefit from university-funded status, only two of the donor-funded teams would be able to sustain a competitive intercollegiate varsity team. Additionally, elevation of water polo to a donor-funded from a club team would be financially disadvantageous since as a club sport, the team receives student activities funding.

At the time Brown's intercollegiate athletic program consisted of 32 teams for 342 female (38.13% of athletes) and 555 male (61.87% of athletes) participants. During that same year [1993-94], the undergraduate enrollment was 5722 students; 2796 men (48.86%) and 2926 women (51.14%).

A key issue in Brown was how to determine the effective accommodation of interests and abilities. Under OCR's Title IX regulations an institution may effectively accommodate the interests and abilities of its students by either:

(1) providing intercollegiate level participation opportunities for male and female students in numbers substantially proportionate to their respective enrollments; or

(2) where the members of one sex have been and are underrepresented in intercollegiate athletics, by showing a history and continuing practice of program expansion which is demonstrably responsive to the developing interest and abilities of the members of that sex; or

(3) where the members of one sex are underrepresented in intercollegiate athletics, and the institution cannot show a continuing practice of program expansion such as that shown above, by demonstrating that the interest and abilities of the members of that sex have been fully and effectively accommodated.

Prong One Applied

Plaintiffs have proven that Brown does not satisfy prong one. The gender balance of Brown's intercollegiate athletic program is far from substantially proportionate to its student enrollment. As discussed above Brown provides 555 (61.87%) intercollegiate athletic opportunities to men and 342 (38.13%) to women, whereas the undergraduate enrollment for the relevant year is 2796 men (48.86%) and 2926 women (51.14%). Brown currently offers 479 university-funded varsity slots for men and 312 for women. It also provides 76 donor-funded varsity slots for men and 30 for women. Thus, because Brown maintains a 13.03% disparity between female participation in intercollegiate athletics and female enrollment, it cannot gain the protection of prong one. Although Brown clearly does not meet the criteria of the first prong, Brown will prevail if they can demonstrate that they satisfy the requirements of the second prong or if plaintiffs are unable to meet their burden of proof on prong three.

Prong Two Applied

Although Brown has an impressive *history* of program expansion, they have failed to demonstrate that the University has maintained a *continuing* practice of intercollegiate program expansion for the underrepresented sex, women. Brown substantially expanded its athletic program for women in the 1970s but, since 1977 only women's indoor track and skiing have been added. Because merely reducing program offerings to the overrepresented sex does not constitute program expansion, the fact that Brown has eliminated or demoted several men's teams does not amount to a continuing practice of program expansion for women. Since the 1970s the percentage of women participating in athletics at Brown has remained steady.

Prong Three Applied

Prong three would excuse Brown's failure to provide substantial proportionality only if Brown fully and effectively accommodated the underrepresented sex. The plaintiffs have successfully established the Brown has not fully and effectively accommodated the interests and abilities of women, the underrepresented sex. The plaintiffs introduced testimony of student athletes, coaches and experts to verify that at least four existing teams have long been participating in competitive schedules and are capable of competing at Brown's highest varsity level. There are interested women able to compete at the university-funded varsity level in gymnastics, fencing, skiing and water polo.

Brown fails to comply with prong three in two respects. First, Brown has failed to increase the number of intercollegiate participation opportunities where it could do so by elevating a team with demonstrated interest and ability from below intercollegiate status to intercollegiate status. Specifically, Brown has failed to do this by maintaining water polo at club status and demoting gymnastics. The women's water polo team operates as a traditional club sport, rather than an "intercollegiate" team under the definition of the OCR Interpretation. Although gymnastics is technically a donor-funded varsity at this time, it will in fact cease to exist, within a few seasons, at an intercollegiate varsity level in the absence of university funding. Neither team can compete as an intercollegiate varsity team if denied university-funded status.

Second, Brown failed to maintain and support women's donor-funded teams at its highest level thus, preventing athletes on the teams from developing fully their abilities and athletic skills. Specifically, Brown failed by maintaining women's fencing and skiing at a donor-funded level when each of these teams demonstrated the interest and ability to operate as a university- funded varsity team and where donor-funded status has prevented each of these teams from reaching its athletic potential. Although both athletic tiers provide participation opportunities in Brown's "intercollegiate" athletic program, there are substantial qualitative differences between university and donor-funded teams which rise to such a level that the women participating on donor-funded varsities are not being fully and effectively accommodated.

This second basis for finding a violation was a new application of prong three. While prong three had not been read by any court to require an institution to upgrade any teams from within its intercollegiate athletic program, no other court had been presented with the factual situation of an officially maintained, two-tiered intercollegiate program. Prong three's "full and effectively accommodation" language could have been read to require only that an institution elevate or create athletic offerings from outside of its present intercollegiate program. However, Brown has created two distinct levels of athletics within the OCR Interpretation's definition of "intercollegiate" athletics and thus, the unique factual situation called for a more comprehensive interpretation of prong three. The court found that Brown's restructured athletic program could not be used to shield it from liability when in truth and in fact it does not fully and effectively accommodate the women athletes participating on donor-funded teams. It would circumvent the spirit and meaning of the OCR's Interpretation if a university could "fully and effectively" accommodate the underrepresented sex by creating a second class varsity status.

Finally, the court noted that Brown could not excuse its failure to accommodate the interest and abilities of the women athletes by citing an absence of "a reasonable expectation that intercollegiate athletic competition in the four sports would be available within the institution's normal competitive region. The evidence demonstrated that adequate intercollegiate competition exists within Brown's normal competitive region.

Equal Treatment Factors Applied

There was an additional Title IX violation. Brown's program offerings, as allocated by gender within the two-tiered structure of the intercollegiate varsity program violate the "treatment" aspect of Title IX. At Brown, far more male athletes are being supported at the university-funded level than are female athletes, and thus, women receive less benefit from the intercollegiate varsity program as a whole. This inequity was a consequence of the qualitative differences between benefits enjoyed by the university versus donor-funded varsity teams. Donor-funded teams are not provided with treatment equivalent with regard to at least the following factors: equipment and supplies, travel and per diem allowance, opportunity to receive coaching, assignment and compensation of coaches, and athletic training services.

References

Appenzeller, H., and Appenzeller, T. (1979). *Sports and the Courts*. Charlottesville, VA: The Michie Co.

Appenzeller, H. (1985). *Sports and Law: Contemporary Issues*. Charlottesville, VA: The Michie Co.

Averill v. Lutress, 311 S.W. 2d 812 (Tenn. Ct. App. 1957).

Baley, J. and Matthews, D. (1989). *Law and Liability in Athletics, Physical Education, and Recreation* (2nd Edition). Dubuque, IA: William C. Brown Publishing.

Banks v. NCAA, 977 F 2d 1081 (7th Cir. 1992)

Berry R., Gould, W., and Staudohar, P. (1986). Labor Relations in Professional Sports. Dover, MA: Auburn House Publishing Co.

Berry, R., and Wong, G. (1986). *Law and Business of the Sports Industries*. Dover, MA: Auburn House Publishing Co.

Bridgeman v. NBA, 675 F. Supp. 960 (D.N.J. 1987)

Brown v. Pro-Football, Inc., 50 F. 3d 1041 (D.C. Cir. 1991)

Brown v. Woolf, 554 F. Supp. 1206 (S.D. Ind. 1983)

Bunger v. Iowa High School Athletic Ass'n, 197 N.W. 2d 555 (Sup. Ct. 1972)

Chicago Bulls and WGN v. NBA, 961 F. 2d 667 (7th Cir. 1992)

Childress by Childress v. Madison County, 777 S.W. 2d 1 (Tenn. Ct. App. 1989)

Christ the King Reg. High School v. Catholic High Schools Athletic Ass'n, 624 N.Y.S. 2d 755 (Sup. 1995)

Clement, A. (1988). *Law in Sport and Physical Activity*. Indianapolis, IN: Benchmark Press, Inc.

Cohen v. Brown University, 879 F. Supp. 185 (D.R.I. 1995)

Cooper v. Peterson, 626 N.Y.S. 2d 432 (Sup. Ct. 1995)

Detroit Lions, Inc. and Sims v. Argovitz, 580 F. Supp. 542 (E.D. Mich. 1984)

Dworkin, J. (1981). *Owners versus Players: Baseball and Collective Bargaining*. Dover, MA: Auburn House Publishing Co.

Federal Baseball Club of Baltimore, Inc. v. National League of Professional Baseball Clubs, et al., 259 U.S. 200 (1922).

Flood v. Kuhn, 407 U.S. 258 (1972).

Franklin v. Gwinnett County School District, 112 S. Ct. 1028 (1992)

Gaines v. NCAA, 746 F. Supp. 738 (M.D. Tenn. 1990)

Greenberg, M.J. (1993). *Sports Law Practice: Vols. I and II*. Charlottesville, VA: The Michie Co.

Grove City College v. Bell, 465 U.S. 555 (1984).

Haywood v. National Basketball Association, 401 U.S. 1204 (1971)

Hennigan v. Chargers Football Co., 431 F. 2d 308 (5th Cir. 1970)

Hill v. NCAA, 273 Cal. Rptr. 402 (1994)

Hochberg, P. and Blackman, M. (1990). *Representing Professional Athletes and Teams*. New York: May 14-16. Practising Law Institute Co-Chairmen.

Kansas City Royals Baseball Corporation v. Major League Baseball Players Association, 409 F. Supp. 233 (W.D. Missouri 1976).

Law v. NCAA, 902 F. Supp. 1394 (D. Kan. 1995)

Los Angeles Memorial Coliseum and the Los Angeles Raiders v. NFL, 726 F. 2d 1381 (9th Cir. 1984)

Ludtke v. Kuhn, 461 F. Supp. 86 (S.D. N.Y. 1979).

Lupien, T. and Lowenfish, L. (1980). *The Imperfect Diamond: The Story of Baseball's Reserve System and the Men Who Fought to Change It*. New York: Stein & Day.

Mackey v. National Football League, 407 F. Sup. 1000 (D. Minn. 1975).

Maloy, B. (1988). *Law in Sport: Liability Cases in Management and Administration*. Indianapolis, IN: Benchmark Press, Inc.

McCourt v. California Sports, Inc., 600 P. 2d 1193 (1979).

McNeil v. NFL, 790 F. Supp. 871 (D. Minn. 1992)

Molinas v. NBA, 190 F. Supp. 241 (S.D.N.Y. 1961)

NBA v. Williams, 43 F. 3d 684 (2d Cir. 1995)

NCAA v. Board of Regents of the University of Oklahoma, 468 U.S. 85 (1984).

Nygaard, G. and Boone, T. (1989). *Law for Physical Educators and Coaches* (2nd Edition). Columbus, OH: Publishing Horizons, Inc.

Piazza v. MLB, 831 F. Supp 420 (E.D.Pa. 1993)

Powell v. NFL, 930 F. 2d 1293 (8th Cir. 1989)

Reed, M. Hutchings (1989). *IEG Legal Guide to Sponsorship*. Chicago IL: Internatnioal Events Group, Inc.

Robertson v. National Basketball Association, 556 F 2d 682 (2nd Cir. 1977).

Rodgers v. Georgia Tech Athletic Association, 303 S.E. 2d 467 (Ga. Ct. App. 1983).

Ross v. Creighton University, 957 F. 2d 410 (7th Cir. 1992)

Ruxin, R. (1989). *An Athlete's Guide to Agents*. Lexington, MA: The Stephen Greene Press.

Schubert, G., Smith, R., and Trentadue, J. (1986). *Sports Law*. St. Paul, MN: West Publishing Co.

Shelton v. National Collegiate Athletic Association, 539 F. 2d 1179 (9th Cir. 1976).

Stanley v. University of Southern California, 13 F 3d 1313 (9th Cir. 1994)

Staudohar, P. (1991). *Collective Bargaining in the Sports Industry*, Second Ed. Ithaca, NY: ILR Press.

Tokarz, K. (1985). *Women, Sports and the Law: A Comprehensive Research Guide to Sex Discrimination in Sports*. Buffalo, NY: William S. Hein Co.

Tomjanovich v. California Sports, Inc., No. H-78-243 (S.D. Tex. 1979).

Trope. M. (1987). *Necessary Roughness: The Other Game of Football Exposed By Its Most Controversial Super Agent*. Chicago: Contemporary Books.

Tunkl v. Regents of the University of California, 383 P. 2d 441 (1963)

Uberstine, G. (1985). *Covering All the Bases: A Comprehensive Guide to Sports Law*. Buffalo, NY: William S. Hein Co.

Uberstine, G. (1988). *Law of Professional and Amateur Sports*. New York: Clark Boardman Co., Ltd.

Uberstine, G. Ed. (1991). *The Law of Professional and Amateur Sports*. Deerfield IL: Clark, Boardman, and Callaghan.

United States v. Burke, 700 F. 2d 70 (2nd Cir. 1983).

University of Colorado v. Derdeyn, 863 P. 2d 929 (Colo. Sup. Ct 1993)

van der Smissen, B. (1990). *Legal Liability and Risk Management for Public and Private Entities*. Cincinnati: Anderson Publishing Co.

Vernonia School District 47J v. Acton, 115 S. Ct. 2386 (1995)

Wagenblast v. Odessa School District, 758 P. 2d 968 (1988)

Weiler, P.C. and Roberts, G.R. (1993). *Cases, Materials and Problems on Sports and the Law*. St. Paul, MN: West Publishing Co.

Weistart, J. and Lowell, C. (1979; 1985 supplement). *The Law of Sports*. Indianapolis, IN: The Bobbs-Merrill Co., Inc.

Wong. G. (1988). *Essentials of Amateur Sports Law*. Dover, MA: Auburn House Publishing Co.

Wong, G. "Sports Law Report," *Athletic Business*. Madison, WI (published monthly).

Wong, G. and Wilde, T. (1991). *Sports Lawyers Guide to Legal Periodicals*. Buffalo, NY: William S. Hein Co.

Wong G.M. and Wilde, T.J. (1994). *The Sport Lawyer's Guide to Legal Periodicals*. Buffalo, NY: William S. Hein & Co., Inc.

Yasser. R., McCurdy, J., Goplerud, P. (1990). *Sports Law*. Cincinnati, OH: Anderson Publishing.

SECTION II

PLANNING AND DECISION-MAKING FUNCTIONS

CHAPTER 5

THE PLANNING FUNCTION

After studying this chapter, **you will know:**

- Why planning is a precedent activity
- The purpose of planning
- Overall benefits of planning
- What a mission statement encompasses
- Kinds of goals (objectives) in organizations
- Major advantages of a Management by Objectives (MBO) program
- How to classify plans by types
- The importance and meaning of organizational guidelines
- The fourteen steps in the Planning Process
- How to distinguish between risks and uncertainties

Introduction

Planning is an integral part of every aspect of sport management. Athletics administrators schedule meets, games and tournaments years ahead. Organizations plan capital fundraising drives well into the future. Coaches develop game plans for each contest; and city planners work with recreation directors to acquire land and facilities in the right areas and at the proper time for future growth. These examples are just a few instances that typify the importance of planning in the athletic world. As we have pointed out, poor planning is the number one cause of organizational failure. Failure to survive; failure to reach desired objectives; failure to operate within budgets; or failure to maximize the use of resources are all the result of poor managerial planning.

While every sport manager will make some planning mistakes, the professional managers will minimize these errors. There is no such thing as perfect planning because of the many risks and uncertainties that can occur when plans are implemented. Planning always deals with the future and managers cannot totally foresee nor perfectly predict what can occur in the future. They cannot always, therefore, be prepared for what does occur. The failure to anticipate and prepare for the unexpected is the major cause of planning mistakes.

Nature of Planning

The planning function is an activity which all people perform. Students plan their weekends, their study schedules and their breaks from school. Managers also plan when they generate ideas and formalize objectives. Plans are developed to achieve these objectives. Planning can be informal or formal depending on the importance of the objectives. Planning also is an activity that is permeated with risks.

The risks derive from the futuristic nature of planning. Making plans about the future, based on today's information, can harm planning efforts if the planner does not stay abreast of current data. Regardless of their experience and skill and in spite of the pertinence of the data, managers make planning mistakes. Often they cannot foresee or control all internal and external variables which affect the plans.

Sometimes firms formulate major objectives, develop plans, weigh the risks and uncertainties, and activate their plans regardless of the potential for loss. Such a case involves the American firm, Toys "R" Us:

> ...Starting from scratch, in just two years Toys "R" Us opened 16 U.S.-style
> toy superstores throughout Japan and within two more years expects to have
> 35. Each Japanese store averages $15 to $20 million in sales a year. The typi-
> cal U.S. store averages $10 million a year in sales.[1]

Toys "R" Us faced many formidable barriers in Japan, but they took the risks and overcame many of the hurdles which discourage other American retailers from entering the Japanese market.

The Importance of Planning

Of all the functions of management, planning is the one which anchors all other managerial responsibilities. Planning is a precedent activity: Planning should occur prior to organizing, implementing, controlling and decision-making. Sound planning is the activity necessary to achieve efficient utilization of resources and effective attainment of end results. Poor planning or no planning at all by managers generates inefficiency, ineffectiveness, and often leads to the failure of the organization as a whole. Without question, poor managerial planning is the primary cause of organizational failure in the U.S.

Figure 5-1 shows that 667,000 new businesses were incorporated in the U.S. in 1992. The table also shows that 97,069 incorporated businesses failed in the same year. Poor planning is a major cause of business failure, but it is not the only cause. Some experts state that half of all new businesses fail in the first year of operations. Many of these are not incorporated and go unreported, but the inability of new owner-managers and/or entrepreneurs to plan for the future, foresee pitfalls, do market research, be properly capitalized and truly ready to run a business can cause early failure. Sound planning is of critical importance when attempting to start a new business.

YEAR	Total concerns in business [1] (1,000)	Index of net business formations[2] (1967=100)	New incorporations (1,000)	FAILURES[3]			YEAR	Total concerns in business [1] (1,000)	Index of net business formations[2] (1967=100)	New incorporations (1,000)	FAILURES[3]		
				Number	Rate per 10,000 concerns	Current liabilities [4] (mil. dol.)					Number	Rate per 10,000 concerns	Current liabilities [4] (mil. dol.)
1970	2,442	108.8	264	10,748	44	1,888	1986	5,119	120.4	702	61,616	120	44,724
1975	2,679	109.9	326	11,432	43	4,380	1987	6,004	121.2	685	61,111	102	34,724
1980	2,780	129.9	532	11,742	42	4,635	1988	5,804	124.1	685	57,098	98	39,126
1981	2,745	124.8	581	16,794	61	6,955	1989	7,694	124.8	677	50,361	65	44,261
1982	2,806	116.4	566	24,908	88	15,611	1990	8,038	120.7	647	60,747	74	56,130
1983	2,851	117.5	602	31,334	110	16,073	1991	8,218	115.3	629	88k,140	107	96,825
1984	4,885	121.3	635	52,078	107	29,269	1992	8,805	116.3	667	97,069	109	94,317
1985	4,990	120.9	663	57,078	115	36,937	1993, prel.	8,966	120.8	(NA)	85,982	90	48,423

NA Not available. [1]Data through 1983 represent number of names listed in July issue of *Dun & Bradstreet Reference Book.* Data for 1984-93 represent the numr of establishments listed in the Dun's Census of American Business. The base has been changed due to expanded business failure coverage. [2]Source: U.S. Bureau of Economic Analysis, *Survey of Current Business.* [3]Includes concerns discontinued following assignment, voluntary or involuntary petition in bankruptcy, attachment, execution, foreclosure, etc.; voluntary withdrawals from business with known loss to creditors; also enterprises involved in court action, such as receivership and reorganization or arrangement which may or may not lead to discontinuance; and businesses making voluntary compromise with creditors out of court. [4]Liabilities exclude long-term publicly held obligations; offsetting assets are not taken into account.

FIGURE 5-1: NEW BUSINESS INCORPORATIONS AND BUSINESS FAILURES: 1970 TO 1993

Source: Except as noted, Dun & Bradstreet Corporation, New York, NY, *New Business Incorporations*, monthly; and *Monthly Failure Report.*

There is no mystery to the function of planning. Planning is a common sense activity that is futuristic in nature. Individually, we plan virtually everything in our lives: We plan our upcoming weekends and vacations, how to spend our money, what television programs to watch, when to write the term paper, and so forth. Organizationally, managers plan for capital expenditures, manpower requirements, cash flow needs, growth of sales and market share, introduction of new products and services, and many more factors. In sport management, plans are made for fundraising campaigns, for expansion of facilities or landscaping fields, for recruiting, for scheduling competition, for cooperative use of multi-use facilities, for adding new sports and joining leagues, for ticket sales growth, and much more. All of these planning activities relate to the future. All of today's activity is the result of past planning. Tomorrow's or next year's activity will result from today's planning.

The future success of an organization correlates closely to the planning skills of the managers running that organization now. An interesting example of futuristic planning occurred in early 1996 when the National Football League owners approved a plan to allow the Cleveland professional franchise to relocate to Baltimore for the 1996 season. The League owners, however, were planning ahead and protecting their interests when they also acted to help finance a new stadium in Cleveland and promised to grant another professional football franchise to the city by 1999. This new franchise would retain the nickname "Browns" and use the original colors of the team.

Planning is not the only factor that directly affects the success or failure of an organization, but planning does represent the first and most important step in achieving future organizational goals, objectives and ultimate success.

The Purpose of Planning

The purpose of planning is to formalize objectives and develop a plan to attain these objectives in the desired period of time in the most efficient and effective way possible with a minimum of problems.

This statement of purpose captures the essence of planning. Whether planning is for the long-run, short-run, a department or the whole organization, the purpose of planning is the same. Look at each point in this purpose of planning statement.

Formalize Objectives. To formalize objectives means first to determine what the goals or objectives are; then, to submit the objectives in writing to higher management for review and approval. When written objectives have been approved by higher management, lower level managers have the authority to proceed.

Time Standards and Efficiency. Planning to reach your goals or objectives in the desired period of time refers to setting a **time standard**. Time standards should accompany the pursuit of any objective. A time standard should be set at a **level of excellence**, which is a time standard well within the average amount of time usually needed to complete the task. Everyone involved in implementing the plan should know the time standard. The key to efficiency when implementing a plan is to produce quality work in the shortest possible time period. Not only does a tight time standard improve efficiency, it also tends to boost the morale of employees performing the work or carrying out the plan. Meeting a tight time standard usually generates a sense of excitement among employees because it denotes that the work is important.

Minimum of Problems. The most effective managerial planners try to formulate plans that, when implemented properly, will reach the desired objectives in the correct period of time with a **minimum of problems**. Sound planning does not eliminate or avoid all problems; there is no such thing as a problem-free plan. But, sound planners try to anticipate **major** problems in advance. When major problems are anticipated, then steps are taken to prepare for them so that the loss or damage will be offset or minimized if they do occur. One of the most common examples of this kind of anticipation is carrying fire insurance on property. Another example is cross-training employees to do more than one job. Managers can anticipate bad weather that may keep part of their work force at home. To offset the potential of loss from being idle or short-handed, managers can reassign employees to other jobs to maintain basic operations. Managers can have additional sources of raw materials in case a supplier fails to deliver on schedule. Managers have no excuses if they fail to anticipate major problems in advance when planning so that the effect can be offset.

Effective End Results. Sound planning leads to effective end results. This point simply means that the **desired** end result is achieved. How is theis acomplished? Sound planners think in advance and answer the questions of who, when , where, how and why? Then, they put these answers in **writing**. When all parties directly involved in implementing plans understand the answers to the above questions and their individual roles in carrying out the plans, the odds are increased that effective end results will be achieved. These points will be discussed in more detail in the section on The Planning Process later in this chapter.

Goals and Objectives

Goals and objectives are words used interchangeably in this chapter. Generally objectives are viewed as more specific than goals, but there is no concensus on this definition.

There are many different kinds of goals (objectives) in organizations. The primary reason an organization exists relates to its purpose. The purpose of an organization is part of its *mission statement.* Top management, including directors of firms, formalize mission statements. *The mission statement is the broadest of objectives and defines the purpose and uniqueness of the organization regarding its products, services, markets and revenues.*

Other kinds of goals (objectives) can be classified as *strategic, tactical* or *operational.*

Strategic goals or objectives, set by top management, tend to be long-run and are introduced to influence overall organizational behavior. Strategic goals are expansive and may relate to profitability, market share or changes in products or services offered customers.

Tactical goals or objectives, usually the responsibility of middle management, have an intermediate time frame for accomplishment. Tactical goals represent the operational objectives needed to be achieved in order to reach strategic goals.

Operational goals or objectives, typically set by first-level managers, are short-run goals (one year or less). Achieving operational objectives is part of the effort to reach tactical goals.

Functional areas where goals can be set may include human resources, physical facilities, research and development, financial activities, product quality, cost control and many more.

Management by Objectives (MBO)

Management by Objectives (MBO) is a philosophical approach used in some organizations to help managers more effectively implement plans. MBO is a popular planning/decision-making aid because managers can use it to convert organizational objectives into group and individual objectives. Many people are reluctant to set personal objectives, but MBO helps to overcome this barrier. When individual employees discuss with managers their objectives and have significant input into establishing their own annual work objectives, they feel more committed and perform better. Managers must manage individuals, not groups, and should learn to know their employees so well that they can allign each employee's goals and objectives with those of the department and the organization as a whole. Theoretically, when all employees, all managers and all parts of the organization achieve their anual objectives under MBO, then the overall organizational goals will be met.

The major disadvantage of an MBO program is that much time must be committed to introducing the program, meeting with all employees, formalizing objectives, and monitoring performance throughout the year. Small organizations, however, find MBO a helpful planning/decision-making aid because the time requirement is much less in introducing and administering the program.

MBO or some similar program has had wide acceptance in every type of American organization since the mid-1950s. Not only does MBO influence management decisions, the program also becomes a control mechanism when actual performance of employees and groups is measured against the mutually derived and agreed upon preset standards. It is a less subjective means of evaluating performance.

MBO or some similar program is ideal for application in sport management because of the relatively small numbers of employees usually involved in most organizations and because of the qualitative and quantitative criteria used as a measure of performance.

Figure 5-2 shows the essential written requirements for an MBO program, but an actual MBO program can be as extensive as management wants it to be. Any MBO program must have full cooperation, top management to lowest employee, to work effectively and must be worth the cost in time and money it takes to implement it.

- The primary objectives (why the organization exists)

- The operating objectives (annual or twelve month objectives)

- Unit objectives (annual objectives for divisions, branches, departments, etc.)

- Individual managerial objectives

- Individual nonmanagement employees' objectives

FIGURE 5-2: ESSENTIAL WRITTEN REQUIREMENTS FOR MBO PROGRAM

Overall Benefits from Planning

The function of planning as practiced by managers at all levels generates many benefits to an organization:

1. **Sound planning gives direction to the efforts of employees.**
   Can you imagine floating in a small boat in the middle of the Pacific Ocean with no motor, no sails, oars, charts, compass, rudder or tiller? What are the odds you will reach some desired objective, such as land? Slim indeed! That's how an organization would operate without planning. Sound planning does give direction to organizational effort through the establishment of purpose, objectives and goals. Detailed plans provide the blueprint for small group and individual effort which, when put together with efforts of others, makes up total organizational effort toward the pursuit of objectives. Policies, procedures, rules and other planning tools provide the influence on employee behavior which makes certain everyone and every part of the whole effort is moving in the right direction toward achieving desired objectives.

2. **Sound planning helps an organization determine its own destiny.**
   Rather than being overly influenced by competitors' actions or trends in an industry or public opinion or changing technology, an organization can use

sound planning to decide what it wishes to do, when it wants to do it, what niche in the marketplace it wishes to fill, what product or service it will provide or delete. Simply, through sound planning, an organization determines its own destiny. Managers decide how much control over the future and subsequent events they wish to have knowing they must accept risks associated with their actions. Then they engage in planning the destiny of the organization rather than letting trends and outside forces, over which they have little or no control, do it for them.

3. **Sound planning is a key to effective control.**
The primary function of controlling is to measure performance against a plan (standard) and take remedial action if the plan (standard) is exceeded. Sound planning leads to effective control programs which minimize wasted efforts, defective quality, loss of time, loss of money and customer dissatisfaction. Clear cut objectives which become standards of control are the result of sound managerial planning. While control programs can be costly activities, the lack of control may cost even more. Without sound controls based on planning standards, organizations would not be capable of adapting to rapid change occurring in today's world. Think of all the changes in the economy, in the political arena, in technology and in the social field that direcly affect success and survival of organizations. On-going activities of an enterprise which are a result of yesterday's planning must be monitored carefully; and if change has occurred which threatens the attainment of goals and objectives, adjustments must be made to insure a greater probability of success. Good control programs are built into plans so that these adjustments to changing conditions can be made at proper times.

4. **Sound planning is essential to managerial success.**
If managers are competent as planners, then the organization will most likely be relatively successful in achieving its desired objectives and goals. The emphasis is that sound planning should precede the manager's efforts to organize, implement, control and make decisions. The managerial function of planning permeates all other management responsibilities. Managers plan what organization structure is best for group effort; they plan how the programs of action will be carried out working through the employees (implementation); they plan the standards against which results are compared (control); and they make all of the decisions in all of these functional areas as need arises. Since the majority of managers are judged on their performance over time, it is logical to conclude that sound planning is critical to achieving desired end results which in turn reflects well on the managers. When managers perform well, the entire organization benefits.

Types of Plans

Classifying plans varies according to the classifier. The jargon in management is not standardized. Most scholars in management agree, however, that plans can be typed as follows:

> Strategic

> Operational

   > Single use

   > Standing

> Functional

> Short-run and long-run

> Contingency

Strategic plans are those that are developed and designed to achieve the broadest objectives of the organization. They encompass every aspect of activity and are directly related to the primary reason the organization exists. Often these plans are called master plans.

Operational plans are those that are very detailed in content and are used in carrying out the strategic plans. Operational plans can be divided into two main types: single use plans and standing plans.

Single use operational plans are designed to implement programs of action that likely will not be repeated. Once these plans have achieved a specific objective, they are withdrawn from further use. For example, designing a plan to enlarge and renovate executive offices would be a single use plan. The most common single use plans are programs, budgets and projects.

Standing operational plans are those that exist to guide managerial actions when organizational activities repeat. For example, a manufacturer may have a standing plan to follow when production managers order additional raw materials.

Standing plans are established to provide managers a standardized and consistent way of handling similar, repetitious occurrences. Standing plans use policies, precedures and rules to guide managerial actions.

Functional plans are plans classified by their use or function. The most common types are marketing plans, manufacturing plans, finance plans and human resource plans. As an example, marketing plans may include how to obtain a larger share of the market; how to advertise more effectively; how to distribute finished goods more efficiently. Functional plans often overlap and interrelate because each major activity is interdependent with every other one. Sales plans, for example, may relate to and affect human resource plans.

Short-run and long-run plans are plans that are classified by periods of time. Although there is no standard period of time which identifies either plan, one-year or less time span is generally considered short-run; longer than one year, long-run.

Short-run plans can have pitfalls. Organizations that pursue short-run objectives intensely may overlook long-run consequences. It is also true, however, that the achievement of short-run goals often is critical to succeeding in the long-run. An organization such as United Way definitely is interested in reaching its annual fundraising objective (one year or short-run plan), but it is also interested in surviving and being needed in the long-run. Many of the airlines which lowered fares drastically to fill empty seats in the short-run are no longer around due to long-run losses.

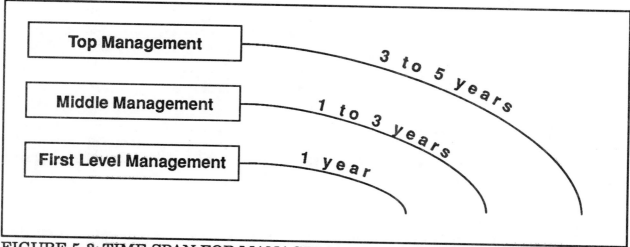

FIGURE 5-3: TIME SPAN FOR MANAGERIAL PLANNING IN SMALL
ORGANIZATIONS

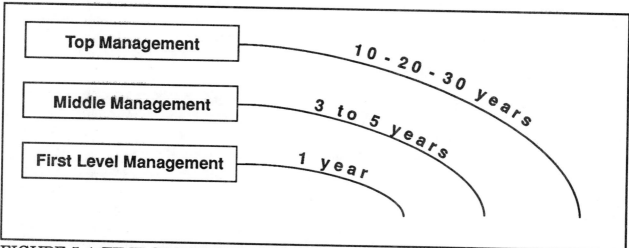

FIGURE 5-4: TIME SPAN FOR MANAGERIAL PLANNING IN LARGE
ORGANIZATIONS

Long-run plans may be from three to five years in relatively small organizations; while in large organizations, such plans may span twenty to thirty years or more. Top management usually formulates long-run plans along with setting long-run objectives.

Roger Smith, former Chairman and Chief Executive Officer of General Motors Corporation, stated in a speech to The Economic Club of Detroit how GM is preparing for the long-run future. In his speech, entitled "The 21st Century Corporation," Mr. Smith explained the acquisition of Electronic Data Systems and Hughes Electronics:

> ...A major reason for bringing our three firms together was to create a computer-integrated 21st Century Corporation such as I've described. Each of the entities— General Motors, EDS, and Hughes has unique properties and strengths which complement the others. We offer each other special synergies, which we hope to use for mutual competitive advantage.[2]

Long-run planning is essential if companies in a highly competitive environment wish to survive over the next twenty to thirty years. As one would expect, General Motors, the largest organization in the U.S. and in one of the highly competitive industries, is preparing now for well into the next century.

Contingency plans are often referred to as "back-up" plans if something renders the original plan inappropriate. The "something" may be an unlikely event that does occur or a planned-for risk that happens. Contingency plans should be viewed as alternative plans that can be followed to achieve the desired objective whenever the original plan must be discarded.

Formulating contingency plans is most important to athletics administrators when staffing key jobs; in undertaking construction projects for facilities; in renting or leasing facilities; when anticipating significant sources of funding; in arranging travel for teams; in scheduling outdoor events, and much more. This is especially true in instances, such as the Olympics, where many years are required to complete the project.

Organizational Guidelines

Regardless of the type of plan, the success of the plan depends on how well it is implemented by the personnel involved. Part of the responsibility of management when formulating plans is to provide guidance to the efforts at implementation. This is accomplished by introducing what is known as organizational guidelines as part of the plan.

Organizational guidelines are anything management introduces to influence the behavior of personnel working to achieve objectives. Organizational guidelines are popularly known as "red tape," and include such examples as rules, procedures, policies, systems, methods, codes, regulations and many more. There are distinct differences in each of these types of organizational guidelines. In sport management, guidelines are such things as league or conference rules and regulations (the NCAA Manual or the drug policy of major league baseball). A good example of subjects involving "red tape" in an athletic organization is shown in Figure 5-5. The University of Oklahoma's athletic manual, reviewed and updated annually, is one of the best. It prescribes the requirements to be followed when conducting oneself on behalf of the University's athletic program. State high school athletic associations generally have specific guidelines for participation, including new rules regarding "no pass - no play" which have been controversial. In a county recreation program, there may be specific rules and regulations about who has access to the county's programs and facilities.

FIGURE 5-5: EXCERPT FROM UNIVERSITY OF OKLAHOMA'S ATHLETIC DEPARTMENT MANUAL. Reprinted with permission.
Written and prepared by Kenneth E. Farris, Associate Director Emeritus of Athletics

Rules are guidelines that demand certain employee action with no room for interpretation. Rules have no flexibility and are the most specific type of organizational guildeline. In effect, rules dictate certain employee behavior. Example: No employee shall smoke on company premises at any time.

Procedures are a series of job tasks or steps to be taken in chronological order to achieve a certain end result. Example: Purchasing requisition procedure which requires filing a form and completing certain steps in sequence before actually buying or contracting to buy anything.

Policies are the most general of organizational guidelines. Policies are flexible, subject to some interpretation by managers, and are introduced primarily to influence managerial actions. Example: A promotion from within the organization policy.

Systems are a group of coordinated procedures that are followed to achieve a major end result. Example: A manufacturing system such as automotive sub-assembly lines feeding into a final assembly line to produce the finished product—an automobile.

Methods are guidelines that specify an exact way to perform a particular task. Example: The exact manner in which one step of work in a procedure is to be done by any employee.

Codes are standards of professional practice or behavior. Example: An organization requiring employees to dress in a prescribed manner.

Regulations are an authoritative issue of guidelines for employees to follow originated by higher management or government. Example: Federal government job safety regulations issued by OSHA.

Recommendations for Organizational Guidelines

Effectively implementing plans requires managers to introduce some organizational guidelines. These guidelines, however, can create confusion and slow achievement of objectives if they are not necessary. Unclear guidelines generate more problems, and all guidelines are expensive to administer. Therefore, a few suggestions are needed to avert problems with organizational guidelines.

First, do not introduce guidelines unless they are absolutely **essential**. Make sure that the proposed guideline is **required** to attain the objective before introducing it. The question of cost versus return always needs to be answered. Will the value of having a particular guideline be greater than the cost of administering it?

Next, keep the guidelines **simple**. All employees expected to follow any guideline should understand it. They should know why such a guideline is needed, the expected value of it, and how they can comply with it.

Third, put guidelines **in writing**. To avoid communication breakdowns, such as possible misunderstanding, put the guidelines in writing. Provide each affected employee a copy with an explanation of the value of the new rule, procedure, etc. Have meetings if necessary to explain the new guidelines. If effect, justify totally the addition of new guidelines (red tape).

Finally, **audit** guidelines periodically. Every year or two management should audit or review the guidelines in their area of responsibility. Anything that has been introduced over time to influence and control employee behavior should be inspected. If any of the prescribed guidelines are no longer serving the original purpose, they should be eliminated or modified. Good managers work continuously to simplify work effort. Removing obsolete guidelines is an essential first step in simplification.

Planning and Control

In 1917, Henry L. Gantt, one of the scientific management pioneers mentioned in Chapter 1, developed the Gantt Chart. The Gantt Chart is a control technique still used throughout the world today in more sophisticated form than his original. The original chart identified individuals and machines along the vertical axis and measured individual and machine output along the horizontal axis. Also included on the horizontal axis was a time scale. By setting work or project standards for a set period of time and by posting work output for a set period of time, a manager could quickly determine whether the work standard was being met or exceeded, and in what period of time and by what quantity. The chart was relatively simple in form and use, but Gantt revolutionized American management's thinking about planning and control with its introduction.

Many sport managers use a modified visual control chart to measure progress against the plan in assessing the effectiveness of fund drives, membership drives, promotional efforts to increase participation and/or attendance, and other measurable objectives. Control programs are designed to measure performance against plans (standards). Therefore, the functions of planning and control are closely related. Control compares what is actually happening to what management hoped would happen when they developed their plans. Any significant deviation from planned results requires corrective or remedial action by management.

Managerial plans to produce a product of a certain quality, in a set quantity, and at a specific per unit cost may have programs of quality control, production (quantity) control, and financial (cost) control to guarantee the planned objectives are met.

Another control device which is important to managers in all types of organizations is budgeting. Budgeting directly relates planning to control. Formalized budgets are part of the planning process and are used to determine expenditures for the allocation of resources in implementing plans. When planned budget allocations are exceeded, it is usually a time for managers to take some corrective or remedial action. When a coach or director of a recreation facility exceeds the budget, they usually find their jobs in jeopardy; and if a coach spends too little in one year, he or she may find the budget reduced the next. Thus, the popularity of zero-base budgeting (refer to discussion in Chapter 15).

Theoretically, if the functions of planning, organizing, implementing and decision-making were performed perfectly, there would be no need for the control function. This does not happen in the real world; however, sound planning does minimize the scope of the control function.

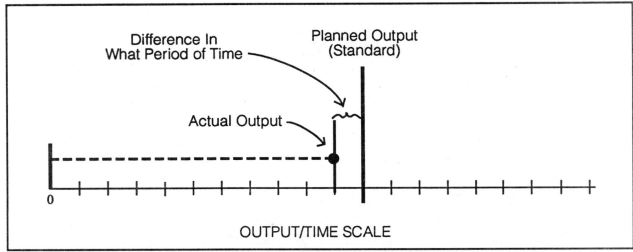

FIGURE 5-6: MODIFIED GANTT CONTROL CHART

Steps in Planning

Suppose an organization wishes to double its revenues over the next five years, an intercollegiate athletic program wishes to establish an endowment fund that will support the annual budget, or an organization wishes to reduce its internal operating costs over the next three years. What are the steps to follow in achieving these goals? The first step is to develop a detailed plan of action that focuses on the goal.

Developing a detailed plan of action requires that management consider all the facts and variables that can affect future performance and make pertinent decisions based on this information. While a generalized plan can give some direction toward the achievement of goals, it is much better to develop a detailed plan of action that specifies who is to do what, when, where, how, and why. As stated before, sound planning will not eliminate all problems or guarantee success, but sound planning does increase the chances of success. The key is to consider a full range of possibilities and decide in advance how to deal with them within the plan.

Steps in planning, sometimes called **the planning process**, are not in a perfectly sequential order. The steps can be arranged in any order depending on the practicality of the situation. Here is a typical sequence of steps to follow in developing a detailed operating plan of action:

1. Generate ideas
2. Select tangible objective(s)
3. Inventory your resources
4. Conduct necessary research
5. Review alternative courses of action
6. Select a course of action

7. Establish a time standard
8. Anticipate major problems in advance
9. Determine your organization structure
10. Decide on essential organizational guidelines
11. Formalize a program of control
12. Blueprint your plan of action
13. Implement the plan
14. Evaluate the results

The Planning Process

These fourteen steps in planning are called **The Planning Process**. This process is extremely useful as a guide when developing specific plans. Students can use the process to plan vacations and fraternity parties. Managers use this process to plan the introduction of new products and/or services plus any other facet of organizational activity. Entrepreneurs use the process to plan opening their own businesses. Athletics directors can use the process when adding a new varsity sport; recreation directors can use the process to plan new parks and facilities; and managers in the sports equipment industry can use the process to introduce new products or open new territories (including international ones).

The planning process is a logical, common sense approach. Adhering to the process does not guarantee the success of your plan, but it does reduce the risk of failure. Each step is explained in detail.

Generate Ideas. This is probably the most overlooked step in formal planning. Higher management needs to encourage lower level managers to generate ideas from employees, customers, students, competitors and any other source available. If the organization has a system for reviewing ideas, through a refinement process the best ideas surface for consideration and intense scrutiny. Ideas which have realistic possibilities can be selected and put into tangible (written) form to become working objectives. Virtually every product or service used by organizations today or produced for consumers began with a new idea. Great organizations are not created by accident; they tend to do something better than their competitors. It all begins with ideas.

Select tangible objective(s). From a review of the ideas generated, tangible objectives are selected. Once selected, the idea(s) need to be approved by higher management and put in writing to avoid confusion about the planning effort which follows (steps 3 - 14). These objectives should be clearly described, concrete, achievable goals.

Inventory your resources. Planning efforts can be wasted unless a careful inventory of resources is conducted prior to the investment of much time or money. The purpose of the inventory is to determine the availability of monies, employee skills, materials, the state of equipment, what management talent is available, and much more. Essentially, the inventory analysis compares the resources available for undertaking a project against what will be needed for maximum success in reaching the objective.

Conduct necessary research. Research takes the form of investigation, review or study about the project or subject under consideration. When planning to reach set objectives, it may be necessary to conduct market research, financial analyses, review historical patterns of the organization, or simply read some literature on the topic. Fast food organizations such as McDonald's always test market new products prior to a full scale introduction. The purpose of research is to uncover potential problems, verify the feasibility of the planning effort, acquire facts pertinent to the subject or project, identify trends, and specifically to determine whether the objective of the plan is realistic or not.

Review alternative courses of action. There are always several possible directions to take in the pursuit of a planning objective. When planning a vacation in Florida, you consider whether to fly, drive, take the bus, or go by train. All can be viable options. The same viable options face managers in charge of planning. A necessary step is to list optional courses of action with the significant advantages and disadvantages associated with each option. The facts should be considered without personal bias or emotional whims when addressing the advantages and disadvantages of options.

Select a course of action. Unless there are announced restrictions that temper a choice of courses, an objective decision maker will select the course of action that appears to be the freest of problems. This will usually be the course of action for which the advantages most outweigh the disadvantages. Factors which influence this decision and do temper the choice are cost considerations, budget limitations, resources available, governance restrictions and requirements, organizational policies, and many other internal and external considerations, any one of which may limit the options it is feasible to take. An ever-present consideration for the planner is to select the course of action that most ideally will achieve the desired end result in the most efficient and effective way possible.

Establish a time standard. A critical step in planning is the determination of the period of time in which the desired end result must be reached. This is called the time standard. Time standards should be set at a level of excellence which focuses all effort in the proper direction, but some leeway must be allowed for the unexpected: breakdowns, bad weather, absenteeism, slow deliveries, etc. Personnel involved in implementing a plan will be more highly motivated if the time standard is tight. Implementing a plan and successfully attaining the desired objective in a shorter period of time than the standard is a measure of efficiency.

Anticipate major problems in advance. Failure by managers to anticipate major problems in advance is the primary cause of planning failure. Planners cannot anticipate every problem that might occur before implementing a plan; however, potential major problems that have a high probability of happening should be considered and preparations for the occurrence made. Managers deal with two types of problems in planning: **risks** and **uncertainties**.

Risks are events or occurrences that managers should be able to predict with reasonable accuracy and plan for so that if they do occur, the loss or damage can be offset. Routine risks that must be anticipated are death of key people, bad weather, a shortage of supplies, breakdown of equipment, trends in the economy, and hazards such as fires and burglary which can be covered by insurance.

Uncertainties are events or occurrences that a manager cannot anticipate with accuracy and plan for so that if they do occur, the organization will either be damaged or benefited. A benefit to the organization is called a windfall; damage, a disaster. Examples of uncertainties from history are the Persian Gulf Conflict in 1990-91, the oil crisis of the

1970s and its subsequent economic upheaval, the surprising recent outbreaks of measles on several college campuses, and the accidental discovery of penicillin. Perhaps many uncertainties should be anticipated, but the probability of certain events happening is so low that no one foresees them. Such things as earthquakes in an area previously not known for having them or a building's being hit by debris from outer space are examples of low probability uncertainties. In 1989, an earthquake in San Francisco, California, caused an expensive postponement of baseball's World Series. While an earthquake in the state of California is a "risk" management should anticipate in planning, the probability of its occurring during a World Series between two Bay-area California teams moves the natural disaster into the realm of an "uncertainty."

The significant point to remember about risks and uncertainties, is that the occurrence of an unanticipated risk reflects badly on management. But the occurrence of an uncertainty affecting the organization, either as a benefit or as a disaster, is not due to good or bad management.

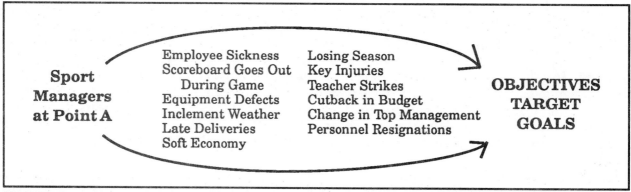

FIGURE 5-7: GOOD PLANNERS ANTICIPATE PROBLEMS IN ADVANCE AND ARE PREPARED FOR THEM

Determine your organization structure. The success of implementing a plan often relates directly to the way the effort is organized. Sound planning includes deciding who is to do what, when, where, and how. Assigning the critical jobs to people with the right qualifications; designing an open communication system; pinpointing responsibility; delegating appropriate authority to accompany responsibility; and coordinating all effort to develop a synchronized flow of work is fundamental to sound planning.

Decide on essential organizational guidelines. Organizational guidelines have been defined previously as anything management introduces to influence employee behavior toward the achievement of objectives. Some guidelines (red tape) may be established early in the planning stages to help control and influence the implementation of the plan. For example, certain rules may be set covering the purchase of equipment [No purchases exceeding $500.00 may be made without approval by a higher manager] or rules may be established regarding who can drive a company vehicle [No one with a speeding ticket or DUI in the past three years may qualify]. Some procedures, policies, rules, and systems incorporated into the plan can be of great value if they help expedite activity and minimize confusion or problems when a plan is implemented.

Formalize a program of control. Preventing the implementation of a plan from getting "out of control" is the purpose of this step. Control programs are designed to measure the actual progress against the planned or expected results. This kind of program should be carefully developed before introducing it as part of the implementation of a plan. Control programs can be costly, but they are valuable if they prevent major problems. Ideally, planners should decide on the control program, perhaps having several critical points throughout the plan where results are measured against the planned progress. The control program should be relatively simple, easy to administer, but still accurately measure the progress at critical stages. The lack of formal controls can cause small problems to blossom into major flaws and can destroy an otherwise good planning effort.

Blueprint your plan of action. When all decisions have been made about each of the steps in the planning process, it is time to write out the complete plan. Writing everything down so that the final plan clearly shows the sequence of steps, the timing of activities, who is to do what, etc. is good common sense. A plan in writing is easier to understand, easier to follow, and easier to change if conditions so dictate.

At this stage in the planning process, you have developed a **master plan** which is ready for implementation once approved by the necessary and appropriate management levels.

Implementation. Put the plan into action! This is easy to say, but may be difficult to do. Individuals involved in implementing the plan, no matter how sound the plan may be, may prove to be effective barriers to good end results. To make sure this is not the case, managerial planners must have competent, motivated individuals carrying out the plan. Those who will implement the plan must be convinced that the plan is the best approach to undertake, need to be totally supportive of the objectives, and should understand clearly the importance of the part they play in the plan. Without question, plans are only as good as the individuals who implement them.

Evaluation. The purpose of evaluation is to review the planning and implementation effort. From this process of evaluating, the strengths and weaknesses of the plan and its implementation will be revealed. Information which will allow managers to do an even better planning job in the future result from the evaluation step, regardless of the degree of success of the current plan.

Summary

Planning is the management function that precedes all other functions. Sound planning is the basis for good organization, implementation, control and decision-making. Poor managerial planning is the number one cause of organizational failure.

The purpose of planning is to formalize objectives and develop a plan to attain the objectives in the desired period of time with a minimum of problems and in the most efficient and effective way possible.

Overall benefits to the organization from sound planning are these:

1. Sound planning gives direction to the efforts of employees.
2. Sound planning helps an organization determine its own destiny.

3. Sound planning is a key to effective control.
4. Sound planning is essential to managerial success.

There are many ways to classify plans. The most common classifications are as strategic, operations, functional, short-run, long-run and contingency. Operational plans may be single-use or standing.

Goals and objectives are words used interchangeably in this chapter. There are many kinds of goals (objectives) in organization. Examples are the mission; strategic, tactical and operations goals.

Managment by Objectives (MBO) is a philosophical approach used in some organizations to help managers more effectively implement plans. MBO allows managers to convert organizational objectives into group and individual objectives.

Organizational guidelines, commonly called "red tape," can be defined as anything management introduces to influence employee behavior toward the achievement of objectives. Common examples of guidelines are rules, procedures, policies and systems. There are many more. Four suggestions are made to managers about introducing organizational guidelines; they are these:

1. Do not introduce guidelines unless they are absolutely essential.
2. Keep the guidelines simple.
3. Put the guidelines in writing.
4. Audit guidelines periodically and eliminate any which are no longer needed.

There are fourteen steps in planning to achieve a specific objective. These steps are called The Planning Process:

1. Generate ideas
2. Select the best ideas and make them tangible objective(s)
3. Inventory resources
4. Conduct necessary research
5. Review alternative courses of action
6. Select a course of action
7. Establish a time standard at a level of excellence
8. Anticipate major problems in advance
9. Determine your organization structure
10. Decide on essential organizational guidelines
11. Formalize a program of control
12. Blueprint the plan of action
13. Implement the plan
14. Evaluate the effort after implementation

Evaluation is the review of what happened, good and bad, so that the managers can do an even better job of planning in the future.

Review Questions

1. Define the purpose of planning.

2. Why is it stated that planning is the primary function of management?

3. Explain the close relationship between the functions of planning and control.

4. Operational plans may be standing plans or one-use plans. What is the difference between the two?

5. Identify the kinds of goals that exist in organizations.

6. What is the primary purpose of an MBO program?

7. What are the four suggestions to managers about organizational guidelines (red tape)?

8. List the steps in planning (The Planning Process).

9. Distinguish between organizational "risks" and "uncertainties."

10. Explain how a "windfall" differs from a "disaster."

11. Outline a classification of types of plans.

12. What are the overall benefits to an organization from sound planning?

Assignments for Personal Development

1. You are a student intern working on a degree in athletic administration. Your boss says that $25,000.00 of outside money is needed to renovate the tennis facility. Your job is to develop a plan to raise this money within three months. If your plan is approved, all personnel will participate in the effort. Develop your plan!

2. If you were appointed to the job of Director of Recreation, Intramurals and Athletics at a new community college that had none of these activities, how much lead time do you think would be necessary for implementing a completely detailed plan that might assure success? Justify your answer.

Incident

OPPORTUNITY UNLIMITED

Mack Knight was a recent graduate with a Master's degree in Sport Administration. He had left a decent job as a teacher and assistant football coach of a local high school to pursue his Master's degree full time. Upon graduation, he had actively sought a position in the sport management world and felt grateful when a national sporting goods chain offered him a position as a marketing manager. He accepted the position and spent the first six weeks learning everything about operations, inventory, merchandising and sales. Shortly thereafter, corporate management called him in and said:

...Mack, we're proud to have you as part of the team! So far you appear to be just what we've been looking for. Someone who can pioneer new market areas and help the organization grow at an expanded clip. Opportunity in unlimited for you if you can produce! Your first assignment is exciting. We want you to develop a complete plan for locating a new retail store in some major city in the midwest. As you know, we have outlets on both coasts in ten major cities, but nothing yet in the midwest. Of our ten active stores, five are profitable and the other five are marginal. We cannot afford to make any more mistakes with new store locations. They have to be profitable from the get-go!

What we would like you to do is recommend the city for a new site and accompany that with a total plan for operating the store for one year. Detail everything!

In other words, Mack, when you present your plan to us in three weeks, be prepared to justify everything you recommend. We don't think you could have a more exciting first assignment. If the plan is accepted, you will be transferred to the new city to oversee the store's operations for at least the first year. Good luck. We'll talk again in three weeks.

Questions:

1. If you were Mack Knight, how would you go about selecting a major city for a new store's location?

2. List the five most important questions that have to be answered in the process of developing a complete plan for a one-year store operation.

Glossary of Key Terms

Contingency Plans: Often referred to as "back up plans," a plan to be implemented if unexpected events render the original plan inappropriate.

Management by Objectives: A philosophical approach used in some organizations to help managers more effectively implement plans. Individual employee, managerial and unit objectives are formalized and pursued toward the achievement of the overall operating objectives.

Mission Statement: The broadest of objectives, it defines the purpose and uniqueness of the organization with regard to its products, services, markets and revenues.

Operational Goals: Typically, short-run goals which are part of the effort to reach tactical goals.

Organizational Guidelines: Anything managers introduce to influence the behavior of personnel working to achieve objectives. Examples are rules, procedures, policies and systems. [A.K.A. "red tape"]

Planning Process: A series of steps to follow when developing specific plans.

The Purpose of Planning: To formalize objectives and develop a plan to attain these objectives within the desired time period with a minimum of problems in the most efficient and effective way possible.

Risks: Events or occurrences that managers should be able to predict with reasonable accuracy and plan for so that if they do occur, the loss or damage can be offset or minimized. Failure to prepare for risks does reflect on management.

Strategic Goals: Set by top management, they tend to be long-run to influence overall organizational behavior.

Tactical Goals: Include the operational objectives needed to be achieved in order to reach strategic goals.

Uncertainties: Events or occurrences that a manager cannot anticipate with accuracy and plan for so that if they do occur, the organization will either receive a benefit (a windfall) or damage (a disaster). Failure to prepare for uncertainties does not reflect on management.

Practical Concepts in Management
Adopt Planning as a Way of Life

The basic process of management consists of planning, organizing, implementing and controlling. It is a process because each function interrelates with the others; but planning is the first function of management and should precede the other three.

The activity of planning consists of looking ahead, generating ideas, establishing objectives, and working out all of the specifics before a plan of action is undertaken. The final plan should be in writing; and it should state who does what, when. where and how.

Sound planning before initiating action will not guarantee a problem-free course to reaching the objective. It is, however, an effort in advance to help you minimize problems and be prepared for those you can anticipate. Failure to plan carefully is the sign of poor management.

Rarely do managers overplan! On the contrary, most managers never come close to the point of diminishing returns for time spent in the planning stage. This would occur when the cost of planning exceeds the value of planning.

In general, you can say that the best planners tend to be the best decision makers; and the best decision makers tend to be the best managers.

Make Progress on Purpose

These are magic words for the successful organization!

Progress is made "on purpose" rather than by accident in the well-managed organization. If top management adopts this philosophy and it permeates the entire organization, all employees at all levels get the positive spirit for bringing about change.

Progress on purpose refers to attacking problems instead of retreating from them. It implies finding ways to improve rather than maintaining the status quo. It requires generating ideas and plans about the future rather than waiting for things to happen. It is a "proactive" rather than a "reactive" stance by management.

Great organizations have great management and leadership, and thus they have great employees. Great organizations always excel at doing something better than their competition. Part of the reason for this is the adoption of the philosophy that progress will be made on purpose. This requires full utilization of resources in the best possible way including brainpower and skillful planning on the part of all management.

References and Chapter Notes

[1] Gale Eisenstadt, "Bull in the Japan Shop," *Forbes*, January 31, 1994, p. 41.

[2] "The 21st Century Corporation," speech by Roger B. Smith before The Economic Club of Detroit, September 6, 1985.

Additional Readings:

Dyson, R. G., and M. J. Foster. "Making Planning More Effective." *Long-Range Planning* 16 (1983): 68-73.

French, Wendel L., and Robert W. Hollmann. "Management by Objectives: The Team Approach." *California Management Review*, Spring 1975, pp. 13-22.

CHAPTER 6

STRATEGIC MANAGEMENT

After studying this chapter, **you will know:**

- The difference between long-term planning and operational planning
- What strategic management is and the role of strategic managers
- Strategic planning by definition and purpose
- The strategic planning process step by step
- The meaning of programs, policies, procedures and objectives
- The value of an organization's **mission**
- Criteria for evaluating strategy
- How to implement and control strategy
- Significance of SWOT Analysis
- A company's Theory of the Business

Introduction

Strategic management includes long run planning, strategy formulation, strategy implementation, managerial decision-making, and the monitoring and control of implemented plans. This statement expresses the planning responsibility of any top level manager. In the field of sport management, strategic managers and thus strategic planners would be those managing league offices, franchise owners, Olympic sport organizations' heads, collegiate directors of athletics programs, and top managers/owners of sports marketing firms and health and fitness clubs/spas among many others.

While top management of all organizations may also be involved in short term or operational planning, the responsibility for long term planning rests solely with them.

This chapter stresses the need for top level managers to consider external or environmental factors as well as internal resources when they plan. In addition, the strategic planning process is detailed. This process is somewhat different from the planning process for formulating short term or operational plans presented in Chapter 5.

In Chapter 5, we discussed the major points about managerial and personal planning, including the importance of planning, the benefits from sound planning, the relationship between planning and control, and The Planning Process. This information is important and useful to any practicing manager as he or she develops plans (tactics) for achieving relatively short-term objectives. This function is called **operational or tactical** planning.

The steps in The Planning Process outlined in Chapter 5 require the manager (planner) to answer some specific questions and gather detailed information in formulating the plan. More precise decisions are required in developing a plan to reach short-term objectives than are required in formulating plans which cover a longer time frame.

Without operational or tactical planning, organizations would have difficulty surviving. Operating objectives must be achieved on a continual basis; otherwise, the organization will not be around over the long-term. The key to short-term survival is sound operational or tactical planning. These types of plans are developed by first- and middle-level managers. In sport management middle and first level managers, such as head coaches, assistant coaches, head trainers, sports information directors, etc., are called operating managers. Every level of management is important; but those managers who are responsible for the quality of performance (and survival) of an organization in the long term are the strategic managers who consider external or environmental factors as well as internal resources when they plan.

Long-Term Planning

Another kind of planning is described as **long-term, long-range** or **strategic**. Upper level managers are more responsible for this kind of planning. Executives of large organizations often set goals and develop plans for the next five to twenty years. Part of their job is to provide direction to the efforts of all personnel so that there is a common purpose in the present as well as in the future. Executives of smaller organizations view the long-term as three to five years, but they plan for the same reasons as those in larger organizations. This type of planning responsibility applies to top managers of **any kind of organization**: government, education, business, industry, manufacturing, service, profit-seeking and non-profit. The vision and acumen needed to plan effectively for the long-term are facets of the conceptual skill that characterize successful top managers.

The value of long term planning in the sport industry is visible each baseball season when certain major league teams consistently compete for the division title in their league. These clubs have developed a long term plan for grooming young players through their farm systems. Many of the current stars are products of a team's farm system where they have been taught and their skills refined over a period of several years. Smart trades and securing free agents help a professional team become competitive; but to stay competitive yearly, it takes a long term commitment to a plan for the future. Other examples of long term planning in the sport industry include collegiate endowment funds built over decades that fund annual scholarship budgets; long term capital funding (sometimes through selling bonds and making loans) for physical facilities; and the type of long term planning it takes to host the Olympic Games (usually more than four years of planning, building and securing corporate sponsorships that must be projected and produced).

In this chapter, we take a closer look at the job of the executive who must formulate plans for the long-term. These people are called **strategic managers**.

Strategic Management

Strategic management is the process of managerial decision-making and implementation of plans that directly affect the quality of performance and survival of an organization in the long-term.

Historically, the study of management has focused on the effective use of internal resources to achieve desired end results. This is still important today for operational managers and those responsible for reaching established short-term objectives. Over the past twenty years, however, top management has given much more attention to the environmental factors that affect an organization's future performance. This is necessary when formulating sound strategy.

Strategic management includes long-term planning, strategy formulation, strategy implementation, managerial decision-making, and the monitoring and control of implemented plans. Today, top-level managers are often called strategic managers, while middle- and first-level managers are usually called operating managers. Every level of management is important; but those managers who are responsible for the quality of performance (and survival) of an organization in the long-term are the strategic managers who consider external or environmental factors as well as internal resources when they plan.

George Steiner and John Miner state that, "The emphasis on strategic management as distinct from operational management reflects the growing significance of environmental impacts on organizations and the need for top managers to react appropriately to them."[1]

Another view of strategic management is provided by Thomas L. Wheeler and J. David Hunger: "The study of strategic management emphasizes the monitoring and evaluating of environmental opportunities and constraints in light of a corporation's strengths and weaknesses."[2]

Both of these statements reflect the need for strategic managers to consider both internal and external factors as they plan for the long-term and formulate an organiztional strategy. The growth of strategic management as a field of study and as a responsibility of management reflects the increasing complexity of an organization's environment.

Strategies can be classified as **grand or corporate strategies, as business strategies,** and as **functional strategies.** Clearly top management is directly involved with corporate strategy which provides overall direction to the entire organization, whether it has one unit or hundreds of units. Business strategies tend to be more narrow is scope and are formulated primarily to help a single organization compete more effectively. Functional strategies pertain to the different activities of a business such as production, sales, finance, human resources and so forth. In collegiate sport management functional strategies might pertain to each varsity sport as well as involve strategies for fundraising, promotions and publicity, and enhancement of physical facilities.

A good example of strategic management where both internal and external factors have been considered in formulating a grand or corporate plan involves Glaxo PLC. In early 1995, Glaxo, the second largest drug producer in the world, cleared the way for a merger with

Wellcome PLC. This merger creates the world's largest drug maker. Glaxo makes the largest-selling prescription drug in the world, the ulcer medication Zantac, and Wellcome is best known as the developer and maker of the AIDS drug AZT. The merger is expected to cut millions in costs once reorganization takes place. The strategy will help offset the problems and reduced revenue expected with the upcoming expiration of the patents each company holds on several key drugs.[3]

Strategic Planning Defined

Strategic planning is a job function of strategic managers which has many different meanings. Management literature gives various definitions of all management topics, including strategic planning. The variations result from semantics problems (different interpretations of word meanings).

Here are several definitions, from leading authorities in the field of management, of strategic planning:

> Strategic planning involves an organization's most basic and important choices—the choice of its mission, objectives, strategy, policies, programs, goals, and major resource allocations.[4]

> Strategic planning comprises the process of setting common purposes, goals, and objectives for the enterprise, breaking them up into specific plans and policies for the operating level and securing the necessary resources to put the plan into action.[5]

> Strategic planning is the 'management of change.' It is a decision-making process, based on empirical evidence and analytical studies, that provides the basic direction and focus of the enterprise.[6]

Now look at the common elements in each of these definitions. All stress the importance of making decisions and choices today which will affect the organization in the future. Strategic planning is long-term in outlook and direction but is based on knowledge currently available.

The definition of **strategic planning** we will use in this text is this:

> *Strategic planning is the process of determining an organization's long-term goals and obejctives in compliance with its mission and formulating the proper plan of action (strategy) , policies and programs which insure that sound decisions will be made about internal resources and environmental factors that affect all effort to achieve the desired end results in the long run.*

Inherent in strategic planning is that the processes and plans should strive to meet goals and objectives in the most effective and efficient way possible.

A good case study relating to this point is presented in Figure 6-1. The United States Naval Academy's Athletic Association developed a strategic plan for the athletic department. The approach involved a re-engineering of the department for alignment with its strategic plan. All members of the athletic department were instrumental in formulating the final plan which was in keeping with its mission and vision.

THE UNITED STATES NAVAL ACADEMY ATHLETIC ASSOCIATION HAS DEVELOPED A STRATEGIC PLAN FOR THE ATHLETIC DEPARTMENT WHICH HAS ALSO CAUSED A RE-ENGINEERING OF THE DEPARTMENT FOR ALIGNMENT WITH ITS STRATEGIC PLAN. THE SENIOR STAFF, OR AS WE NOW CALL IT FOR STRATEGIC PLANNING PURPOSES, THE EXECUTIVE STEERING COMMITTEE, MET FOR THREE DAYS OFF CAMPUS AND DEVELOPED THE MISSION AND VISION FOR THE ATHLETIC DEPARTMENT. THEY THEN DEVELOPED A LIST OF KEY VALUES AND GUIDING BEHAVIORS AND TENTATIVE STRATEGIC PLANS FOR ALL OF ITS AREAS.

EACH DEPARTMENT HEAD THEN RETURNED TO THE NAVAL ACADEMY ATHLETIC ASSOCIATION AND MET WITH THEIR STAFFS TO SHARE THE MISSION AND VISION WITH EACH STAFF MEMBER. THEN THEY PROCEEDED TO DEVELOP AND REFINE KEY VALUES AND GUIDING BEHAVIORS WITH EACH STAFF MEMBER. ONCE THERE WAS CONSENSUS ON THE KEY VALUES AND GUIDING BEHAVIORS, THE STAFF THEN PROCEEDED TO DEVELOP THEIR STRATEGIES AND OBJECTS FOR THEIR SPECIFIC DEPARTMENTS. WHEN THIS WAS ALL ACCOMPLISHED, THE DEPARTMENT HEADS BROUGHT BACK THAT INFORMATION TO THE EXECUTIVE STEERING COMMITTEE, AND IT WAS REVIEWED AND ALIGNED WITH THE MISSION AND VISION AND THEN RETURNED TO THE STAFF FOR THEIR DEVELOPMENT OF COMPLETE CONSENSUS AND FINAL APPROVAL. WITH THIS CONSENSUS AND FINAL APPROVAL, THE STRATEGIC PLAN HAD OWNERSHIP BY ALL MEMBERS OF THE ATHLETIC DEPARTMENT AND WAS THEN PRINTED IN BOOKLET FORM AND DISTRIBUTED TO THE ENTIRE STAFF.

THIS STRATEGIC PLAN IS A LIVING DOCUMENT AND WILL CONTINUE TO CHANGE EACH YEAR AS GOALS ARE ACCOMPLISHED AND STRATEGIES CHANGE. IT WILL BE OUR ROAD MAP TO SUCCESS IN THE FUTURE.

DURING THIS PROCESS, AN EDUCATION BUY-IN WHICH REFLECTED THE CULTURAL CHANGE WITHIN THE DEPARTMENT WAS ALSO TAKING PLACE BY THE ENTIRE STAFF . AS THE STRATEGIC PLAN DEVELOPED, IT REQUIRED A RE-ENGINEERING OF DEPARTMENTS AND STAFF RESPONSIBILITIES; AND, FOR OTHERS, THE ENTIRE PARADIGM OF THE OPERATION WAS CHANGE. NEW INDIVIDUALS WERE INCORPORATED IN THE NEW STRUCTURE TO MEET THE GOALS AND OBJECTIVES OF THE NEW STRATEGIC PLAN.

THE COVER OF THE NEW STRATEGIC PLAN HAS ONE STATEMENT IN THE MIDDLE WHICH IS OUR STRATEGIC PLAN. EVERYONE IN THE DEPARTMENT HAS PUT THEIR SIGNATURE ON THE COVER, FRONT AND BACK, TO SIGNIFY INDIVIDUAL OWNERSHIP; AND IT TRULY WILL BE OUR STRATEGIC PLAN.

THE PROCESS OF DEVELOPING A STRATEGIC PLAN CREATES MANY OPPORTUNITIES FOR OPEN, FRANK DISCUSSIONS AND THE DEVELOPMENT OF CONSENSUS ON GOALS FOR EACH DEPARTMENT. THESE GOALS MUST BE MEASURABLE; AND WHEN THEY ARE ACCOMPLISHED, NEW GOALS MUST COME INTO PLAY. THIS MEANS THAT THE STRATEGIC PLAN WILL CONTIMUE TO CHANGE AND CONTRIBUTE TO THE SUCCESS OF THE OVERALL ATHLETIC DEPARTMENT.

FIGURE 6-1: STRATEGIC PLANNING PROCESS OF THE UNITED STATES NAVAL ACADEMY'S ATHLETIC ASSOCIATION

Source: Jack Lengyel, Director of Athletics, United States Naval Academy Athletic Association.

Why Strategic Planning?

If you will review what happens to an organization over the long-term without strategic planning, then you can identify the reasons for it. Without strategic planning an organization would have no direction, no course to follow, no protection, and no goals or objectives to achieve. You would not know if you had accomplished anything, and the organization would be adrift, subject to environmental factors that could not be controlled.

Strategic planners, like all planners, anticipate the future; but strategic planners look farther ahead. They define the purpose, set the course, anticipate problems, prepare for contingencies, evaluate the environment, formulate plans of action (strategy), structure the organization properly, and introduce the policies and procedures needed to implement the plans. Good strategic managers also evaluate and contol strategies once they are implemented as an on-going part of the process.

The common sense objectives of good strategic planning are the following:

1. Increase the odds that the firm will survive over the long-term
2. Increase the probability that the firm will more nearly achieve its stated objectives
3. Increase the possibility of operating more efficiently and effectively
4. Provide a plan for harmonizing the activities of all elements within the organization toward its stated mission
5. Provide a long-run planning framework within which short-run plans can fit and be used to move the plan toward culmination
6. Become the model for continued organization growth and expansion.

It makes sense for managers to formulate short-term (operating) plans and follow them to achieve specific objectives. But these operating plans must conform to some type of overall scheme that leads the organization somewhere. This is the purpose of strategic planning: a grand plan that forms the boundaries which guide organizational activity toward the attainment of long-term goals and objectives (those set five or more years into the future).

Strategic planning is often overlooked or minimized in the sport world because of the problems and pressures of the short term. Certainly short term planning such as developing an annual budget, hiring (and sometimes firing) personnel, handling personnel problems, scheduling events as well as many daily crises will keep any sport administrator busy. If an organization is to grow and prosper, however, strategic or long term planning must take just as important a place in the manager's routine.

An organization must have both kinds of plans to survive. Strategic planning by nature and purpose requires more conceptual skill of the manager. Thus, top level managers generally tend to be the strategic planners.

The Strategic Planning Process

While there is no sacred sequence of steps to follow in strategic planning, a practical approach is listed below. (Note that the steps might vary depending on the size and nature of the organization, the kind of industry, the organization's history, the volatile nature of the industry or environment, and many more factors.)

Step 1.   Define the goals and mission of the organization.
Step 2.   Identify the long-term objectives.
Step 3.   Review the existing strategy to achieve these goals.
Step 4.   Evaluate current environmental factors.
Step 5.   Inventory the organization's resources.
Step 6.   Identify strategic strengths and weaknesses of the organization.
Step 7.   Compare current strategy against current information.
Step 8.   Formulate new strategy if needed.
Step 9.   Develop policies, procedures, and programs to accompany new strategy.
Step 10. Implement and control the strategy.

Step 1: Define the goals and mission of the organization. Logic dictates that a firm know where it wants to go and why before it develops detailed plans and a strategy. Where a firm wants to go, we call goals. Goals provide the sense of direction that influences all organizational efforts. For example, the goal of a firm may be to become number one in industry sales.

Why an organization wants to achieve its goals relates to its mission. The mission of an organization evolves from its particular, unique characteristics; from its philosophy or culture, and is a function of its reason for existing. The organization may exist to achieve a reasonable net profit and to survive. But its mission may be to provide the finest possible product quality and services among competitors so that it not only will reach its goal (become number one among competitors), but will also achieve its purpose of existence (being profitable and surviving). To do this, the organization must establish a mission which all employees understand and endorse.

The goals and mission of the organization should be in writing. They should be formal statements that clearly focus the direction of all effort. The goals and mission should be based on the uniqueness of the organization. The uniqueness is the "edge" that the organization has or is trying to develop which will enable it to achieve its goals effectively and efficiently.

Written mission statements may be generalized and vague or formal and detailed. The latter is preferred so that employees, customers, patrons, members or other interested parties who read it have no questions about the direction of effort and the unique qualities of the organization that set it apart from others of its type.

Many sport organizations have a mission statement. An excellent example of one is shown in Figure 6-3 from Georgetown University.

Step 2: Identify Long-Term Objectives. The purpose of strategic planning is to formalize long-term objectives. Then, through the process of analysis, research and strategy formulation, implement plans that allow an organization to achieve its objectives in an efficient and effective way. A major influence on the determination of specific long-term objectives is the mission of the organization.

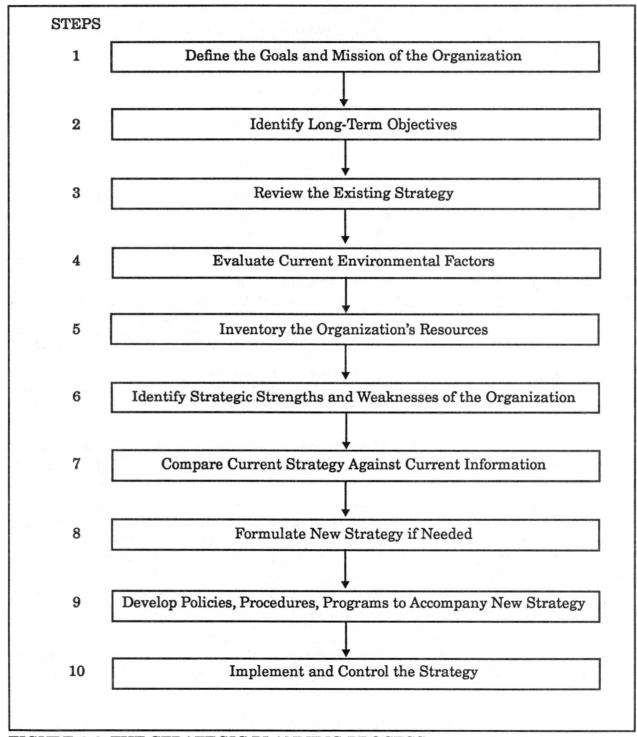

STEPS

1 — Define the Goals and Mission of the Organization

2 — Identify Long-Term Objectives

3 — Review the Existing Strategy

4 — Evaluate Current Environmental Factors

5 — Inventory the Organization's Resources

6 — Identify Strategic Strengths and Weaknesses of the Organization

7 — Compare Current Strategy Against Current Information

8 — Formulate New Strategy if Needed

9 — Develop Policies, Procedures, Programs to Accompany New Strategy

10 — Implement and Control the Strategy

FIGURE 6-2: THE STRATEGIC PLANNING PROCESS

1.2 Athletic Department Mission and Goals Statement

1.2.1 Mission and Goals. The Georgetown University Athletic Department, as a part of a university with roots in the Jesuit tradition of education, commits itself to the comprehensive development of the student. The interdependence of the physical, emotional, moral and intellectual aspects of personal growth requires simultaneous and balanced focus. This objective does not imply that each facet of an individual's growth is of equal importance. It does require that Georgetown provide the means and encouragement for each person to develop according to his or her own interests and abilities, whether at the recreational, intercollegiate, intramural or instructional level. In addition to physical development, the Athletic Department promotes principals of character development within the framework of an abiding and broadened commitment to community.

FIGURE 6-3: MISSION STATEMENT OF GEORGETOWN UNIVERSITY'S INTERCOLLEGIATE ATHLETIC PROGRAM

Reprinted with permission from Georgetown University Department of Athletics.

The mission provides purpose and reason for the organization to exist, and it includes the general organizational goals. Objectives, however, are more specific than goals and can be more easily quantified to make measuring progress simpler.

Identifying long-term objectives is the second step in the strategic planning process.

Step 3: Review the Existing Strategy. A further step in formalizing strategic planning is to review the existing strategy. Questions such as these must be answered: What are the current objectives? What plans are being or have been implemented to achieve these objectives? Is this current strategy viable and compatible with existing resources, environmental factors, and current objectives? The answers to these kinds of questions tell the organization if conditions have changed enough to warrant formulating a new strategy.

One test strategic managers can use to evaluate the need for changing strategy is whether performance (end results) meets the original objectives. Any significant difference between the two suggests a review of the existing strategy and probable implementation of a new one.

Step 4: Evaluate Current Environmental Factors. A major step in strategic planning is evaluating the environmental or external factors that can affect management's plans and decisions. This activity is often called an environmental analysis.

Strategic managers who stay current on changes in the environment have a valuable attribute called **awareness**. That is, they know what is changing in the political, social, technological, and economic arenas. Collectively, all managers directly involved in strategic planning must have awareness. Knowing the current trends in the important environmental areas is critical to the formulation of sound strategy.

Major technological advances such as the development of microprocessors for computers a few years ago can have a major impact on the plans and long-term objectives of an organization. Certainly specific legislation enacted at the local, state or federal level can alter plans and decision. In the social sphere, the great influx of foreign-born people into the American work force and in the market place can affect everything from employee relations programs to advertising decisions. And economically, managers need to maintain a current sensitivity to economic indicators (such as the consumer price index, the prime rate, unemployment figures, inflation rates and more) as well as international factors (such as OPEC's actions and any trade or tariff changes with trading countries). College administrators should be aware of legislation affecting funding for research, Pell Grants and construction projects.

These are relatively simple examples to emphasize the need for managers to stay current on a wide variety of environmental factors. It is important to remember, however, that an organization's strategy cannot respond to every change or event in the environment. Critical factors must be identified and watched. Not every move or action will affect the organization, but those that impact the formulation of strategy must be monitored. This is where some managers become brilliant and others fail. Thorough analysis of the key factors in the formulation of strategy is a must.

Step 5: Inventory Organization Resources. Early in the strategic planning process, an analysis of internal resources must be conducted. This means taking an inventory of the strengths and weaknesses of the organization.

The purpose of inventorying internal resources is to isolate the significant strengths, often called the competitive advantages, which can be used more effectively in formulating future strategy.

Specifically, an inventory of internal resources should answer questions such as these:

1. What are the skills and capabilities of our personnel?
2. What is the state of our physical resources plant, equipment, etc.? Is it updated; properly maintained; and are we using it at full capacity?
3. Are our work layout and space needs being met in every functional area so that we can operate at maximum efficiency?
4. Do we have sufficient funds to support our efforts to achieve desired objectives? Is the cash flow adequate? Can and do we have sources available for additional funds for short-term and long-term needs without costly delays?
5. Are activities and resources properly controlled to insure conformance to whatever standards must be met (nondiscrimination laws, regulatory guidelines, safety standards, etc.)?
6. Have we clearly identified the organization's competitive advantages and disadvantages?

Clearly owners of a professional sport franchise would answer all of these questions when formulating a long term strategy.

Step 6: Identifying Strategic Strengths and Weaknesses of the Organization. Strategy is also called a master plan. Reviewing the master plan that has been followed to achieve current results should identify the significant strengths and weaknesses of that strategy.

A list of strategic strengths of the organization might be in order. For example, during the past eighteen months the organization may have had personnel totally enthused about their activities; more than willing to work extra hard, if necessary; sensitive about the quality of their performance; and excited about the status and future of the organization. This major strength should be used by the organization in a positive way in formulating plans. But if a major weakness in the strategy is revealed by the organization's performance, an overall problem with the strategy may exist. The effort and enthusiasm of personnel may have resulted in little, if any, success to the organization if, for example, the organization is overmatched by its competition or severely underfunded.

An objective review and listing of all strengths and weaknesses of any strategy that have developed during operations explains why results have been good or bad. Organization strengths and weaknesses, however, are relative to that of the competition.

An effective analytical tool to implement this step in strategic management is **"SWOT" analysis**. In "SWOT" analysis, the planner lists the organization's internal **Strengths** and **Weaknesses** and external **Opportunities** and **Threats**; then, evaluates these factors.

Internal Strengths	External Opportunities
Experienced Management	Explore International Markets
Modernized Equipment	Acquire Successful Competitors
Loyal Labor Force	Diversify Product Line
Financial Stability	Market Products and Services Nationally
Well-Known Organization	Recruit Younger Replacements
Internal Weaknesses	**External Threats**
Limited Capacity	Economic Recession
Aged Labor Force	New Governmental Regulations
High Overhead Costs	Entry of Foreign Competition
Low Profit Margins	Product Obsolescence
Limited Resources	Legal Liability Claims by Customers

FIGURE 6-4: SWOT ANALYSIS OF THE XYZ GOLF PRODUCTS MANUFACTURING COMPANY

Step 7: Compare Current Strategy Against Current Information. Results obtained by following current strategy suggest whether the strategy is adequate or needs to be modified. A wide difference between organization performance and strategic expectations emphasizes the need for new strategy. Changes in the environment or in internal factors may have prevented the attainment of expected or desired objectives.

Following the first six steps in the strategic planning process will provide much information about the organization's mission, goals, objectives, environmental factors, internal resources, strategic strengths and weaknesses, and more. When all this information is reviewed, strategic managers know what the current strategy is, what is good and bad about it, and how the organization has performed using it. Now the strategic managers need to know if a new strategy is needed.

In order to determine the overall effectiveness of the current strategy and the need or desirability of changing to a new one, the following questions must be answered:

1. Are the organizational objectives still the same?
2. Is there new information available today, environmental or internal, that has not been considered previously and may affect future performance?
3. Do we have any better means of analyzing current information than was available when the current strategy was formed and does sharper analysis affect the projections and/or conclusions reached earlier?
4. Are our competitors likely to change their strategies? Are we well-informed about the strategies used by our competitors?
5. Is current performance within acceptable deviations from desired results? Are we satisfied with our current performance under the current strategy?

Answering these questions compares current strategy with current information and indicates whether a new strategy is needed. Figure 6-5 summarizes the reasons for altering strategy.

Step 8: Formulate New Strategy if Needed. In Step 7, it was determined whether a new strategy is needed. If management decides performance has not met criteria or if changes in the environment or internal factors dictate a change in strategy, then managers must review alternatives and set a new strategy.

Choosing among alternatives must be related to maximizing organizational strengths or minimizing organizational weaknesses or related to objectives which, if achieved, will show improved organizational performance.

Strategic alternatives should be realistic options that parlay the strengths of the organization into greater success in achieving predetermined objectives.

When strategic managers must select among alternative courses of action, they should evaluate each option. New strategy should be right for the organization with regard to the following:

1. Internal consistency
2. Consistency with the environment
3. Appropriateness in light of available resources
4. Satisfactory degree of risk
5. Appropriate time horizon
6. Workability[7]

Internal consistency refers to the strategy's being compatible with internal policies and organization goals.

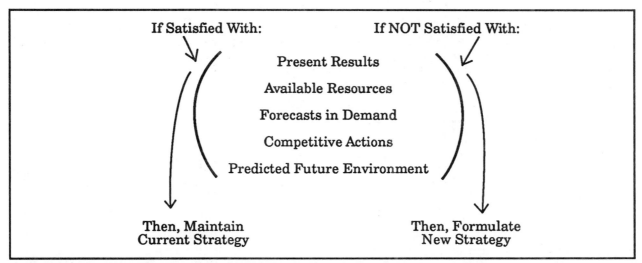

FIGURE 6-5: MAINTAIN CURRENT STRATEGY OR CHANGE?

Consistency with the environment suggests that the selected strategy, which includes plans, policies, tactics, etc., be compatible with governmental regulations, industry trade practices, patron expectations, competitors' actions, and any other outside or external factors that influence strategic planners decisions including ethical and social responsibility considerations and union agreements.

Appropriateness in light of available resources refers to how realistic and appropriate the strategy is considering funding available, competency of personnel, physical facilities, and so forth.

Satisfactory degree of risk emphasizes that all strategy implementation has risk associated with it. How much risk management wishes to expose the organization to in pursuing the objective is the crucial question. Ideally risk is calculated for each strategic alternative under consideration. The degree of risk any organization takes with a particular strategy is a function of the soundness of the strategy and the resources of the organization. That strategy finally accepted should be the one that meets or most nearly meets the degree of risk which the organization defines as acceptable.

Appropriate time horizon means that every strategy should be accompanied by a time standard so all involved know when certain results are to be achieved. The time horizon or standard should be realistic in view of the internal resources and environmental factors but set at a level of excellence.

Workability means simply that if the strategy implemented produces the desired results, then it works. But how do you evaluate strategy for workability without encountering risks? The answer is that you will never really know until you apply the strategy.

Step 9: Develop Policies, Procedures, Programs to Accompany New Strategy. A strategy is composed of a plan or plans which, if followed, will provide direction toward the attainment of predetermined objectives. Strategic managers develop the plans which consist of programs, procedures, policies, and many more forms of organizational guidelines.

A program is a statement of activities that need to be implemented to accomplish a plan. Programs are the action oriented part of strategy.

Procedures are a series of steps or tasks in a logical order. Procedures detail how certain specific results are to be obtained. Procedures are parts of a program.

Policies are general guidelines to influence the behavior of all personnel. They have flexibility and room for interpretation built into them. Policies are important parts of programs which are the substance of strategies. Policies guide and influence management actions toward organization objectives but provide latitude for interpretation and adaptation to changing situations or conditions.

Other organizational guidelines (also called "red tape") may be essential to the formulation and implementation of a good program and sound strategy. Budgets, rules and systems are examples of guidelines that must be included in specific programs.

Step 10: Implement and Control the Strategy. The implementation of strategy activates its component plans and programs. Sound strategic planning should deliver excellent end results; however, managers can insure the performance of the strategy by reviewing all facets of the plan—programs, procedures, budgets, policies, objectives, tactics, etc.— before initiating action. In addition, management must answer such questions as these:

1. Are all personnel involved thoroughly educated and trained for implementing the strategy?
2. Is the proper organizational structure in place to generate coordination of effort and efficiency?
3. Are required resources on hand and readily available for effective utilization?

Once these points have been checked and compliance satisfied, the strategy can be implemented. Thereafter, the control function becomes the manager's chief role.

Control is the function of measuring actual performance against the expected results or the desired standard. Programs of control must be included in the formulation of strategy. At critical stages of progress, a quantitative evaluation should be made.

A comparison is made between results achieved and results desired, and any unusual deviation pinpointed. These lapses in the implementation of the strategy require managerial action.

Such managerial action may be a product redesign, an adjustment in ticket prices, a change in personnel or reassignment of personnel, a change in the time and/or location of an event to draw a larger crowd, or any number of other options.

Also, at critical stages of progress, management should evaluate whether the strategy is being implemented **as designed**. Failure to do this can generate poor performance without the strategy's being the reason and lead to faulting the strategy erroneously. One consequence of failing to implement the strategy properly is unnecessarily changing a strategy that has not been accurately tested first.

Contemporary Views on Strategic Planning

Henry Mintzberg, recognized as a scholar and author in management, challenges traditional strategic planning activities. Mintzberg contends that strategic planning, as currently practiced, is really *strategic programming*, which he calls the articulation and elaboration of strategies or visions that already exist. He also points out that today's strategic planning is not strategic thinking, labeling one "analysis" and the other "synthesis." Strategic thinking (synthesis) involves intuition, creativity and a vision of the direction the organization should take. Strategic planning cannot generate strategies; but, given viable strategies, it can program them and make them operational. Mintzberg further states that sometimes strategies must be left as broad visions with flexibility not precisely articulated in order to allow adaptation to a changing environment.[8]

Another highly regarded management scholar and author, Peter F. Drucker, has his own atypical views of strategic planning. Professor Drucker denotes that many large organizations that have enjoyed long-term success up to now are stagnating, frustrated and in trouble. Top management faces the challenge of "What to do?" Drucker includes labor unions, government agencies, hospitals, churches and other types of organizations as facing the same challenges as many profit-seeking businesses. He suggests that the root problem here is not that things are being done poorly and is not because the wrong things are being done. Rather, he states that the assumptions on which the organization has been built and are being operated no longer fit reality. These are assumptions that shape any organization's behavior, dictate its decisions, and define what the organization considers meaningful results. The assumptions concern markets, competitors, customers, technology and the company's strengths and weaknesses. Together these assumptions are what Drucker calls a company's *Theory of the Business*.

Sometimes a company's Theory of the Business may be viable for a long time, but eventually every Theory of the Business becomes obsolete and invalid. His examples of this are General Motors, IBM and AT&T in recent years.

Drucker believes that it may take years of hard work to reach a clear, consistent and valid Theory of the Business for any organization, but to be successful, every organization must develop one. The four specifications of a valid Theory of the Business are these:

1. The assumptions about environment, mission and core competition must fit reality.
2. The assumptions in all three areas have to fit one another.
3. The Theory of the Business must be known and understood throughout the organization.
4. The Theory of the Business has to be tested constantly.

Drucker suggests that, if an organization's Theory of the Business is stagnating, it is time to rethink a theory, change policies and practices, and bring the organization's behavior in line with the new realities of its environment. Along with this a new definition of its mission is needed and new core competencies developed and acquired.[9]

The contemporary views of Mintzberg and Drucker are "food for thought" and should be considered by any top level manager in the sport industry who engages in strategic planning.

Summary

Strategic management is long-term planning, not operational or tactical planning which is relatively short-term (see Chapter 5). Upper level managers do long-term planning and are called strategic managers. Long-term planning usually covers three to five years, but it can be for as long a time period as ten to twenty years.

Strategic management is defined as the process of managerial decision-making and implementation of plans that directly affect the quality of performance and survival of an organization in the long-run. Strategic managers, also called strategic planners, focus their attention on long-term planning, strategy formulation, strategy implementation, managerial decision-making, and the monitoring and control of implemented plans.

Strategic planning is defined as a process which involves the following: determining an organization's long-term goals and objectives to conform to its mission and formulating the strategy, policies and programs that insure reaching the desired end results in the long-run. The strategy, policies and programs guide decision-making so that internal resources and environmental factors can be used in the most efficient and effective way to achieve predetermined goals and objectives.

A strategic planning process is outlined and discussed. This process, when followed by strategic managers, leads to the formulation of new strategy as required and includes the implementation and control of such strategy.

These are the ten steps in the strategic planning process:

1. Define the goals and mission of the organziation.

2. Identify the long-term objectives.

3. Review the existing strategy to achieve these goals.

4. Evaluate current environmental factors.

5. Inventory the organization's resources.

6. Identify strategic strengths and weaknesses of the organization.

7. Compare current strategy against current information.

8. Formulate new strategy if needed.

9. Develop policies, procedures and programs to accompany new strategy.

10. Implement and control the strategy.

New strategy formulated should be right for the organization and should be eveluated by these criteria:

1. Internal consistency

2. Consistency with the environment

3. Appropriateness in light of available resources

4. Satisfactory degree of risk

5. Appropriate time horizon

6. Workability

A generalization managers should heed is that sound long-term planning, using the strategic planning process, will produce sound strategy which, if followed, will yield the best possible results in the future one can reach using currently available information. Implemented strategy should be carefully monitored and adjusted to fit new internal and external information.

Contemporary management scholars express a contrary view of strategic management and strategic planning. One such author, Peter F. Drucker, suggests a more appropriate term for this activity is developing a "Theory of the Business," which every organization should have.

Review Questions

1. Distinguish between operational planning and long-term planning.

2. Define strategic management.

3. Discuss why long-term planners should be so concerned with environmental factors.

4. Define strategic planning.

5. What are the objectives of good strategic planning?

6. List and explain the steps in the strategic planning process.

7. What is the difference between programs, policies, procedures and objectives?

8. When should an organization consider changing strategy?

9. How do managers evaluate strategy?

10. Once implemented, can strategy ever be changed?

11. Discuss the control of implemented strategy.

Assignments for Personal Development

1. Review the Sunday Business Section of your city's newspaper and find five or six economic indicators listed which will be of major importance to consider when planning a long term strategy. (Example: CPI - Consumer Price Index) Explain the importance of each one you choose.

2. Give an example of a professional sport team in football, baseball, basketball or hockey that is following a long term strategy to achieve a major objective (such as winning the Superbowl, the World Series, etc.).

Incident

CRITICAL JUNCTURE

Twenty-five coaches and staff members had been called to an emergency meeting on short notice by the newly appointed Director of Intercollegiate Athletics. This was the first meeting where all key personnel had been present.

The Director was new, having been appointed by the University's President following the recommendation of a search committee set up to screen and interview applicants.

The Director opened the meeting with a statement that, after three months on the job during which most of his time was spent reviewing performance records, financial data, and the history of the program, he felt an urgency to bring the group together. The thrust of his message centered on how the program planned to survive when so little had been done in the past to prepare for the future. Specifically, he pointed out that annual operating costs had exceeded income for the last several years; outside gifts to the scholarship fund had diminished significantly; student support for the athletic program was lukewarm; and the won-loss records of the varsity teams are one of the worst in their conference. There were other negatives as well. He described the three options that he saw open for the program:

1. Recommend a replacement of many of the present employees. Bring in new blood with some motivation and creativity.

2. Recommend dropping the athletic program to a lower level classification and resigning from the conference.

3. Formulating a long term strategy that possibly could make the program solvent and competitive in three to five years.

Questions:

1. If you were picked as one of a committee to formulate a long term strategy, where would you begin and how would you go about it?

2. List four or five external or environmental factors that have to be considered in the formulation of a long term intercollegiate athletic strategy.

Glossary of Key Terms

Business Strategies: Plans formulated primarily to help a single organization compete more effectively.

Functional Strategies: Plans that pertain to the different activities of a business such as production, sales, finance and human resources.

Grand (Corporate) Strategies: Plans which provide overall direction to the entire organization.

Long-Term Planning: Focuses on achieving goals or objectives for three to twenty years, depepnding on the size of the organization.

Mission: The broadest goal of an organization; it evolves from the particular unique characteristics of the organization; from its philosophy or culture, and is a function of its reason for existing.

Strategic Management: The process of managerial decision-making and implementation of plans that directly affect the quality of performance and survival of an organization in the long-run.

Strategic Planning: The process of determining an organization's long-term goals and objectives in compliance with its mission and formulating the proper plan of action (strategy), policies and programs which insure that sound decisions will be made regarding internal resources and environmental factors that affect all effort to achieve the desired end results over the long-run.

Strategic Programming: The articulation and elaboration of strategies or visions that already exist.

SWOT Analysis: An analytical tool that lists the organization internal strengths and weaknesses and external opportunities and threats.

Tactical Planning: Can be called "operational planning;" it focuses on achieving short-term objectives (usually for one year or less).

Theory of the Business: A concept promoted by Peter Drucker which includes assumptions by an organization about its markets, competitors, customers, technology and core competencies.

Practical Concepts in Management
Generating Ideas and Objectives

Probably the most overlooked responsibility in management is that of generating ideas. Few organizations stress this as part of a manager's job. It is, however, and you as a new manager can get ahead by realizing it.

New ideas are the forerunners of new products, designs, work methods, advertising, product improvements and hundreds of other things which make some organizations much more sucessful than others. A new idea can put additional revenue into the coffers or save money by cost-effectiveness. If the idea is yours, you have made your mark on top management.

Few people use more than five or ten percent of their creative ability. Yet, practically everything around us is wide open for improvement including the activities in any kind of organization.

The most successful organizations are filtering hundreds of ideas annually to bring about change and improvement. Some sponsor contests to encourage creative thinking. These organizations make changes by design—not by accident! Business firms like this encourage "fresh thinking," and they lead their industries.

You can find new ideas anywhere. There is no illegitimate source. You should use your creative ability to generate ideas yourself, learn to stimulate the creative talents of your employees, read trade journals, watch what competitors do, listen to customers and keep up with technological advances. All are fertile sources for new ideas.

Once you have learned to generate and uncover ideas, you must differentiate between them until the best is selected. These best ideas in tangible form become the working objectives of the organization.

Be Aware of Both Risks and Uncertainties

The failure to anticipate major problems in advance is probably the main weakness of most planners. When looking ahead and speculating about what might happen as you pursue objectives, you must be aware of **risks and uncertainties**.

An organizational **risk** is any event, occurence or act that a manager ought to be able to anticipate and plan for. Doing this means that, if the possible problem becomes a reality, you can offset or minimize the effect.

An **uncertainty** is any event, occurrence or act that a manager cannot anticipate nor plan for. If one of these occurs, the organization will either benefit by a windfall or be harmed by a disaster. But is does not relate directly to good or bad management.

Risks have to be calculated. That is, if a manager believes there is a reasonable probability an event will occur, such as a strike, mangers should plan in depth and be prepared. If the probability is slight for such an event, the planning time invested in preparing for it is minimal or none.

Uncertainties are rare! Nearly everything that happens in the future which affects an organization's efforts to achieve an objective should have been uncovered, anticipated and prepared for. Failure to be ready for the obvious possibilities is inexcusable. An uncertainty encompasses such things as an earthquake in an area where no faults are known and no previous earthquakes have occurred. A terrorist bombing, such as the one in Oklahoma City in 1995, with no warning at a randomly selected site is an uncertainty.

Often the single difference between the professional manager and the average (mediocre) one is the ability to anticipate and prepare for major problems in advance. Learn to examine every aspect and to acknowledge every possible problem. Then, master the habit of planning properly for each likely event.

References and Chapter Notes:

[1] George A. Steiner and John B. Miner, *Management Policy and Strategy* (New York: Macmillan Publishing Co., INc., 1977), p. 7.

[2] Thomas L. Wheeler and J. David Hunger, *Strategic Management* (Reading, Mass.: Addison-Wesley Publishing Company, 1984), p. 4.

[3] "Glaxo Wins: Wellcome OKs $15 Billion Bid," from Associated Press, London, as reprinted in *The Atlanta Journal/The Atlanta Constitution*, March 7, 1995, p. E-1.

[4] John H. Grant and William R. King, *The Logic of Strategic Planning* (Boston: Little, Brown and Company, 1982), p. 3.

[5] Alan J. Rowe, Richard O. Mason, and Karl E. Dickel, *Strategic Management and Business Policy* (Reading, Mass.: Addison-Wesley Publishing Company, 1982), p. 6.

[6] T. Mitchell Ford, *Long Range Planning*, Vol. 14, No. 6 (December, 1981), pp. 9-11.

[7] Seymour Tilles, "How to Evaluate Corporate Strategy," *Harvard Business Review*, Vol. 41, No. 4 (July-August, 1963), pp. 111-121.

[8] Henry Mintzberg, "The Fall and Rise of Strategic Planning," *Harvard Business Review*, January-February, 1994, pp. 107-113.

[9] Peter F. Drucker, "The Theory of the Business," *Harvard Business Review*, September-October, 1994, pp. 95-101.

Additional Readings:

Certo, Samuel C., and J. Paul Peter, *Strategic Management: Concepts and Applications.* New York: Random House, 1988.

Scarborough, Norman M., and Thomas W. Zimmerer, "Strategic Planning for the Small Business." *Business* 37 (April/May/June 1987): 11-20.

CHAPTER 7

SOLVING PROBLEMS AND MAKING DECISIONS

After studying this chapter, **you will know:**

- The definition of decision-making

- The distinction between problem-solving and decision-making

- What are programmed and nonprogrammed decisions

- Three conditions of uncertainty

- Major decision-making approaches

- Steps in the rational decision-making approach

- What optimizing and satisficing mean in decision-making

- The importance of "crisis" and "purposeful" creativity

- Techniques used to stimulate group creativity

Introduction

Every manager confronts problems and makes decisions. Decision-making is the essential activity that justifies the existence of managers. Formulating plans, structuring an organization, implementing programs and controlling activities all involve continuous decision-making.

Solving problems is another expectation of managers. Without problems there would be no reason to have managers. Solving problems requires an analysis of facts and information that leads to determining a course of action (making a decision).

This chapter presents information which can aid a manager as he or she plans, analyzes and decides what action to follow when facing a problem. Typically, sound planning precedes sound decision-making, and most often the best managers are the most effective decision-makers. They are the ones who achieve the desired results most effectively and efficiently.

A distinction should be made between problem-solving and decision-making although the two are usually grouped together. *Problem-solving involves determining the proper response to a situation which is judged to be nonstandard or unacceptable. Decision-making involves selecting a course of action among alternative choices.*

One example of problem-solving is the situation that faced major league baseball owners when the players association (a union) called a strike during the 1994 season. What should be the proper response? The owners responded by "locking out" the players. This solution led to the loss of the entire 1994 baseball season. The decision-making process involved reviewing alternative courses of action and selecting one of the available choices. When the strike issues were not settled before the beginning of the 1995 season, the owners chose to form teams using "replacement" players. Eventually, both sides modified their positions enough to allow the delayed season to begin with regular players in place.

This chapter is of special value to managers who interrelate with many different groups of people. "People relationships" often generate problems which require careful analysis of many factors as a prelude to making a decision which will optimize results.

Decision-Making Responsibility

Within the formal organization, managers make a majority of the decisions. While individual nonmanagement employees may choose a best way to do a task from their available choices or workers may proceed with their work according to their own self-determination, managers make the significant decisions, including the decisions to allow the employees this type of freedom.

The autonomy to make decisions depends on the individual manager's level of authority; the nature and tradition of the organizaton; the personalities of bosses, peers and employees; and the expectations or pressure placed on a manager by his or her superior managers. One cardinal rule managers must remember is that every decision must be based on what is good for the organization. Making decisions that benefit one group of employees or oneself, but not the organization, is a good way to lose a job.

Perhaps the most difficult situation a manager faces in his or her career is determining a course of action when it is good for the organization or department but the choice conflicts with the action the manager would prefer personally. Non-management employees must realize that when they become managers, they become the organization and every action they take should be for the benefit of the organization.

Managers make many different kinds of decisions. Some affect the entire organization and other decisions may be routine such as deciding if an employee can leave work early. Whatever the magnitude of the decision, all decisions are important and carry some degree of risk.

As discussed in Chapter 6, decisions affecting long-term objectives are made by strategic managers who are upper-level executives. Functional decisions regarding sales, finance and production usually are made by middle managers. Detailed operating decisions tend to be made by first-level managers.

Types of Decisions

There are several ways to describe the types of decisions managers must make. Depending on the situation, decisions may be considered **programmed** or **nonprogrammed**.

Programmed decisions are those that are repetitive and routine. The decision is influenced by some traditional habit or practice, a defined rule or set procedure. "Red tape" in the organization dictates the decision to make when problems are routine. For example, when supplies must be ordered, a purchasing requisition procedure outlines the steps that one must follow. There is an employment process that a manager must follow in order to fill a vacant position in his or her area of responsibility. Programmed decisions based on predetermined **decision rules** allow managers to concentrate on the unusual problems and decisions rather than worry about handling these routine matters. Many of the decision rules are included in employee manuals which clearly state action prescribed in certain situations. Decision rules, carefully developed, can eliminate wasted time in the decision-making process.

Nonprogrammed decisions are those that apply to unusual problems or situations that are unique or have never occurred previously. Generally higher level managers handle these problems and decide what to do. Situations requiring nonprogrammed decisions are those that require special consideration. Such a problem might include the refusal of a student-athlete on a particular team to play for a coach; a professional athlete who refuses to conform to a league requirement, such as standing attentively during the playing of the national anthem; deciding which sport or activity to eliminate in a drastic budget crisis; or perhaps a claim by a club member or spa client of discrimination against an employee. Most of the major problems managers face will require nonprogrammed decisions which incorporate risk.

Programmed	Nonprogrammed
When to pay overtime	How to overcome low employee morale
How to purchase supplies	Improving the organization's image
Determining employee holidays	Gaining support of higher administration
Hiring new employees	Selecting new programs
Who drives organization vehicles	Storm damage to facilities

FIGURE 7-1: EXAMPLES OF PROGRAMMED AND NONPROGRAMMED DECISION SITUATIONS

Conditions of Uncertainty

Managers are required to make decisions that affect the future based on today's climate and information. Managers attempt to achieve stated goals and desired end results at some future time with each decision made in the present time. Today's decisions do not always result in meeting the goals. The amount of information available to managers at any time varies widely. Circumstances change rapidly, and no person or organization operates in a static environment. The dynamics of the environment dictate that varying degrees of uncertainty accompany decision-making. The primary conditions of uncertainty are **certainty, risk** and **uncertainty**.

If a manager knows exactly what will happen when a decision is made, the manager operates under conditions of **certainty**. Under a condition of certainty, the manager has accurate, factual information on which to base a decision. The outcome is known in advance. While the condition of certainty may be more theoretical than actual since nothing in the future can be absolutely guaranteed, the probability of predicting the outcome relative to the other conditions of uncertainty is much higher (see Figure 7-2).

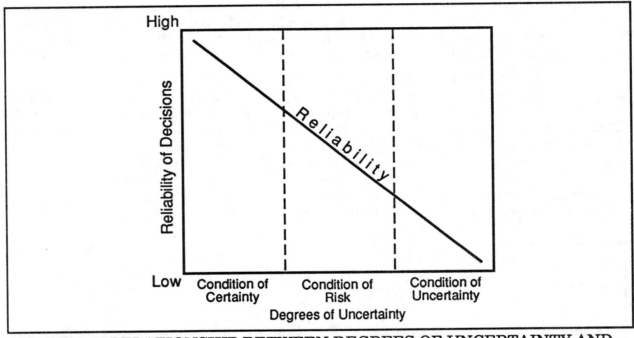

FIGURE 7-2: RELATIONSHIP BETWEEN DEGREES OF UNCERTAINTY AND RELIABILITY OF DECISIONS

Risk is a condition under which a manager can predict with reasonable accuracy future occurrences and assign relative probabilities to them. Gathering information as a basis for predicting probabilities may be costly so some type of value analysis must be made by the decision maker to determine if the cost of information will be more than offset by the outcome. A reasonable probability can be assigned to most of these factors, and the decision maker can proceed.

Uncertainty is a condition which exists under which the manager has little or no information. There is no accurate or totally reliable way to calculate objectively the probabilities. Managers, however, still must use subjective reasoning or a "feel" of the situation as a basis for decisions. Decisions made under conditions of uncertainty carry a high degree of unreliability (refer to Figure 7-2). It is a responsibility of managers to attempt to anticipate uncertainty as much as possible and prepare to offset its effect. Such ability to calculate and prepare for these situations is a reflection of the quality and capability of the manager and decision maker.

Certainty	Risk	Uncertainty
• Ordering office supplies	• Predicting the weather	• Employee resignations
• Granting a pay increase	• Life expectancy	• Acceptance of a new product
• Faxing a message	• Normal employee attrition	• Starting a new business
• Availability of monies in bank account	• Risk of injuries	• Anticipating revenues ten years in advance

FIGURE 7-3: TYPES OF DECISIONS UNDER CONDITIONS OF UNCERTAINTY

The Nature of Problems

It is clear that managers face existing problems that they must handle. Other problems, however, must be defined by the managers. Finding and anticipating problems can be an opportunistic activity. Preventing a problem from occurring may be a cost-saving action. Finding a problem may in reality be an opportunity to bring about gain to the organization beyond normal expectations.

Henry A. Mintzberg, Duru Raisingham and Andre Theoret distinguish among **crises**, **problems** and **opportunities**. Their research indicates that crisis decisions are usually triggered by a sudden, single event (a fire, death of a top manager, bankruptcy of a key supplier, for example) that requires immediate attention. Problems become evident through a stream of ambiguous and frequently verbal data stimulated by the accumulation of multiple events. Opportunities are often evoked by an idea or single, non-crisis event. When handling problems and opportunities, managers accumulate and process information until they reach a certain threshold. When that threshold is reached, the manager is prepared to make a decision. The threshold varies among managers and with the nature of the decision being made.[1]

Remember that problems not handled appropriately can prevent an organization from reaching its desired objectives.

Decision-Making Approaches

Many decision-making approaches are used by managers for the purpose of achieving desired results. Some are laughable; others are more objective. No approach to decision-making, however, can guarantee a correct solution to general management problems. *A general management problem is any kind of problem within an organization about anything so long as people (the human element) are part of the problem.* General management problems account for about ninety (90) percent of the kinds of problems managers face daily versus technical or nonhuman problems which represent about ten (10) percent of a manager's daily problems. The division or breakdown of general problems to technical problems varies with the nature of the organization.

Where variables in a problem can be quantified, often a mathematical or quantitative method of decision-making can be used. Accountants, architects, engineers and quality control specialists are typical of personnel who employ quanititative methods in making daily decisions. Examples of quantitative decision-making methods are linear programming, queuing theory, simulation models, Program Evaluation and Review Technique (PERT) and Critical Path Method (CPM). These techniques are part of a **management science approach to decision-making**.

Management Science Approach. According to Thomas M. Cook and Robert A. Russell, *management science (MS) is the discipline devoted to studying and developing procedures to help in the process of making decisions.*[2] *Management science is also called operations research (OR).* The distinguishing characteristic of MS/OR is the use of the scientific method for decision making and the use of scientific methodology to solve problems.

Examples of the use of management science techniques go back thousands of years to such historical events as the construction of the pyramids in Egypt. In Chapter 1 there is a review of the work of some individuals who applied scientific methodology to solving problems—Adam Smith, Eli Whitney, Charles Babbage, Frederick W. Taylor, Frank Gilbreth, Henry L. Gantt and many others.

World War II marked the beginning of operations research/management science as a recognized discipline. The British government, facing a shortage of skilled personnel to solve problems in wartime, recruited scientists with different specializations to be on teams which studied major operational problems. These OR teams with multi-disciplinary backgrounds succeeded in solving problems such as convoy routes, the development of radar, and many others that enabled Britain to survive the crisis.

By 1950, the OR/MS approach was in vogue in the U.S. military and accepted by U.S. industry. With the advent of high-speed electronic computers, complex problems were analyzed and solved more quickly. The recognition of the discipline was complete with the organization of professional operations research associations and the publication of professional journals.

Management science methods are based on the use of the historic *scientific method*. *Steps in the scientific method are observation, definition of the problem, formulation of a hypothesis, experimentation and verification.*

Also, management science decision-makers often use a systems approach when studying organizational problems. They view individual parts of an organization in relation to the whole. The control of quality of products, for example, impacts sales, costs and prices.

Cook and Russell summarize management science applications by stating that any approach to problem-solving incorporates all or most of the following characteristics:

1. Viewing the problem within a system perspective.

2. Applying the scientific method to develop the solution methodology.

3. Using a team or interdisciplinary approach.

4. Using a mathematical model.

5. Using a high-speed electronic computer.[3]

Intuitive Approach. The intuitive approach to decision-making cannot be ignored or deemed unimportant. Everyone has made decisions based on a "hunch," "feel," "vibes," or some form of personal judgement. Many successful entrepreneurs have started businesses based on a hunch; upper-level executives have made major decisions based on a "feel" of the situation; students sometimes characterize instructors because of "bad vibes," etc. The decision to hire an applicant for a job usually is determined at the final stage of the personnel selection process by a manager who bases his or her choice on personal judgement (a "feel" or intuition about the person in question). The information available on any job applicant cannot absolutely predict whether that person will become an outstanding employee if hired. Figure 7-4 lists some of the intuitive approaches to decision-making used on occasion by virtually everyone.

Intuition is defined as the immediate and instinctive perception of a truth. It is also defined as direct understanding without reasoning.[4] Clearly, managers who rely wholly on intuitive approaches may make some bad decisions.

When might an intuitive approach to managerial decision-making be appropriate? K. J. Radford suggests that, when decision situations are classified as ill-structured, the experience and intuition of those involved in decisions becomes personalistic as contrasted to the use of a well-structured and logical procedure.[5]

The four main characteristics of ill-structured decision situations are these:

1. Lack of complete information regarding the decision situation and its environment.

2. Lack of quantitative measures that truly and completely describe the costs and benefits of the available alternatives.

3. The existence of multiple objectives on the part of the organization, individual, or group concerned.

4. The existence of more than one participant in the decision situation with power to influence the outcome.[6]

Undoubtedly, a large proportion of business decisions are based upon pure guess or hunches, according to Leanard W. Hein. He continues by saying that the successful business person is one who guesses right more than fifty (50) percent of the time.[7]

Intuition and other forms of personal judgement are important in the decision-making process, but problems can occur if the decision-maker ignores available facts and relevant information. All the speed and help computers and other information processing equipment can give a manager are of little value if the manager misuses the information when making a decision.

Based on:		
• Hunch	—	"We'll take the next exit."
• "Gut" feeling	—	"I've got a feeling this is wrong."
• Vibes	—	"Something tells me he is not be be trusted."
• Emotion	—	"I know we can't afford it but I want it."

FIGURE 7-4: EXAMPLES OF INTUITIVE DECISIONS

The Rational Approach to Decision-Making

Since decision-makers are people whose actions and decisions are influenced by many things (time of day, food intake, weather, attire and the environment in general), a rational decision-making approach is presented. The use of this approach does not guarantee a more correct decision or recommendation in every case. What the rational decision-making approach does guarantee is that, on average, a manager will make sounder decisions and recommendations with this approach than if he or she uses some other approach when confronting **general management problems**.

Decision-makers are people, and people are not totally rational and objective when analyzing problems every time. The use of the rational approach to decision-making is an effort to offset the influence of biases, tradition, emotion and all other personal and environmental factors which can warp decisions. The rational decision-making approach forces the manager to focus on a more logical and more objective method to making decisions. It involves the use of a seven-step approach. These are the seven steps in the rational decision-making approach:

1. Clearly identify the fundamental management problem
2. List all the facts pertinent to the problem
3. List alternative courses of action to solve the problem
4. List advantages and disadvantages of each alternative (evaluate)
5. Review all of the above
6. Draw conclusions, make recommendations and/or decisions
7. Follow-up after the decision has been implemented to ascertain if the desired results have been achieved.

Step 1: Clearly identify the fundamental management problem. This is a critical step. No progress can be made in any organization unless the fundamental or causal issue is defined and overcome, eliminated or modified. Symptoms of causal problems must be separated from the fundamental problem in order to effect a conclusive solution. Employee absenteeism or tardiness may be causing delays and costly difficulties, but the underlying or cause problem leading to this symptom must be identified before corrective action can be significant and lasting. Fundamental management problems are those that have occurred in the past; are occurring now; and more than likely will show up again within the organization in the future. Threats or punitive action may temporarily stem the absenteeism, but no truly effective solution will be found until the fundamental reason for the employee's attitude and behavior is identified and addressed.

Step 2: All factual data and pertinent information should be gathered prior to continued analysis. Because factual data may be limited, the rational decision-making approach sometimes is called the subjective decision-making approach. Using factual data is important but facts can be scarce when analyzing general management problems.

Step 3: The identification of alternative courses of action refers to the choices of action a manager has to eliminate or overcome the fundamental problem. If a manager has difficulty finding alternative courses of action, it may indicate that the manager does not have a problem to solve. All real management problems have several ways of being handled. Situations which many people call problems, but where nothing can be done about them, are really conditions that exist that create a negative atmosphere. Each alternative carries risks and must be evaluated for its potential effect on all phases of the organization's effort. Many managers forget that doing nothing about an existing problem is always one alternative.

Step 4: Listing advantages and disadvantages of each alternative is something nearly every individual goes through when making a thoughtful personal decision. Questions such as to buy or lease; rent or purchase; keep a current job or try to find a new one or accept an offered one are examples. The purpose of Steps 3 and 4 is to force a manager or individual to review all sides of a problem and all consequences of any action before reaching a conclusion.

Step 5: Review all of the above is a suggestion for managerial decision-makers to slow down and carefully rethink everything one more time before implementing a decision. This step does not suggest a long delay, but it does emphasize that a conclusion drawn now may not be the same as one drawn tomorrow. Wise decision-makers allow a little time to pass before implementing important decisions. The old saying, "Haste makes waste," has some validity.

Step 6: After Step 5, if a manager feels comfortable with the analysis and review, he or she draws conclusions and makes a decision or recommends a course of action to higher management for implementation.

Step 7: Following up after a decision has been made is an act of a truly professional manager. Decisions should not be implemented and left unattended. It behooves the manager to check on the effect of the decision and measure results against expectations. In this step managers take corrective or remedial action if necessary.

Limitations of Rational Decision-Making. Rational decision-making uses a logical approach (sometimes called the scientific method) when analyzing general management problems. The approach is superior to the intuitive approach in most situations, but it has limitations. The objective of the rational decision-making approach is to optimize. *Optimizing means selecting the best possible alternative (decision) in light of all the facts, considerations and options.* Critics of this approach point out that decision-makers are not always objective; often do not have all the facts; can be easily influenced by emotions or prejudices; may not consider all available alternatives; and may not evaluate available information properly.

Herbert A. Simon, American scholar and former Nobel Prize recipient, originated the **Principle of Bounded Rationality** that recognizes that decisions are not always made rationally and logically. His *Principle of Bounded Rationality states "The capacity of the human mind for formulating and solving complex problems is very small compared with the size of the problems whose solutions are required for objectively rational behavior—or even for a reasonable approximation to such objective rationality.*[8] Simon's *administrative model* describes how decisions often are actually made. He suggests that people do not exhaustively search for the optimum alternative but instead select the first alternative that meets some minimum standard of satisfaction. This is called *satisficing.*

The optimizing and satisficing approaches to decision-making both have value. Using the rational decision-making approach in an effort to optimize provides the manager a model for rational and objective analysis even though it is imperfect. The satisficing approach reminds managers of their inherent weaknesses as decision-makers. Satisficing is a more realistic approach to decision-making while optimizing is a more ideal approach. Often the crucial difference in choosing between the two approaches is determined by how much time the manager has to gather information and facts, formulate alternatives and decide.

Group Decision-Making

Most decisions are made by individuals although it is not uncommon to find groups making decisions. Examples of group decision-making include the U.S. Congress and state legislative bodies, committees, corporate boards of directors, trustees of nonprofit organizations and juries in the legal system. The great advantage of this approach is the pooling of thoughts, experiences and ideas of many to provide a consensus. The major disadvantages are that the approach can be time consuming and the group decision nearly always is based on compromise, which may or may not be the best decision for the problem at hand.

Group decision-making is a form of participative management. Everyone in the group has an opportunity to participate and identify with group decisions. Resistance to decisions by group members is minimized since all members have had a chance for input, and all group members have been privy to the discussions and the rationale. Nevertheless, there are limitations to group decision-making.

These potential limitations include the group can be dominated by a member of upper management; the members may not be qualified to deal with the problem at hand; personalities of members may clash, which could lead to irrational decisions; and time constraints might force hasty analysis and decisions not well conceived.

Theoretically, group decision-making should be superior to that made by a single person because of the great base of knowledge a group would have about a subject and the larger number of alternatives or ideas generated by group members. Group decision-making generally takes longer, however, and the timeliness of the decision may be more important to the organization.

Creative Problem-Solving and Decision-Making

Making Progress on Purpose. It is well known that individuals and organizations become more creative in a time of crisis. During World War II, the U.S. created the atom bomb to end the war with Japan. During the oil and gasoline crisis of the 1970s, any number of alternative fuel sources sprang to life for cars and homes. Materials using petroleum by-products, such as polyester, were replaced by newly developed cottons and blends that use natural fibers. When you have a flat tire on a lonely road in the middle of the night and your flashlight will not work, you become more creative and build a small fire so you can see even if you have to rub two sticks together. *Crisis creativity* is important, but the progressive leaders of industry today do not rely on this kind of creativity to give them the competitive "edge" in their field. Rather, modern managers do not merely *react* to conflict and problems to find novel solutions and better methods, they are progressive managers who encourage creativity in a proactive way. This can be called *purposeful creativity*, and the distinction is clear!

Purposeful creativity is a planned, continuous effort by management to encourage creativity. The end result is new products, improved existing products, greater market share, better methods of operation, more efficient systems of activity, and general improvement in all aspects of running an organization. Managers in these kinds of organizations have adopted the philosophy of **"Making progress on purpose"** instead of by accident. Progress comes through a deliberate, designed effort not simply by reacting to organizational needs and conflict.

Booster groups of high school athletic teams and parents of recreation and little league teams are prime examples of creative people who proactively develop plans for fundraising to support their teams and programs.

To achieve purposeful creativity, managers must establish a climate for individual and group creativity. The following steps lead to such a climate:

1. Top management must totally endorse and continually support the concept of change if it will prove beneficial and economically sound to the organization.

2. A program encouraging creativity (new ideas and new ways of doing things) must be introduced with full support of management and complete understanding by the employees.

3. Individual employees and groups must be given the opportunity to learn more about the creative process. This should include training sessions, literature and exercises that stress idea generation.

4. A formal organization should be created to administer the creative/idea program properly on a continual basis. This effort, composed of full-time employees or administered by a committee of employees, should develop a system of idea encouragement; a procedure for reviewing submitted ideas; a manner for recognizing selected ideas; and a reward program for employees whose ideas are implemented.

5. Finally, there should be a program to implement the best of the ideas. Often this requires a mix of functional specialists under the direction of an administrator who coordinates all aspects of the new activity.

Many ideas submitted by individuals or groups will not have practical value. But some will, and the important point to remember is that the effort must be formally recognized and the participants encouraged to continue to think creatively.

Creation and Implementation of New Ideas. *Creativity is the generation of new ideas. Innovation is the practical application of new ideas.* Obviously, ideas without implementation lead nowhere. Years ago children with worn out roller skates often took the wheels and nailed them on a plank of wood to make a homemade scooter. Ultimately someone had the "idea" of calling such things skateboards, making them sleek and colorful, and selling them as terrific "new" toys. The result of commercializing this product is millions in sales annually, new contests between highly-skilled practicioners, and a whole new sport— all because an "idea" was implemented.

Ideas come to all people at odd times and in strange places. Many highly creative people keep a notepad or recorder handy at all times to jot down their ideas as they come. Most employees are not this creative, but each one is more creative than he or she imagines. The role of the manager is to encourage employees to use their full creative potential for the good of the organization.

A common sense creative process which one can apply to individuals is this:

1. Identify the subject to resolve.
2. Research the subject.
3. Review all information over a period of time.
4. Project alternative ways to achieve objective.
5. Test alternatives.
6. Select and implement an alternative.

The six steps in this creative process which can be applied to an individual are a form of scientific methodology. Using such a process to generate ideas and improvements when analyzing organizational problems and making decisions is similar to the approaches used by Frederick W. Taylor, Frank Gilbreth and other management science pioneers to improve shop operations early in the 20th Century. This approach is still valid today.

Another creative process for generating ideas that lead to solutions to organizational problems has four stages: preparation, incubation, illumination and verification. *Preparation* involves gathering and studying information about the subject. This may include information from reports, research findings and direct observation as well as other sources. *Incubation* is a stage of not consciously thinking about the problem but letting the subconcious mind review the problem. *Illumination* occurs, often suddenly, when a solution to the problem is recognized. *Verification*, the final stage, is the act of fine-tuning and testing the solution.

Once a solution has been determined, decisions can be implemented to resolve the problem.

Generating ideas is the first step in The Planning Process (see Chapter 5). Managers should take the best of these ideas, put them in tangible form, and make them working objectives. To say that all good ideas will come only from the employees or the managers is misleading. Many good ideas can be generated by customers, clients, vendors, competitors, and other sources. A company determined to "make progress on purpose" does not overlook any source of new ideas. Even complaints and criticism of products and/or services can be the source of a new idea for improvement or modification.

Stimulating Creativity

Organizations that encourage employees and managers to be creative have established an environment in the workplace that fosters creativity. Through participative management practices, the use of committees, quality circles and more self-directed work groups, opportunities are provided for new ideas and solutions to existing problems. Additionally, on occasion management may select employees to be part of groups that employ special techniques to stimulate creativity. The three best known techniques are *brainstorming, synectics and the nominal group process.*

Brainstorming[9] was developed by Alexander F. Osborn, who at the time was a principal with the New York advertising agency of Batten, Barton, Durstine & Osborn. The technique has enjoyed wide use for over 25 years. Brainstorming attempts to generate many ideas in a relatively short period of time. A small group of seven or eight people are brought together, presented a problem, and asked to recommend solutions to the problem (spontaneously). It does not matter how absurd the suggested solutions may be. The purpose is to generate a large quantity of ideas about a problem in an unrestricted setting in a brief period of time. From the large number of proposed solutions, perhaps one or two may be acceptable and workable once refined.

Synectics[10] means "holding together continuously." The technique, developed by William J. J. Gordon, is somewhat similar to brainstorming except participants in the group may have different specialized backgrounds and the experienced leader carefully explains the problem to be discussed. As participants recommend solutions, the leader encourages them to think more creatively about the problem and to develop more nontraditional approaches to the problem. The leader structures the discussion suggesting direct analogies be applied in consideration of a solution to a problem. For example, how sea gulls glide over the ocean might be valuable in overcoming some of the problems of ultralight aircraft.

Synectics is a group process where all participants get involved in evaluating solutions, and the leader "holds together" all of the ideas and recommended solutions which are used in the final determination of a solution.

Nominal group process[11] is a technique developed by Andre Delbecq and Andrew H. Van de Ven for the purpose of finding creative alternatives to solving problems. The process begins when a problem is clearly explained to the group.

Then, each group member working alone prepares a list of ideas or possible solutions to the problem. Following this, each member of the group presents his or her ideas or solutions to the problem to the other members. These ideas are recorded. After all members have made their presentations, an open discussion follows and each idea or recommendation is evaluated. Next, the members vote privately on each other's ideas and rank the ideas in order of importance. The results are anounced to all and a brief discussion follows. Lastly, a final secret vote is cast by each member of the group to determine the group's preference.

The nominal group process technique, unlike brainstorming and synectics, does not generate an open discussion of ideas. Much of the work within the group is done privately by each member, and there is a limit placed on participants' verbal interaction. Still this process, like the others, generates many good ideas and creative solutions to organizational problems.

Summary

Every manager confronts problems and makes decisions. Decision-making is the essential activity that justifies the existence of managers. In the strictest sense decision-making involves selecting a course of action from alternative choices. Problem-solving involves determining the proper response to a situation which is considered to be nonstandard or not acceptable.

Decisions may be described as programmed or nonprogrammed. Programmed decisions are those that are repetitive and routine. Nonprogrammed decisions are those that apply to unusual problems or situations that are non-routine. Generally higher level managers handle non-routine problems.

Varying degrees of uncertainty accompany decision-making. The primary conditions of uncertainty in decision-making are certainty, risk and uncertainty.

Major decision-making approaches include the management science approach, the intuitive approach, the rational approach, the creative approach and the group decision-making approach. The rational decision-making approach involves the application of the scientific method to general management problems. General management problems are those which involve people (the human element).

Management Science (MS) is the discipline devoted to studying and developing procedures to help in the process of making decisions. Management Science is also called Operations Research (OR). Scientific methodology is used to solve problems.

The intuitive approach to decision-making is based on an individual's perception of the truth without much reasoning involved.

All decision-making approaches have limitations. Herbert Simon's "Principle of Bounded Rationality" recognizes that decisions are not always made rationally and logically.

Group decision-making is a form of participative management where everyone in the group has an opportunity to participant and identify with the decision(s). Theoretically, group decision-making should be superior to that of a single person because of the greater knowledge of the subject a group would have and the larger number of alternatives or ideas submitted by group members.

Creativity is the generation of new ideas. Innovation is the application of new ideas. Creative problem-solving and decision-making are important to organizations that wish to make progress on purpose and stay ahead of their competitors. Good ideas can come from employees, customers, vendors, competitors and many other sources. Organizations that want to stimulate group creativity have a number of techniques available. The three best known techniques are brainstorming, synectics and the nominal group process.

Review Questions

1. Make a clear distinction between decision-making and problem-solving.

2. Discuss why higher-level managers generally make the nonprogrammed decisions.

3. Clearly explain the three conditions of uncertainty which affect managerial decision-making.

4. Outline and briefly discuss each step in the rational decision-making approach.

5. Review the origin of Operations Research (OR).

6. Under what conditions might intuitive decision-making be acceptable?

7. Distinguish between "crisis" and "purposeful" creativity.

8. What is the Principle of Bounded Rationality?

9. Why might group decision-making be superior to individual decision-making? What are the limitations of group decision-making?

10. Briefly discuss the three best known techniques for stimulating group creativity.

Assignments for Personal Development

1. Assume that you need twenty-four (24) semester or quarter hours of course work to graduate after the current term. Each course carries three hours of credit if completed satisfactorily.

   Using the *rational decision-making* approach determine whether you should take 2, 3 or 4 courses per term in order to graduate in 1, 1½ or 2 years.

2. One of the complaints about professional baseball games is that they take too long to complete; they drag on with many delays throughout the game. Using "purposeful creativity," suggest some creative ways the games might be improved to stimulate fan enthusiasm, improve attendance and benefit all parties concerned.

Incident

FRUSTRATED A.D.

Wallace Fieldhouse was the newly appointed athletics director of a mid-sized university. His first three months on the job had been a nightmare. He was working ten to twelve hours daily and getting more behind with the work. Most of his days were filled with problem situations and making decisions. It seemed that every staff member came to him for either a solution or recommendation about every problem they encountered, or they wanted him to approve or make a decision before they took any action. He was flattered by the confidence and attention they showed him, but something was going to have to give!

Questions:

1. What is wrong with Wallace Fieldhouse as a decision-maker? List four things.

2. Would it make a difference if Wallace Fieldhouse understood the distinction between programmed decisions and nonprogrammed decisions? Discuss.

Glossary of Key Terms

Brainstorming: Technique to encourage a small group to generate many ideas for solving a problem in a short period of time.

Crisis creativity: Generating ideas and novel solution to problems in an emergency situation.

Decision-making: Selecting a course of action among alternative choices.

General Management Problems: Any kind of problem within an organization about anything so long as people are part of the problem.

Intuition: The immediate and instinctive perception of a truth. Also defined as a direct understanding without reasoning.

Management Science (MS): The discipline devoted to studying and developing procedures to help in the process of making decisions.

Nominal group process: Technique for developing creative alternatives to solving problems in which participants work independently initially and avoid influence from other members of the group.

Nonprogrammed decisions: Those that apply to unusual problems or situations that are unique or that have never occurred previously.

Operations Research (OR): Study of large operational problems by a team of individuals from different disciplines and backgrounds.

Optimizing: Selecting the best possible alternative in light of all facts, considerations and options.

Principle of Bounded Rationality: The capacity of the human mind for formulating and solving complex problems is very small compared with the size of the problems whose solutions require objectively rational behavior.

Problem-solving: Determining the proper response to a situation which is judged to be nonstandard or unacceptable.

Programmed decisions: Decisions that are repetitive and routine.

Purposeful creativity: Planned, deliberate continuous effort by management to encourage and promote creativity.

Risk: A condition under which a manager can predict with reasonable accuracy future occurrences and assign relative probabilities to them.

Satisficing: A decision-maker's selection of the first alternative solution to a problem situation that meets some minimum standards of satisfaction.

Synectics: Creative problem-solving technique that encourages group members to develop more nontraditional approaches to solving the problem.

Uncertainty: A condition which exists for which the manager making a decision has little or no information; a future occurrence that cannot be predicted with any reasonable degree of probability.

Practical Concepts in Management

Management Is the Significant Difference

Every organization has competition. If you are part of a business firm, you have much head-on competition. Even the U. S. Postal Service has competition. There are few monopolies left.

When you review successful organizations in a highly competitive field, you wonder why some are more profitable or successful than others. If they provide about the same services or similar product lines with prices that do not vary much, you invariably think: What makes the difference? You wonder because inevitably one organization *is* better, more successful, more profitable than the others.

The significant difference between competing organizations originates in the hundreds of decisions managers make over a period of time. Decisions in any organization flow downward and create action which results in change. Changes affecting pricing, styling, merchandising, packaging, advertising, customer services, location, efficiency, product lines, and hundreds of other things that over time make the significant difference between competing organizations. All these change-initiating decisions have one common factor:the managers who made and implemented them. It is the quality of those managers' decisions that makes the critical difference.

Management Is Decision-Making

The most common activity in management is decision-making. Every manager makes decisions, good or bad, and stands on the results. Decision-making is an unavoidable responsibility that leads to action. This action, multiplied by every decision made, brings about the results which are the goal of the manager's job.

Most decisions in management are subjective in nature and concern problems that include people. These are called *general management problems*. Nonpeople problems or technical problems can be difficult, but they represent only about ten percent of a manager's total problems.

Decision-making is not very scientific and many factors affect how a manager acts under certain circumstances. Mathematical decision-making is used in some organizations if the variables in the problem can be quantified. But this is not always the case, and such precise decision-making is therefore limited in use.

A general notion is that the best management planners tend to be the best decision-makers who, in turn, tend to be the best managers.

References and Chapter Notes:

[1] Henry A. Mintzberg, Duru Raisingham, and Andre Theoret, "The Structure of 'Unstructured' Decision Processes," *Administrative Science Quarterly*, 21, No. 2 (June 1976), 246-275.

[2] Thomas M. Cook and Robert A. Russell, *Introduction to Management Science*, Third edition (Englewood Cliffs, NJ: Prentice-Hall, Inc., 1985), pp. 2-3.

[3] Cook and Russell, Introduction, p. 9.

[4] "Intuition," *Webster's Encyclopedia of Dictionaries*, New American edition (Ottenheimer Publishers, Inc., 1972), p. 199.

[5] K. J. Radford, *Modern Managerial Decision Making* (Reston, VA: Reston Publishing Company, Inc., 1981), pp. 15-19.

[6] Radford, *Modern*, p. 16.

[7] Leonard W. Hein, *The Quantitative Approach to Managerial Decisions* (Englewood Cliffs, NJ: Prentice-Hall, Inc., 1967), p. 3.

[8] Herbert A. Simon, *Model of Man* (New York: John Wiley & Sons, 1957), p. 198.

[9] Alexander F. Osborn, *Applied Imagination: Principles and Procedures for Creative Problem-Solving*, 3rd ed. (New York: Scribners, 1963).

[10] William J. J. Gordon, *Synectics: the Development of Creative Capacity* (New York: Harter, 1961).

[11] Andre L. Delbecq and Andrew H. Van de Ven, "A Group Process Model for Problem Identification and Program Planning," *Journal of Applied Behavioral Science* 7, No. 4 (July-August, 1971), 466-492.

SECTION III

ORGANIZING THE WORK FORCE

CHAPTER 8

THE FUNCTION OF ORGANIZING

After studying this chapter, **you will know:**

- The purpose of organizing
- The benefits of organizing
- The history of organizing
- Some theories of organizing
- Traditional principles of organization
- The definition of a formal organization
- How to design and structure an organization
- Types of organization structures
- Steps in organizing
- Importance of organization charts

Introduction

Every formal work or sport effort requires good organization if success is the objective. Lack of sound organization causes disorder, confusion, frustration, duplicated effort and often chaos. Good organization generates efficiency of effort and harmony in the combination of resources, both human and nonhuman, involved. Defects in the organization become the primary cause of daily management problems.

Coordination of effort does not happen by accident. Students should learn that only good organization leads to the proper level of coordination required to reach objectives. Sound organization provides two benefits to management that are essential for the success of any type endeavor: First, the right people will be in the right jobs; and second, the proper amount of resources (human and nonhuman) of the right quality will be avilable at the time they are needed.

The responsibility to organize effectively is a function of management. Comments you will hear that reflect on the organization skills of managers are similar to these:

- They really work well together.
- Everyone knows their job and when to do it.
- Have you ever seen such team effort?
- There are no weak links.
- They have a great game plan.
- They may be unbeatable.

As you study Chapter 8, remember that practicing managers probably know less about the subject of organization than any of the other subjects in management.

The Importance of Organizing

"Organizing" comes from the word "Organism" and refers to parts separate in function which are interdependent. Applied to today's organization, **organizing is a managerial effort to assign work and allocate resources; then, arrange the work and resources in such an orderly way that a group's effort generates the desired end result in the most efficient manner possible.**

Organizing is a main function of management which is often not a separate managerial act. Organizing may be part of planning or mixed with other management functions as well. Collectively, the activities of planning, organizing, deciding, implementing and controlling are called **managing.** Students should view organizing as the managerial effort to create order from chaos in the workplace, generating operating efficiency in the process.

Organizing is important in management because of the following benefits:

1. Generating effective group action
2. Synergizing resources
3. Pinpointing individual responsibilities
4. Facilitating the functions of implementing and control.

Generating effective group action. Reaching desired work objectives requires the efforts of many individual employees. When employees' efforts are coordinated so that the group reaches its goals and individual employees fully use their knowledge and skills, the organization as a whole benefits as well as individual employees.

Synergizing Resources. Sound organization leads to the proper use of resources (people, money, inventories, supplies, equipment, etc.) so that over time the value of end results is greater than the combined starting values of the resources. This point reflects on efficiency of effort which is the primary purpose of organizing work.

Pinpointing individual responsibilities. A major reason for organizing is to specify the duties and responsibilities of individual employees. Doing this eliminates doubt about any employee's purpose and relationship to other work being performed. Lines of authority and accountability (reporting relationships and dependencies) are defined and clarified. Every member of the work unit wants to know who is in charge of what; where to go for answers to each kind of question; how each employee's actions affect others; and who judges work performance.

Facilitating the implementing and control functions. Today, good organizing considers interpersonal relationships, the work environment, and the control of results. It is well accepted that the majority of workers perform best when the following conditions are met: (1) Their job skills and knowledge are right for the job; (2) working conditions are pleasant, and (3) they have a clear understanding of their duties and responsibilities. Organizing efforts support the implementation of plans and programs and facilitate the control function by communicating work expectations that become a standard for evaluation of performance.

History of Organizing

Organizing has a long history as a recognized function of management. Whether studying the prehistoric era or ancient civilization, it is clear that there were organization structures, there were superior/subordinate relationships, there were centers of authority, and there were duties delegated to subordinates.

Construction of the pyramids in Egypt from 5000 to 525 B.C. provides a vivid example of good organizational technique:

> During the New Empire under the reign of Ramses IV, one expedition to quarry stone at Hammamat was carried out in quite a regal style. The expedition was under the titular leadership of the high priest of Amon (because the monuments were for a god) and other attendants of the king, none of whom made any consequential contribution. The men who, in effect, were in charge were military officers inasmuch [sic] work of this nature usually fell on the army. On this expedition one hundred ten officers of each rank, fifty civil officials and ecclesiastics, one hundred thirty stone masons, two painters, and four engravers furnished the leadership. The work of transport was done by five thousand common soldiers, two hundred members of the king's court, eight hundred barbarians, and two thousand bondservants of the temple. Altogether, the expedition consisted of 8,368 men.

> By using masses of organized labor the Egyptians were able to accomplish tasks that astonish us. While their system of organization may appear unwieldy, cumbersome, and even wasteful, they actually had no reason to economize on labor since more peasants, mercenaries, and slaves were always available simply for the asking.[1]

Many individuals, civilizations and governments have contributed to the subject of organization over time. This includes the feudal organization, the organizational genius of the Romans, Alexander the Great, Niccolo Machiavelli and many more.

In more modern times, Sir James Steuart, Adam Smith, Thomas Jefferson and Eli Whitney introduced important organizational concepts in the eighteenth century. Steuart developed a source of authority theory based on dependency; Adam Smith introduced the principle of work specialization in 1776 (also known as the "division of labor" principle).[2] The concept of interchangeable parts was one of Thomas Jefferson's suggestions, and Eli Whitney was the first American to apply the concept of interchangeable parts and the specialization principle when he manufactured muskets for the government in the 1790s.

During the late nineteenth century and early twentieth century, the subject of management took on new importance. The so-called "pioneers" of modern management emerged with their writings, theories and practical applications. People like Frederick W. Taylor, Frank Gilbreth, Henry L. Gantt, Harrington Emerson and others applied their management ideas successfully and became nationally famous.

Taylor introduced an organization structure called **functional foremanship** (See Figure 8-1) which exchanged multiple accountability for intense specialization to support the work of individual employees. This contribution, while not universally popular in Taylor's day, is similar to matrix organization as practiced today in multi-project organizations.

In 1931, James D. Mooney and Alan C. Reiley published *Onward Industry.*[3] This represented the first effort in the United States to present a systematic approach to organization. Many principles or "universals" of organization were included.

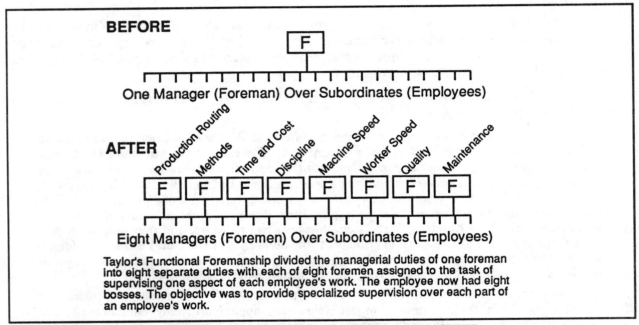

FIGURE 8-1: F. W. TAYLOR'S FUNCTIONAL FOREMANSHIP

Source: Based on material in F. W. Taylor, *The Principles of Scientific Management,* New York: Harper & Brothers, 1911.

Theories of Organizing[4]

Historically speaking, organization theory is identified as **classical, neoclassical** and **modern.** None of the theories is complete or neatly packaged. None is totally accepted by researchers in management; however, the theoretical approaches provide students some insight into the evolutionary development of management thought about organizing.

Classical theory. Classical organization theory or doctrine relates to the early work of Taylor, Fayol, Mooney and Reiley, Weber and others. Importance is placed on organization structure or the hierarchy. Principles of organization have been developed to provide guidance to practicing managers. The main elements of classical organization are the division of labor, the scalar principle, the functional management process, organization structure, and the concept of span of management (control) [see Figure 8-2].

The *division of labor principle refers to breaking work down into basic components and emphasizing specialization of effort.* Workers become expert at one job and output and efficiency increase. This element directly influences the others, and thus is considered the foundation of classical organization.

The *scalar principle pertains to vertical growth of an organization (the hierarchy or chain of command), while functional process pertains to horizontal growth (the functional processes of management).* Within these elements in classical organization you find the subjects of delegation of authority and responsibility, unity of command, accountability, and the separation of the organization into specialized (functional) parts, from which evolved line and staff activities.

Division of Labor—refers to breaking work down into basic components and emphasizing specialization of effort.

Parity Principle—states that authority and responsibility must be equal or coincide.

Scalar Principle—authority in the formal organization flows one link at a time from the highest level to the lowest level.

Span of Control (also called the span of management)—there is a limit to the number of employees a manager can effectively supervise.

Unity of Command—No employee should report to more than one immediate superior (boss).

Exception Principle (also called management by exception)—managers should concentrate their efforts on matters that deviate significantly from normal and let subordinates handle routine matters.

Graicunas' Theorem (also called the principle of increasing organizational relationships)—states that as you add people to an organization arithmetically (1, 2, 3, etc.) the number of organizational relationships increase geometrically (at a much faster rate). Also explained as: the complexities of managing increase geometrically as the number of subordinates increase arithmetically. (Developed by V. A. Graicunas.)

FIGURE 8-2: TRADITIONAL PRINCIPLES OF ORGANIZATION

The organization structure refers to clearly established lines of authority, responsibility, accountability and communication that logically relate work functions to each other. A sound organization structure is a system that balances functional activities and creates consistent relationships between work groups. The goal of organization structure is to achieve an end result in the most efficient, effective manner.

Span of management (sometimes called span of control) defines the number of employees a manager can effectively supervise. There is no set number, but the number for any given management situation depends on four factors: (1) the talent of the manager; (2) the type of work being performed by subordinates; (3) the worker's skill at the job, educational level, background and work ethic; and (4) physical factors in the work area. The importance of this concept is that the span of management directly affects the organization structure. A wide span of management creates a flat organization structure; a short span, a tall structure. The shape of the organization structure affects human and departmental interrelationships and organizational complexity.

Max Weber, a German sociologist, was a major contributor to classical organization theory. Weber was a social theorist who developed the bureaucratic model of organizations. Unlike his contemporaries Taylor and Fayol, Weber dealt secondarily with applied management problems even though he is regarded today as a major contributor to management theory. Weber viewed the bureaucratic form of organization as logical, rational and efficient. His model of organization design is based on a formal and legitimate system of authority with distinct divisions of labor; expert personnel to fill each job; clear-cut rules and procedures to follow when performing tasks; and a formal hierarchy of positions from the top to the bottom in an organization.[5] Educational institutions as well as various levels of government in the U.S. are examples of bureaucracies.

While bureaucracies are criticized today as inefficient and self-serving, Weber's ideas were revolutionary in his time and presented organizations a model to follow if they wished to improve performance and create efficiency of effort. Weber's work, along with that of the pioneers mentioned, is a starting point in studying and understanding organization design.

Neoclassical theory. The neoclassical theory of organization is an effort to offset some of the shortcomings of the classical theory by expanding into the behavioral sciences. The underlying elements of classical organization theory are modified by emphasis on the importance of individual behavior and the impact of the informal organization which operates within the framework of the formal organization. Earlier contributors to this approach were Henry L. Gantt and Lillian Gilbreth. Most researchers agree, however, that the Hawthorne Studies led to the evolvement of the neoclassical school.[6]

The neoclassical approach focuses on problems such as employee monotony, fatigue, isolation and insignificance (which results from specialization of work). Neoclassical theory stresses subjects such as motivation, coordination and leadership as responsibilities of managers.

While classical organization theory implies perfection from assignment of duties (delegation), communication, control and other managerial and employee functions, the neoclassical school identifies human frailties and expects some errors in managerial judgment. Neoclassical theory views classical theory as sound but impossible to apply perfectly because of the human element. Neoclassicists have devised tools, techniques and additional theory to overcome the problems which result from delegation of duties; interpersonal conflicts between workers and between managers and nonmanagers; employees' job frustration and boredom; motivation of employees and many other troublesome areas.

Neoclassicists also pay special attention to the informal organization. *The informal organization is an indigenous grouping of employees in the work place.* Informal organizations, which will not show up on an organization chart, are created around work locations, around similar work being performed, by common interests of the employees (the company softball team), or by special problems or issues affecting a group of employees (such as a group of older employees who believe they are being discriminated against in pay increases).

Management's recognition of the informal organization and accepting it as an important part of the formal organization are part of neoclassical theory. Each informal organization has its own leaders, communication system (grapevine) and standards.

The formal and informal organizations are distinct entities which may or may not work well together. Collectively, the two organizations along with individuals, jobs, the work environment and more make up the social system which can be studied as a whole.

Modern organization theory. The uniqueness of this theory is that it studies the organization as a system. Modern organization theory goes beyond classical and neoclassical approaches and treats the organization as a system of interdependent variables.

According to William G. Scott, the key questions to ask are these:

1. What are the strategic parts of the system?

2. What is the nature of their mutual dependency?

3. What are the main processes in the system which link parts together and facilitate their adjustment to each other?

4. What are the goals sought by systems?[7]

While these are important questions to answer, the student should realize that there is no unified body of thought. Researchers stress and analyze different segments of the system depending on their special interests.

Modern theorists consider the organization to be a system composed of the following strategic parts: the individual; the formal structure; the informal organization; status and role patterns; and the physical environment of work. All together these parts compose the organizational system.

Factors Affecting Organization Structure and Design

Traditionally the *formal organization is described as a group of people working together toward common objectives with a clearly defined hierarchy* (i.e., clear lines of authority, responsibility, accountability and communication).

But, the question arises: How do you group people and develop a sound hierarchy?

To design a sound organization structure, managers must consider the organization strategy, the current environment, the dynamics of the industry and other variables before determining the appropriate organization structure. Stephen P. Robbins states that "organization design is concerned with constructing and changing an organization's structure to achieve the organization's goals."[8] Having a mission statement which clarifies organizational goals is an important first step in organization design.

Sometimes managers use a contingency approach when structuring an organization. This approach is based on the assumption there is no one best way to design and structure an organization. The situation or the variables affecting the efficient operation of an organization as it attempts to achieve its objectives change periodically; thus, the structure may need to change also. The contingency approach requires management to stay abreast of "changes" to determine if the existing structure remains appropriate.

A traditional second step when designing an organization structure involves *departmentation*. Nearly every organization structure is based on the idea of departmentation or grouping jobs into related work units. Related work units may be grouped according to function, product, service, location, customer or some other criteria.

Functional Departmentation. This is the most basic form of structuring an organization. The word *function* here refers to an activity like sales, production or finance. Employees who do the same or similar jobs are brought together in one department. A manager heads each functional department and is responsible for achieving departmental goals. Often small organizations are structured functionally, and every employee is considered a line employee. Staff employees do not appear until the organization grows larger.

There are four major advantages of organizing by functional departments: Each employee can be a specialist or expert in his or her job; the manager's tasks are more narrow and limited to more specific duties and responsibilities; the job of coordinating work and talents is relatively easy; and the success or failure of a department's efforts can be measured more precisely. An example of structuring an organization by functions in intercollegiate athletics can be seen in Figure 8-3.

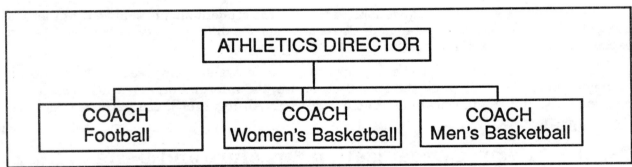

FIGURE 8-3: SIMPLIFIED FUNCTIONAL DEPARTMENTATION
            ORGANIZATION STRUCTURE

Product Departmentation. In large organizations with a diverse product line most departments are structured around major products or products of a similar nature. This includes large service organizations as well. Employees identify with their departmental product line such as General Motors employees who work in the Pontiac Division. Within the product departments, managers are assigned to functional duties and pursue the objectives of that department. Often the structuring of an organization by products provides the basis for identifying the revenue generating areas, usually called profit centers. Being a manager of a profit center provides an unusual opportunity for managers to demonstrate managerial competency (or incompetency). Organizing by product often is the forerunner of decentralizing authority, responsibility, decision making and control in management The ultimate authority and responsibility, however, never leaves top management.

The four major advantages of organizing by product departmentation are the relative ease of coordinating all of the work and activity associated with the isolated product or product line; the promptness in decision-making associated with that product area; the work and results achieved by product departments are more visible and readily available for objective evaluation; and product managers have the opportunity to demonstrate their functional skills.

The inherent weakness in product departmentation is that managers can become so engrossed in the success of their part of the organization that department goals and needs may take precedent over what is good for the organization as a whole. In addition, organizing by product or product line leads to the creation of multiple line specialists since each department must have its own specialists. The result is an increase in overall operating costs. Figure 8-4 shows a typical product departmentation organization structure.

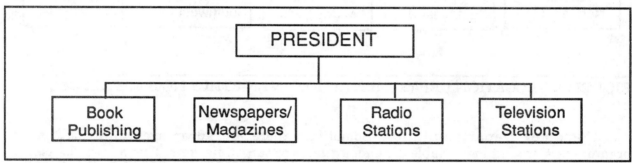

FIGURE 8-4: PRODUCT DEPARTMENTATION OF A LARGE
COMMUNICATIONS COMPANY

Location Departmentation. Some large multiunit organizations tend to structure their departments, divisions or plants around the locations they serve. These locations may be small geographic areas such as the northwest side of a city, or they may be continents such as Europe, Australia or North America. Usually these sub-organizations have corporate line support from the home office but function independently on a daily basis. Much like product departmentation, each geographic area can be viewed as a revenue generating part of the whole, and individual managers can be held responsible for the results in their location. Again, there can be some duplication in providing line specialists in each geographic area, but normally this occurs only when distance between markets is large.

The major advantage of organizing by location departmentation is that managers can respond quickly to problems that occur in their geographic area. These managers are nearer the action; control is more assured; and problems can be pinpointed more accurately, leading to quicker resolutions.

Typically in higher education, Alumni Associations or Athletic Booster Clubs would be organized by location departmentation based on regions in the U.S. Organizing fundraising campaigns along geographic lines helps the participants to feel more involved and contributes to the identification with the cause. An example of an alumni fund drive structured by location departmentation is shown in Figure 8-5.

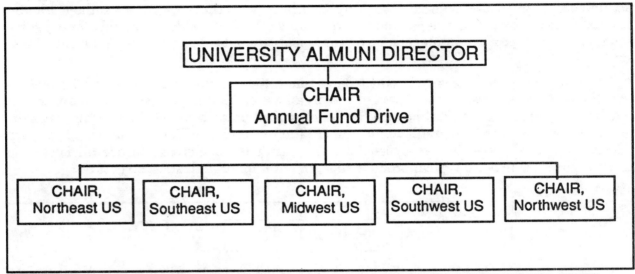

FIGURE 8-5: LOCATION DEPARTMENTATION IN AN ATHLETIC BOOSTER CLUB

Customer Departmentation. Sometimes there are advantages to structuring an organization around identifiable customer groups or target markets. This allows the personnel in that customer area to specialize in meeting the unique needs and demands of that group. In an international sporting goods company, major customers may be separated and identified by the particular sport's equipment they use such as skiers, tennis players, golfers, etc. A manager becomes a specialist in that sport's total equipment line. In a sales campaign for season tickets, a baseball team might identify customers by such factors as local businesses, regional businesses, national corporate clients, repeat buyers, single game ticket buyers, former buyers, etc. In Figure 8-6, see an example of customer departmentation in an intercollgiate atheltic scholarship foundation.

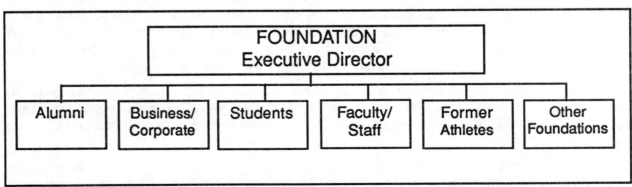

FIGURE 8-6: CUSTOMER DEPARTMENTATION IN AN ATHLETIC SCHOLARSHIP
        FOUNDATION

Other Types of Departmentation. Two other types of departmentation are used occasionally to group jobs in organizations. The first is departmentation by **time**. Many companies operate on work shifts such as airlines; nurses and other staff in a hospital; utility companies that operate some services (such as telephone operators) on a twenty-four hour basis; and manufacturers which operate more than one eight-hour work crew daily. Each shift will have its own personnel, supervisors and organization structure.

A second type of additional departmentation is by **number** or **sequence**. For example, an elementary school may limit the number of children in a single class to twenty; in the army, the number of soldiers in a squad, a company or battalion may be fixed.

Summary Comments. The word **departmentation** has been used repeatedly to denote the grouping of jobs by functions, products, location, customers, time, sequence and numbers. Students should understand also that **departments** may refer to divisions, plants, sections, branches, bureaus, regions or other synonyms. The selected word depends on the growth, size or nature of the organization.

Finally, depending on the size and nature of the organization, departmentation of jobs may be grouped in one area or at one level by product and in another area by function, etc. There can be departmentation mixes within the same organization to gain advantages of specialization and control.

Major Organization Structures

The field of management, especially in the area of organization, is full of jargon. When studying the major forms of organization structure, students may be perplexed to read about so many types. Writers identify major organization structures as line, line and staff, matrix, classical, tall, flat, functional and more. In addition, organizations are called highly centralized or highly decentralized. To students this can become confusing. To clarify this subject, this text will discuss three major types of organization structure: line, line and staff, and matrix. Nearly every type of organization structure is one of these or a variation of one of the three. A fourth major type, committee organization structure, will be discussed in detail in Chapter 9.

The Line Structure. *The line structure is built around activities essential to the attainment of the primary objectives of the organization.* All work of all employees in all departments directly relates to the production, financing and marketing of goods and/or services produced. The goods and/or services produced are designed for a market; and in the case of a profit-seeking business, the output is intended to generate revenues which will cover costs and produce a profit. Profit becomes the primary objective of a business so that it can survive.

Those organizations which do not have profit as the major goal, called nonprofit or not-for-profit organizations, must clearly define primary objectives so that all employees and all customers/clients (who may be supporters, members, users of services, volunteers, etc.) know why the organization exists and what it should achieve.

Every sport organization should have a written statement expressing the primary reason for its existence. Every employee and participants in the organization's activities should be familiar with this statement. Sometimes this is called the mission statement (refer to Figure 6-3 for an example of an intercollegiate athletic program's mission statement). Another example of a mission statement is shown in Figure 8-7; this one for a not-for-profit hospital.

> The mission of our medical center is to contribute to the well being and the quality of life of our community by providing in partnership with our physician practices high value health and wellness services for those whom we serve.

FIGURE 8-7: MISSION STATEMENT OF A MAJOR URBAN MEDICAL CENTER

The line structure is used primarily by small organizations. It is relatively simple to construct with vertical lines connecting the various levels of the organization (see Figure 8-8).

The major advantage of the line structure is the clarity associated with pinpointing authority and responsibility. Decision-making can be quick in response to a problem, and responsibility for results is clear. A major disadvantage is that line managers may not possess all the special skills needed to run an organization. The talent and ability of the line managers are often limited, but they are frequently required to perform many jobs whether qualified to do so or not.

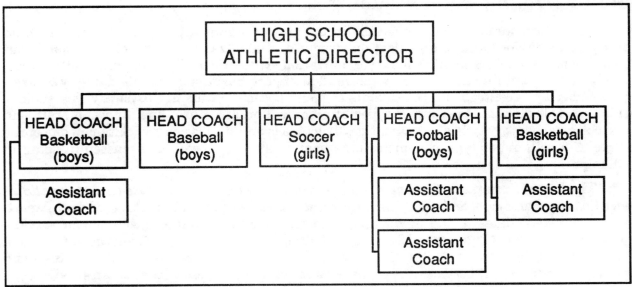

FIGURE 8-8: SIMPLE LINE STRUCTURE ORGANIZATION CHART

The Line and Staff Structure. As organizations grow in size and complexity, staff positions and departments evolve. **Staff functions relate indirectly to the primary purpose of an organization.** Prior to the creation of "staff," line managers or line employees performed the now-called staff activities. Typical staff functions are personnel, industrial relations, research and development, public relations, control activities, and the technical assistance or "how-to" positions. Except in unusual cases, staff personnel have no direct authority over "line" employees. The job of staff personnel is to support line managers by providing assistance, advice, counsel, coordination, specialized knowledge or technical skills. Figure 8-9 shows a line and staff organization chart for intercollegiate athletics at the Community College of Rhode Island which has a two-campus system.

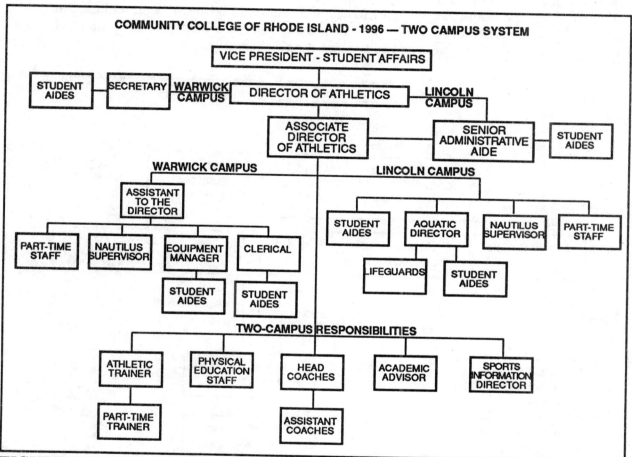

FIGURE 8-9: LINE AND STAFF ORGANIZATION STRUCTURE CHART
Source: Vin Cullen, Director of Athletics, community College of Rhode Island, 1996 (used with permission).

Staff positions are created by higher line managers to enlarge knowledge and skills in specialized areas. Once staff positions are added to line positions, the organization structure becomes line and staff. Most organizations beyond the smallest in size are structured this way.

Functional Staff. A special kind of staff position or department is sometimes created by higher line managers and given **limited line authority.** This is called **functional** or **specialized staff.** Examples of specialized staff are inspectors in quality control, plant maintenance personnel, safety specialists and security personnel. They operate as pure staff (described above); but in special situations, they can exert "limited line authority." An athletic trainer in a sports program is a functional staff person. The athletic trainer working

under the auspices of a physician can tell a coach that a player is not medically fit to participate. Safety and security personnel would have primary authority over an event or athletic
contest at which a fight or riot erupts until order is restored.

    Advantages and problems with staff. The major advantage of the line and staff
organization structure is that of providing specialized support to line managers. Staff personnel free the line managers to concentrate on immediate issues as well as long-run problems. Staff positions allow more flexibility in the organization. Line managers do not have to
become specialists in every area of the organization's operations.

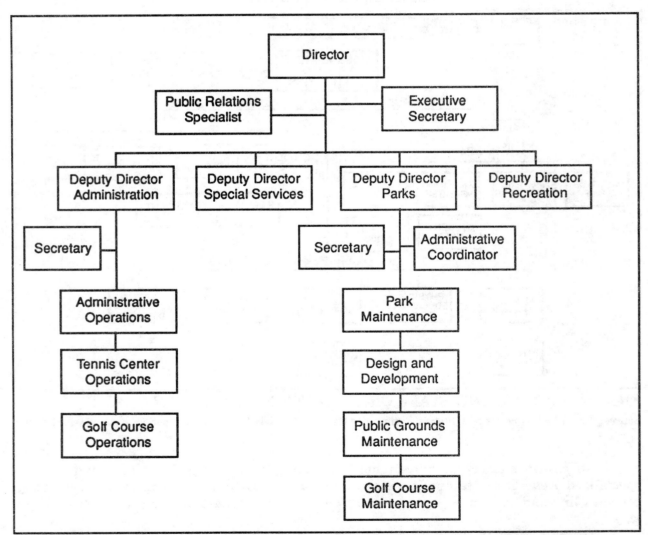

FIGURE 8-10: PARTIAL LINE AND STAFF ORGANIZATION STRUCTURE OF A
COUNTY RECREATION AND PARKS DEPARTMENT

Potential conflict does arise when staff is added to a line organization structure. There is opportunity for contention between line managers and staff managers over who is in charge of what. For example, staff personnel specialists have no authority to hire new employees for a line manager. The job of personnel may be to advertise, interview, test and screen applicants on behalf of line managers, but the line manager interviews and approves the applicant before employment.

Staff personnel make suggestions to line managers as part of their function, and they may become upset if line managers do not accept and follow these suggestions. Being highly specialized then having expert advice ignored can irritate staff personnel. Often staff people are regarded as internal consultants who are sensitive to their area of expertise. If line managers do not understand the staff person's point of view, and the staff person does not fully understand the function of the line manager; trouble will develop.

Figure 8-10 shows another simple line and staff organization structure. In this example, the Public Relations Specialist, all secretaries, and the Administrative Coordinator are staff positions. Two points are important about staff positions or departments in an organization. One, staff is always offset from the line of authority with the staff person or department head reporting directly to a line manager above the staff position. Second is that the staff person or department is located on an organization chart in the area that it serves. The Public Relations Specialist serves the Director and is located below and offset from the line directly under the Director. The Executive Secretary does the same. Each staff person in this example serves administrators and participants under the direction of his or her higher line manager. The position of staff on an organization chart does not reflect its relative importance, but the location of line positions on a chart does reflect power, status and importance.

The Matrix Structure. The matrix organization structure is two directional, based on the mathematical concept of **matrix** (an array of both vertical columns and horizontal rows). Large companies that are involved in multi-projects often structure part of the organization as a matrix.

These are the characteristics of matrix organization:

1. Employees are assigned to work on a project while maintaining entity in a functional department.
2. Employees have accountability to more than one boss.
3. Specialized knowledge and skills are more readily available to assist in project work.
4. Communication is more open to access information.
5. Managers are more flexible and better able to adjust to changes in technology and in the market.

Large companies engaged in several major projects found it difficult to set up a line and staff organization structure for each project. Furthermore, they were duplicating staff skills and not fully utilizing the talents of line employees. Matrix organization evolved primarily at the insistence of government. When projects involved government contracts, the government wanted a means to fix responsibility for progress and performance. The outcome was matrix organization structure.

Several of the characteristics of matrix organization structure have roots in Frederick W. Taylor's functional foremanship organization structure. Functional foremanship created multiple accountability to provide intense specialization to workers on the line.

Matrix organization structure has proved valuable to many companies, but its popularity has waned. The major disadvantages are the violation of the scalar principle, parity principle and unity of command.

The scalar principle is violated because the matrix structure encourages lateral or horizontal communication in addition to or in place of vertical (chain of command) communication. When authority and responsibility is divided between project and functional managers, the parity principle is violated. Anytime an employee reports to more than one supervisor (boss), the unity of command principle is violated; and the matrix structure is based on multiple accountability.

The matrix structure can also create problems between line managers and project managers over the control of employees and resources. Power struggles sometimes arise over the final source of decision-making.

Figure 8-11 shows an example of matrix organization. Note the vertical columns and horizontal rows, multiple accountability, and the identity of functional departments and projects.

Some large companies that have abandoned matrix organization structure have gone toward a decentralized structure of independent units. These units operate much like subsidiaries or profit centers and concentrate on specially assigned projects. This approach eliminates some of the disadvantages of matrix organization structure but often increases operating costs due to duplication of skills and personnel.

Matrix Organization in the Sport World

It would be rare to find an example of matrix organization in the world of sport except in large manufacturing companies that produce a variety of sporting goods and equipment.

Forms of matrix organization do show up, however, in sport programs when a head coach of one sport serves as an assistant coach in another sport. This is a common practice in high schools. The coach also may be a teacher. In effect, the head coach reports to the principal (as a teacher), the athletics director (as a head coach), and the head coach of the other sport (as an assistant coach). This is multiple accountability (several bosses), yet the expertise of the individual is fully used without hiring new personnel.

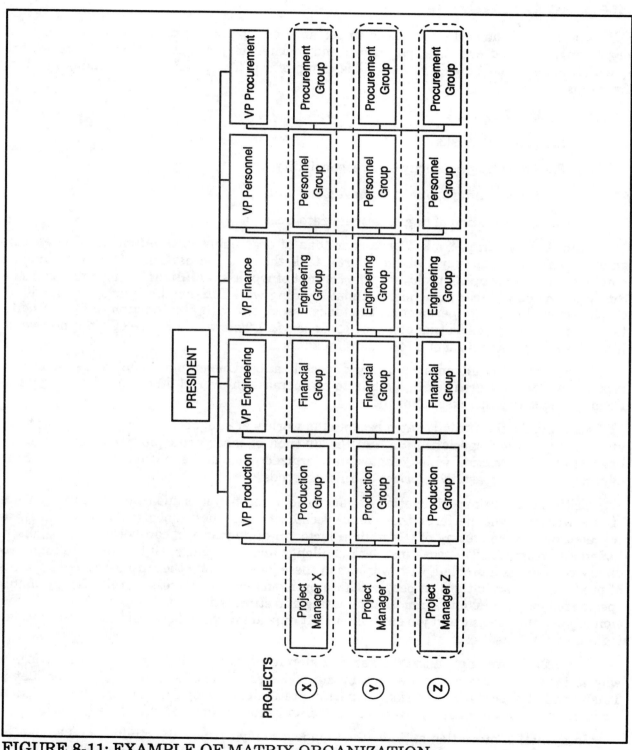

FIGURE 8-11: EXAMPLE OF MATRIX ORGANIZATION

Steps in Organizing

Now that we have discussed the importance of organizing, reviewed some history of organizing, sampled organization theory and learned major organization structures, the question arises: Just how do you organize group effort? The process of organizing involves five steps:

1. Dividing work

2. Grouping tasks

3. Activating authority and responsibility

4. Determining spans of management

5. Coordination of organizational resources

Step 1: Dividing Work. The cornerstone of organizing is the division of work into smaller parts. Smaller parts of the overall task then can be performed by an individual employee or by a group of employees. The concept of **work specialization** is based on Adam Smith's division of labor principle. Without dividing work into smaller parts, an individual employee would have to perform all the tasks associated with any function (all the production, or financing or marketing of a product or service). This would not be efficient nor would it mesh with the definition of a formal organization.

There are many advantages to work specialization. One employee doing the same task repeatedly develops great skill, leading to an increase in overall efficiency. Total organizational productivity increases sharply.

Historically, the United States became the world's greatest economic power through the application of work specialization and the division of labor principle. This concept is the basis of mass production which creates standardized parts and end products, low unit costs of production, and reasonable prices of finished goods.

Criticism of work specialization has surfaced in recent years and centers on the attitude of the workers who perform the same specialized jobs continuously. These workers, as revealed by closer scrutiny of the human factor in organizations, can become bored, dissatisfied and resentful. The work may lack challenge and eventually fail to stimulate high productivity. There is a problem with workers in these jobs thinking they are perceived as "units of production" rather than as people. These problems led to progress in redesigning highly specialized jobs to make them more interesting and stimulating (see Chapter 11 for a discussion of job enlargement and job enrichment). It appears certain, however, that work specialization will not disappear.

Step 2: Grouping Tasks. The second step in organizing is to group jobs in a logical way so that managers can more soundly supervise employees in identifiable departments. This is called *departmentalization*. Departmentation can be by function, product, location, customer and, less frequently, by time, number or sequence (as we have already discussed).

In a small organization an individual manager may oversee all activities and be in complete control of all work effort. As growth occurs, however, it is necessary to appoint managers to supervise the work of parts of the total organization. Called departments in small organizations, they may be divisions, plants, regions, districts or overseas markets in large ones.

Step 3: Activating Authority and Responsibility. After dividing work into smaller parts through the application of the division of labor principle and after grouping tasks in some logical way with a manager assigned to each department, the next step in organizing is to activate the authority and responsibility of each manager.

Authority in management is associated with *power*. Alvin Brown, a pioneer in the study of modern organizations wrote

> That aspect of responsibility which represents its power of performance has been called authority. In common usage, the word is not always given so broad a sense, being often limited to the power exercised by one member of enterprise over another. It is also defined, however, as the right to act officially—the personal power that commands influence, respect, or confidence—so that it is not confined to its exercise toward particular persons. In this sense, as has been said, authority is the exact reciprocal of responsibility. It cannot be less in extent since responsibility without authority would be an empty duty. It cannot be greater in extent, since authority without responsibility would be an empty power.[9]

While there are many interpretations of authority, the *right to act officially* is most often associated with managers. Managers have *formal authority which is a form of power.* This authority or power originates from higher up and is legally passed downward one level at a time. In business individuals have the legal right to incorporate, elect directors, select a president, appoint people as managers, etc. The authority or power of the manager originates from above the position. According to many writers authority is power that has been formalized by the organization.

A second view of the origin of formal authority comes from Chester I. Barnard who advocated the **acceptance theory.**[10] This view holds that the employee, the subordinate or the influencee determines whether the manager has any authority or not. If employees below do not comply with the manager's request, demand, order or directive, the manager has no authority or power.

In American organizations the vast majority of workers accept the legitimacy of authority which a manager has and they willingly comply with the manager's directions. In practice, however, there are two tests to determine if a manager has any real authority:

> First, is the manager being accepted from below? That is, are the employees responding positively to the directions and orders delegated to them by the manager? (This is the Acceptance Theory.)

> Second, is the manager being supported from above. A manager has no authority whatsoever if the boss above does not back him or her. (This is the Authority Theory—source of power from the top down.)

Responsibility accompanies authority. There is no need to delegate authority unless there is a job to do, an obligation to meet, and you wish to accomplish more work by assigning part of it to subordinate employees. *Responsibility is an acceptance of accountability for doing a particular job.* In the case of the manager, the job is to achieve desired goals and objectives working with and through employees and other resources.

Delegating is the assignment of authority and responsibility to a person or group of people at the next lower level in the organization. The Chair of a committee may appoint a subcommittee and assign part of the overall committee's work to it. A manager may tell an employee what to do, when to do it, and why the work is important. In each of these cases, there is an assignment of authority and responsibility from one management level to the next lower level to do specific jobs. This is *delegating*.

In management, the process of delegating involves these four steps:

1. **Assign responsibility.** A person or group is told exactly what to do verbally or in writing or both.

2. **Assign authority.** A person or group is given the power needed to get the job done.

3. **Assign a time standard.** A person or group is told exactly when the job or task is to be completed.

4. **Assign accountability.** A person or group must accept the assignment and report to the manager above (the delegator) on progress and problems.

Delegation of authority and responsibility flows downward in a formal organization. Some writers argue that responsibility cannot be delegated. This view is based on the concept that ultimate responsibility for results below is never relinquished by managers at the higher level. This is true! It is also true, however, that any manager or employee who has a job to perform has responsibility for that job. The question arises: Where did the employee get that responsibility? And the answer is from someone at the level above him or her. The responsibility for accomplishing the assignment was delegated downward along with the authority needed to do the job. Employees at one level work on behalf of bosses above them. Both have responsibility for the work assigned. But the employee's responsibility is limited to specific tasks and jobs, while the boss' responsibility encompasses many tasks assigned to various different employees. The boss still retains the ultimate responsibility that the work delegated to employees will be done properly and on schedule.

Step 4.: Determining Spans of Management. In the logical sequence of developing an organization which will generate efficient group effort and reach common objectives, we have divided the work into smaller parts, departmentalized tasks, and activated authority and responsibility. Now, we must discuss how many employees should be assigned to individual managers.

The number of employees reporting to a single manager is called the span of management. Because the number also affects supervisory effectiveness, the question of control also arises. The ideal number of employees a manager can effectively supervise and control has been debated for many years.

It is important to recognize that if a manager supervises too few employees, inefficiency can be the result. If the manager supervises too many employees, inefficiency and ineffectiveness can result due to the loss of control.

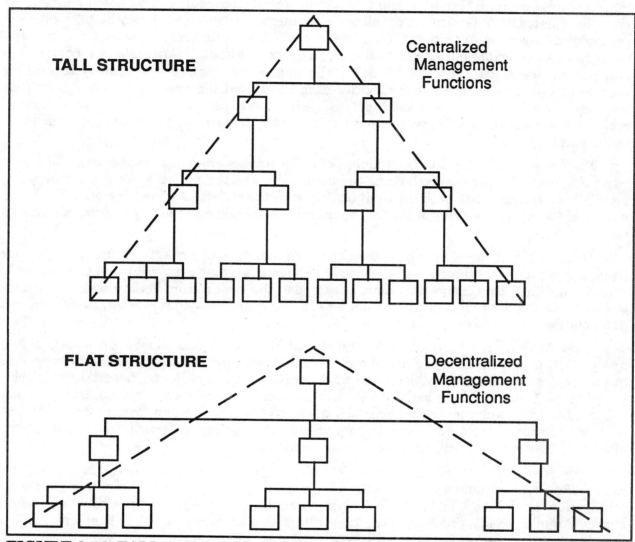

FIGURE 8-12: TALL AND FLAT ORGANIZATION STRUCTURE
SHOWING DIFFERENT SPANS OF MANAGEMENT

Determining the span of management directly affects the shape of the organization structure. If there is a wide span of management, the structure will be flat with fewer levels of management. Also, the organization will most likely have decentralized its decision-making, authority, responsibility and control. If the span of management is narrow, the organization structure will be more vertical or tall. This indicates more levels of management and more centralization of management functions. See Figure 8-12 for a graphic representation of these two extremes.

General Ian Hamilton of the British Army (post-World War I), Lyndall F. Urwick and V. A. Graicunas (both in the 1930s) were management pioneers who researched the span of management question. Hamilton and Urwick suggested an executive span should not exceed six subordinates. V. A. Graicunas developed a mathematically sound theory in 1933 which is pertinent to this question today. Called *Graicunas' Theorem, it says as you add employees to an organization arithmetically (1 + 1 + 1), the organizational relationships increase at a much faster (geometric) rate (4, 16, 64).*[11] The impact for managers is that by increasing employees one at a time, the complexities of management increase at a much faster rate because of the increase in relationships. Interactions between individuals, between managers and individuals, and between groups of subordinates are all expanded for each additional employee added.

The question of a limit to the number of subordinates any one manager can effectively supervise remains unanswered. Some organizations, like the military, have a set number; most other organizations base the limit on four significant factors. These factors involve the nature of the work, the skills of the manager and the worker, and the physical work environment.

The exact number of subordinates any given manager can effectively supervise is not fixed, but it should be apparent that there is a theoretical limit even if it cannot be precisely calculated. When this theoretical limit is exceeded the result is ineffectiveness. The symptoms are results not realized, frustration for the managers, wasted resources, loss of control, and poor overall performance by employees.

Step 5: Coordination of Organizational Resources. The last step in organizing group effort is coordinating the use of resources so that organizational objectives can be met in the most efficient way possible. When work is divided into smaller parts and grouped logically (Steps 1 and 2), these separate work components must be coordinated. Coordination refers to the blending, matching or synchronizing of individual and group effort. Without coordination individuals and departments would act independently with no regard for the effort of others or for overall organizational objectives.

Coordination is needed when there is a high degree of interdependence among departments. If one department's work directly affects another's in a sequential manner, good communication is the key to effective coordination. Providing knowledge about schedules, expected quality, costs, problems, etc., to each interdependent department is essential. This is called *sequential interdependence.*

Another type of departmental interdependence which requires coordination occurs when one department works directly with another department. This is called *parallel interdependence.* An example is the food services unit of a hospital which must coordinate patients' meals with doctors instructions. Each must keep the other informed and follow directions and procedures to coordinate and control departmental activities (or the safety and well-being of patients suffers).

The least amount of required coordination occurs when departments do not work directly with each other and do not depend on the work of each other. These departments are *autonomous* in their efforts to achieve organizational goals, but the lack of productivity and efficiency within each unit can affect the well-being of other departments.

Coordination is best achieved when all managers and all employees in departments understand the overall objectives, the departmental objectives, their own objectives, the importance of their work, the time schedules, the organizational guidelines (rules, procedures and policies) influencing their actions, and when all receive adequate information to support their work efforts.

Good communication is essential to effective coordination and sound organization.

Organization Charts

Organization charts are useful to most organizations because they present a picture of the formal organization structure and show the following:

1. Positions of responsibility (who is in charge of what)

2. Lines of authority (who has the power to do what)

3. Superior-subordinate relationships (levels of management)

4. Formal communication channels

5. Lines of accountability (reportability)

6. Grouping of related work activities

There are many ways to construct an organization chart which shows the above information, but not one ideal way. Location of positions and functions on a chart may vary firm to firm because of the relative importance attached to work activities and because of such factors as a shortage of resources including personnel. Despite their shortcomings, organization charts are valuable if they are *correctly drawn, made visible and kept current.*

Steps in construction of organization charts are these:

1. Clearly define the primary objective(s) of the organization.

2. List all jobs by title and function.

3. Identify whether each job is "line" or "staff."

4. Group jobs with similar work activity together.

5. Logically draw the chart.

Experience and common sense play an important role in construction of organization charts. Also, knowing the difference between line and staff activities and understanding where to locate staff positions or departments on the chart make a significant difference.

Summary

Organizing is a managerial effort to assign work and allocate resources; then arrange work and resources in an orderly way so that group effort generates the desired end result efficiently.

Organizing is a primary function of management but is not usually a separate managerial act. Organizing may be part of planning or mixed with other management functions.

Organizing can be viewed as a managerial effort to bring order to the work place and generate efficiency of effort.

Organizing is important in management because of the following benefits: It generates effective group action; it synergizes resources; it pinpoints individual responsibility; and it facilitates the implementing and control functions.

Recognition of the organizing function has a long history. Organization structure existed in prehistoric and ancient civilizations which had superior-subordinate relationships, centers of authority, and duties delegated to subordinates.

Organization theory is identified as **classical, neoclassical** and **modern**. None of the theories are complete nor totally accepted by researchers in management. The theoretical approaches do provide students some insight into the evolutionary development of management thought about organizing.

Traditionally the formal organization is described as a group of people working together toward common objectives with a clearly defined hierarchy (lines of authority, responsibility, accountability and communication). A sound hierarchy results when the organization's departments are structured into efficient and effective work groups or units. Departmental work groups can be categorized by function, product, location, customer, time, number and/or sequence.

The major types of organization structure are line, line and staff, matrix and committees (see Chapter 9). Nearly all small organizations are line structured. Large organizations tend to be structured line and staff, and very large, multi-project organizations may have some form of matrix structure as part of the formal organization.

Delegating is a major activity of a manager. The process of delegating involves four steps: Assign responsibility, assign authority to accompany responsibility, assign a time standard, and assign accountability.

The steps in organizing group effort are the following:

1. Dividing work into smaller parts based on the concept of work specialization

2. Grouping tasks in a logical way so that managers can more soundly supervise employees in identifiable departments, called departmentalizing

3. Activating authority and responsibility by delegating both downward

4. Determining spans of management (the number of employees which should report to a single manager) without losing any efficiency and effectiveness of effort

5. The coordination of organization resources between departments that have a high degree of interdependence.

Organization charts are useful to most organizations because they present a visual image of the formal organization showing lines of authority, responsibility, accountability and communication.

Review Questions

1. Why is organizing so important to the managerial functions of planning and implementing?

2. Can you name the important managerial benefits of organizing? Which of the benefits do you consider most important?

3. Name and briefly explain the traditional principles of organization mentioned in this chapter.

4. What subject of interest did Adam Smith, Thomas Jefferson and Eli Whitney have in common? Explain.

5. Is the classical theory of organization still in vogue? Discuss completely.

6. What is the contribution of Max Weber to organization design?

7. Matrix organization is widely used in multi-project organizations. What are the advantages and disadvantages of this form of organization?

8. How do you go about organizing group effort? Name and explain each step.

9. Name the benefits of having an organization chart to an employee in that organization.

Assignments for Personal Development

1. Visit any kind of sport organization and ask a manager to list the ten most common daily problems that he or she has to handle. Identify which of the ten problems occurs because of defects or weaknesses in the existing organizational structure.

2. Some major athletic programs reorganize every four or five years. Why? Present the reasons you find or think of and exchange points of view in a class discussion.

Incident

DISGRUNTLED EMPLOYEES

Ms. Pam Petite had just returned from lunch with several of her colleagues. The luncheon was a celebration of her first year of employment with a large public relations firm. Her division concentrated on the promotion of major sporting events, exhibitions and a major bowl game annually played around January 1.

She was disgusted with the conversation around the lunch table. Instead of talking about her and her experiences during this past year on the job, her colleagues spent most of the time complaining about the management of the organization. Everyone at the luncheon had a few choice complaints!

Pam decided to write down the complaints she could remember:

- Communication misunderstandings
- Ineffective delegation of work assignments
- Jurisdictional disputes over work responsibilities
- Conflicts between line and staff personnel
- Bosses failing to support employees when problems arise
- Employees bypassing their managers
- Failure of employees to report everything that happens to their bosses
- "Fuzzy" job descriptions
- Lack of excitement in the workplace.

The more Pam thought about the complaints, the more she realized that she was part of a badly organized organization which is managed by some less than competent managers.

Questions:

1. Is there anything Pam Petite can do to help the public relations firm become better organized?

2. Assuming Pam Petite was appointed to an employee committee to come up with recommendations for improving the organization—what should she recommend? (List five things as a start.)

Glossary of Key Terms

Bureaucratic Model: An organizational design developed by Max Weber that created a hierarchical structure; clear lines of authority from top to bottom; expert workers; distinct divisions of labor; and clear rules and procedures for workers to follow when performing their tasks.

Contingency Approach: Sometimes used in organizing when there is not one best way to design and structure an organization. Depends on the situation and the variables affecting organizational activity.

Delegating: The assignment of authority and responsibility to a person or group of people at the next lower level in the organization.

Division of Labor: Breaking work down into basic components and emphasizing specialization of effort.

Exception Principle: (Also called management by exception) The concept that managers should concentrate their efforts on matters that deviate significantly from normal and let subordinates handle routine matters.

Flat Organization Structure: An organization that is horizontal or decentralized with respect to authority, responsibility, decision-making and control.

Formal Organization: A group of people working together toward common objectives with a clearly defined hierarchy.

Functional Foremanship: An organization structure originated by F. W. Taylor that breaks the job of a foreman down into eight jobs with each of eight foremen having responsibility for one part of each employee's work.

Functional Staff: (Also called specialized staff) A type of staff position created by higher line management and given limited line authority.

Graicunas's Theorem: (Also called the principle of increasing organizational relationships) A premise that as you add people to an organization arithmetically (1, 2, 3, etc.), the number of organizational relationships increases geometrically (at the faster rate of 4, 16, 64, etc.) Also explained as the complexities of managing increase geometrically as the number of subordinates increases arithmetically. An actual mathematical formula developed by V. A. Graicunas.

Line and Staff Structure: An organization structure similar to the line structure but with "staff" positions or departments added to provide support to line managers.

Line Function: Activities that relate directly to the attainment of the organization's primary objective(s).

Line Structure: Organization structure built around activities essential to the attainment of the primary objectives of the organization.

Matrix Structure: An organization structure that is two directional, based on the mathematical concept of matrix.

Mission Statement: A written statement expressing the primary reason for the existence of an organization.

Organization Chart: A visual depiction of the formal organization which shows the lines of authority, responsibility, accountability and communication.

Organizing: The managerial effort to assign work and allocate resources; then, arrange the work and resources in such an orderly way that a group's effort generates the desired end result in the most efficient manner possible.

Parity Principle: Authority and responsibility must be equal or coincide.

Scalar Principle: Authority in the formal organization flows one link at a time from the highest level to the lowest level.

Span of Management (Control): There is a limit to the number of employees a manager can effectively supervise.

Staff Functions: Activities that relate indirectly to the attainment of the primary objectives of the organization.

Tall Organization Structure: An organization that is vertical or highly centralized with respect to authority, responsibility, decision-making and control.

Unity of Command: No employee should report to more than one immediate supervisor (boss).

Practical Concepts in Management

The Difference Between Line and Staff Functions

New managers sometimes have difficulty distinguishing "line" from "staff" activities. The distinction is important because it affects the flow of authority, responsibility, accountability and communication in the organization.

Line activities are those which are related **directly** to the attainment of the primary objectives of the organizaiton. For example, in a business firm, sales, production and finance are essential line functions. The business would not exist without these activities, and all relate directly to the profit and survival objectives. Employees in these departments are "line" employees.

Staff activities and staff positions are an outgrowth of needs of "line" managers. Whenever a line manager needs help because of a shortage of time, lack of specialized knowledge, absence of technical expertise, or desire for counseling or coordination assistance, "staff" positions are created under that line manager to fill the need. These staff positions will report only to the line manager which they serve. Pure "staff" personnel have no direct authority over line employes. They may act on behalf of a line manager, if instructed to do so, but they have no authority of their own. They contribute to the organization's reaching its objectives, but do so **indirectly**.

There are instances when "specialized staff" employees are given limited line authority. The conditions are usually a critical problem arising in their area of expertise, and they are given authority to act and correct the situation in place of the appropriate line manager. Such examples as security personnel handling serious theft problems or quality control specialists correcting a product defect come to mind. These cases are not too common, and the line authority given staff specialists is limited and only lasts until the crisis is over.

The factor to learn and remember is the limit of "staff" functions. Do not use "staff" employees improperly, and see that "staff" personnel do not usurp any line authority (maybe yours).

The Organization Chart

Not every formal organization has an organization chart. The chart is a picture of the formal organization and provides a new manager much information.

If the chart is correctly drawn and current, it will show your position and the relationship of your job to every other job. Additionally, it shows your scope of authority and responsibility and your line of accountability to the position and person above you. The formal communication system follows the lines on the organization chart.

If names of people holding the various jobs are put on the chart, you have a way of identifying who does what in the organization. If positions are open, the chart will show this. You can also visualize your route of promotion on the chart.

All in all, an accurately drawn chart made available to all employees provides much information about the jobs, the interrelationships of people and work, the communication system, and who has authority and reponsibility over what.

Information such as that provided by an accurate organization chart is invaluable to a new manager. Learn to understand the organization chart of your organization and develop one for your area of responsibility. It will give recognition to your employees, providing them with a feeling of importance, and it will be useful in showing them how important they are to the organization as a whole.

References and Chapter Notes:

[1] Adolf Erman, *Life in Ancient Egypt*, trans. from the German by Helen M. Tirard (London: MacMillan and Company, 1894), p. 492, as quoted in Claude S. George, Jr., *The History of Management Thought* (Englewood Cliffs, NJ: Prentice-Hall, Inc., 1968), p. 5.

[2] Adam Smith, *An Inquiry into the Nature and Cause of the Wealth of Nations* (London: A. Strahan and T. Cadell, 1793), Vol. 1, pp. 7-8.

[3] James D. Mooney and Alan C. Reiley, *Onward Industry* (New York: Harper and Brothers, 1931).

[4] Many of the points and ideas presented are drawn from William G. Scott, "Organization Theory: An Overview and an Appraisal," *Journal of the Academy of Management*, Vol. 4, No. 1, April, 1961, pp. 7-26.

[5] Max Weber, *Theory of Social and Economic Organizations*, trans. by T. Parsons (New York: Free Press, 1947).

[6] For review see F. J. Roethlisberger and William J. Dickson, *Management and the Worker* (Cambridge: Harvard University Press, 1939).

[7] Scott, "Organization Theory," pp. 7-26.

[8] Stephen P. Robbins, *Organization Theory, Structure, Design and Applications* (Englewood Cliffs, NJ: Prentice-Hall, Inc., 1990), p. 6.

[9] Alvin Brown, *Organization of Industry* (Englewood Cliffs, NJ: Prentice-Hall, Inc., 1947), p. 61.

[10] Chester I. Barnard, *The Functions of an Executive* (Cambridge: Harvard University Press, 1938).

[11] V. A. Graicunas, "Relationships in Organizations," *Bulletin of the International Management Institute*, March 7, 1933, pp. 39-42.

CHAPTER 9

ORGANIZING WORK EFFORT OF INDIVIDUALS AND GROUPS

After studying this chapter, **you will know:**

- What job design is

- Factors that affect job design

- Job design methods

- How to implement job design

- The types of groups to manage

- The value of work groups to the organization

- About task forces and special groups

- Steps to make committees more effective

- The importance of informal groups that have norms, cohesiveness and conformity

Introduction

The implementation of plans and programs through individuals and groups is the focus of this chapter. Chapter 8 presented organization structure, principles and theory. This organization structure provides the framework for all activities of individuals and groups as they strive to achieve organizational objectives.

To create efficiency of effort a firm must have a sound organization structure with individual employees and groups in jobs that are meaningful and rewarding to them and to the organization. The managerial effort that addresses this goal is called job design.

Formal and informal groups are also discussed in this chapter. Managers must understand the importance of groups and know how to manage them effectively. Groups which have special management significance are task forces and committees.

In sport management, the subjects presented in this chapter have special significance. Players' associations (unions) in professional sports have player representatives who, as a committee, bargain and negotiate with a committee of owners to finalize agreements. Manufacturers of sporting goods equipment are concerned with job design and employee satisfaction which affects efficiency and productivity. Directors of intercollegiate athletics programs often recommend the formation of task forces to pursue objectives such as raising capital for facility expansion. Athletics directors also work with and report to faculty athletic committees and to trustees of athletic associations. In addition, every type of organization in the sports world has informal groups within the formal organization which should be identified and understood. Every subject in this chapter is of importance to future managers in the sport industry.

Organizing Jobs

American businesses, governmental agencies and other nonprofit organizations have been startled in recent years by an apparent lag in worker productivity, reduced efficiency of output, and increased foreign competition. Many industries, formerly dominated by American manufacturers, have been overwhelmed by foreign competitors. The nature of the American economy has changed along with the characteristics of American employees. Today, there is a renewed interest among American managers in the individual employee and the specific job he or she performs. This interest is justified by the premise that the more satisfied an employee is on the job, the more positively that employee will respond. The end result will be greater productivity and improvement in the efficiency of output.

Some management experts have suggested that waste in time, effort and monies in the typical business organization might reach as high as twenty (20) percent. In the typical nonprofit organization, it has been suggested that this figure might be as high as thirty (30) percent (in government agencies, large educational institutions and certain social agencies). There is no doubt that most organizations could improve performance and generate greater efficiency if management approached the task in a more professional way.

The beginning point for improving overall organizational effort is the design of individual jobs.

Job design is the process of specifying the tasks to be performed; the work methods to be used in performance; and the relationship of that job to other jobs in the organization for the purpose of improving the quality and quantity of work.

There are five phases of job design:

1. Specifying individual job tasks.

2. Identifying the work methods of performing each task.

3. Combining individual tasks into specific jobs.

4. Assigning specific jobs to qualified employees.

5. Coordinating all work activity to achieve efficiency of effort.

Current interest in job design stems from work specialization. Historically, the United States became a great economic power because of the principle of division of labor (work specialization) as advocated by Adam Smith and Thomas Jefferson and applied by Eli Whitney. The result of division of labor was mass production of standardized products at low unit costs. Mass production drastically improved the standard of living of workers in this country; however, after nearly one hundred years of benefits from its application, American employees, managers, organized labor and researchers now question the continued value of work specialization in relation to greater productivity and increased efficiency.

A common view of repetitive work is that it is dull and dehumanizing with the end result of alienating the individual employee from the workplace. Thus, there is new interest in job design for the purpose of improving the quantity and quality of work while providing greater job satisfaction to the employee. Many approaches to job design are available to managers. Nearly all these approaches are aimed at reducing the need for job specialization.

Factors Affecting Job Design

Job design is a product of many factors. The greatest impact on structuring any job comes from job depth and job scope, the type of available employees, economic restrictions, union limitations, and the management philosophy of the organization.

Job Depth and Job Scope. Before designing or redesigning a job, a manager should determine how specialized the job is or should be. Determining the **job depth** and **job scope** is one approach. **Job depth** refers to the individual employee's flexibility to control his or her work performance. If the job must be performed in a set sequential fashion, then job depth is low. If the employee has the flexibility to determine the order of work and the work pace and make many decisions affecting job performance, then job depth is high. Obviously, if job depth is high, there is less specialization of work.

Job scope refers to how specialized and narrow the work activity is. If an employee concentrates on doing a single task repeatedly, job scope is low. If the employee's job involves doing five or ten different tasks, job scope is broader no matter now much repetition there is.

In collegiate athletics, the job of sports information director has high job depth and high job scope. Work is not performed in a sequential fashion and the SID is able to control his or her work activities in light of the demands of the job. On the other hand, an accounting employee in the business office of a collegiate athletic program has relatively low job depth and job scope. Work activities are prescribed in a specific manner, and the employee has little autonomy or control over the work performed.

Job specialization varies inversely with the degree of job depth and job scope. Low job depth and low job scope produce the most specialized job. As job depth becomes higher and job scope broadens, specialization decreases. Figure 9-1 illustrates the characteristics of high and low job depth and scope.

Types of Employees. The availability of labor is a major factor in designing jobs. If an organization is located in a large city, the labor pool will usually include many potential employees who can be trained to operate machinery or perform job duties with a minimum of supervision. Such employees can perform high quality work with less specialization of tasks. Where the available labor force is less skilled or the supply more limited, jobs may need to be designed with a high degree of specialization and more repetition of limited tasks. Of concern to management in both these cases is the degree of supervision required which is a consequence of job design.

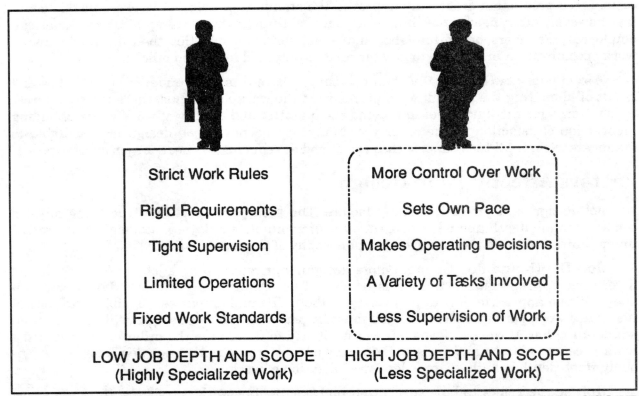

LOW JOB DEPTH AND SCOPE	HIGH JOB DEPTH AND SCOPE
Strict Work Rules	More Control Over Work
Rigid Requirements	Sets Own Pace
Tight Supervision	Makes Operating Decisions
Limited Operations	A Variety of Tasks Involved
Fixed Work Standards	Less Supervision of Work
LOW JOB DEPTH AND SCOPE (Highly Specialized Work)	**HIGH JOB DEPTH AND SCOPE** (Less Specialized Work)

FIGURE 9-1: CHARACTERISTICS OF HIGH AND LOW JOB DEPTH AND SCOPE

Economic Restrictions. Resources available to a manager, both for personnel as well as equipment and facilities, may dictate job design. Restricted budgets and space limitation directly affect the flexibility of a manager in designing jobs. A manager's intentions may be idealistic, but a lack of funding to initiate change can limit the design of a job. Further, if facilities and equipment are old and nearly obsolete, job design can be severely restricted.

Union Limitations. Union philosophy often conflicts with management's thinking about job design. If the union-management contract specifies work standards which in turn set pay rates, the option for redesign of jobs will be limited. In recent years, however, many unions have cooperated with management in redesigning jobs because of competitive pressure and fears that more jobs would be lost without such cooperation. Usually if unions are assured of job security and no decrease in wage rates, they will cooperate in the redesign of jobs, and in some cases encourage the effort.

Organization Philosophy. Managerial philosophies vary among organizations. But, in organizations where managers view employee job satisfaction as a major priority and where the philosophy includes genuine concern for the individual employee, job design is directly affected. Most managers who hold these views believe that job satisfaction leads to greater productivity, less absenteeism, little turnover, and overall higher efficiency. While results such as these have occurred in many organizations, some researchers see a different cause-and-effect relationship. March and Simon conclude that high job satisfaction does not necessarily stimulate productivity. They state that motivation to produce "stems from a present or anticipated state of discontent and a perception of a direct connection between individual production and a new state of satisfaction."[1]

Fortunately most people who are employed by organizations are individuals who desire and have chosen to work in that industry. This is especially true of most employees in the sports industry. Higher level managers already have employees who view the work and industry in a positive light. This is a plus for managers who have as part of their philosophy the objective of creating job-satisfied employees. On the contrary, poor managerial practices can quickly change an employee's positive attitude into one that is negative which will eventually be reflected in marginal performance.

Job Design Methods

Managers may use any of several job design methods. The specific method chosen will be influenced by all the factors affecting job design and how the manager weights them in his or her deliberation. Some of the more widely used job design methods are time and motion analysis, job rotation, job enlargement, the sociotechnical approach, and job enrichment.

Time and Motion Analysis. This method of designing jobs, also called **job engineering,** originated with the scientific management movement pioneered by Frederick W. Taylor and Frank Gilbreth (see Chapter 1). Time studies are made of repetitive work cycles, and motion analysis is conducted to improve the way tasks are to be performed. From these two types of studies a work standard and the correct way to perform the job are established. This approach leads to improved efficiency of output but also creates intense specialization of work. A significant disadvantage of this method is that the individual employee must adapt to the machine, leaving little room for individuality or creativity in the workplace. Jobs designed using time and motion analysis have low job depth and scope and often lead to employee job dissatisfaction. This employee discontent is generally thought to come from frustration over workers' having little input about standards and work methods; however, William Gomberg stated years ago that worker participation in the setting of production standards does not necessarily lead to a more peaceful and productive relationship.[2]

Job Rotation. To maintain employees' interest in work, some managers introduce a job design method called job rotation. Employees, including managers, are moved from one job to another. Job rotation often reduces the boredom of a task and stimulates interest in the new work. The rotation can also be from a day work schedule to an evening work schedule and can include a new job as well as new associates, supervisors, etc. Job rotation also has the advantage of cross training employees to insure more depth at each job in case of an emergency.

Job rotation or cross training not only is a form of good planning and insurance in case key employees leave, get ill or are promoted; but it also provides employees a new perspective about total operations. Cross training adds value to the individual as well as provides benefits to the organization.

Job Enlargement. Job enlargement is a design method that adds more responsibilities to a worker's existing job. Instead of three or four functions, the worker's job may be increased to ten or twelve functions. Theoretically, depending on the nature of the job, the worker's sense of importance may be greater. The goal is to reduce boredom and increase output and job satisfaction. Job depth and scope will be higher. This method may work well in organizations where machines do not control the output and where individual initiative is encouraged. Employees who aspire to advance within the organization willingly accept additional duties.

Sociotechnical Approach (Work Teams). The sociotechnical approach to job design is a method in which both the technical system and its related social system are considered. From the workplace a group or team of employees is formed and given total responsibility for achieving job goals.

This approach emphasizes the social values in the workplace, sometimes called the work climate, and stresses mutual respect between management and the employees. Decision-making is a joint endeavor. One popular example of this approach is quality control circles, which solicit workers' ideas regarding changes.

It does not automatically follow, however, that jobs designed on the basis of both social and technical aspects increase productivity, raise morale and/or generate higher efficiency. As Haynes and Massie noted:

> There are no simple generalizations on the superiority of group endeavor. The problem
> for management is to determine whether the task at hand is one for which group endeavor
> will in fact carry benefits which exceed the costs.[3]

Job Enrichment. Job enrichment is a job design method that originated from the work of Frederick Herzberg on factors affecting motivation. Herzberg's hygiene/motivator theory of motivation established factors that motivate employees and factors that maintain them (hygiene factors) but do not motivate them. Herzberg identified motivating factors as achievement, recognition, work itself, responsibility and advancement.[4]

In a practical sense job enrichment is the design of a job which psychologically benefits the employee by allowing greater self-direction, more opportunity to perform interesting work, and added responsibilities. The employee has more control over the job and sinks or swims based on the results.

Without question, job enrichment increases job depth. High employee motivation, a higher quality of performance, greater job satisfaction, less absenteeism, and much lower turnover can result from this approach to job design.

While enriching jobs may benefit the employees involved, the organization must gain also. There are always specific costs associated with job enrichment, such as equipment and layout changes, salary increases, training costs, etc. Realistically, organizations that introduce job enrichment programs wish the value of benefits from such programs to far exceed the costs of implementing them. These cost savings or increased revenues are generated by the greater efficiency and increased output and other factors previously discussed.

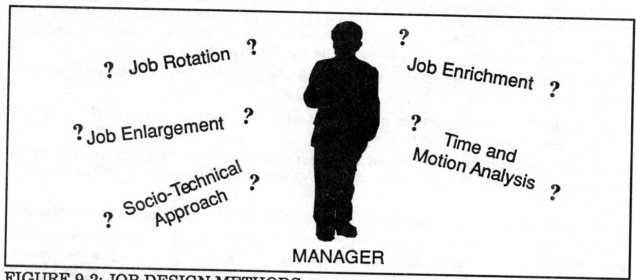

FIGURE 9-2: JOB DESIGN METHODS

Perhaps the most unique example in America of a company that has designed every job from top to bottom to be enriched is W. L. Gore and Associates, Inc., headquartered in Newark, Delaware. The term job enrichment is not used by sponsors (managers) in this organization, but the nature of each job matches the definition of job enrichment.

W. L. Gore and Associates, Inc., was founded in 1958 by W. L. Gore, a former researcher with E. I. DuPont de Nemours.

The company's sales currently exceed $700 million with over two dozen plants located throughout the United States. Of the five basic product groups, Gore-Tex fabrics is the best known to the general public. Gore-Tex produces a waterproof yet "breathable" fabric for making tents, outdoor clothing and other such equipment.

W. L. Gore and Associates, Inc., is unique because no one has a job title of "manager." Every employee is an "associate," and Mr. Gore describes the un-management company as a "lattice organization."

Unlike traditional "pyramid" management structures with carefully defined chains of command, the lattice organization contains no titles, no orders and no bosses. "Associates" (employees) are allowed to identify an area where they feel they will be able to make their best contribution. Then, they are encouraged to maximize their individual accomplishments.

Mr. Gore says, "People manage themselves. We organize ourselves around voluntary commitments. There is a fundamental difference in philosophy between a commitment and a command."[5]

Implementing Job Design

Once jobs have been designed, managers must carefully select the most qualified employees to perform the job. The selected employees must possess the desired qualifications; they must understand job content; they must understand methods of performance; and they must be motivated to do the job. When employees are selected to fill certain jobs, it is helpful if managers tell them why they were selected, the importance of the work, and how their work will relate to other jobs, departments and the ultimate consumer.

It is easier to establish this **role clarity** with new employees if the manager has developed **job descriptions** and **job specifications**.

A *job description* is a written statement of all the duties and responsibilities to be performed on a particular job. [See Figure 9-4]

A *job specification* is a written statement of the personal qualities an individual should possess to perform a particular job (such things as skills, abilities, knowledge, etc.). [See Figure 9-5]

Job descriptions and job specifications are developed after performing a **job analysis**.

Job analysis is the collection of data about a job through observation, interviewing, questionnaires, charting, and other means. The purpose of job analysis is to provide factual, objective data about the major duties and responsibilities involved in performing the job; the tools and equipment used in doing the job; the physical activities involved; the skills, knowledge and abilities required; and to include a description of the work environment. From this collected data, called **job analysis**, job descriptions and job specifications are developed.

Job specifications are important in the selection of the right employees to fill particular jobs. Equally important is the use of job descriptions to clarify the work role of the employee selected to fill the job.

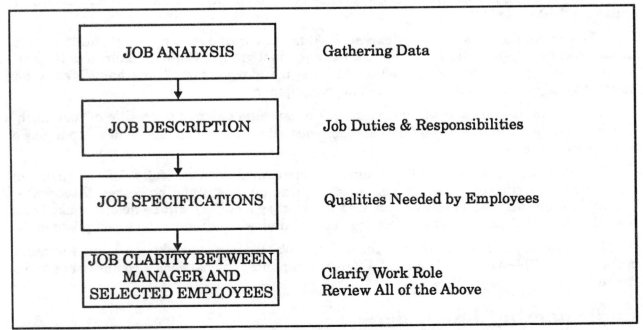

FIGURE 9-3: STEPS IN IMPLEMENTING JOB DESIGN

IDENTIFICATION

Computer Programmer
Job Title

April 10, 1981
Date

Arthur Allen
Written By

Juanita Montgomery
Approved By

Programming Supervisor
Title of Immediate Supervisor

Nonexempt
Status

007.167
Job Code

Olympia, Inc.—Main Office
Plant/Division

Data Processing—Information Systems
Department/Section

21   2,480
Grade   Points

22,500-25,850-29,200
Pay Range

SUMMARY

Performs studies, develops and maintains program concerned with employee benefits, focusing specifically on life, medical and hospitalization, accident and disability, and retirement insurance for all divisions of Olympia.

RESPONSIBILITIES AND DUTIES

1.0 Serves as a member of the Employee benefits team of programmers.
  1.1 Updates, modifies, and designs new applications in such areas as enrollment, premium costs, premium collections.
  1.2 Maintains existing programs that constitute employee health and retirement benefits program for employees of Olympia.
  1.3 Develops reports on the status of existing program for which responsible.

2.0 Recommends needed redesign studies.
  2.1 Reviews proposed changes in legislation.
  2.2 Consults with user representatives on proposed changes in existing benefit: programs, constraints, and potentially relevant developments.
  2.3 Discusses with other programmers and software specialists use of most suitable application programming technology.
  2.4 Identifies impact of program changes on existing computer programs.
  2.5 Recommends to supervisor changes that should be made in applicable software.

3.0 Carries out study projects.
  3.1 Investigates feasibility of alternate design approaches with a view to determining best solution within constraints set by available resources and future demands.
  3.2 Explores desirability of various possible outputs, considering both EDP and non-EDP costs, benefits, and trade-offs.
  3.3 Identifies types and designation of inputs needed, system interrelationships, processing logic involved.
  3.4 Develops programming specifications.
  3.5 Informs supervisor of progress, unusual problems, and resources required.

4.0 Designs internal program structure of files and records and reviews its operation.
  4.1 Determines detailed sequences of actions in program logic.
  4.2 Codes, tests, debugs, and documents programs.
  4.3 Writes and maintains computer operator instructions for assigned programs.
  4.4 Monitors existing programs to ensure operation as required.
  4.5 Responds to problems by diagnosing and correcting errors of logic and coding.

FIGURE 9-4: SAMPLE JOB DESCRIPTION

Source: Richard I. Henderson, *Compensation Management: Rewarding Performance*, 4th ed. (Reston, Virginia: Reston Publishing Company, Inc., 1985), p. 202

CLASS TITLE: Systems Project Leader

CHARACTERISTICS OF THE CLASS:

Under direction, is responsible for work of considerable difficulty in supervising a project team in the plan, design, and implementation of a major data processing project.
Incumbents are responsible for supervising a team of programmer/analysts in the design, installation, and implementation of a system and functions with complete independence within the framework of the assignment. This level is distinguished from the EDP Programmer/Analyst III by having responsibility for planning, designing and implementing a total project and may assign responsibility at the job level to EDP Programmer/Analyst III. This level is distinguished from the EDP Systems Project Manager who has the responsibility for managing several project teams.

EXAMPLES OF DUTIES:

Supervises and participates as a member of a project team in systems design and implementation; plans and design automated processes determining applications and computer requirements, conducting feasibility studies, scheduling projects and implementation of activities; coordinates the development and implementation of projects working with users and DP personnel to maintain schedules, to identify/resolve problems, and to maintain effective communication with users and DP management; assists users in planning and the development of new systems and maintenance, modification and enhancement of existing systems to identify/resolve problems, assure that schedules are being met, provide better service, and maintain effective communication links; prepares written instructions/descriptions for use in developing user procedures and programming specifications; supervises the activities of programming staff in the development of coded instructions for digital computer processing and may perform programming functions as required; plans and develops test data files, testing sequence and reviews test results for adherence to programming and operations standards.

KNOWLEDGE, ABILITIES AND SKILLS:

Considerable knowledge of electronic data processing equipment capabilities; considerable knowledge of application systems design techniques and procedures; considerable knowledge of project organization, management and control; good knowledge of the principles and techniques of programming and digital computers; good knowledge of the principles of supervision; some knowledge of statistics. Ability to analyze data and situations, reason logically, draw valid conclusions and develop effective solutions to systems problems; ability to design procedures for processing data with digital computers; ability to prepare comprehensive reports; ability to analyze and evaluate the progress of the system being developed; ability to speak and write effectively.

MINIMUM QUALIFICATIONS:

Two years experience equivalent to an EDP Programmer/Analyst III

FIGURE 9-5: SAMPLE JOB DESCRIPTION/SPECIFICATION COMBINATION

Source: Robert L. Mathis and John H. Jackson, *Personnel*, 3rd. ed. (St. Paul: West Publishing Company, 1982), p. 160

UNLV

Director of Intercollegiate Athletics

RESPONSIBILITIES: The Director of Intercollegiate Athletics will be responsible for the supervision and direction of coaches and staff and operation of athletic facilities; the planning and administration of the athletic budget; the advocacy and continued development of 14 sports (7 men – 7 women) in a highly successful NCAA Division 1-A athletic program; compliance with requirements and standards of NCAA Division 1-A athletic governing bodies; the hiring, supervision, and evaluation of personnel; academic standards and personal growth for student-athletes; and the effective negotiation of radio and television contracts.

QUALIFICATIONS: Successful candidates should have exceptional organizational, administrative, marketing, communications, and interpersonal skills; and demonstrated leadership, public relations, and fund-raising abilities. Candidates should have administrative experience in athletics in increasingly responsible positions, possess creative and motivational skills, and have evidence of personal integrity and high ethical standards. A bachelor's degree is required with a master's degree preferred.

SALARY: Competitive. Commensurate with qualifications and experience.

THE SETTING: UNLV is one of the fastest growing universities in the nation with a current enrollment of more than 18,200 students. UNLV was recently cited by U.S. NEWS & WORLD REPORT (1990-92) as one of the "up-and-coming" colleges and universities in the U.S. Located in cosmopolitan Las Vegas, the university has the strong support of the community's rapidly growing population of 850,000 residents.

APPLICATION: Applications and/or nominations and a complete file including current resume, and three letters of reference must be received by October 2, 1991. Applications and a complete file should be sent to: University of Nevada, Las Vegas; John C. Unrue and Dwaine Knight, Co-chairs; Athletic Director Search Committee; c/o Senior Vice President and Provost's Office; 4504 Maryland Parkway, Las Vegas, NV 89154-1002. Additional inquiries may be directed by phone to the office of the Senior Vice President and Provost at 702-739-3301.

The University of Nevada, Las Vegas is an equal opportunity/affirmative action employer. UNLV employs only U.S. citizens and aliens authorized to work in the U.S.

A YOUNG, PROUD, AND GROWING UNIVERSITY

FIGURE 9-6: PRACTICAL EXAMPLE OF JOB ANNOUNCEMENT INCLUDING THE RESPONSIBILTIES OF THE JOB AND QUALIFICATIONS OF THE APPLICANT

Source: *Athletics Administration*, October, 1991, p. 24 (Advertisement).

Organizing Groups

Management faces the on-going challenge of running an efficient organization. To meet this goal, full utilization of employee potential is essential. Four steps aid the manager in maximizing use of employees:

Step 1.   Design jobs effectively and fill them with qualified personnel.

Step 2.   Group similar jobs together to form departments.

Step 3.   Coordinate the activities of machines and employees into harmonious group effort which generates efficiency.

Step 4.   Structure all departments into an effective and efficient working "whole" (the ideal end result).

In the process of organizing, managers have many options for action. For example, managers have choices about job design, about structuring the organization, about employee selection, and about what groups, if any, they wish to use to achieve the ideal end result.

Groups play an important role in most organizations. Boards of Directors, committees, task forces, and teams are some examples. Groups can be formal or informal. Members of formal groups can be elected, appointed or volunteer. Members of informal groups have the freedom to enter or exit at will. Understanding the types of **groups** and the roles they can play to benefit overall organizational effort is important to a manager.

Identifying groups. Many types of groups have been identified in management, but there is no standardization of terms. Groups have been called formal, informal, functional, task forces, permanent or standing, ad hoc, committees, boards, commissions, teams, projects, directors and more. For the purposes of this text, groups will be identified as **formal** or **informal** with attention given to specialized groups, such as committees, which affect management practices.

A *group is two or more individuals who through interaction and mutual dependency work together to achieve common goals.*

Formal Groups. Formal groups are created purposely by management to achieve specific objectives. Employees in a payroll department would be an example. Specialists from functional departments assigned to work on a special project (see Matrix Organization in Chapter 8) would be another. Management sometimes establishes task forces to work on a complex organizational problem. When the work is completed, the task force is dissolved. A task force is a formal group and can also be called an ad hoc committee. Some organizations also have standing (permanent) committees which function continuously (although membership may change periodically).

Informal Groups. Informal groups emerge spontaneously, created by the members themselves for the purpose of sharing some common interest. The interest may be personal, social, recreational or work-related. Employees on a softball team or the gang that eats lunch together each day are examples of informal groups.

Informal groups are part of the informal organization which has its own leaders and its own communication network, known as the "grapevine." The informal organization never appears on the formal organization chart, but it has a significant presence just the same. Management must consider the informal organization and use it to advantage in performing daily management functions.

FORMAL GROUPS CREATED BY MANAGEMENT
Board of Directors
Departments
Standing Committees
Task Forces
Project Teams

INFORMAL GROUPS CREATED BY MEMBERS
Lunch Gang
Car Poolers
Office "Cliques"
Softball Team
Disgruntled Employees

FIGURE 9-7: EXAMPLES OF FORMAL AND INFORMAL GROUPS

Value of Work Groups to the Members. Whether the work group is formal or informal, the members may receive benefits in the following areas from belonging:

Social satisfaction can be obtained through interaction with group members. Sharing problems or joys of mutual interest; discussing common objectives; listening to other opinions; and developing camaraderie with colleagues can be sources of social satisfaction.

Safety needs in the form of job security may be realized by membership in a group. This is the case when an employee joins a union. As a group, members are stronger in a confrontation with management than they would be as individuals. Departments often protect members from other departments in a period of crisis or conflict.

Self esteem and dignity are often increased through group participation and involvement. Realizing new goals through team effort or acquiring new skills from on the job training can increase a feeling of self-worth and importance.

Value of Work Groups to the Organization. Groups become the foundation of organized effort within the organization. Work groups provide these major values to the organization:

The Synergistic Effect. Grouping employees in an orderly way, when proper skills and equipment are in place, allows the output (end result) to be far greater in value than the output of isolated individuals. Group formations begin the process of increasing the efficiency and productivity of work effort.

Value in decision-making. Managers can use groups as participants in decision-making. New ideas and approaches may come from within the group that will be more readily accepted by the group if the decision affects them. Also, members' knowledge of a subject may be greater than that of management when the problem directly involves them. Additionally, group recommendations often provide new alternatives for management to consider.

Orientation and socialization of new employees. Groups often provide the means for orienting new employees to the workplace. Explaining work expectations, job requirements, standards of conduct, the philosophy of management which is actually practiced, and even helping the new employee learn the job are all of great value to the organization. The act of introducing new employees to older workers and making them feel comfortable in the work environment helps the new employee adjust more quickly to the workplace.

Special Groups

Task Forces. Task forces are created by management to concentrate their time and talents on specific problems determined by management. Often the members of a task force are drawn from different subunits or functional areas to address a problem that is interdepartmental. Once the work of the task force has been completed, the group is disbanded.

An early example of task forces is found in England during World War II. The British government set up teams of specialists to work on complex operational problems important to the war effort. Because of a shortage of skilled scientists/researchers from specific areas, the groups were composed of individuals with different backgrounds and skills. This multidisciplinary approach to solving complex operational problems proved highly successful, and a new management field, called **operations research**, was begun.

Task forces are used in organizations today for these purposes:

1. Make recommendations to management;
2. Reach decisions and initiate action under the authority of higher management;
3. Draw conclusions and implement the results in individual areas of managerial influence.

Task forces are also called **ad hoc** or temporary committees, but the designation "task force" with its implication of action and authority (power) may be preferred, if management wishes to convey a sense of urgency about a problem.

Two common examples of using "task forces" are these: a Mayor appoints a "task force" to raise funds for building a multipurpose arena to serve the needs of a city; a "task force" may be established by university officials to double the endowment funds over a five-year period.

Committees. An old adage, reprinted on plaques and various business-related bric-a-brac, says this:

>If something is urgent, do it yourself.
>
>If you have time, delegate it.
>
>If you have forever, form a committee.

Unfortunately, this is what committees signify to many people. Service on a committee is often viewed as a waste of time and energy. This does not have to be the case, however, if management applies the guidelines suggested here to the formation and administration of committees.

A committee is a formally appointed group of two or more people to consider and satisfy some organizational need.

Committees are either **standing** or **permanent**, or they are **ad hoc** or **temporary**. Since **ad hoc** or **temporary** committees are similar to task forces in operation, this discussion will concentrate on **standing committees**. Suggestions for improving use of all committees applies to both types.

Standing committees are permanent. While membership on the committee rotates periodically, the committee and its function stay. Standing committees play an important role in all types of American organizations. Standing committees run the United States Senate; trustees often formulate policies and goals of some private American universities; boards of directors oversee the management practices of business firms; and a finance committee may review all budgets and expenditures of management above a certain dollar limit. Standing committees function at all levels of an organization, i.e., an employee safety committee.

Although there are conflicting views about the worth of committees, most managers agree that committees can play a valuable part in meeting certain organizational needs. Advantages and disadvantages of committees are summarized in Figure 9-8.

ADVANTAGES	DISADVANTAGES
1. "Two heads are better than one" when dealing with major organizational problems.	1. Committees compromise findings.
2. Functional specialists from different areas provide expertise.	2. Committees can generate conflict where none existed before.
3. Committee decisions or recommendations may be more readily accepted by members.	3. Committees are time consuming and therefore expensive.
4. Diverse membership communicates information quickly.	4. Committees do not pinpoint responsibility on any one individual.
5. Creation of a committee stresses the importance of the work.	5. Committees can be viewed as a tool to avoid individual managerial responsibility.
6. Committee decisions are shared by the group rather than being the action of one person.	6. Talent of committee members may be better used on other activities.
7. Committee involvement often motivates members.	
8. Membership on a committee provides opportunities for training, growth, and the acquisition of more knowledge.	

FIGURE 9-8: ADVANTAGES AND DISADVANTAGES OF COMMITTEES COMPARED

1. Members not qualified to serve
2. Dominated by people with rank and title
3. Objectives not specified by higher management
4. Members' interest not stimulated by higher management
5. Chairperson is incompetent
6. Absenteeism
7. Committee work viewed as unimportant
8. Incompatibility of members
9. Meets too often or not often enough
10. Members receive no reward or recognition
11. Committee membership is too large

FIGURE 9-9: SOME CAUSES OF COMMITTEE FAILURE

Managers often view the pros and cons of forming a committee before they act. There are many potential advantages and disadvantages to the use of committees, but the committee form of organization structure is widely used.

Committees should be formed as needed, constructed properly, administered correctly, and rewarded fairly for the contribution made by the members. Figure 9-9 lists some of the causes of committee failure which must be overcome if committees are to prove effective. In Figure 9-10 major suggestions for improving committee effectiveness are listed. After reviewing these suggestions, you can evaluate your next experience on a committee.

Summary Comments about Committees. Committees should be groups that management can use effectively for the good of the total organization. Individuals who have served on committees should feel that the experience was educational, pleasant, personally rewarding, and important. They should look forward to serving on another committee in the future.

Effective committees benefit everyone. Managers should plan the formation of committees as carefully as they plan budget expenditures.

Using committees poorly is expensive, time consuming, and a detriment to the morale of employees involved. Poor committee implementation is as bad a management practice as the improper use of any other resources, such as equipment and inventories.

Management of Group Behavior. The previous discussion has concentrated on committees as groups whether they are task forces, standing committees, project teams, boards or other designations. Managers have a responsibility to manage groups as well as they do individual employees.

Managers also need to recognize the influence of *informal groups* in the organization. While managers cannot control informal groups, they can be aware of their existence and use them on occasion for the benefit of the organization.

Step I: **Have Competent Members**

Make certain that committee members are qualified, competent and motivated to serve on the committee and that they can deal effectively with the specific objectives assigned to the committee. Committee members can be appointed, elected, or can volunteer. Regardless of job title, salary level, and length of experience in the organization or how the committee is selected, the committee will not function well with incompetents as members. Remember, thoroughbreds run in the Kentucky Derby — not mules!

Step II: **The Committee Must Be Properly "Charged"**

Someone in higher management who carries authority and has the respect of the committee members should "charge" the committee. The "charge" should include why the committee has been formed; the importance of the work; the importance of the individuals selected; and the time-table for completing the assignment. The "charge" should include not only the act of entrusting the committee with their duty, but also energize them.

Step III: **Select or Elect a Competent "Chairperson"**

The "chair" of a committee is the key to success in implementing the committee's work. The "chair" needs to be an effective manager who can plan, organize, implement, and control committee activities. The "chair" delegates, sets time schedules, coordinates work, recognizes accomplishments, follows-up on assignments and much more. The "chair" also must be an effective leader who can instill enthusiasm among the members, develop loyalty within the group, and generate high morale and motivation during the committee's existence.

Step IV: **Recognize/Reward Committee Accomplishments**

Once the work of the committee has been completed or the work of the committee has reached a certain benchmark, then recognize the results. Recognition or reward may be in the form of a company-sponsored dinner; a personal letter to each member; a report of the committee's accomplishments in the company newsletter; or a visit by top management to the committee where each member is thanked personally for his or her contribution. Committee members deserve recognition for outstanding accomplishments.

FIGURE 9-10: STEPS IN IMPROVING THE EFFECTIVENESS OF COMMITTEES

Informal work groups play an important role in the success or failure of an organization. Managing the establishment of informal groups is not an option facing managers since they have no direct authority over the groups; however, managers can easily identify informal groups through direct observation.

Groups that develop over time on their own create specific group norms, cohesiveness and conformity. *Group norms refer to behavior expectations of the members.* There may be informal rules or codes of conduct which members voluntarily observe. *Group cohesiveness can be seen when individuals stick together or back each other in time of need.* Members of a group that relate well together demonstrate cohesiveness by eating lunch together, socializing after work and other group activities on and off the job. *Group conformity occurs when individuals abide by the group norms.* Without group conformity, the cohesiveness of the group disappears and the informal group can disintegrate.

One of the most important research studies regarding group behavior was conducted by Bernard Berelson and Gary A. Steiner who published an inventory of scientific findings about human behavior. In effect, these findings (reproduced as an extract in Figure 9-11) are principles of behavior of individuals as members of a group. Managers may gain more meaningful insight into group interaction and individual behavior within groups after reviewing these points. They are valuable tools to the student of management who seeks to understand group behavior better.

Summary

American managers have a renewed interest in the American employee and the jobs they hold. This concern has been spurred by declining productivity and efficiency in some industries and increased foreign competition. Justification for management's interest in employees and their jobs is based on the premise that the more satisfied an employee is on the job, the greater productivity and efficiency of output will be.

The starting point for improving overall organizational effort is the design of individual jobs. Job design is the process of specifying the tasks to be performed, the work methods to be used in performance, and the relationship of the job to other jobs in the organization for the purpose of improving the quality and quantity of work.

Factors affecting job design are job depth and job scope, types of employees available to work, economic restrictions, union limitations, and company philosophy.

Many job design methods are available to the manager. Specifically the method selected will be the result of considering all the factors affecting job design. The job design methods are time and motion analysis, job rotation, job enlargement, sociotechnical, and job enrichment.

Implementing job design and clarifying the work role of the employee are made easier if the manager develops job descriptions and job specifications.

Groups play an important role in most organizations. Groups can be formal or informal. Understanding the types of groups and the roles they can play to benefit overall organizational effort are important to a manager.

Extract A

HUMAN BEHAVIOR: AN INVENTORY OF SCIENTIFIC FINDINGS
Bernard Berelson and Gary A. Steiner

A1. The more people associate with one another under conditions of equality, the more they come to share values and norms and the more they come to like one another.

A3. The more interaction or overlap there is between related groups, the more similar they become in their norms and values; the less communication or interaction between them, the more tendency there is for conflict to arise between them. And vice versa: the more conflict, the less interaction.

B1. The small group strongly influences the behavior of its members by setting and/or enforcing standards (norms) for proper behavior by its members—including standards for a variety of situations not directly involved in the activities of the group itself.

B2. The less certain the group is about the right standards, the less control it can exercise over its members.

C1. In most groups, there is a rough ranking of members, implicit or explicit, depending on the extent to which the members represent or realize the norms and values of the group: the more they do, the higher they rank.

C9. In general, there is an alternation within groups, especially those having tasks to perform, between communications (interactions) dealing directly with the task and communications dealing with emotional or social relations among the members—the former tending to create tensions within the group and the latter tending to reduce them and achieve harmony.

C10. Both the effectiveness of the group and the satisfaction of its members are increased when the members see their personal goals as being advanced by the group's goals, i.e., when the two are perceived as being in harmony.

C11. The more threatened the individual members feel (i.e., the more they think they will personally lose something by the group's performance), the more concerned they become about being accepted in the group and the less effective the group as a whole becomes, with regard to both efficiency of performance and satisfaction of the members.

C12. The more compatible the members are, in norms, skills, personality, status, etc., and the more the procedures of the group are accepted and understood, the more effective and satisfying is the performance of the group in its tasks.

C13. Active discussion by a small group to determine goals, to choose methods of work, to reshape operations, or to solve other problems is more effective in changing group practice than is separate instruction of the individual members, external requests, or the imposition of new practices by superior authority—more effective, that is, in bringing about better motivation and support for the change and better implementation and productivity of the new practice.

FIGURE 9-11: EXTRACT ON BEHAVIOR OF INDIVIDUALS WITHIN GROUPS

Source: Bernard Berelson and Gary A. Steiner, *Human Behavior: An Inventory of Scientific Findings* (New York: Harcourt, Brace and World, Inc., 1964), pp. 325-360, as reproduced in Haynes and Massie, *Management*, pp. 173-74.

A group is defined as two or more individuals who, through interaction and mutual dependency, work together to achieve common goals.

Formal groups are created purposely by management to achieve specific objectives. Informal groups emerge spontaneously, created by the members themselves, for the purpose of sharing some common interest.

Members of groups may receive great benefits from being part of a group. Some are social satisfaction, safety needs being realized, and an increase in self-esteem and dignity. Work groups also may be of value to the organization by providing help in decision-making, by orienting and socializing new employees to the organization, by creating the synergistic effect in the workplace. In addition, special groups such as task forces and standing committees provide assistance to managers. Task forces are formed by management to concentrate their time and talents on specific problems. Once the work of the task force has been completed, the group is dissolved. Standing committees are permanent groups even if members change over time.

Committee effectiveness can be improved by having competent committee members, having the committee properly "charged," having a competent chairperson who is a good manager/leader, and by recognizing or rewarding a committee after its work has been completed.

Informal groups exist in organizations, but they are not under the direct authority of a manager. Informal groups can be identified by their norms, cohesiveness and conformity to the norms. They play an important role in the success or failure of organizational effort.

Review Questions

1. Explain each factor that affects job design. Which of the factors do you consider the most important?

2. Which of the job design methods is an offshoot of Frederick Herzberg's hygiene/motivation theory? Explain.

3. How important is job analysis to the development of job descriptions and job specifications? Discuss.

4. Distinguish clearly informal groups from formal groups. Identify how each type of group is formed and for what purposes.

5. Why is intense specialization of work not popular today with American employees?

6. What recommendations are given for improving committee effectiveness?

7. What is meant by an informal group's having norms, cohesiveness and conformity?

Assignments for Personal Development

1. Select a job that is considered mundane or dull (such as that of a clerk or secretary). Write a plan to enrich the job through job enlargement.

2. Compare your experience on a committee with the suggestions to make committees more effective (see Figure 9-10). Were all of the suggestions met or not? List the good and bad about your committee experience. [Hint: Working on a group project for a class would be like a committee.]

Incident

THE DYSFUNCTIONAL COMMITTEE

Hazel Upshaw was one of twelve committee members appointed by the President. The committee's purpose was to generate suggestions about how to market more effectively and creatively the company's line of sportswear and equipment. Hazel had been on the committee for three months, and nothing had come forth from the committee. They met once a month and did nothing more than gossip and complain about the management. She thought being on the committee was a total waste of time. The chair of the committee was inept but worked overtime to stay popular with committee members.

Just yesterday, each committee member received a memo from the President announcing the transfer of the chair to a new job located elsewhere which removed the chair from the committee. At the conclusion of the memo, the President recommended Hazel Upshaw to become the new chair. He also charged the committee to become productive quickly, or the committee would be disbanded.

Questions:

1. Give Hazel some suggestions for improving committee effectiveness.

2. What is the role of a committee? Does committee action ever replace the duties and responsibilities of higher management?

Glossary of Key Terms

Committee: Formally appointed group of two or more people to consider and satisfy some organizational need.

Group: Two or more individuals who through interaction and mutual dependency work together to achieve common goals.

Job Analysis: Collection of data about a job through observation, interviewing, questionnaires, charting and other means.

Job Depth: Refers to the individual employee's flexibility to control his or her work performance.

Job Description: Written statement of all the duties and responsibilities to be performed on a particular job.

Job Design: The process of specifying the tasks to be performed; the work methods to be used in performance; and the relationship of one job to other jobs in the organization.

Job Enlargement: A job design method that adds more responsibilities to a worker's existing job.

Job Enrichment: The design of a job which psychologically benefits the employee by allowing greater self-determination, more opportunity to perform interesting work and added responsibilities.

Job Rotation: Moving employees from one job to another to maintain employees' interest in work.

Job Scope: Refers to how specialized and narrow the work activity is.

Job Specification: Written statement of the personal qualities an individual should possess to perform a particular job.

Operations Research: Multi-disciplinary approach to solving complex operational problems.

Task Force(s): Special group(s) of individuals created by management to concentrate their time and talents on specific problems.

Time and Motion Analysis: Time studies are made of repetitive work cycles, and motion analysis is conducted to improve the way tasks are to be performed.

Work Teams: A sociotechnical approach to job design which forms teams of employees who are given total responsibility for achieving job goals.

Practical Concepts in Management
The Informal Organization

We have defined the formal organization as a group of people who work together toward common objectives with clearly defined lines of authority, responsibility, accountability and communication. Note that the first half of the definition refers to the grouping of people—employees—working together toward common goals. Among the formal group of employees in any kind of organization you will have what is called the "informal organization."

Identifying the informal organization is important to a new manager. Often the informal organization, led by informal leaders, is a persuasive factor in determining attitudes and morale of the employees. "Informal" simply means that the leaders and the employee associations do not appear on the formal organization chart and are not outwardly recognized by management. It is a major mistake, however, to overlook or underplay the power and influence of the informal organization.

Groups of employees who lunch together or socialize after work are examples of the informal organization. Each of these groups has its natural leader who consciously or not exerts much influence on the behavior and attitudes of other employees.

If these leaders are positive about the organization, the working conditions, the job benefits, etc., then much of this will rub off on the group members. The opposite holds true as well.

This is why a manager should quickly identify the natural leaders of the informal organization. After doing so, he or she should insure that these leaders are job satisfied, positive in attitude, and optimistic about the future. Done sincerely by the manager, this action can generate many fringe benefits to the organization and help minimize employee problems and conflicts in the future. It should not be overdone, however, and no new manager should allow these natural leaders to "blackmail" him or her into favoritism. Remember, the point is for you to use the informal group and its leader, not vice versa.

Make Perfectionism a Disease

The definition of management includes working "through others" to achieve objectives. It is a totally people-oriented activity. Management is also a largely inexact science full of risks, uncertainty, and the unpredictable behavior of people.

Any manager at any level who expects or demands perfection from employees is living in an unrealistic world. It is professional to aim high, to encourage the perfect job, to strive to maximize profits and minimize costs; but mistakes and errors are bound to occur. There are too many variables which managers cannot control and cannot foresee with pinpoint precision to expect perfection.

Perfectionism is a disease that destroys people. Keep standards high, but as a manager learn to adjust to the imperfections of your employees, peers and bosses. And learn to adjust to the imperfections in *you*.

Organizations are imperfect entities as well. The structure may not be right; job descriptions may be obsolete; jobs may be poorly designed, and some equipment may be outdated. Managers must perform to the best of their ability within the confines of the flawed environment around them.

References and Chapter Notes:

[1] James G. March and Herbert A. Simon, *Organization* (New York: John Wiley & Sons, Inc., 1958), p. 51.

[2] William Gomberg, *A Trade Union Analysis of Time Study* (Englewood Cliffs, NJ: Prentice-Hall, Inc., 1955), pp. 25, 271-272.

[3] W. Warren Haynes and Joseph L. Massie, *Management: Analysis, Concepts, and Cases*, 2nd ed., (Englewood Cliffs, NJ: Prentice-Hall, Inc., 1969), p. 151.

[4] Frederick Herzberg et al, *The Motivation to Work* (New York: John Wiley and Sons, 1959).

[5] Lucien Rhodes, "The Un-Manager," *Inc.*, August, 1982, p. 34.

CHAPTER 10

STAFFING THE ORGANIZATION

After studying this chapter, you will know:

- The Meaning of Staffing
- The Personnel Management Process
- How to Audit Human Resources
- Steps in Human Resource Planning
- Major Legislation Affecting Staffing
- Recruitment Sources and the Process
- The Personnel Selection Process
- About Assessment Centers
- The Value of New Employee Orientation
- Types of Training Programs
- The Importance of Compensation and Benefits

Introduction

This chapter stresses the importance of staffing positions with the most qualified personnel available. Whether an organization has a personnel department or not, the responsibility to hire, integrate, develop and maintain employees rests with the management. There is no shortage of applicants for open positions, especially in the sport industry. The important point to remember is that every job should be filled by a competent, motivated professional individual. Often the new employee is less than the "best," but with management's guidance, training, encouragement, and support, the new employee may develop into the "best." Many consider the development of employees to their full potential the number one responsibility of managers.

No activity is more important in management than **staffing**. *Staffing is the acquisition and placement of qualified employees in jobs that fully utilize the talents and skills of the individual.* The staffing activity is essential because it directly impacts the economic success of the organization.

Managers may structurally organize soundly, design jobs effectively, and even develop an impressive organization chart; but no aspect of organization can work well if jobs are not filled with qualified people at the right times.

The sport world historically has relied heavily on the "buddy system" to fill jobs such as coaches, administrators and management personnel. This often-criticized networking approach, however, has been tempered somewhat with the advent of government regulations on employment discrimination. In many cases a **search committee** is formed to recruit, screen, interview and recommend applicants for vacant positions. Search committees tend to consist of people from a cross section of functional areas, appointed by someone in higher administration, to perform the functions of a personnel department for a specific job opening. The search committee will advertise the job and the desired experience, qualifications and skills needed; screen applications; interview selected applicants; check references and work histories (as well as personal and academic histories in some cases), and recommend candidates to higher management. Search committees are in common use in the field of education but are used by other types of organizations as well. The creation of search committees is in part due to legal and public pressure to encourage the active recruitment of a cross-section of applicants. Also, members of a search committee may be more objective in the evaluation of applicants since they have no personal ties to the applicants.

Regardless of the method used to choose personnel to fill vacant jobs, each job should be filled by a qualified person.

Personnel Management

Staffing is a function of personnel management. Usually organizations that have one hundred or more employees create personnel management positions. These positions tend to be filled by personnel management specialists who assist line managers in performing all of the personnel functions. When organizations grow larger, personnel management departments (sometimes called human resource departments) are created and perform all of the personnel functions on behalf of line managers. Personnel managers and personnel management or human resource departments are traditional staff activities and have no direct line authority in the organization.

Line and Staff Conflict. Ultimate responsibility for the success or failure of any organization rests with line managers. As discussed in Chapter 8, staff persons and departments are internal specialists employed to provide some form of specialized aid to line managers. Line managers should make the actual hiring and firing personnel decisions, not personnel managers or departments. Personnel managers and departments provide the necessary skills and expertise to assist line managers in staffing decisions. Confusion can occur about the role of personnel because line managers become dependent on the skills of personnel managers while they perform their line responsibilities. All managers are, in fact, "personnel managers."

Staffing and Personnel Management. Personnel management is the process of supporting the accomplishment of organizational objectives by continually **acquiring** human resources; **integrating** employees into the organization; **developing** employee potential; and **maintaining** the work force.[1] Staffing involves the acquisition of human resources. This is the first step in building a strong organization, but new employees also must be integrated, developed and maintained to build a "great" organization.

Human Resource Planning (HRP). Human resource planning includes two steps. One is a projection of future human skills and talents that the organization will need to meet its strategic objectives. The second is the formulation of a detailed plan to recruit and staff the jobs so that the organization can satisfy its strategic objectives.

Knowing the strategic objectives is essential to HRP. Human resource planners must coordinate their efforts with higher management (who develop strategy) so that they are informed about changes in goals or direction of the organization. Internal and external environmental factors that may directly affect staffing needs must also be considered. For example, changing technology in the industry may make existing equipment and current job skills obsolete (internal environment); or a declining national economy may affect revenues, resulting in personnel cutbacks (external environment).

Auditing Human Resources. Essential to HRP is an audit of existing talent and skills of current employees. Information about each employee can be obtained from interviews, questionnaires, and a review of personnel files. Audit results show whether new employees with different job skills should be sought or if, with training, present employees can meet the future needs of the organization. An audit can indicate the need for both. In addition, HRP should focus on turnover trends, normal attrition rates, and expected retirements in some defined time period (say, two to five years). Normally it would be wise to project or forecast human resource needs for the next twelve months (short run) and also for the next five years (long run). The audit should include a review of management personnel as well as nonmanagement employees.

Step 1. Determine Strategic Objectives

Step 2. Establish the Time Standard for Reaching Objectives

Step 3. Review Internal and External Environmental Factors That Affect Staffing Needs

Step 4. Project Human Talents/Skills Needed for Achieving Strategic Objectives

Step 5. Audit Human Resources in the Organization

Step 6. Determine Human Resource Needs in the Short-Run and Long-Run to Meet Projected Needs

Step 7. Plan a Program of Recruitment and Selection to Fulfill Human Resource Needs

---

FIGURE 10-1: STEPS IN HUMAN RESOURCE PLANNING (HRP)

Staffing and the Legal Environment

Many local, state and federal laws affect personnel management decisions, especially those decisions which pertain to staffing the organization. A brief review of the more important federal legislation is presented to indicate the complexity legal constraints add to management's staffing activities.

Social Security Act of 1935. This act established a federal tax on payrolls and provides disability and retirement benefits. The rate of the tax has been changed many times, and employers are responsible for collecting the portion paid by employees and depositing this amount into the employee's account with the Social Security Administration.

Fair Labor Standards Act of 1938. This law set minimum wages (amended many times), overtime pay and child-labor standards.

Labor-Management Relations Act of 1947 (Taft-Hartley Act). This act was an amendment to the National Labor Relations Act of 1935 (the Wagner Act) and was designed to balance some aspects of the Wagner Act, which guaranteed employees the right to self-organization and to bargain collectively. The Taft-Hartley Act lists unfair labor practices by labor unions; provides management more rights to speak against unions during an organizing campaign (as long as employees are not threatened); and established the National Emergency Strike provision (an eighty-day cooling off period invoked by Presidential court injunction if a strike endangers the national health and safety).

Equal Pay Act of 1963 – Amended 1972. This prohibits wage discrimination on the basis of sex when the jobs require equal skills, effort and responsibility and are performed under similar working conditions.

Civil Rights Act of 1964 – Amended 1972 and 1978. Title VII of the Civil Rights Act of 1964 prohibits discrimination in employment (hiring, discharge, recruitment, assignment, compensation, and other terms and conditions of employment) on the basis of race, color, religion, sex or national origin in organizations that conduct interstate commerce. As amended in 1972, the Act extended coverage to state and municipal employees and to employers in educational institutions. In 1978, the Act was amended to prohibit discrimination in employment because of pregnancy, childbirth or related medical conditions and to reduce the number of employees necessary to comply with the Civil Rights Act (to fifteen or more). The Act created the Equal Employment Opportunity Commission (EEOC) and the Office of Federal Contract Compliance Programs (OFCCP) to hear complaints filed under the provisions of the Act and to enforce equal opportunity legislation.

Age Discrimination in Employment Act of 1967 – Amended 1978 and 1986. This act prohibits employers from discriminating in employment against individuals on the basis of age between ages 40 and 65. A 1978 amendment extended the age to 70; and in 1986, the Act was amended to remove the age limitations.

Occupational Safety and Health Act of 1970 (OSHA). OSHA mandates that employers provide their employees with a healthy and safe work environment that is free from recognized hazards that cause or are likely to cause death or serious physical harm. In addition, employers must conform to the safety and health standards set by the Occupational Safety and Health Administration, established by the Act.

Vocational Rehabilitation Act of 1973. This act prohibits discrimination in employment against individuals who are mentally and/or physically handicapped. It requires government contractors to take affirmative action to employ and advance in employment physically and mentally handicapped individuals who are qualified. Employers must also make reasonable accommodations to provide accessibility for handicapped employees (i.e., ramps and elevators rather than stairs and aisles wide enough for wheelchairs to move freely). Employers must also allow applicants and current employees to self-identify themselves as handicapped. The government's affirmative action requirement means organizations must not only cease any form of discrimination in employment practices but also actively seek handicapped employees in recruitment programs. This Act is administered by the OFCCP (refer to Civil Right Act of 1964).

Federal Privacy Act of 1974. This act applies only to the Federal Government and its contractors. It provides certain safeguards for an individual against invasion of privacy. The Act requires that individuals be permitted access to any personal records concerning them.

Employee Retirement Income Security Act of 1974 (ERISA). This act was designed to protect the interests of participants in employee benefit plans and their beneficiaries. The Act establishes standards of conduct, responsibility and obligations for fiduciaries of employee benefit plans.

Vietnam Era Veterans Readjustment Assistance Act of 1974. This act requires government contractors to take affirmative action (actively seek) to employ and advance in employment qualified disabled veterans and Vietnam-era veterans (who may or may not be disabled). Those prospective employees and current employees who are eligible to be classified under this Act may be given special consideration. It is administered by the OFCCP.

Immigration Reform and Control Act of 1986. This law seeks to protect jobs for those who are legally entitled to hold them, specifically American citizens and aliens who are authorized to work in this country. To enforce the hiring provisions of the law, employers must verify employment eligibility of anyone hired after November 6, 1986, and complete and retain a form (titled I-9, see Figure 10-2) on each employee for three years from the hiring date or for one year after termination (whichever is longer). The Act creates a tremendous record-keeping burden for employers. If you examine the form reproduced in Figure 10-2, you will see the various documents which may be used to verify eligibility. The Department of Justice and the EEOC administer this law.

Americans with Disabilities Act (ADA) of 1990. This act relates to persons with physical and mental disabilities. Employers may not discriminate in hiring or firing if persons are otherwise qualified for jobs; may not limit advancement opportunities; use tests or job requirements to screen out the disabled, and much more. The purpose of the Act is to increase access to services and jobs for the disabled. Employers do not have to provide accomodations for disabled persons, however, if doing so imposes undue hardship on business operations.

Civil Rights Act of 1991. This is a law which permits women, minorities, persons with disabilities, and persons who are religious minorities to have a jury trial and to sue for punitive damages if they can prove intentional hiring and workplace discrimination. The law places a cap on the amount of damages a victim can collect which depends on the size of the employer and the nature of the discrimination. The law applies to all employers with fifteen (15) or more employees.

┌───┐

1 **EMPLOYEE INFORMATION AND VERIFICATION:** (to be completed and signed by employee.)

Name: (Print or Type) Last	First	Middle	Birth Name

Address: Street name and Number	City	State	ZIP Code

Date of Birth (Month/Day/Year)	Social Security Number

I attest, under penalty of perjury, that I am (check a box):

☐ 1. A citizen or national of the United States.

☐ 2. An alien lawfully admitted for permanent residence (Alien Number A_____).

☐ 3. An alien authorized by the Immigration and Naturalization Service to work in the United States (Alien Number A_____.
   or Admission Number _____expiration of employment authorization, if any_____).

I attest, under penalty of perjury, the documents that I have presented as evidence of identity and employment eligibility are genuine and relate to me. I am aware that federal law provides for imprisonment and/or fine for any false statements or use of false documents in connection with this certificate.

Signature	Date (Month/Day/Year)

PREPARER TRANSLATOR CERTIFICATION (To be completed if prepared by person other than the employee) I attest under penalty of perjury, that the above was prepared by me at the request of the named individual and is based on all information of which I have any knowledge.

Signature	Name (Print or Type)
Address (Street Name and Number)	City	State	Zip Code

2 **EMPLOYER REVIEW AND VERIFICATION:** (To be completed and signed by employer.)

Instructions:
Examine one document from List A and check the appropriate box, **OR** examine one document from List B *and* one from List C and check the appropriate boxes. Provide the Document Identification Number and Expiration Date for the document checked.

List A	List B	List B
Documents that Establish Identity and Employment Eligibility	Documents that Establish Identity	and Documents that Establish Employment Eligibility

List A

☐ 1. United States Passport

☐ 2. Certificate of United States Citizenship

☐ 3. Certificate of Naturalization

☐ 4. Unexpired foreign passport with attached Employment Authorization

☐ 5. Alien Registration Card with photograph

Document Identification

_____

Expiration Date (if any)

_____

List B

☐ 1. A State-issued driver's license or a State-issued I.D. card with a photograph, or information, including name, sex, date of birth, height, weight, and color of eyes.

(Specify State_____)

☐ 2. U.S. Military Card

☐ 3. Other (Specify document and issuing authority

Document Identification

_____

Expiration Date (if any)

List B

☐ 1. Original Social Security Number Card (other than a card stating it is not valid for employment

☐ 2. A birth certificate issued by State, county, or municipal authority bearing a seal or other certification

☐ 3. Unexpired INS Employment Authorization

Specify form

_____

Document Identification

_____

Expiration Date (if any)

CERTIFICATION: I attest, under penalty of perjury, that I have examined the documents presented by the above individual, that they appear to be genuine and to relate to the individual named, and that the individual, to the best of my knowledge, is eligibly to work in the United States.

Signature	Name (Print or Type)	Title
Employer name	Address	Date

Form I-9 (05/07/87)
OMB No. 1115-0136

U.S. Department of Justice
Immigration and Naturalization Service

└───┘

FIGURE 10-2: EMPLOYMENT ELIGIBILITY VERIFICATION (FORM I-9). Federal form to be completed on every employee hired after November 6, 1986, must be retained in files and reverified if documents list expiration.

Acquiring Human Resources

Once human resource needs are determined, personnel managers must develop a program to attract people with the desired skills, experience and talent to apply for job openings. This is called recruitment. Once a pool of applicants has been assembled, the right person must be chosen for the job. This activity is called selection.

Recruitment. A recruitment plan requires a job analysis which leads to job descriptions and job specifications, if they do not already exist.[2]

The most useful tool in planning a recruitment program is the job specification. Job specifications detail the human traits, education, experience and skills an individual must have to qualify for a particular job. Job descriptions are a written explanation of all the duties and responsibilities of a job. As Wendell L. French points, "...one use of job descriptions is in the development of job specifications. These specifications, in turn, are useful in recruitment, hiring people with appropriate skills, in promotion and transfer decisions, and in job evaluation.[3]

The last step in planning a recruitment program is to review sources of applicants that may have the desired qualifications to fill the jobs. Two general sources of supply are available: People from within the organization and people from outside the organization.

Sources from Within. Promoting or transferring employees from within the organization to fill job openings is an excellent source of people. Using existing personnel to fill jobs has many advantages:

1. It tends to boost employee morale.
2. It provides incentive to others.
3. You already know the work habits of the employee.
4. The organization is using an individual's skills to the fullest.
5. It minimizes new employee orientation and training.
6. It benefits both the employee and the organization.

Many companies post job openings to allow any employee who thinks he or she is qualified to apply for the position. Sometimes managers nominate employees for the position, or individuals may be chosen by management after a complete assessment of the individual's work record, training received, experience, potential and personal motivation.

Outside Sources. There are an abundance of outside sources for recruitment. But good human resource planners must pick sources carefully so that they may attract enough applicants of the right qualifications without overdoing it. Advertising in the newspaper "Help Wanted" section may bring in a torrent of applicants; however, the cost of processing applications may offset any benefit from the size of the applicant pool. Recruitment programs must involve sources which will supply job candidates with the desired skills.

For nonmanagement or nonprofessional jobs recruitment may be through newspapers; "word-of-mouth;" the union; employment agencies; vocational or trade schools, or local magazine ads. One of the best sources of applicants is from friends of current employees. This type of "word-of-mouth" recruitment tends to attract potential employees whose values, life style and work ethic are similar to existing employees.

For the more professional or technical jobs, including middle and top management, major sources of applicants would be graduate schools, specialized employment agencies, other companies, trade association journal ads, and friends of current employees who are in professional positions.

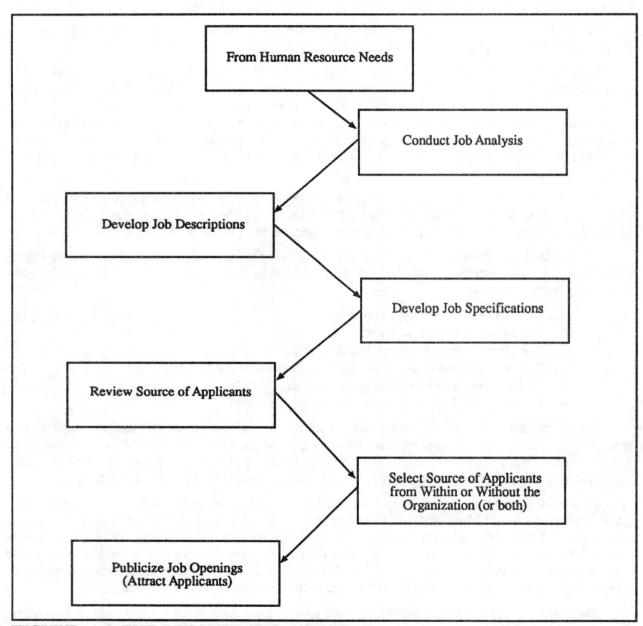

FIGURE 10-3: THE RECRUITMENT PROCESS

Selection. *Selection is the process of reviewing the qualifications of applicants for specific jobs and hiring those that appear most qualified to do a particular job.*

The personnel selection process is not a solution to all the problems that may plague a labor force. Hiring better qualified people is one step in the right direction. But the reception a newly hired employee gets once on the job can offset the benefits of a good selection process. New employees must be properly integrated into the organization, properly developed to their full potential, and properly maintained while on the job.

Selection processes vary with organizations. Some are detailed, elaborate, and expensive to administer. Other selection processes are so simple that they do not justify the title "process." When a person is hired, regardless of the complexity of the selection procedure, it means that someone in management has made a judgment, based on some criteria, that the applicant will be able to perform the job. He or she has been **selected**.

The Selection Process. Three points need to be emphasized about the selection process:

1. The selection process is not scientific. The use of the process does not guarantee that the person selected for employment will be the best available for the job; nor does it guarantee that the new employee will be steady, dependable, a self-starter, loyal, able to work well with colleagues and bosses, ready to accept responsibility and handle pressure well, and much more.

2. The last step in any selection process is "personal judgment" by the hirer. The various criteria used in selection do not guarantee that information obtained will accurately predict future performance. The person doing the choosing reviews the selection process data and makes a final personal judgment about the applicant for the job.

3. Every step in the selection process is a point that can disqualify an applicant. When an applicant under consideration for employment reaches the final interview stage, it means that the applicant has not been disqualified at any step in the selection process. Reaching the final stage in the process does not mean that the applicant should be hired, only that he or she is still available to be hired.

One interesting point of view about the selection process was presented years ago by Eli Ginzberg. While at Columbia University in New York, he was coordinator of a major project studying manpower resources in the United States. Dr. Ginzberg studied how men were selected for the military and how these selected personnel performed once in the service. One conclusion of the study was that about one of every three individuals show an unstable pattern of performance at some time in their lives, and there is no reliable way of predicting when it will occur. Dr. Ginzberg wrote that the most important lesson to management concerning the selection of employees is the need to establish a modest objective for screening. Management must realize that one inherent limitation of the selection process is that people's performance is likely to change over time.[4]

Steps in the Selection Process. The traditional steps in the personnel selection process are **reception, initial screening interview, application form, testing, background investigation, in-depth selection interview, physical examination, and final interview/job offer.**[5]

Reception. Whenever an applicant contacts an organization about employment, the reception should be positive. Each applicant should be treated fairly and honestly in a respectful manner. First impressions are important to both parties, and the applicant should be told if job positions are available. This step emphasizes the importance of the person within the organization who handles this initial contact.

Initial Screening Interview. Prior to an applicant's completing the application form, the interviewer can conduct an initial screening by asking certain questions. These questions would pertain to job interests, nature of skills, experience, desired location, salary expectations, and other general information. This is the time to inform the applicant about job openings, benefits, work schedules, salary, and other things. The purpose of the initial interview is to compare the job applicant's interests and skills with any job openings to justify moving to the next step in the selection process.

Application Form. Application forms, also called application blanks, must be completed by job candidates. The forms provide the organization biographical data about the applicant. The information on the forms is useful to an interviewer and also important in performing a background investigation. Today's forms request applicant information about work interest, work location desired, work skills possessed, education, previous work history, list of references or former supervisors, citizenship status, any disabilities, and possibly other miscellaneous items relating to the job. It is illegal to ask questions about sex, race, age, religion, marital status and number of children, native language, and national origin because application forms must comply with EEOC (Equal Employment Opportunity Commission) guidelines. An identification document with a photograph is now required to establish citizenship (see discussion of Immigration Control and Reform Act of 1986), but no information that might be used to discriminate against applicants is allowed.

Data provided by the applicant on the application form determines whether the selection process continues.

Testing. Tests may be used to help select new employees. Not all organizations use them; however, because tests are legally subject to requirements of validity and reliability and because tests are controversial as predictors in the selection process.

Test validity occurs when performance on the job closely relates to performance on the tests. **Test reliability** exists when the individual taking the test scores about the same on the test when taken a second or third time.

Tests that measure ability, skill, aptitude, or knowledge relevant to a particular job best predict the performance of a new or prospective employee. Tests, properly validated, can be of value in the selection process.

Background Investigation. Before an in-depth selection interview, a background investigation of the applicant should be conducted. This step insures that information provided in the initial interview and on the application form is correct. It is an important, precautionary measure.

Reference checking is the most common way to verify background information. Organizations can run credit checks, contact school references (obtain transcripts), contact personal references, or verify prior work experience with former supervisors. Information from personal references is probably the least important source to check because applicants will not list people who may write or say anything negative about them.

Conducting a credit check and verifying educational information are routine steps that take some time and cost money, but the information obtained may be valuable in evaluating an applicant. It is more difficult to investigate work background.

Employers are aware of the various federal and state laws which protect the privacy of personal information. The major law, already discussed in this chapter, is the Federal Privacy Act of 1974 which applies to government agencies and units; however, some states have similar laws.

Before contacting former employers, an organization should obtain written releases from the job applicant giving the organization permission to request personal information about his or her work experience. When contact is made with a former employer, only information that relates to the job performance should be requested. Information received in writing from former employers should be available for the applicant to see, if he or she desires to do so.

In-Depth Selection Interview. The in-depth selection interview should concentrate on the information provided by the applicant (during the prior steps in the process) and the information obtained from the background investigation. All this information should be compared with the requirements of the job by the interviewer in this step. There should be a "match" between the skills and abilities of the applicant and the job needs of the organization. A skilled interviewer provides a positive picture of the organization, yet is realistic in describing job expectations. The applicant should objectively "sell" himself or herself based on work experience and actual ability. Any additional information gained from tests may be discussed during this interview.

The interview may be highly structured, semi-structured, or unstructured. Semi-structured interviews may be the best at this stage in the selection process. In the semi-structured interview, the interviewer plans major questions in advance; but, depending on the responses of the candidate, other subjects and questions may arise which were not pre-planned.

If the interviewer finds no cause to disqualify the applicant and all information appears accurate, the selection process proceeds to the next stage.

Physical Examination. Physical examinations may be at the expense of the applicant or provided by the organization. Public school teachers in many states must provide evidence of a physical examination, at their expense, annually to qualify for continued employment. Most business organizations pay for a required physical examination for a job applicant.

Among the purposes of a physical examination are these:

1. To make sure that workers are physically able to perform the work required on a job
2. To detect any contagious diseases
3. To have the health record of each employee
4. To identify injuries and illnesses, past and present, to protect against invalid worker's compensation claims in the future.

Many jobs have physical standards that can be met by a majority of job applicants. Some jobs, however, require lifting, strenuous physical activity, or working in areas with extraordinary temperatures. The work environment of some organizations may be dirty, with a heavy concentration of dust or fumes. Physical restrictions that prevent satisfactory job performance or endanger the health of an applicant (such as asthma to a person who will work in a dusty area) must be identified.

The physical examination can also provide vital information in projecting health care costs of employees under a medical insurance benefit program. The cost of medical insurance programs is escalating, and more organizations provide such benefits to their employees. The federal government has proposed a massive overhaul of the nation's healthcare system, which would include changes in the way health benefits are delivered to employees and in how requirements for such benefits are to be met. As of now, organizations providing health insurance coverage as a benefit for employees are spending billions: According to Richard I. Henderson, in 1987 General Motors spent more than $2 billion on medical care coverage for its employees, retirees and their dependents.[6] One of the major bargaining points in virtually every union contract negotiation is improvement of healthcare benefits.

If an applicant successfully passes the physical examination and matches the physical requirements of the job, he or she moves to the last step of the selection process.

Final Interview/Job Offer. Managers who hire employees often allow personnel specialists to process an applicant for employment up to the point of hiring. Then, the manager reviews all of the information obtained from the steps in the selection process, hears the findings and recommendations of personnel, and reaches an agreement on the position to be filled, starting salary and benefits to be provided, and date employee will report. The final interview and job offer should be handled by the new employee's immediate supervisor.

In some organizations the manager is involved throughout the selection process, but the above scenario is also common.

The final interview is intended to clarify job questions about work expectations, pay, benefits, starting date of employment, opportunity in the organization, and the importance of the work. The interview is open for free discussion and complete understanding of the job situation by both parties.

If the manager is satisfied with the information on the applicant and the responses from the applicant, then a job offer is made. If the applicant understands the conditions of employment and the work expectations and is satisfied with the offer, then the job offer is accepted.

Assessment Centers. Assessment centers are a special method of selecting managers for employment or promotion. Originated by the military in World War II, assessment centers have grown in popularity and are used extensively in large organizations. The purpose of assessment centers is to predict management potential of participants through a variety of techniques such as in-basket exercises, role playing, incident analysis, and gaming simulations.

Information gained about management potential from assessment center exercises should be reviewed along with other sources of information in the selection process before a final decision is made about hiring or promoting a manager.

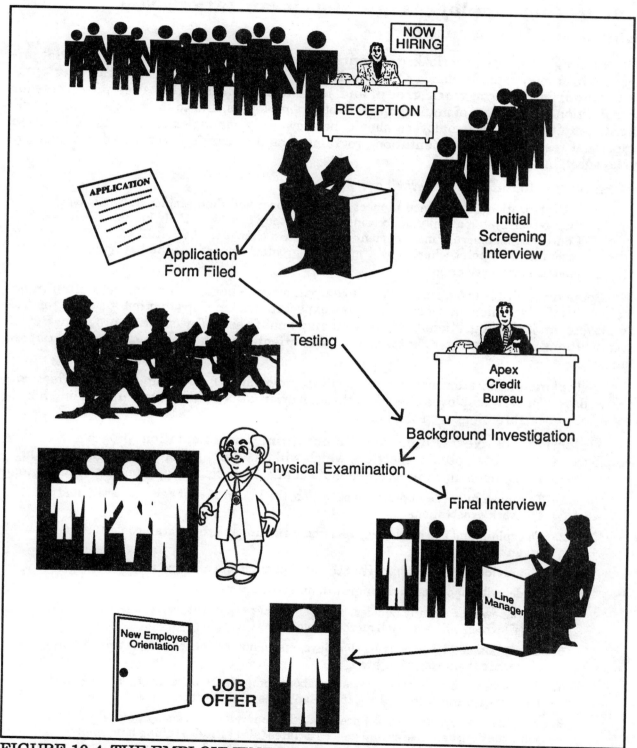

FIGURE 10-4: THE EMPLOYMENT PROCEDURE

Integrating Employees into the Organization: New Employee Orientation

Although it is often overlooked, **orientation** of new employees makes a significant difference in employee performance. **Orientation is a process of integrating the employee into the organization, work group, and job.** Included in the orientation program is an introduction to members of management, to other employees, and to the immediate supervisor. Orientation of new employees should be viewed by management as one of its most important responsibilities. Orientation programs should be carefully conceived and planned to be effective.

According to Kanouse and Warihay:

> ...Organizations determined to meet both their own and their employees' goals need a method for systematically addressing the way they deal with their human resources. Concerned members of management can initiate a change in their utilization of human resources at a point where it will make the greatest impact—at the beginning—with effective employee orientation.[7]

Some orientation programs in small companies are short in duration and often informal. A brief discussion of work rules, job expectations, an introduction to some of the employees, and a few questions and answers may qualify as the orientation program. But in organizations where managers know the value of orientation, the program has added importance.

Well planned and administered orientation programs for new employees may last one or two days. The new employee should go through orientation immediately upon being hired, not after two or three weeks on the job.

Objectives of New Employee Orientation. The orientation program for new employees should have specific objectives which will dictate much of the content of the program. The most common objectives/components of effective orientation programs are these:

1. To convey fully the importance of the job, the importance of being selected, and the work expectations
2. To explain and clarify the organization structure and the overall goals of the organization
3. To provide a complete history of the organization and a projection of the future
4. To describe opportunities for growth and advancement
5. To review all company policies, rules, and other organizational guidelines ("red tape") which will affect job performance
6. To explain employee benefits (holidays, insurance, social security, retirement program, profit sharing plan, etc.)
7. To discuss and answer any question about compensation (rates of pay, wage and salary programs, bonus plans, incentive plans, and merit increases)
8. To offset any uneasiness or uncertainty the new employees may have about the job situation, new bosses and new associates (also includes telling new employees where to go for advice or to seek answers to job-related questions)
9. To familiarize new employees with work stations, layouts, offices, locations of

departments and activities, and to explain products or services offered by the organization

10. To introduce new employees to their fellow workers and immediate bosses as well as to other selected personnel who may have a relationship to their job performance

Potential Benefits of New Employee Orientation. While the administration of an effective orientation program for new employees may take some time and will cost an organization money, the potential benefits far outweigh these costs. The primary benefits are as follows:

1. Reduced start-up costs because less time is involved in workers' reaching standard levels of performance

2. A more positive attitude toward work and the organization which creates more loyalty, less absenteeism, and less turnover

3. Good orientation reduces new employee anxiety and increases feelings of self-worth and dignity

4. New employee operates with more confidence, based on acquired knowledge of the organization, clear work expectations, familiarity with operations, and introduction to fellow workers and bosses

For many companies the development of an organization **handbook**, sometimes called a policies and procedures manual, is helpful to use in an orientation program. A **handbook** contains, in writing for future reference, much of the same information given the new employee orally during orientation. The employee receives a copy to refer to any subject for review at any time. Other organizations distribute the handbook and many other written documents for employees to use as well (i.e., company newsletters, directory of employees, maps of physical layout, etc.). Altogether such items constitute an **orientation kit.**

Orientation Follow-Up. Initial orientation, before new employees actually begin work, should be followed with a continuing or follow-up orientation in the future. To integrate the employees fully into the organization a follow-up orientation session should be held within three to six months of employment. After the employee has been on the job for this length of time, there may be a need to answer questions, listen to problems, explain any changes, and offer continued support. This would provide continuity to the integration process and insure that new employee orientation programs are effective.

Developing Employee Potential

Human resource effectiveness depends largely on developing the capabilities of employees. Rapid change in all aspects of business, from technology to social interaction, demands constant efforts to keep employees informed of new policies, techniques, and developments in the organization and in the economy. Because of the variegated composition of the work force, management faces a real challenge and responsibility in developing the full potential of every employee.[8]

We have discussed the importance of staffing; the legal environment; the recruitment and selection of employees; and the integration of employees into the organization through orientation programs. Now, we look at developing employees through training, performance appraisals, promotions, transfers, and disciplinary action.

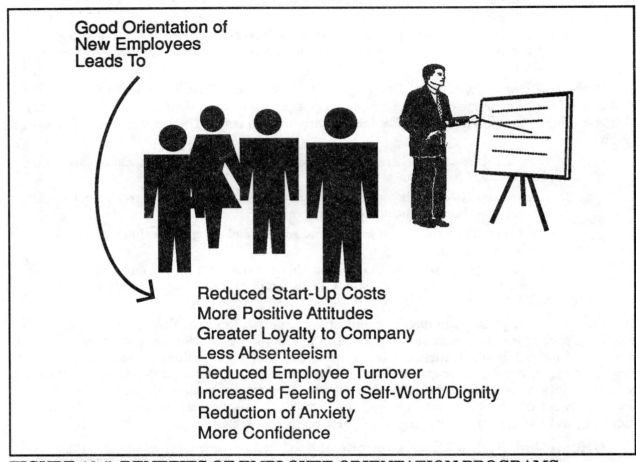

Good Orientation of
New Employees
Leads To

Reduced Start-Up Costs
More Positive Attitudes
Greater Loyalty to Company
Less Absenteeism
Reduced Employee Turnover
Increased Feeling of Self-Worth/Dignity
Reduction of Anxiety
More Confidence

FIGURE 10-5: BENEFITS OF EMPLOYEE ORIENTATION PROGRAMS

Training. Training is a process in which employees acquire new skills and knowledge that will enable them to be more effective in the performance of their jobs. The management responsibility to train employees and develop them to their full potential is the number one job of American managers, according to Crawford Greenwalt, former President and Chief Executive Officer of DuPont.[9]

Training efforts are directed at both nonmanagement and management employees. Nonmanagement training usually concentrates on teaching technical skills. Management training focuses on teaching or developing personal and conceptual skills.

Determining Training Needs. Training needs can be established through observation of individual employee performance, group performance, and overall organizational performance. If individuals have difficulty meeting work quantity standards on a consistent basis, they may need additional training. If a department as a whole fails to generate quality work, there may be a need for training. If the whole organization misses its desired annual goals or objectives, there may be a need for training. Poor results can be a clue to encourage further investigation of individual, group, and total organizational performance to evaluate the need for training.

Training needs of individual employees can be assessed through **performance appraisals. Performance appraisals compare the employee's work against the work standards or the objectives of the job (for management).** If work standards or objectives do not exist, then managers are wasting time evaluating employees. If an employee's work performance repeatedly fails to match or exceed the standard, he or she becomes a candidate for training. Since other factors, both personal and organizational, can affect job performance, more training may not be the answer in every case. For a detailed discussion of performance appraisals, see Chapter 16.

Another method for determining training needs is to conduct a questionnaire survey or personal interviews of selected personnel to determine the problems they have and their suggestions for overcoming them. Often, more training is the solution.

When training is indicated, management has several options for types of training programs: on-the-job training (OJT), apprenticeship training, vestibule training, programmed training, and classroom training.

On-the-job training (OJT) is the most common form of training, occurring daily under the direction of an experienced employee or the immediate supervisor. The employee performs his or her work assignment while the "trainer" watches and teaches.

Apprenticeship training dates back to ancient times and is often related in today's organizations to unions. Apprentices work under a skilled craftsperson who teaches the trade to the individual who performs the work (normally at a lower wage level). Apprenticeships vary in length of time, but usually last from two to five years.

Vestibule training takes place in a separate work environment that simulates real working conditions. Under these conditions, using identical equipment and supplies, the trainer stresses correctness of technique, procedure, and quality rather than quantity of output. Once an employee is properly trained, he or she fills a job as part of the regular work force.

Programmed training includes correspondence courses available through colleges, trade associations, and educational organizations. Also included are study courses on video and/or audio cassette tapes and computer video displays. Programmed training is a process of studying material and being tested at periodic intervals to check satisfactory progress. It is a sequential process of going through stages of learning and satisfactorily acquiring knowledge until the course is completed.

Classroom training is normally conducted away from the work location, but many organizations today maintain their own classroom facilities. Groups of employees can be trained at one time; they receive the same information; and they have the opportunity to participate in question and answer sessions on topics of shared interest. Usually classroom training is part of orientation, a management development program, safety seminars, technical training programs on new equipment, and so forth. Training may be done by company personnel or by outside specialists.

Management Training. Management training is introduced when a need is established at the supervisory, middle management, or top level. Managers tend to need technical, human or personal, and conceptual skills in varying combinations at each different management level. First level managers or supervisors need much technical knowledge plus good human or personal skills. Middle managers tend to need even more human or personal skills, some technical knowledge, and a growing amount of conceptual skill. Top managers primarily need conceptual skill with the amount of technical knowledge required based on the nature of the organization. Management training programs are structured with these skills in mind to provide or reinforce the skills managers need.

Supervisory training is growing in popularity today because of the manner by which most new supervisors are selected. They are primarily promoted from within the organization based on technical knowledge and skills but without confirmed management knowledge or skill. Training for supervisors often is conducted in a classroom setting on or off the premises by company personnel or by a professional management trainer. The major topics covered in a typical supervisory management seminar are the basic functions of management (such as planning and control, principles of communication, concepts of organization, and the management of people).

Middle managers and top level managers have opportunities to attend advanced management training programs. Many major colleges and universities offer these programs at off-site locations. Training time varies from one week to two months. Subjects stressed in these programs are centered on the conceptual skills needed by top managers in areas such as strategic planning, policy formulation, and corporate finance.

Promotions. Competent individual performance over a sustained period of time deserves recognition. Sometimes that recognition takes the form of a promotion. Promoting an employee, whether a manager or nonmanagement employee, can be a development technique that benefits the person and the organization. Moving into a position that requires new skills or talents with added responsibilities becomes a growth experience. Caution should prevail, however, because not every excellent employee at one level will perform as well at a higher level. It is important that the person under consideration for promotion have the experience, talent, and skills needed to do the new job.

Transfers. Transfers (sometimes called job rotation) can provide a development opportunity for individuals. Relocating to a new work environment with new responsibilities and new associates can be stimulating. While some transfers occur because an individual is not being considered for promotion, most occur for the benefit of the organization and the individual. An opportunistic person should view a transfer as a chance to demonstrate competency in another area, showcasing his or her multiple talents and skills and confirming his or her value to the organization.

Disciplinary Action. Disciplinary action can be a verbal or written reprimand, a suspension, or a demotion. It must be carefully considered before applied. Many employees resent such action especially when they think they are being singled out, unfairly treated, or have a personality conflict with the manager. If disciplinary action is fair and based on known rules of the organization, however, the individual may learn from the experience and become a better employee.

Written reprimands are a form of **documentation**. Documentation is important today because of the growing number of lawsuits filed against former employers by discharged employees. To document properly, a manager should objectively write exactly the situation involving the employee as it occurred (time, date, place, etc.) and have a statement at the bottom of the page which reads: "I have read the above and have been given a copy." The employee signs this document and receives one of the copies. Other copies go to the manager, the manager's boss and possibly personnel (for filing in the employee's personnel records).

While disciplinary action is justifiably viewed as negative, the results gained sometimes are not. Often it provides the stimulus needed by an employee to "snap out" of the destructive work behavior before it is too late.

Maintaining the Work Force

Two things that work best to maintain a competent work force are compensation and benefits. Compensation programs enable organizations to attract, maintain, and develop the best available talent. Benefits are a form of supplementary compensation and one that grows in importance constantly.

Compensation and benefits together form what is called monetary income received by an individual employee. The fundamental purposes of compensation are to do the following:

1. Obtain qualified talent
2. Retain good employees
3. Provide equal pay for equal work
4. Reward performance
5. Provide incentive.[10]

High compensation "attracts" applicants and "holds" employees in the work force, but there are other factors important to the maintenance of the work force. These factors (discussed more fully in Chapter 16) revolve around the concept of "psychic income" and are some of the more important job needs, wants, and desires of employees. These factors include job security, opportunity for advancement, recognition, better supervision, safe and pleasant work environment, and many more.

It is important to properly recruit, select, integrate, and develop employees. But all these activities are useless if employees are not maintained. Maintenance of the work force should follow a well planned and carefully constructed program balancing the best interests of the organization and the employees. This planning effort should be based on a fair compensation program, with desirable benefits, and a reasonable satisfaction of basic employee job needs, wants, and desires beyond monetary income.

Summary

Staffing is the acquisition and placement of qualified employees in jobs that fully utilize the talents and skills of the individual.

Staffing is a function of personnel management and normally is performed by staff specialists operating under the authority of higher line management.

Human resource planning is essential to the effective achievement of desired staffing results. Human resource planning includes two steps: projecting human skills and talents needed to satisfy strategic objectives and forming a detailed plan to recruit and staff the jobs so that strategic objectives are met.

The staffing function is directly influenced by state, local, and federal laws. Major federal legislation includes the Social Security Act of 1935; the Fair Labor Standards Act of 1938; the Labor-Management Relations Act of 1947 (Taft-Hartley Act); the Equal Pay Act of 1963, amended 1972; the Civil Rights Act of 1964, amended 1972 and 1978; the Age Discrimination in Employment Act of 1967, amended 1978 and 1986; the Occupational Safety and Health Act of 1970 (OSHA); the Vocational Rehabilitation Act of 1973; the Federal Privacy Act of 1974; the Employee Retirement Income Security Act of 1974 (ERISA); the Vietnam Era Veterans Readjustment Assistance Act of 1974; the Immigration Reform and Control Act of 1986, the Americans with Disabilities Act of 1990; and the Civil Rights Act of 1991.

Recruitment is the task of attracting people with the desired skills, experience, and talent to fill jobs. The recruitment process requires the development of job descriptions and job specifications from job analyses. Job specifications refer to the human traits such as education, experience, and skills an individual must have to qualify to perform a certain job. Sources of qualified applicants for jobs come from within and from outside the organization. Promoting from within has many advantages if the people are fully qualified for the job. Major outside sources include "friends of employees," newspaper ads, campuses, employment agencies, the union, and other companies.

Selection is the process of reviewing the qualifications of applicants for specific jobs and hiring those that appear most qualified. The selection process is not scientific nor does it guarantee that the person selected will be the best available for the job. The last step in any selection process involves "personal judgment." Traditional steps in the personnel selection process are reception, initial screening interview, application form, testing, background investigation, in-depth selection interview, physical examination, and final interview/job offer.

Assessment centers are special methods of selecting managers for employment or promotion. The purpose of assessment centers is to predict management potential of participants through a variety of techniques such as in-basket exercises, role playing, incident analysis, and gaming simulation.

Orientation is a process of integrating the employee into the organization, their work group, and their jobs. It is often overlooked by organizations but can make a significant difference in employee performance and attitude. Good new employee orientation programs can lead to reduced start-up costs, more positive attitudes, greater loyalty to the organization, less absenteeism, and much more.

Training is the process in which employees acquire new skills and knowledge that will enable them to be more effective in the performance of their jobs. The management responsibility to train employees and develop them to their full potential is the number one job of American managers. Types of training programs are on-the-job training (OJT), apprenticeship, vestibule, programmed, and classroom training. Management training typically is classroom training. In addition to formal training efforts, employees can be developed through promotions, transfers, or disciplinary action.

Two things that best maintain a work force are compensation and benefits, which together comprise monetary income. Other factors, which generally revolve around "psychic income," have a maintenance influence, too. These factors include job security; opportunity for advancement; recognition; and other job needs, wants, and desires of employees.

Review Questions

1. Name the steps in the personnel management process. How does each step relate to the other steps?

2. How is a futuristic projection of human skills and talents needed in an organization determined?

3. Are you familiar with steps in human resource planning (HRP)? List them.

4. Starting with the passage of the Social Security Act of 1935, identify the major federal legislation enacted which affects the staffing of personnel.

5. Distinguish between job descriptions and job specifications.

6. Recruiting from within an organization is an excellent source of people. Explain the advantages of this source of personnel.

7. Discuss the personnel selection process. Why is the process not considered scientific and why is it not an absolute predictor of future performance?

8. Identify types of training programs available for nonmanagement personnel.

Assignments for Personal Development

1. Everyone who holds or has held a job write out the steps he or she remembers in the selection process prior to being offered the job. Compare experiences in open discussion and relate what occurred with the steps in the selection process in this chapter.

2. Job descriptions are a written statement of the duties and responsibilities of a person holding a job. In one or two paragraphs write a job description of the professor teaching your class. Compare yours with other students in open class discussion. Afterward, let the professor tell you what is right and what is missing!

Incident

HOW TO RECRUIT!

Pete Gray was elated! After a month of interviews, reference checks and a physical exam, he had been offered the position of City Recreation Director. He quickly accepted the offer even though he had never held a management position. The small town of 20,000 people had grown overnight from a "sleepy" town of 5,000 because of several major construction projects in the vicinity. The town had never had a formal recreation department, but the citizens demanded recreational services as part of a package to help justify increased local taxes.

When Pete was offered the job, the town fathers pointed out the budget constraints and the need to develop a quality program quickly. Five staff positions were funded in the budget, one of which was to be a receptionist/secretary. The other four positions and job titles would be left up to Pete. Pete realized he needed to do some planning and organizing quickly. Additionally a couple of other problems faced him: (1) The starting salaries of the four positions were fixed and were relatively low; and (2) the small town was over 100 miles from a major metropolitan marketplace and people with the job skills he needed were not in the small town.

Questions:

1. What should Pete Gray do before he starts trying to attract applicants for the open positions?

2. What recommendations can you give Pete Gray on how to recruit applicants for jobs in a small town when the pay is low and the location not the most desirable in the world?

Glossary of Key Terms

Age Discrimination in Employment Act of 1967, Amended 1978 and 1986: Prohibits employers from discriminating in employment based on an individual's age.

Americans with Disabilities Act (ADA) of 1990: Prohibits employers from discriminating against disabled persons in hiring or firing if an individual is otherwise qualified; by limiting advancement opportunities; by using tests or job requirements to screen out the disabled, and much more.

Apprenticeship training: A type of job training in which an apprentice works under a skilled craftsman who teaches the trade to him or her while he or she performs the work; usually lasts from two to five years.

Assessment Centers: Special method of selecting managers for employment or promotion. Through the use of a variety of techniques, the management potential of a participant is predicted.

Civil Rights Act of 1964, Amended 1972 and 1978: Title VII of the Civil Rights Act of 1964 prohibits discrimination in employment (hiring, discharge, recruitment, assignment, compensation and other terms and conditions of employment) on the basis of race, color, religion, sex or national origin in organizations that conduct interstate commerce; state and municipal employees and employers in educational institutions (1972); 1978 amendment added pregnancy, childbirth or related medical conditions to prohibitions and reduced the number of employees required for compliance to 15.

Civil Rights Act of 1991: Permits women, minorities, persons with disabilities and persons who are religious minorities to have a jury trial and to sue for punitive damages if they can prove intentional hiring and workplace discrimination.

Employee Retirement Income Security Act of 1974 (ERISA): Protects the interests of participants in employee benefit plans and their beneficiaries.

Equal Pay Act of 1963, Amended 1972: Prohibits wage discrimination on the basis of sex when the jobs require equal skills, effort and responsibility and are performed under similar working conditions.

Fair Labor Standards Act of 1938: Set minimum wages (amended many times since 1938), overtime pay and child-labor standards.

Federal Privacy Act of 1974: Applies only to the Federal Government and its contractors, provides certain safeguards for an individual against invasion of privacy and permits access to any personal records concerning them to that individual.

Human Resource Planning (HRP): Includes two steps: first, a projection of future human skills and talents that the organizaiton will need to meet its strategic objectives; second, the formulation of a detailed plan to recruit and staff jobs so that the organization can satisfy its strategic objectives.

Immigration Reform and Control Act of 1986: Seeks to protect jobs for those who are legally entitled to hold them, specifically American citizens and aliens who are authorized to work in this country.

Labor-Management Relations Act of 1947 (a.k.a. Taft-Hartley Act): Amendement to the National Labor Relations Act of 1935 (the Wagner Act) which was designed to balance some aspects of the Wagner Act. The Wagner Act guaranteed employees the right to self-organization and collective bargaining; Taft-Hartley lists unfair labor practices by labor unions, provides management more rights to speak against unions during an organization campaign; and established the National Emergency Strike provision (80-day cooling-off period invoked by the President).

Occupational Safety and Health Act of 1970 (OSHA): Mandates that employers provide their employees a healthy and safe work environment free from recognized hazards that can cause death or serious injury.

On-the job training (OJT): Most common form of training, an experienced employee or the immediate supervisor directs the work of a newcomer who does the work while the trainer watches and teaches.

Orientation: Process of integrating the employee into the organization, work group and job.

Performance Appraisal: An evaluation method that compares the employee's work performance against the work standards or the objectives of the job.

Programed training: Study courses available through colleges, trade associations, educational organizations, in the form of study courses or video/audio cassettes or computer programs that provide stages of learning and a means of periodically measuring progress.

Search Committe: A group from a cross section of functional areas formed to recruit, screen, interview and recommend applicants for vacant positions.

Selection: The process of reviewing the qualifications of applicants for specific jobs and hiring those that appear most qualified to do a particular job.

Social Security Act of 1935: Established a federal tax on payrolls to provide retirement and disability benefits to workers who contribute to the system.

Staffing: The acquisition and placement of qualified employees in jobs that fully utilize the talents and skills of the individual.

Test reliability: Exists when the individual taking the test scores about the same on the test when taken a second or third time.

Test validity: Occurs when performance on the job closely relates to performance on the test.

Training: A process in which employees acquire new skills and knowledge that will enable them to be more effective in the performance of their jobs.

Vestibule training: Training set up in a situation separate from the work environment which simulates the real working conditions.

Vietnam Era Veterans Readjustment Assistance Act of 1974: Requires government contractors to take affirmative action (actively seek) to employ and advance in employment qualified disabled veterans and Vietnam-era veterans who may or may not be disabled.

Vocational Rehabilitation Act of 1973: Prohibits discrimination in employment against individuals who are mentally and/or physically handicapped and requires government contractors to take affirmative action (actively seek) to employ and advance in employment such persons who are qualified.

Practical Concepts in Management

Practice Personnel Preventive Maintenance

About ninety percent of all management problems involve people in some way. These may be employees, other managers, customers, suppliers or others. Problems involving people are called *general management problems.*

A lot of time and effort is spent by managers on people problems. The practical approach is to try to prevent these problems before they occur. Anticipating many of these problems in advance requires a program of personnel preventive maintenance.

Companies budget millions of dollars annually for physical plant maintenance. Why not budget monies for personnel maintenance and avoid some of the human problems before they occur and cost even more? Such an expenditure should produce a large return on investment.

A personnel preventive maintenance program requires management to organize a department or group for the sole purpose of continuously reviewing employee job needs, wants and desires. Its objective would be to achieve complete job satisfaction among employees while insuring good employee performance, efficient operations and increased loyalty to the company. It is a very good concept.

You as a manager can perform much the same function individually, in the absence of such an organized effort, by knowing your personnel and practicing effective leadership and communication techniques.

Above all, do not wait until a problem develops; be proactive—try to prevent it!

Develop Employees to Their Fullest

Of all the factors of production only "people" can grow and develop into something **more** valuable than they were originally.

Managers have a major responsibility to develop employees to their fullest. This is a twenty-four hour a day job.

Since people are the number one resource of any organization, a number one priority of every manager is to guide, direct, educate, train, inspire, stimulate and encourage all employees to grow and develop to their maximum potential.

The benefits of this are obvious. The employee becomes more valuable and will either gain more job security, a promotion or both. The manager benefits because all employee efforts reflect on him or her. Finally, the organization benefits from having a more productive and valuable employee.

It is economically and socially sound to develop employees to their fullest. You do this through practicing positive leadership techniques and professional management.

References and Chapter Notes:

[1] Donald P. Crane, *Personnel, The Management of Human Resources*, 3rd ed. (Boston: Kent Publishing Company, 1982), p. 11.

[2] For a complete definition and discussion of job analysis, job description and job specification, see Chapter 9.

[3] Wendell L. French, *The Personnel Management Process*, 5th ed. (Boston: Houghton Mifflin Company, 1982), p. 189.

[4] Eli Ginzberg, "The Ineffective Soldier," *Advanced Management*, Vol. 24-26, June, 1960, pp. 16-21.

[5] Comments based on selected material from Robert L. Mathis and John H. Jackson, *Personnel, Contemporary Perspectives and Applications* (St. Paul: West Publishing Company, 1982), pp. 194-216.

[6] Richard I. Henderson, *Compensation Management: Rewarding Performance*, 6th ed. (Englewood Cliffs, NJ: Prentice-Hall, Inc., 1994), p. 551.

[7] Daniel N. Kanouse and Philomena I. Warihay, "A New Look at Employee Orientation," *Training and Development Journal*, 1980, p. 38.

[8] Donald P. Crane, *Personnel, The Management of Human Resources*, 4th ed. (Boston: Kent Publishing Company, 1986), p. 283.

[9] Crawford H. Greenwalt, *The Uncommon Man* (New York: McGraw-Hill Book Company, Inc., 1959), p. 32.

[10] Crane, *Personnel*, 3rd ed., p. 538.

SECTION IV

THE HUMAN SIDE OF ADMINISTRATION

CHAPTER 11

MOTIVATION AND EMPLOYEE PERFORMANCE

After studying this chapter, **you will know:**

- The meaning of motivation
- Managers control the work environment
- Scientific management's approach to motivation
- The significance of the Hawthorne Studies
- The Equity Theory of motivation
- The Need Hierarchy Theory of motivation
- Need-based motivation theory
- Motivation-Maintenance Theory
- Theory X and Theory Y
- Preference-Expectancy Theory
- Reinforcement Theory
- Common factors that tend to promote motivation
- The meaning of *morale*
- How job satisfaction relates to performance

Introduction

Previous chapters have presented information on the management functions of planning and organizing. These important functions are major activities of every manager. After developing plans and programs, structuring the organization properly to achieve objectives and goals; then, managers are ready to put their plans and programs into action. This activity is called *implementing* or *directing*. *Implementing is working through others (employees) to achieve the goals and objectives.* Most often managers are judged not by what they do but rather by what they cause to happen—by what they cause others to do. An essential part of a manager's job is to stimulate motivated employees to want to perform job assignments and reach the goals and objectives.

According to Professor David Schwartz, the *goal of motivation is to cause people to put forth their best efforts with enthusiasm and effectiveness, in order to achieve and hopefully surpass organizational objectives.*[1]

Highly motivated employees can effect significant increases in performance and significant decreases in problems that plague management such as absenteeism, tardiness, chronic complaining and low morale. Managers in sport administration strive hard to get student-athletes, player personnel and all other employees or participants to perform near their full ability. The sports pages regularly include stories about highly-paid professional athletes who perform well below their potential or cause continuous problems for professional teams.

This chapter is designed to clarify the meaning of motivation; to define the basic factors that affect motivation; present motivation theories, and to show the importance of employee morale to worker productivity.

Professional managers understand that low employee motivation is a common problem in many American organizations. Better comprehension of the subject is the first step to assist managers who wish to make changes that will influence employee motivation positively.

Understanding Motivation

The word "motivation" comes from the Latin word movere, which means "to move." It is difficult to evaluate a person's motivation, however, until the person does something. Motivation pertains to what activates human behavior. Some motives originate from physiological needs such as basic human survival needs like food and water. Other motives stem from psychological needs. For example, *motivation can be regarded as the psychological process that gives behavior purpose and direction.* Some employees have motives that begin with such psychological needs as a desire for recognition, status, self-esteem and achievement.

Hersey and Blanchard define *motives as needs, wants, drives or impulses within the individual.* They continue by saying that managers who wish to predict and control employee activities must know which motives or needs evoke certain actions at a particular time.[2]

Professor Stan Kossen defines a *need as something that gives a person a feeling of deprivation when it is missing.*[3] If a need is not being met, the individual becomes motivated to satisfy the need. An example might be an employee who feels deprived because he or she does not have medical benefits associated the job. This person might appeal to the union or to management to add such benefits as soon as possible, or the employee may actively seek another job where medical benefits are provided.

Managers have considerable control over the work environment. Managers set the tome and create the work climate which can be positive or negative. A worker who needs to have his or her work recognized and appreciated can be satisfied by the proper attitude of the manager.

Where the work climate is positive, employees feel secure, have open communication with their boss, understand the importance of their work, and feel they are being treated fairly. Basic conditions exist for high motivation. In addition, managers design and implement monetary reward programs, which include salaries, bonuses and fringe benefits, as well as psychological incentive programs. Psychological incentives include recognition, appreciation, status, promotion and added responsibilities which can motivate employees.

Victor Vroom, a management scholar and researcher, states that a manager's basic job may be to have highly motivated employees performing at near peak capacity; however, this will not happen unless two other conditions are met: (1) the employees must have the ability to do the work and (2) the work environment must be satisfactory. The work environment includes the space, equipment, supplies and support needed to perform a job well. The lack of any one of these conditions leads to less than desirable performance.[4]

Theories of Motivation

There are many theories of motivation that have application for managers. This discussion focuses on those that can be applied by managers at any level.

Punishment-Reward. Perhaps the most widely used theory of motivation, and certainly the oldest, provides reward for good performance or behavior and punishment for bad. In today's organizations, reward can be pay increases, bonuses, promotions, titles, special "perks," "attaboys," and more. Examples of punishment are bad evaluations, demotions, missing a pay increase or job promotion, transfers, bad work assignments, and the ultimate punishment—loss of job. Most modern motivational theories include rewards as a motivating factor, either in monetary or psychological form. But punishment is rarely mentioned as a basis for motivation since most researchers believe that punishment has no long-lasting positive effect on the improvement of performance or behavior modification.

Punishment used as a motivator has a short-term effect but creates resentment and low morale if used excessively. On the other hand, when psychological rewards are given for outstanding performance, employees respond positively and the effect last longer.

This theory is still in vogue and will not disappear. Students who make high marks on quizzes usually receive grades to match (such as an "A") while those who do not perform as well receive grades of "C" or lower. Parents still rear children and try to control behavior with praise and reward or with punishment like "time out," loss of privileges or scolding.

Many coaches have student-athletes run laps when performance is not satisfactory. This form of punishment used as a motivator has a short term effect but creates resentment and low morale if used excessively. On the other hand, when psychological rewards are handed out for outstanding performance, such as a coach's praise printed in the newspaper, the student-athletes respond positively and the effect is more lasting.

Traditional Theory (The Scientific Management Approach). Traditional theory of motivation evolved from the work of Frederick W. Taylor (refer to Chapter 1). Taylor, called the "Father of Scientific Management," made many contributions to management. One of his most important was the development of the Taylor Differential Piece Rate Incentive Plan around the turn of the century (1900). Taylor believed in rewarding employees who performed above the work standard. His plan established two wage curves for the payment of employees' wages (see Figure 11-1). When an employee's performance exceeded the work standard, his or her pay was calculated using the higher wage curve. If the employee produced less than the standard, the wage was calculated using the lower wage curve. Taylor believed that paying a highly productive employee the same wage as a less productive one would lead to a decrease in the former's performance and result in overall low performance by the employees. Thus, the need to reward performers who produced above the work standard. One basic assumption Taylor made was that money was a motivating factor when directly related to individual employee performance. If the potential financial reward was great enough, employees would produce more.

Most motivation theories used around this time (1900) were based on monetary rewards tied directly to job productivity or output. The nature of workers and more complex issues did not surface until well into the century.

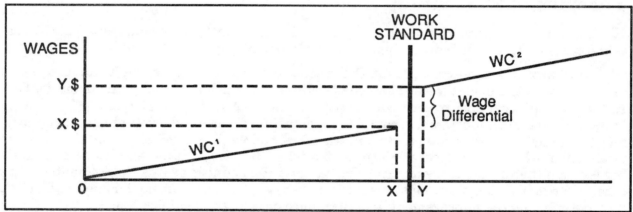

FIGURE 11-1: MODIFIED TAYLOR DIFFERENTIAL PIECE RATE INCENTIVE PLAN

The Hawthorne Studies. *The Hawthorne Studies* represent the beginning of the *Human Relations Movement* in American management. *Human relations* is the way managers relate to their employees. When employee performance is at a high level because of the way managers interact with their subordinates, we say there is good human relations in that organization. When employee performance and morale are low, we say there is bad human relations.

The Hawthorne Studies began in 1924 at the Hawthorne Plant of the Western Electric Company in Cicero, Illinois and ended in 1932. The original researchers conducted experiments that produced some unexpected results. For example, they lowered the level of lighting in the workplace, expecting productivity to decline. Instead productivity increased. In 1927 Elton Mayo, Fritz Roethlisberger and William J. Dickson, psychologists from Harvard University, were called in to continue the studies. Mayo and his associates conducted hundreds of experiments over the next five years. They improved the working conditions of female employees by scheduling rest periods, company lunches and shorter work weeks. The researchers found that productivity increased. Then, when they eliminated all improved working conditions, the researchers found that productivity continued to increase.

After much analysis the researchers concluded that other factors, beyond the physical environment, affected worker productivity. The other factors that stimulated performance were the social and psychological aspects of the job. The women were being paid attention and felt important. They were working together rather than being isolated, and they were allowed to participate as part of a congenial work group.

Hundreds of other studies and employee interviews were conducted by Mayo and his staff. The same conclusions were drawn that indicated employee performance was affected most by the interpersonal relationships developed on the job, not by the physical working conditions or pay.

Mayo recommended that management study and understand relationships among people; that management get employees to identify with management through participation (interviews, etc.); and that management strive to get group goals of employees aligned with those of management.

Mayo deplored the authoritarian, task-oriented approach that many managers used in that era. Managers who assumed people work only for pay and are self-serving in their interests have what Mayo called the "Rabble Hypothesis."

The findings of the Hawthorne Studies stress the importance of effective supervision on productivity and morale and on lessening human problems in the workplace.[5] While the Hawthorne Studies do not represent a theory of motivation, the results of these studies added greatly to the knowledge about the factors that can influence employee motivation.

Equity Theory. Developed by J. Stacey Adams, this theory concerns fairness among employees.[6] Fairness is based on an employee's perception of his or her job inputs and outcomes, regardless of how realistic such perceptions are. *Inputs relate to job requirements and outputs relate to what employees receive in exchange for their efforts.* Inputs may be the training, skill, experience and effort put into the job while outcomes are the rewards received by the employee such as pay, status, recognition, benefits and more.

Inequity occurs when an employee perceives his or her inputs and outcomes to be less than the job inputs and outcomes of another employee.

When employee outcomes (expectations) are not met, the employee tends to become dissatisfied. This can lead to lesser motivation, or the employee may strive to eliminate the inequity which would lead to higher motivation. If the employee perceives the inequity to be so great that it cannot be corrected, he or she may quit the job.

Need Hierarchy Theory. The most familiar motivation theory is Abraham Maslow's Need Hierarchy Theory. This theory is studied in a wide variety of academic disciplines, such as sociology and behavior psychology, as well as in management. In 1943, Maslow presented a paper, which has been reprinted by the American Psychological Association, in which he listed thirteen propositions that he believed would have to be included in any theory of human motivation. His proposition seven appears to be the foundation of his hierarchy theory:

> Human needs arrange themselves in hierarchies of pre-potency. That is to say, the appearance of one need usually rests on the prior satisfaction of another, more prepotent need. Man is a perpetually wanting animal. Also no need or drive can be treated as if it were isolated or discrete; every drive is related to the state of satisfaction or dissatisfaction of other drives.[7]

The term "pre-potent" is used here to mean a more dominant or stronger, more preeminent need.

Maslow's Need Hierarchy Theory consists of five levels of needs that must be satisfied. As each level of needs is met, the individual is able to focus more attention on fulfilling the higher level needs. Most people move up the hierarchy as they attempt to satisfy unmet needs. These five levels are Physiological and Survival Needs, Safety and Security, Love (also referred to as Social Needs), Ego and Esteem, and the need for Self-actualization.

Maslow's proposition number seven states that the appearance of one need usually rests on the prior satisfaction of another, more pre-potent need. Managers sometimes believe this means one focuses on one level of needs until it is fully satisfied; then moves upward. Maslow never constrained this theory that closely. He said that the lowest unmet need receives the majority of attention while other needs receive less attention. A manager therefore would understand that the basic physiological needs of an employee would have to be fully satisfied before the safety need becomes a motivating factor and so on up the scale. Society and the environment act with an individual's need structure to affect human behavior. If an individual, such as a celebrity or world-class athlete, is operating at self-actualization level but for some reason fears assault or invasion of privacy (a lower level safety need), that safety need becomes pre-potent and receives the most attention.

The thrust of Maslow's theory is that a satisfied need is no longer a motivator. When a need is satisfied, at once other and higher needs emerge and become the motivating factors.

Figure 11-2 shows Maslow's Need Hierarchy. Here is a brief explanation of each level:

Physiological and Survival Needs. These needs include the satisfaction of hunger, thirst, sleep and other basic bodily needs.

Safety and Security Needs. When physiological needs are met, safety and security needs become dominant. Safety needs include a safe work environment; security and safety from threats and criminal acts; protection and economic security.

Love (Social) Needs. According to Maslow's Theory, when both physiological and safety needs are satisfied, the need for affiliation and a sense of belonging becomes preeminent. These are such emotional needs as the desire for social acceptance, love and affection, and friendship.

Ego and Esteem Needs. If the three lower level needs are gratified, the need for esteem arises. Esteem relates to self-respect which comes from being accepted and respected by others. Good self-esteem also occurs when people view themselves as worthwhile individuals. A person at this level strives for the high regard of others.

Self-actualization. This is considered the highest order of need once all other individual needs have been satisfied. Self-actualization has been interpreted in many ways: realizing one's full potential; doing what one most wants to do with one's life; and feeling good about what you have accomplished with the resources at hand. This is the only need that cannot be completely met. Maslow believed one will always strive to become better and achieve more.

Value of Maslow's Theory for Managers. The value of Maslow's Theory to managers is that it emphasizes people's needs and allows managers to work toward providing employees the means to satisfy these needs and become more productive. Since management's task is to activate the desired human behavior to achieve goals, every manager must know each employee well enough to determine the needs and the need level that will trigger the most positive motivation.

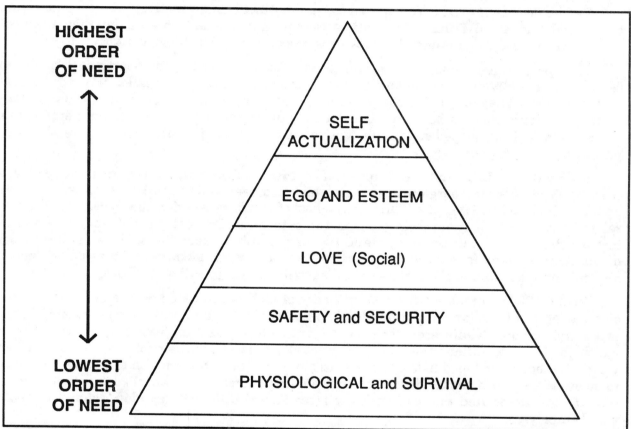

FIGURE 11-2: MASLOW'S HIERARCHY OF NEEDS

This theory is of great value in a general sense, but it does not apply universally to all people at all times. Current research demonstrates that the lower level needs (Physiological and Survival and Safety and Security) may be in sequential order; but beyond that, people may be motivated separately or simultaneously by several needs which are not necessarily in the order of Maslow's Hierarchy.

Need-Based Motivation Theory. David C. McClelland and associates at Harvard University developed a theory of motivation based on human beings' having three basic motivational needs: *power, affiliation and achievement.* Needs in this theory can be taught and developed in people according to McClelland.[8]

The *power need* can be observed when people try to change the course of events, influence other people or take strong positions. People who are strongly motivated by the need for power often are effective communicators and persuasive individuals.

The *affiliation need* refers to wanting to be liked, accepted, loved or have friendly relationships with others. It goes to the basic desire in most people to be a part of the group; to be accepted by associates.

The *achievement need* is considered to be a distinct human motive. It is the motivation to succeed and avoid failure. The satisfaction from personal achievement may be more important to these people than other rewards associated with achievement.

Most people have some desire for all three of these needs, but the degree each need can be used as a motivator varies considerably. High achievers, for example, may not become good managers. They may enjoy the power of the position of manager, but their intense motivation to achieve may not be compatible with the drive and complacency of their employees. Individuals with developed needs are motivated to look for job situations where they can pursue their need goals.

Motivation-Maintenance Theory. The **Motivation-Maintenance Theory** developed by Frederick Herzberg and associates has also been called the **Dual-Factor Theory** and the **Motivation-Hygiene Theory**. The basis for this motivation theory is that all work-related factors can be grouped into one of two categories. One category of work-related factors is called **maintenance or hygiene factors or job dissatisfiers.** The second category of work-related factors is called **motivation factors or job satisfiers.** To avoid confusion, students should think of the factors as **job satisfiers and job dissatisfiers.**

In the 1950s Herzberg presented a theory of motivation based on the results of extensive, in-depth interviews with approximately 200 engineers and accountants working in the Pittsburgh, Pennsylvania area. The participants were asked to describe job situations in which they felt exceptionally bad or exceptionally good about their jobs. From these interviews Herzberg developed lists of job dissatisfiers and job satisfiers. Job dissatisfiers tended to be associated with the conditions or environment surrounding the job. Job satisfiers were those factors associated with the work itself (see Figure 11-3) and included factors that motivated employees.

Job satisfiers, such as achievement, recognition, the work itself, opportunity for growth and advancement, are motivator factors. Factors associated with the work environment, such as job security, salary, supervision and working conditions, do not promote motivation, but they can prevent it from occurring. These dissatisfier factors (the maintenance or hygiene factors) must be given all the attention necessary to prevent employee dissatisfaction. Employees will not become highly motivated, however, unless both sets of factors are reasonably satisfied. No matter how well the maintenance work factors are satisfied, employee needs are recurrent and take many forms so that managers are constantly faced with the demand for more and more.

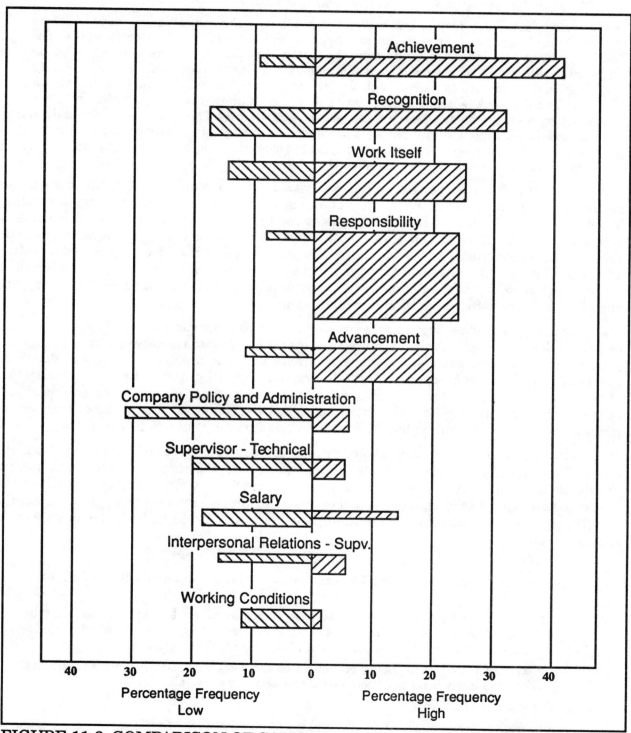

FIGURE 11-3: COMPARISON OF SATISFIERS AND DISSATISFIERS The wider the box the longer the duration of the attitude.

Reproduced from *The Motivation To Work*, Frederick Herzberg et al. John Wiley and Sons, New York, 1959.

Professor Herzberg explained motivation this way:

> The motivator factors are a direct derivation of the connections I have observed between the quality of motivation and hygiene and the quality of job performance. The basis of the idea is that motivators are the factors that meet man's need for psychological growth, especially achievement, recognition, responsibility, advancement, and opportunity. [Hygiene] factors are concerned with the job environment—conditions and treatment surrounding the work, specifically company policy and administration, supervision, relationships with others, salary, personal life, status, and security. Their underlying dynamic is the avoidance of pain within the work environment. Motivators are concerned with using people well and, when combined with a good hygiene program, with treating people well. The result will be motivated performance.[9]

Herzberg's theory of motivation has many critics, but his study and publications about motivation have encouraged much additional research. Perhaps the most valuable result of Herzberg's research to practicing managers is the emphasis placed on the work itself as a starting point for generating employee motivation. Today job enrichment programs, based on the Motivation-Maintenance Theory, have been introduced to increase employee motivation on the job. Job enrichment includes upgrading a job; increasing a worker's job-related challenges, responsibility and autonomy; and providing jobs that have meaningful work with opportunity for growth, recognition and advancement.

Any manager holding any supervisory position has the opportunity to enrich the jobs of his or her employees. Job enrichment requires a manager to use some creative skills to change the work environment. For example, an employee in marketing and promotions may be delegated more responsibilities with added authority to work on a special project with the temporary title of Director until the project is completed. After the project is finished, proper recognition should be given for a job well done! The job has been enriched, the employee feels good about the accomplishments, and the recognition provides the incentive for future outstanding work.

Theory X and Theory Y. In 1960 Professor Douglas McGregor of Massachusetts Institute of Technology wrote a book entitled, *The Human Side of Enterprise.* In his book McGregor developed a motivation theory called Theory X and Theory Y. This theory identifies two styles of managing based on the manager's view of human nature: Theory X or autocratic and Theory Y or participative. The assumptions made about human behavior in each style include these:

Assumptions for Theory X:

- The average human being has an inherent dislike of work and will avoid it if he or she can.

- Because of this human characteristic of dislike of work, most people must be coerced, controlled, or threatened with punishment to get them to put forth adequate effort toward the achievement of organizational objectives.

- The average human being prefers to be directed, wishes to avoid responsibility, has relatively little ambition, and wants security above all.

Assumptions for Theory Y:

- Work is a source of satisfaction and is as normal as play or rest.

- Threat of punishment is only one way to induce people to work, and it is not usually the best way. People who are committed to achieving the organization's objectives will display self-motivation and self-direction.

- A person's commitment to objectives depends on the rewards he or she expects to receive when goals are achieved.
- Under the right conditions, the average person will both accept and seek responsibility.
- The abilities to think creatively, to innovate, and to solve problems is widely, not narrowly, distributed among people.
- The intellectual abilities of most people are underutilized.[10]

McGregor's assumptions about human behavior in the workplace have been challenged as being too extreme to account for all situations and all human behavior. The popularity of the Theory Y approach, however, did encourage managers to practice more participative management, become more concerned with employee morale, and to concentrate on enlarging and enriching the jobs of employees to add challenge to the work and make it more rewarding.

The popularity of participative management today is a direct result of McGregor's Theory X and Theory Y and the publicity given it years ago. The technique of getting employees more involved in subjects which directly affect them is potentially valuable to employees, to the managers, and to the organization. When a head football coach asks an assistant coach to start drafting a game plan for the big game two weeks away, you can be assured the assistant coach will view that as a vote of confidence and put his best work into the project. Even if the game plan is altered later, the assistant feels more important, is more involved, and will be less resistant to the final plan.

Preference-Expectancy Theory. Victor Vroom published his preference-expectancy theory in *Work and Motivation*, a book published in 1964. Vroom suggests that employee motivation relates to preference and expectancy on the job. *Preference is what a person wishes to have happen. Expectancy is the subjective probability of what will happen if certain behavior patterns are followed.*[11]

Employees often have to make rational choices, based on their perception of a situation, to achieve rewards. For example if an employee thinks that working hard and working long hours will bring a significant pay increase, then he or she will be motivated to do this. An athlete trying to earn a spot on the starting team will perform as well as possible to get that reward.

Three relationships enhance motivated behavior: a positive relationship between effort and performance; a positive relationships between good performance and rewards; and the delivery or achievement of valued outcomes as rewards.

Reinforcement Theory. The late B. F. Skinner of Harvard University was the leading proponent of behavior modification as a motivational tool.

Basically, behavior that leads to a positive consequence (reward) tends to be repeated, while behavior that leads to a negative consequence (punishment) tends not to be repeated.[12]

Positive reinforcement practices include rewards such as a promotion, better pay or transfer to a better job. Skinner believed that rewards or positive reinforcement was the best motivational stimulus to change behavior. Negative consequences or punishment can likely lead to undesirable behavior.

A manager who practices positive reinforcement is generous with earned praise, encouragement, and allowing employee participation in problem-solving and decision-making that affects them.

Positive reinforcement in the form of rewards should be based on performance. In order to make rewards a meaningful and motivating factor, they should correspond with the level of performance and be issued shortly after they are earned so that there can be no doubt about the correlation.

Classifying Motivation Theories

Motivation theories tend to be classified as either **content theories, process theories, or reinforcement theories.**

Content theories such as those proposed by Maslow, Herzberg, McClelland and McGregor focus on the needs within individuals that cause them to act in certain ways. **Process theories** such as Vroom's expectancy theory and Adams' equity theory concentrate on rewards that individuals will possibly receive if they behave or work in a certain way. **Reinforcement theories** associated with B. F. Skinner and others base motivation on consequences of past action influencing future actions.

From a review of all types of motivation theories, some common threads emerge that can be valuable to practicing managers. See Figure 11-4 for a list of the most important.

- The Employee's skills match the requirements of the job
- There is open communication between the employee and the manager (boss)
- The work is challenging and stimulating
- Participation is encouraged in problem-solving and decision-making
- Managers provide positive feedback (recognition)
- Employees are allowed some autonomy or independence of action
- There is opportunity for personal growth
- There is opportunity for promotion
- Compensation, monetary and psychological, is fair as it relates to employee performance
- Jobs are secure (steady employment and benefits)
- Good working conditions and necessary resources exist

FIGURE 11-4: COMMON FACTORS THAT TEND TO PROMOTE MOTIVATION

Morale

The American Heritage Dictionary defines *morale* as *"the state of mind of an individual or group in regard to confidence, cheerfulness, and discipline."*[13] Management theorists have a slightly different view of morale.

David J. Schwartz defines high morale as *"the confident, resolute, often self-sacrificing attitude of a group that has strong faith in its leadership and believes organizational goals can be achieved."*[14] Rue and Byars define (organizational) morale as *"an individual's feeling of being accepted by, and belonging to, a group of employees through common goals, confidence in the desirability of these goals, and progress toward these goals."*[15] The latter definitions refer to morale as an intangible factor that relates to a group of employees, not to an individual. Perhaps the most useful way to view *morale is as the mental and emotional state of an individual or a group relative to the tasks or functions they perform at any given point in time.* This definition incorporates the total feeling of enthusiasm, worth and confidence that an individual or group feels while allowing one to know that this attitude can be fleeting. A common way to express group morale is as *esprit de corps* where a group of employees feels a common sense and degree of purpose and confidence in the future. A classic example of team members' having *esprit de corps* occurs when two baseball teams make it to the World Series. All team members have a common sense and degree of purpose and confidence in themselves. Personal rivalries and differences are put aside, and group morale is high!

Organizations are interested in the subject of employee morale because of the possible relationship to performance and outcome. Other questions that need answering are these: (1) Do highly motivated personnel have high morale? and (2) Does satisfaction with a job or a situation equate with high performance?

Morale and Performance

There is a belief among practicing managers that high productivity results from high morale. There may be a tendency for morale and productivity to correlate positively over the long-run, but there are many exceptions to this generalization. A common case of low morale and high productivity often appears among remaining employees after an organization begins layoffs and personnel cutbacks due to economic difficulties. Fear of dismissal, which does not lead to high morale, will cause these employees to perform better and take their work more seriously.

There is general agreement that high morale in a work group will decrease absences, tardiness, turnover and accidents; however, morale is an intangible factor and is difficult to measure objectively. Determinants that can stimulate high morale include positive recognition of a group's efforts; organizational goals that align with the goals of the group; group participation in the decision-making process; and interesting work assignments. A famous research project that focused attention on morale and productivity is the Hawthorne Studies.

We now know that motivation is a process that gives behavior purpose and direction. Motivation is based on the satisfaction of human needs. Employees may be highly motivated to perform well in order to be recognized, get promoted or improve their self-esteem; however, this motivation may or may not be accompanied by high morale. It is possible to have highly motivated performers not be in harmony with the objectives of their work group, and therefore be a contributing cause of low group morale. Conversely, it is also possible to have a group of highly motivated employees working together harmoniously with high group morale. There seems to be no direct, continuing correlation between motivation, morale, and performance in the short-run.

Job Satisfaction and Performance

Job satisfaction, unlike the definition of morale, refers specifically to **the state of mind an individual has about his or her work environment**. Morale of the group can affect an individual's job satisfaction just as job satisfaction can have an influence on morale. Managers in the 1990s spend considerable time and effort trying to create job satisfaction among employees. The thesis is that job-satisfied (happy) employees will be better workers. Employees who like their current work situation are considered job-satisfied. Management scholars do not agree on the impact of job satisfaction on performance, but most practicing managers think there is a positive, direct correlation.

Methods introduced to increase job satisfaction in the workplace include *job rotation, job enlargement and job enrichment.*

Job rotation involves employees' being moved from one job to another periodically to reduce boredom and to increase skills and experience. This approach was popular after World War II in assembly plants where skills might be interchangeable. Today, with operational activities more complex and sophisticated, the options for job rotation are fewer.

Job enlargement is the expansion of jobs to give the employee a greater variety of tasks to perform with added responsibility. The redesign of jobs is an effort to minimize dissatisfaction among employees who are in boring, repetitive work cycle situations. Critics say that job enlargement may still result in boring jobs and may be interpreted by employees as a management ploy to get more work and greater output using fewer employees. Proponents of job enlargement point out that some employees respond favorably to job enlargement because they can learn and use new skills, have more responsibility, and feel a greater sense of importance in the total scheme of things.

Job enrichment is the process of designing jobs to include motivators (Herzberg) which can lead to more job satisfaction. Motivators include making the work more interesting and challenging, giving workers more freedom or self-direction on the job, and allowing more participation in the planning and decision-making. Students should remember that motivators or job satisfiers are not effective unless the hygiene factors or dissatisfiers are reasonably satisfied as well.

In recent years some organizations have introduced several concepts to enrich jobs and influence the job satisfaction and morale of employees. These techniques include *flextime, four-day work weeks* and *"casual Friday."*

Flextime allows selected employees to determine their own daily work schedule as long as they are on the job during certain hours called core time. Core time may be from 10:00 AM until 2:00 PM, but beyond that certain employees can set their own schedule. Many employees, such as working mothers, like flextime.

Four-day work weeks are popular with some organizations if the nature of the work allows this. Employees work four ten-hour days instead of five eight-hour days. This gives the employees a three-day weekend every week and is attractive to many employees; but problems can occur when determining which employee gets which day off.

Casual Friday is also called "dress-down day." In office complexes where employees are required to dress smartly every day, many organizations allow personnel to wear whatever they like on Fridays. Typically, dressing down means employees may wear jeans and a jacket rather than a suit or dress. Casual Friday is very popular in "white collar" work settings, but it has no value in industrial workplaces. It is interesting to note that in other cultures around the world, Friday is considered to be "dress-up" day for working employees. This is true in Puerto Rico and Mexico in the corporate world.

Summary

The most common problem managers face is how to get certain employees motivated to do a better job. Highly motivated employees can bring about significant increases in performance and equally significant decreases in problems. Motivation is concerned with what activates human behavior. Some motives originate from physiological needs (such as survival); other motives stem from psychological needs (such as recognition, status and self-esteem).

Many theories of motivation have been developed. The oldest is reward for good performance and punishment for bad performance. The traditional theory is exemplified by F. W. Taylor's wage incentive plan which pays employees who produce above the standard a much higher wage than those who fail to exceed the standard. Taylor assumed money was the primary motivating factor if the potential financial reward was high enough.

Abraham Maslow's Hierarchy of Needs Theory is well known to students. This theory consists of five levels of need: Physiological, Safety, Love, Esteem and Self-Actualization. Maslow said that the appearance of one need usually rests on the prior satisfaction of another starting with the lowest (physiological) needs and moving up the scale. He said that, regardless of any individual's position on the scale, the lowest unmet need would dominate.

Frederick Herzberg developed the Motivation-Maintenance Theory based on job satisfiers and job dissatisfiers. Job satisfiers relate to the nature of the job such as achievement, recognition and the work itself. Job dissatisfiers tend to be part of the conditions that surround the job such as salary, working conditions, supervision and company policy. Dissatisfiers must be adequately satisfied, but they do not promote motivation. Job satisfiers, along with adequate satisfaction of the hygiene or dissatisfier factors, are motivators.

Other motivation theories in this chapter are Douglas McGregor's Theory X and Theory Y, Victor Vroom's Preference Expectancy Theory, and B. F. Skinner's Reinforcement Theory, J. Stacey Adams' Equity Theory and Need-Based Motivation Theory by David C. McClelland. Motivation theories tend to be classified as either content, process or reinforcement theories.

Morale is defined in several ways. One definition is "an individual's feeling of being accepted by and belonging to a group of employees through common goals, confidence in the desirability of these goals, and progress toward these goals." Morale is an intangible and has an impact on employee performance in many cases. Motivation and morale may or may not have a correlation although there is not a direct correlation.

The Hawthorne Studies represent the beginning of the Human Relations Movement in American management. The findings of researchers are significant because these studies demonstrated that factors other than working conditions affect employee performance.

Job satisfaction refers to the state of mind an individual may have about his or her work environment. Job satisfied, "happy" employees tend to be good workers although there is some disagreement on this point. Methods to bring about more job satisfaction in the workplace include job rotation, job enlargement and job enrichment. Job enrichment is the process of designing jobs to include motivators.

Review Questions

1. Discuss the meaning of motivation and the three conditions which must exist for employees to become highly motivated.

2. Highlight the important differences between Taylor's Traditional Motivation Theory and the theories of Maslow and Herzberg.

3. Theory X and Theory Y are based on assumptions about human behavior. What are these assumptions? Do you think all employees are either an "X" or "Y" type?

4. Review the common threads that emerge from a study of motivation theories. Can you add to this list?

5. Define morale and discuss the relationship to employee performance and motivation.

6. Explain why the Hawthorne Studies mark the beginning of the Human Relations Movement in management.

7. Distinguish between morale and job satisfaction. What are some of the methods used to increase employee job satisfaction in the workplace?

8. Motivation theories tend to be classified as either content theories, process theories or reinforcement theories. Distinguish between these three classifications.

9. Explain how B. F. Skinner's Reinforcement Theory can modify behavior and motivate individuals.

Assignments for Personal Development

1. Conduct a small survey involving four or five friends who are employed on a regular basis. Much like Herzberg's study, ask each one to give examples of what he or she most likes and dislikes about his or her job. Review all of the responses and see if what your friends say matches up with Herzberg's job satisfiers and job dissatisfiers. (Remember that all theories have critics and none is "sacred.")

2. Researchers have said that marginal employees only work twenty to thirty percent of their ability whereas highly motivated employees work eighty to ninety percent of their ability. Make a list of five factors or conditions that highly motivate you in your present job or in a past job. Be prepared to discuss.

Incident

STUDENT PETITION

Rufus Stone, Athletics Director of Cascade College, had just left the office of the College's President. He had been called earlier that morning to discuss the student petition which was being circulated demanding the immediate discharge of Coach "Slim" Turner. Coach Turner had been basketball coach for 12 years. In earlier years, his teams had always been in contention for the conference championship; but for the past four or five years, Cascade College had been a "loser."

Rufus Stone accepted the students' complaints as valid because it was true that the team had performed poorly for several years. Yet, he also knew that the students did not realize that athletic costs, tuition, travel expenses, meals and such had been rising and money available for athletic scholarships was at a new low. Furthermore, the students did not know that Coach Turner had several family problems that took up a great deal of his time and worried him considerably.

Rufus Stone had conveyed this information to the President at the morning meeting. The President's response was curt and brief: "Stone, either stop that petition or get rid of Turner! I have got major problems to deal with and don't intend to become an athletic director at my age. What you need to do is quit taking care of Turner and demonstrate some ability that will help Turner become more motivated to do his job! Work on improving the morale of the student body and stop feeling sorry for Coach Turner."

Questions

1. What suggestions can you give Rufus Stone for improving his ability to help Coach Turner become more motivated to do his job?

2. How would you go about boosting the morale of the student body toward the athletic program.?

Glossary of Key Terms

Content theories: Motivational theories that focus on the needs within individuals that cause them to act in certain ways.

Equity Theory: Motivation theory that concerns fairness among employees.

Expectancy: Subjective probability of what willl happen if certain behavior patterns are followed.

Goal of motivation: To cause people to put forth their best efforts with enthusiasm and effectiveness in order to achieve and hopefully surpass organizational objectives.

Hawthorne Studies: Research conducted by Elton Mayo and others from 1924 to 1932 which represents the beginning of the human relations movement in American mangement; led to emphasis of worker morale.

Job enlargement: Expansion of jobs to give the employee a greater variety of tasks to perform with added responsibility.

Job enrichment: Process of designing jobs to include motivators which can lead to more job satisfaction.

Job rotation: Moving employees from one job to another periodically to maintain or generate enthusiasm or motivation.

Job satisfaction: State of mind an individual has about his or her work environment.

Morale: Mental and emotional state of an individual or a group relative to the tasks or functions they perform at any given point in time.

Motivation: The psychological process that gives behavior purpose and direction.

Motives (also called needs): Needs, wants, desires or impulses within the organization and/or the individual.

Motivation-Maintenance Theory: Motivation theory based on two categories of work-related factors: job satisfiers and job dissatisfiers

Need-Based Motivation Theory: Theory of motivation based on human beings' having three basic motivational needs: power, affiliation and achievement.

Need-Hierarchy Theory: Five levels of needs in a hierarchy that must be satisfied one before the other to motivate individuals; needs in the hierarchy do not become effective as motivators until a lower "pre-potent" need is satisfied.

Preference-Expectancy Theory: Employee motivation relates to preference and expectancy on the job.

Preference: What a person wishes to have happen.

Process theories: Type of motivational theories that concentrate on rewards that individuals will possibly receive if they behave or perform in a certain way.

Reinforcement theories: Those that base motivation on consequences of past action to influence future actions.

Skinner's Reinforcement Theory: Behavior that leads to a positive consequence tends to be repeated; behavior that leads to a negative consequence tends not to be repeated. Foundation of behavior modification (sociology and psychology).

Theory X and Theory Y: View of human behavior and motivation that identifies two styles of managing based on a manager's perception of human nature.

Traditional Theory: Scientific management approach to motivating using money as a motivating factor.

Practical Concepts in Management

How Do You Motivate?

New managers are interested in their employees' becoming highly motivated. Employees who are highly motivated are excited about their jobs, the objectives, the assignment, their responsibilities, the mission, etc.

People who are highly motivated tend to like what they are doing and have confidence they can do their jobs well. If employees are not highly motivated, the manager has a responsibility to stimulate them.

Since motivation comes from within a person, a manager cannot motivate someone else. What a manager does is inspire, stimulate and generate an enthusiasm in employees so that they become more highly motivated.

The best technique to use to achieve this is to inspire someone positively about the importance of his or her job. Stress that the work is essential; emphasize the value of what each is doing and its importance to the department, the organization and other employees; and generously recognize outstanding performance after the fact. Encourage outstanding performance to continue. Do not engage in negative stimuli such as coercion or threats of doom to get people motivated, even if it might work in the short-run. Employees motivated by fear or from threats will leave an organization when they get a chance, and any effect on performance is short-lived at best. You are seeking permanent change in motivation and long-lasting results.

Motivation tends to be the highest when morale is high. Employees who have a good feeling about the importance of their work, their place in the organization, and their future normally will be highly motivated and satisfied.

KNOW YOUR PERSONNEL

If you ask managers the questions: Do you really know and understand your employees? Most will say, "Yes." If a third party talks confidentially with the employees about how they think about their jobs, the company, what they want, need and desire from the job and company; then, often you get a different set of answers from those given by the managers.

When this is the case, and it too often is, there exists a conflict area between management's thinking and that of the employees. The employees and the managers are on different wave lengths. The results are that management bases its employee relations efforts on what it **perceives,** not on what employees truly think and feel.

Do you think this could cause problems? You better believe it does!

When managers take action based on their concept of employees' needs, interests, and desires and the expected results are disappointing, management has proved they really do not know their employees as well as they think. Every manager should work hard to understand each individual employee.

Know your personnel! Talk to them; listen to them; seek their thoughts; try to draw out their needs, wants and desires as employees under your supervision.

This will help you minimize internal problems in the future.

References and Chapter Notes:

[1] David Schwartz, *Introduction to Management* (New York: Harcourt Brace Jovanovich, Inc., 1980), p. 465.

[2] Paul Hersey and Kenneth H. Blanchard, *Management of Organizational Behavior*, sixth edition, (Englewood Cliffs, NJ: Prentice-Hall, Inc., 1993), pp. 19-20.

[3] Stan Kossen, *The Human Side of Organization*, sixth edition, (New York: Harper Collins College Publishers, 1994), p. 156.

[4] Victor H. Vroom, *Work and Motivation* (New York: John Wiley and Sons, 1967).

[5] Hersey and Blanchard, *Organizational Behavior*, pp. 56-59.

[6] J. Stacey Adams, "Toward an Understanding of Inequity," *Journal of Abnormal and Social Psychology*, November, 1963, pp. 422-436.

[7] A. H. Maslow, "A Theory of Human Motivation." Copyright 1943 by the American Psychological Association. Reprinted by permission in *Critical Incidents in Organizational Behavior* by Francis J. Bridges and James E. Chapman (Englewood Cliffs, NJ: Prentice-Hall, Inc., 1977), p. 195.

[8] See David C. McClelland, *The Achievement Motive* (New York: Halsted Press, 1976).

[9] Frederick Herzberg, "The Wise Old turk," *Harvard Business Review*, September-October 1974, p. 71.

[10] Douglas McGregor, *The Human Side of Enterprise* (New York: McGraw-Hill Book Company, 1960), pp 33-34, 47-48.

[11] See Victor H. Vroom, *Work and Motivation* (New York: John Wiley and Sons, 1964).

[12] See B. F. Skinner, *About Behaviorism* (New York: Random House, 1976).

[13] "Morale," *The American Heritage Dictionary* (New York: Dell Publishing Co., Inc., 1983), p. 444.

[14] Schwartz, *Management*, p. 481.

[15] Leslie W. Rue and Lloyd L. Byars, *Management, Theory and Applications* (Homewood, IL: Richard D. Irwin, 1989), p. 381.

Additional Readings:

Davis, Keith, and John W. Newstrom. *Human Behavior at Work: Organizational Behavior.* 7th ed. New York: McGraw-Hill, 1985.

McGregor, Douglas. *Leadership and Motivation.* Cambridge, Ma: M.I.T. Press, 1966.

CHAPTER 12

LEADERSHIP

After studying this chapter, **you will know:**

- The importance of effective leadership
- The definition of leadership
- The distinction between leaders and managers
- Five sources of managerial (leader's) power
- The fallacy of the trait theory of leadership
- Leadership styles
- What the *self-fulfilling prophecy* concept is
- Important leadership studies
- What situational or contingency leadership is
- The difference between transformational and transactional leaders

Introduction

Perhaps no subject in the field of management is less delineated than that of leadership. Interest in the subject of leadership has led to a proliferation of studies, research and theories. According to Professor Gary Yukl, "…the field of leadership is presently in a state of ferment and confusion. Most of the leadership theories are beset with conceptual weaknesses and lack strong empirical support."

The "leadership literature includes over 5,000 studies; but the confused state of the field can be attributed in large part to the sheer volume of publications, the disparity of approaches, confusing terms, many trivial studies and the preference for simplistic explanations."[1]

Despite the confusion and controversy, the study of leadership is important to students who will be placed in leadership roles in the future. According to Mr. Robert Turknett of the Turknett Associates Leadership Group, organizations of the future will require all employees, management and nonmanagement alike, to be leaders. He states the reason for this is the flatter organizational hierarchy with its shrinking management ranks and less bureaucracy coupled with the push for greater speed, better customer responsiveness and on-going innovation. Every employee will be required to think and act like an owner: lead one day, follow the next; be fully informed and able to evaluate all aspects of the business, without regard for the individual's position in the organization; take greater risks, make more decisions and accept responsibility for the results. Mr. Turknett's summary is that all employees in the future will have to use leadership in its most basic form by accomplishing the objectives through influencing and persuading others.[2]

The importance of effective leaders in helping groups and organizations reach their objectives has been demonstrated repeatedly throughout history. Great leaders in government, the military and business emerge as people who influenced the character and future of the nation. Examples go back as far as George Washington and include Abraham Lincoln, Franklin Roosevelt, Dwight Eisenhower, Henry Ford, John D. Rockefeller and others. In a more modern sense, the majority of Americans view Lee Iacocca, Ronald Reagan and Colin Powell as effective leaders in business, government and the military. In the history of football, select leaders would include Knute Rockne of Notre Dame; Bud Wilkinson of Oklahoma; Vince Lombardi of the Green Bay Packers and Paul "Bear" Bryant of Alabama.

Effective leaders are more easily identified by the results of their efforts and by the enthusiasm they generate among followers than by any other means. The qualities associated with effective leaders, however, vary with individuals. No set of common traits has yet been identified that can be used with consistent success when selecting people for leadership roles.

There is general agreement that leadership is essential to managerial and organizational success. This chapter provides an overview of the subject and reviews some of the more important studies in the field.

Leadership Defined

Students cannot study and review the subject of leadership without an understanding of its meaning. But there are many definitions of *leadership*:

◆ George Terry says, "Leadership is the activity of influencing people to strive willingly for group objectives."[3]

◆ Stoner defines managerial leadership as "the process of directing and influencing the task-related activities of group members."[4]

◆ Rue and Byars define leadership as "the ability to influence people to willingly follow one's guidance or adhere to one's decisions."[5]

The common thread in these definitions is that leaders must have the ability to influence people to perform activities *willingly*.

We will define *leadership as the process of inspiring or influencing members of a group to perform their tasks enthusiastically and competently.*

The ability to inspire or influence others is the "undefinable ingredient" in a leader according to Professor Robert Fulmer. He states that "the undefinable ingredient in leadership cannot be bought, sold, or built into an individual. If one has it, it can be nurtured and cultivated. If one does not have it, all the leadership training courses in the world cannot make one a leader."[6]

Leadership has been a subject studied and discussed by scholars in various disciplines for centuries. Consider the words of Lao-tsu, a Chinese philosopher who lived about 2,500 years ago:

> To lead the people, walk behind them....As for the best leaders, the people do not notice their existence. The next best, the people honor and praise. The next, the people fear; and the next, the people hate... When the best leader's work is done the people say, "We did it ourselves!"[7]

Do we have a shortage of effective leaders in this country? Most people agree that we do. Effective leaders are needed in every type of organization and at every level.

Leaders and Managers

The words "leader" and "manager" are often used as if they were interchangeable or synonymous. Managers should be, but may not be, effective leaders. Many effective leaders are not in management positions. Managers have "employees" who work under their direction and are accountable to them. Managers are totally responsible for the actions of these employees. Leaders have "followers" who are loyal to them as long as they do not become disillusioned with the goals or tactics of the leader. Employees receive pay and benefits for performing work assignments as directed by managers. Followers of a leader receive personal satisfaction and a sense of value from being part of the leader's group as they work toward achieving goals.

Managers who are effective leaders are clearly identified because of employee enthusiasm, loyalty and dedication to reaching the work obejctives. Keith Davis expresses the difference between management and leadership as follows:

> Leadership is a part of management but not all of it... Leadership is the ability to persuade others to seek defined objectives enthusiastically. It is the human factor which binds a group together and motivates it toward goals. Management activities such as planning, organizing, and decision-making are dormant cocoons until the leader triggers the power of motivation in people and guides them toward goals.[8]

In the simplest terms, a manager who is an effective leader has employees who not only perform as the managers directs them, but do so because they *want* to work for that manager.

Abraham Zaleznik, while a professor of social psychology at the Harvard Business School, wrote that "managers and leaders are very different kinds of people. They differ in motivation, personal history, and in how they think and act.[9]

Zaleznik differentiates between managers as they perceive themselves and leaders:

> Managers see themselves as conservators and regulators of an existing order of affairs with which they personally identify and from which they gain rewards. Perpetuating and strengthening existing institutions enhances a manager's sense of self-worth; he or she is performing in a role that harmonizes with the ideals of duty and responsibility. [Leaders] tend to be...people who feel separate from their environment, including other people. They may work in organizations, but they never belong to them. Their sense of who they are does not depend upon memberships, work roles, or other social indicators of identity.[10]

Hersey and Blanchard distinguish between management and leadership in a different manner:

> In essence, leadership is a broader concept than management. Management is thought of as a special kind of leadership in which the achievement of organizational goals is paramount. The key difference between the two concepts, therefore, lies in the word organization. Leadership occurs any time one attempts to influence the behavior of an individual or group, regardless of the reason. It may be for one's own goals or for those of others, and they may or may not be congruent with organizational goals.[11]

Sources of Power, Authority and Influence

Understanding how managers influence employee performance requires an understanding of the sources of power. Figure 12-1 shows types of power with an explanation of each. Power refers to a manager's capacity to influence employee attitudes and behavior.[12] Power may also be over material things, but the emphasis here is on influence over people.

Managers in formal organizations have *legitimate power* because of their position in the organizational hierarchy. *Authority* commensurate with the position accompanies this form of power. Managers may exert full authority over employees and resources to achieve objectives, but they may not be viewed as effective leaders. Typically, the amount of *legitimate reward* and *coercive power* a manager has determines the amount of their authority.

Effective managerial leaders rely heavily on *reward* and *referent power* to influence individual and group behavior and performance. *Indigenous* (native) leaders generally use *expert* and *referent power* to influence followers since they have no formal position of authority from which to exercise reward and coercive power. Political leaders, such as Presidents John Kennedy and Ronald Reagan, rely heavily on referent power to influence public attitudes. Great athletes are often indigenous leaders during a competitve contest. They have great skills (expert power) and unique personalities (referent power) which inspire teammates to perform at a peak level.

Early Interest in Leadership

Scientific Management Era. During the time of management pioneers Frederick W. Taylor, Lawrence Gantt, Frank Gilbreth, Harrington Emerson and others, the subject of leadership was given little attention. As the U.S. was quickly becoming a major industrial power in the early 1900s, the emphasis of owners, managers and consultants was on increasing output and decreasing costs in manufacturing operations. Employee wages were low, and the supply of labor was large in the major industrial cities. Concern with employee needs was secondary to the importance of achieving performance objectives set by operational managers. The so-called manager/leader of that day influenced workers to meet organizational goals by using a combination of legitimate (positional) power and coercive power. Later, when Taylor and Gantt introduced their incentive wage plans, they originated the modern practice of rewarding employees for outstanding work performance. Taylor's Differential Piece Rate Incentive Plan is considered the classical example of using money (pay) as a motivating factor to improve employee performance. As more firms introduced monetary incentive plans, the role of the manager/leader in such firms was modified to include emphasis on meeting employee needs as well as organizational needs by increased productivity.

Hawthorne Studies. As mentioned in Chapter 11, these studies spanned years and were significant because Elton Mayo and his associates concluded that social and psychological factors as well as other things affected employee work performance. These studies marked the beginning of the human relations movement in American management. From 1940 until the present, American managers have paid more attention to employee job needs, individual and group relationships in the workplace, the subject of morale, and to providing more opportunity for employee growth on the job. Manager/leaders still focus their efforts on achieving output objectives, but do so now through a process of providing more job satisfaction to employees by concentraing on employees' individual needs.

Reward power	Person's ability to provide rewards
Coercive power	Person's ability to punish
Legitimate power	Person's formal position in the organization
Expert power	Person's expertise, knowledge and skill
Referent power	Person's unique personal characteristics that are appealing to others

FIGURE 12-1: SOURCES OF POWER

Source: Based on the work of J. R. P. French and B. H. Raven, *Studies of Social Power*, (Ann Arbor, MI: Institute for Social Research, 1959) pp. 15-167.

Trait Theory. One of the oldest and most popular approaches to the study of leadership has concentrated on identifying the common traits that effective leaders possess. These traits may be physical, social or personality traits such as height, attractiveness, intelligence, creativity, enthusiasm, self-confidence, knowledge, tact, empathy, etc.

Trait theorists have believed that individuals who are effective leaders have identifiable traits that can be transferred from one situation or location to another. In addition, these theorists believe that all effective leaders have certain common traits. If this were the case, individuals who have these common traits (assuming such traits could be identified) could be selected and be groomed as potential leaders. The implication is that potential leaders have inborn traits which allow them to be separated from those who lack the traits and qualities to become leaders.

The trait approach to leadership has been challenged by many scholars who doubt the predictive value of traits. Eugene Jennings states that "fifty years of study have failed to produce one personality trait or set of qualities that can be used to discriminate leaders from nonleaders."[13]

Continuing this theme, Gary Yukl writes that "the old assumption that 'leaders are born' has been discredited completely, and the premise that certain leader traits are absolutely necessary for effective leadership has never been substantiated in several decades of trait research."[14]

It is likely that individuals who possess certain traits may have greater potential to be effective leaders than others; but there are no universal, identifiable traits which guarantee this. Furthermore, leadership situations vary widely, and the personal traits required in one scenario may not match the need in another.

Leadership Styles and Attitudes

Leadership styles vary with the individual leader. But the person's attitude toward people, the situation in which the leader finds himself or herself, and the type of followers the leader faces greatly influence the style of his or her leadership.

Charismatic Leadership. Some individuals are *charismatic*. They have the power and exceptional ability to gain the devotion of large numbers of people. Examples of this type of leadership are former presidents John Kennedy and Ronald Reagan, two people who had great charisma (personal magnetism) and were effective leaders. Charisma is a quality that is difficult to define but easy to identify when observed in someone. Often charismatic leaders do not hold management positions, but they wield tremendous influence over others who respect them and place great confidence in them. Charismatic leaders rely heavily on their personalities and unique skills to influence the behavior of their followers.

Negative Leadership. A negative leadership style relates to the leader's attitude toward people. Negative managers doubt an employee's desire to work; they use force and fear techniques to motivate and generally "over supervise" the work activities of the employees. Negative leaders subscribe to Douglas McGregor's Theory X attitude toward employees. Their view is that the typical worker is self-centered and has little concern for organizational goals.

Participative Leadership. The participative style of leadership involves allowing employees to have greater input in the decision-making process when the subject directly affects them. The participative leader understands that when employees participate (P) in a decision, they will identify (I) with what happens; and there should be little if any resistance to the outcome. The P and I concept is the basis for employee involvement (EI). Another name for this style of leadership is *democratic*. The foundation of participative leadership rests with Douglas McGregor's Theory Y assumptions about people. That is, people view work as natural as play or rest and willingly look forward to achieving organizational goals when they can directly identify with the objectives.

Participative leadership is concerned with sharing power with followers. One of the current buzz words in management, *empowerment*, refers to this, taking the form of self-managed teams as one example.

Leadership and the Pygmalion Effect. Years ago, J. Sterling Livingston wrote an article entitled, "Pygmalion in Management" which stresses that a manager's expectations are the key to a subordinate's performance and development.[15] This concept is based on George Bernard Shaw's play, *Pygmalion*, and its musical adaptation, *My Fair Lady*. In Greek mythology, a sculptor named Pygmalion created a statue of a beautiful woman, with whom he fell in love, that was brought to life with the help of the goddess Venus. In the play and musical, Professor Henry Higgins takes an ordinary, ill-mannered, Cockney flower girl off the streets of London and, through tremendous effort and sheer will, transforms her into a beautiful lady who passes for royalty. The moral of the story is that one person can transform another by the way he or she treats the person or by *expectation of behavior*.

From Professor Livingston's article and the work of others has come a management concept known as the *Pygmalion Effect* or the *Self-fulfilling Prophecy*.

This popular concept states that the *expectation of an event or behavior* can *actually cause it to happen*. Significant research in the field of education has shown that a teacher's expectations for students can serve as an educational self-fulfilling prophecy.

Applied to management or leadership, the leader who takes a positive attitude toward his or her employees and instills in them the confidence to achieve, while demonstrating the expectation that they will succeed, is a powerful influence on employee performance and behavior. Outstanding coaches usually employ this approach.

Classifying Leadership Styles. There is no specific way to classify leadership styles. One could say some leaders are positive and some are negative. One could list the traditional three styles of leaders as *autocratic or authoritarian*; *participative or democratic*; and *free-rein or laissez-faire*.

An autocratic leader makes all the decisions for the group. One who is a democratic leader encourages and allows the group members to participate in the decision-making process. The laissez-faire leader simply allows followers in the group to make the decisions themselves.

Leadership styles may overlap: a leader may be participative on some occasions and autocratic on others, depending on the situation. An effective leader will tailor his or her style to the situation, to the type of followers, to their own personal traits, and to their attitude toward people. This is known as *situational leadership*.

Leadership Studies

As of 1996, some 5,000 leadership studies have been conducted and the results published. Here are brief summaries of some of the most notable of these studies. Each study has contributed to the understanding of leadership; however, many questions about leadership remain unanswered.

Ohio State Leadership Studies. Conducted in 1945 by the Bureau of Business Research at Ohio State University and directed by Ralph Stogdill, these studies involved questionnaire research which attempted to identify effective leadership behavior. The eventual conclusion described leader behavior as two dimensional: *Initiating Structure and Consideration. Initiating Structure refers to the degree the leader structures the roles of the employees/followers toward the achievement of organizational objectives.* This includes the sound application of management practices such as coordinating, delegating, controlling and communicating.

Consideration concerns the leader's behavior toward the employees/followers. Examples include the development of mutual trust, respect for employees, willingness to listen and support employees, friendliness and acceptance of employee input and suggestions.

The Studies concluded that *Initiating Structure* and *Consideration* are separate and distinct dimensions. A high score on one dimension does not necessarily mean a low score on the other. Leader behavior is a mix of both dimensions. Whether a leader should be more concerned with Initiating Structure (i.e., be task-oriented) or pay more attention to Consideration (be employee-oriented) depends greatly on the situation, the type of work environment, and the urgency to reach objectives.

University of Michigan Studies. These studies at the University of Michigan's Institute for Social Research were under the direction of Rensis Likert. The goal of the studies was to determine the general pattern of management used by highly productive managers as contrasted with the pattern used by other, less productive managers. Professor Likert found that "employee-centered" managers, those who focus on employees' problems, relationships and the human aspects of work, had the best performance records. Managers who closely supervised employee work and kept constant pressure on employees to perform, which he called "job-centered" managers, led low-producing departments.

Likert identified four patterns or styles of leadership in his classic book, *New Patterns of Management*:

> System 1: **Exploitative authoritative.** Authoritarian form of management that attempts to exploit subordinates.

> System 2: **Benevolent authoritative.** Authoritarian form of management, but paternalistic in nature.

> System 3: **Consultative.** Manager requests and receives inputs from subordinates but maintains the right to make the final decision.

> System 4: **Participative.** Manager gives some direction, but decisions are made by consensus and majority, based on total participation.[16]

Likert concluded that System 4 was the most effective style of leadership/ management. Since Likert's studies, many scholars have challenged his conclusion by pointing out that in numerous settings managers have been high producers using a leadership style quite different from System 4. In fact, Hersey and Blanchard challenge the concept of one leadership style's being more effective consistently: "Evidence suggesting that a single ideal or normative style of leader behavior is unrealistic was provided when a study was done in an industrial setting in Nigeria [by Paul Hersey]. The results were almost the exact opposite of Likert's findings.[17]

The Managerial Grid®. Robert Blake and Jane Mouton developed The Managerial Grid, a method of classifying the leadership style of an individual. The Managerial Grid is widely used in management development programs.

Blake and Mouton's Managerial Grid identifies seven basic styles of management and rates a leader on the basis of *Concern for People* and *Concern for Production*. See Figure 12-2 for a visual representation of the Managerial Grid.

Concern for People (relationship) is measured on the vertical axis; Concern for Production (task) on the horizontal one. Each scale runs from 1 to 9, indicating more importance to the leader of each concern as the number goes up. Each individual is ranked for both concerns on a scale of 1 to 9. The ideal leadership style, according to the Grid, is point "9,9," which identifies an individual as a "Team Management" type of leader. This individual ranks "9" on the Concern for People Scale (demonstrating that he or she shows great concern for employees leading to relationships of trust and respect) and "9" on the Concern for Production Scale (he or she has maximum concern for achieving tasks and objectives). Figure 12-2 provides an explanation of the seven leadership styles identified by Blake and Mouton in The Leadership Grid.

There are similarities between the Ohio State studies and The Managerial Grid. Each measures human concerns or relationship matters on one scale; work-related or task concerns on the other and arrives at intersecting points which define individual attitudes about both areas. The Ohio State studies do attempt, however, to integrate behavior with the attitudinal items, while The Managerial Grid focuses only on attitudinal dimensions.

Fiedler's Contingency Theory of Leadership. Professor Fred Fiedler's research on leadership styles involved many different groups with diverse backgrounds and work experiences. He concluded that the success of a leader is not based on personality traits alone. Other factors such as the nature of the work, types of employees being managed, kind of organization and so forth have an impact on leadership effectiveness.

Fiedler isolated three major factors that influence a leader's style:

Position Power: That power the leader has because of the organizational hierarchy and his/her position of authority.

Task Structure: Refers to the clarity with which tasks or work are defined.

Leader-Member Relations: Concerns the trust, confidence and loyalty employees/followers have in the leader. Fiedler names this the most important factor.

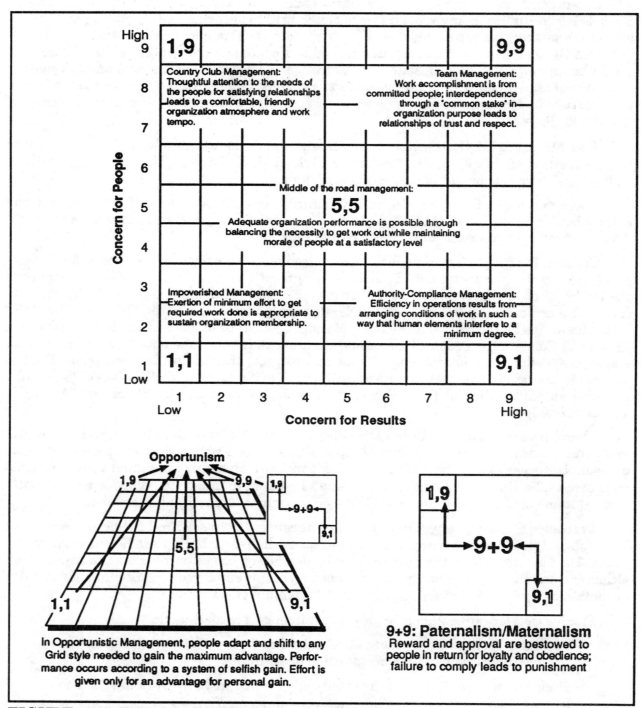

FIGURE 12-2: THE LEADERSHIP GRID FIGURE

Managers who have high position power with work objectives clearly defined have less difficulty inducing employee performance than those with less position power working toward vague or hazy objectives.

Fiedler's research led to the development of a *contingency or situational theory of leadership*. In his book, *A Theory of Leadership Effectiveness*, Fiedler says, "Except perhaps for the unusual case, it is simply not meaningful to speak of an effective leader or an ineffective leader; we can only speak of a leader who tends to be effective in one situation and ineffective in another."[18]

A Path-Goal Approach. The Path-Goal Approach to leadership is a contingency approach which tries to predict leadership effectiveness in different situations. Martin G. Evans and Robert J. House originally developed this approach which says that an individual's motivation depends on his or her expectation of reward and the attractiveness of that reward.[19] The leader is the source of rewards and the path-goal theory attempts to predict how types of rewards and different leadership styles affect the motivation, performance and satisfaction of employees.[20]

According to path-goal theory, the impact of leader behavior on employee satisfaction and effort depends on the situation, the task or work characteristics, and subordinate or employee characteristics. These situational conditions determine the potential for increased employee motivation and influence the action leaders must take to improve motivation.

In the path-goal theory, leader behaviors have been identified as these: supportive leadership, directive leadership, participative leadership, and achievement-oriented leadership.

Selecting the proper leader behavior to influence employee motivation now depends on the situational conditions mentioned previously. For example, if an employee's work is boring and monotonous, supportive leadership tends to increase performance and generate more employee satisfaction. When new employees are in an unstructured job with little formalization of work methods and procedures, directive leadership can achieve the best results.

Under this theory, each of the leadership behaviors is important. But any one of them can fail to gain the desired subordinate performance when applied because of the dynamics of the situational variable.

Transformational and Transactional Leaders. More recent studies on the subject of leadership have focused on *transformational leadership which concerns the leader's effect on followers.* Followers of a transformational leader feel trust, admiration, loyalty and respect toward the leader; and they are motivated to do more than they originally expected to do.[21] *Transformational leaders cultivate the acceptance of the group mission by their employees/followers.* Often such leaders are quite charismatic and inspire their followers through intellectual stimulation and individualized consideration.[22]

Transactional leadership studies are based on the concept that leaders can bargain with their employees/followers and provide rewards if performance criteria are met. This means that employees or followers must know clearly what is required to obtain rewards, i. e., what task or work or what behavior. The manager/leader would only take corrective action if employees/followers failed to meet performance objectives effectively. Some scholars have said that *transactional leadership is an exchange of rewards for compliance.*

Although transformational leadership and transactional leadership are distinct, different processes, a leader/manager may employ both types of leadership at different times, depending on the situation.

Application of Leadership Theories

Perhaps the greatest value of leadership theory to practicing managers and to students of management is to provide more insight into the subject. Leadership theories encourage more research and debate; however, leadership theory does not seem to provide a process to predict accurately effective, successful leaders nor does it provide a basis for training managers to become such leader/managers.

Leadership training can be of value in helping managers become more aware of situations that require leadership and in suggesting alternative ways of leading. Leadership is an art, however, and as such, relies heavily on the intelligence, experience, personality and knowledge of the individual who is in the leadership role. Most scholars and practicioners agree that leadership is a difficult if not impossible quality to define—that "undefinable ingredient" as Professor Robert Fulmer calls it (see Figure 12-3).[23]

From a review of leadership studies and from an evaluation of effective leaders, after the fact, certain common personal characteristics emerge. These points are not to be construed as personal traits which can be measured in advance to predict leadership potential. They are the personal characteristics that most managers demonstrate when they are performing as effective leaders that members of a group follow enthusiastically while competently achieving tasks and objectives.

Essential Leadership Characteristics. A study conducted at Yale and reported in *Psychology Today*[24] lists ten primary characteristics of leadership that are factors in being an effective leader:

> **First, be tolerant.** Try to stay calm during times of crisis; remain unflustered so that your emotions will not interfere with your thinking and actions.
>
> **Encourage others to participate.** Solicit ideas and suggestions about work that affects employees/followers from them; allow them to develop and implement their ideas. This is putting the P and I concept into practice.
>
> **Do not become obsolete.** Question yourself; look for new ideas; seek and eliminate mistakes in yourself and your thinking; elicit feedback from others.
>
> **Compete fairly and properly.** Know there is competition, but compete without hostility. Set your own goals and achieve them; do not go after the goals of others.
>
> **Watch the impulse for vengeance.** Being vindictive or seeking to "get even" for the actions of others is wasteful. Be honest in informing others you know what is happening, but there is no true payoff in revenge.
>
> **Be a good winner.** Win without exulting and share the victory with your followers/employees.
>
> **Lose gracefully.** Do not mope or dwell on defeats; move quickly on to the next task or project. Accept responsibility for your actions and do not blame others, but learn

from failures and mistakes. It is essential that manager/leaders learn the fallacy of doing the same thing the same way over and over expecting the results to be different.

Obey legal restrictions. Work within the law and organizational policies and rules/restrictions.

Be loyal to your associations. Work to help and/or advance the groups to which you belong, inside and outside of the business environment (such as church affiliations, civic associations, homeowners' associations, social clubs, etc.)

Set goals at a level of excellence but make them achievable. Perhaps this is one of the most important factors in leadership. Goals should require hard work and dedication, but they should be realistic. Employees/followers should be able to focus on the attainment of the goal as well as the effort to get there.

Effective managers know leadership does not require a magnetic personality or a special talent for making friends out of employees/followers. Effective leaders do have to influence people to produce their best efforts. Toward that end, effective managers have mastered a set of leadership techniques or practices that enable them to lift a person's vision to a greater goal, raise employee/follower performance standards, focus on the strengths of their employees/followers and minimize the weaknesses. Effective manager/leaders generate excitement toward achieving the goals and inspire their employees/followers to meet challenges and perform at their peak consistently. Figure 12-3 lists certain common personal characteristics of effective leaders that enable them to recognize and use sound leadership practices.

- **Leaders have the ability to inspire.** This is the "undefinable ingredient" in leadership which cannot be bought, sold, or built into an individual. If one has it, it can be nurtured and cultivated. If one does not have it, all the leadership training courses in the world cannot make one a leader.

- **Leaders have good human relations skills.** They respect for people; they have integrity; they stress cooperation and fairness; and they are not afraid to praise people.

- **Leaders have good verbal skills.** They know how to present facts and ideas effectively and how to persuade others in a confident manner.

- **Leaders are totally dedicated to the group's goals.** The actions of a leader through hard work and personal sacrifice demonstrate commitment. Leaders set the example for others to follow. Leaders also have the ability to project the group's goals as exciting, important and essential.

- **Leaders often are risk-takers** who influence others to go beyond normal bounds in achieving objectives. Followers respond to leaders who challenge new horizons without a guarantee of success. Such action usually generates excitement among followers and a feeling of being "special."

- **Leaders take full responsibility** for whatever happens and totally support their personnel through encouragement, showing an interest in problems, and representing them before higher levels of management.

FIGURE 12-3: COMMON PERSONAL CHARACTERISTICS OF EFFECTIVE
        LEADERS

One fact that managers must remember is that they represent all there is about management to their immediate nonmanagement employees. The influence one has as a manager and a leader constitutes the whole work climate and environment for your employees, for better or worse. Leaders have this influence over people around them whether they are consciously trying to exert influence or not. It is this climate or environment that one creates through leadership and management skills that determines productivity, quality of products and/or services, the commitment, teamwork and ultimate achievements of employees.

Factors Affecting Leadership. Many factors affect the opportunity for quality leadership to emerge. For example, if the organization is highly centralized or bureaucratic, there will be less flexibility for individual action and more reliance on following the prescribed course of conduct. Where activities in management are more decentralized, managers have the opportunity to do things their way and exercise leadership skills. Decentralized organizations provide more accessibility to employees and less control over managerial action by higher-level management.

Secondly, groups have personality characteristics. If the majority of the employees in a department are professional and "self-starters," a certain style of leadership, such as participative, might be most effective. If employees are passive and satisfied just to do their jobs and go home on time, the same manager might be more effective with a different leadership style, such as more autocratic. This is called *situational leadership* and involves assessing the nature of the individual or personality of the group before choosing and implementing a leadership style.

Finally, it is important that all members of a group share in the enthusiasm to work toward common goals. MBO (Management by Objectives) is one program that is designed to create this. If individuals work toward their own objectives contrary to what is good for the whole, there will be excess tension and conflict and an absence of effective leadership. A primary management objective is to have every employee working toward common goals which are important to the employee and to the group. This is called "harmonizing the objectives," and is one of management's top priorities.

Leadership Situations. In a leadership situation, employees are followers of a leader by choice. Each individual decides whether he or she wishes to be a follower or not. This "easy entrance/easy exit" of followers is a characteristic of all leadership situations. Followers must be interested, even fanatical, about the goals of the leader and group. The leader must heap praise and glory on the followers and make them feel important to keep them (such as Moses' "Chosen People" concept).

Summary

Leadership literature includes over 5,000 studies; but the sheer volume of publications, the many theories put forth, and the disparity of approaches to leader-ship leave the field in a state of confusion. Nevertheless, the study of leadership is important to students who will be placed in leadership roles in the future.

Leadership is defined as the process of inspiring or influencing members of a group to perform their assigned tasks willingly, enthusiastically and competently.

Life is like a dog sled team. If you ain't the lead dog, the scenery never changes.

Humorist and writer Lewis Grizzard

Leadership is the ability to get men to do what they don't want to do and like it.

President Harry S. Truman

If you want to soar with the eagles, don't trot with the turkeys

Anonymous

In the simplest terms, a leader is one who knows where he wants to go, and gets up and goes.

John Erskine

Sometimes it is better to plough around obstacles rather than waste time going through them.

President Abraham Lincoln

Never in the field of human conflict was so much owed by so many to so few.

Winston Churchill

Great leaders are almost always great simplifiers, who cut through argument, debate and doubt, to offer a solution everybody can understand.

Editor and Author Michael Korda

Leadership is the ability to motivate people to achieve objectives. [It is] the ability to solve problems.

General Colin Powell, USA, Retired

FIGURE 12-4: QUOTES ABOUT LEADERSHIP

The words "leader" and "manager" are often used interchangeably. Managers should be, but may not be, effective leaders. Many effective leaders do not hold management jobs. Managers have "employees" who work under their direction and are accountable to them. Managers are totally responsible for the actions of these employees. Leaders have "followers" who are loyal to them as long as they do not become disillusioned with the goals or tactics of the leader. Employees receive pay and benefits for performing work assignments as directed by managers. Followers of a leader receive personal satisfaction and a sense of value from being part of the leader's group as they work toward achieving common goals.

Comprehending how managers influence employee performance requires an understanding of sources of power. Sources of power are classified as: reward power (a person's ability to provide rewards); coercive power (a person's ability to punish); legitimate power (a person's formal position in the organization); expert power (a person's expertise, knowledge and skill); and referent power (a person's unique personal characteristics).

During the early twentieth century in the U.S., little attention was given to the study of leadership. By mid-century, the trait theory of leadership was popular. This theory says that effective leaders have common traits, and they can be transferred, i.e., an effective leader in one location will be effective in another. This trait theory has never been substantiated.

Leadership styles vary with individual leaders. Also the leader's attitude toward people, the situation in which the leader functions, and the type of followers the leader has greatly influence the style of leadership. Leadership styles can be called charismatic, negative, participative, positive, and self-fulfilling (Pygmalion Effect). Leadership styles also can be classified as autocratic or authoritarian; participative or democratic; free-rein or *laissez-faire*.

The most important leadership studies reviewed in this chapter are the Ohio State Leadership Studies; the University of Michigan Studies directed by Rensis Likert; the Managerial Grid by Blake and Mouton; Fiedler's Contingency Theory of Leadership; A Path-Goal Approach; and comments about Transformational and Transactional Leaders.

Perhaps the greatest value of leadership theory to practicing managers is to provide more insight into the subject. Leadership theories encourage more research and debate; however, leadership theory does not seem to provide a process to predict accurately effective, successful leaders before the fact nor does it provide a basis for training managers to become such leader/managers.

Leadership training can be of value in helping managers become more aware of situations that require leadership and in suggesting alternative ways of leading. Leadership is an art, however, which relies heavily on the intelligence, experience, personality and knowledge of the individual who is in the leadership role.

From a review of leadership studies and observations of effective leaders, certain common characteristics can be found:

- Leaders have the ability to inspire.
- Leaders have good human relations skills.
- Leaders have good verbal skills.
- Leaders are totally dedicated to the group's goals.
- Leaders are risk-takers.
- Leaders accept full responsibility for whatever happens.

It is most important to remember that manager/leaders set the tone and control the climate of the work environment for their employees.

The main characteristics of a leadership situation are easy entrance/easy exit; appealing goals; and followers who feel special or important.

Review Questions

1. Define leadership.

2. Distinguish between leaders and managers.

3. Describe sources of power in organizations.

4. Explain the trait theory of leadership. Why has it been discounted?

5. What is *charisma*? How important is having charisma to being an effective leader?

6. A participative style of leadership is based on the P and I Concept. Explain.

7. Explain the "Pygmalion Effect," also known as the "Self-fulfilling Prophecy." How does it relate to leadership?

8. Describe the following leadership styles: (a) autocratic; (b) democratic; (c) Laissez-faire.

9. What are some of the important results from the Ohio State and University of Michigan leadership studies?

10. Discuss the importance of Fiedler's Contingency Theory of Leadership.

11. What is the Path-Goal Theory of leadership?

12. Define transformational and transactional leadership.

Assignments for Personal Development

1. Using your professor as the model, relate which sources of power (reward, coercive, legitimate, expert and referent) he or she has as the instructor of your class.

2. Which of the common personal characteristics of leaders listed in this chapter apply to President Bill Clinton, Rev. Martin Luther King, Jr., and General Colin Powell. Be prepared to defend and justify your choices.

Incident

THE COFFEE BREAK!

As manager of a department of ten men and women classified as "professional staff personnel," you are uncertain how to enforce a decision handed down concerning the enforcement of the fifteen minutes coffee break (mornings and afternoons). Your boss has made it very clear that no employee shall be exempt from adhering to the rule regardless of seniority or the nature of his or her work. You know that your people are professionals and self-starters who work at their own pace. You also know that they will undoubtedly resent strict enforcement of this rule.

You have scheduled a meeting of all ten of the employees for this afternoon.

Questions:

1. Review the various styles of leadership you could employ at the afternoon meeting.

2. Select the appropriate style and justify its use.

Glossary of Key Terms

Autocratic leader: One who makes the decisions for the group.

Charisma: A power some individuals have to secure the devotion of large numbers of people.

Coercive Power: A person's ability to punish.

Contingency Theory of Leadership: Based on using the most appropriate leadership style in view of the current situation and conditions: Also called situational leadership.

Democratic leader: One who encourages group participation in the decision-making process.

Expert Power: A person's expertise, knowledge and skill.

Indigenous leader: A natural or native leader.

Laissez-faire leader: One who allows followers in the group to make the decisions.

Leadership: The process of inspiring or influencing members of a group to perform their tasks enthusiastically and competently.

Legitimate Power: A person's formal position in the organization.

Participative leadership: Involves letting subordinates have in-put into the decision-making process when the subject directly affects them.

Power: Refers to a manager's capacity to influence employee attitudes and behavior.

Pygmalion Effect (aka the Self-Fulfilling Prophecy): States that the expectation of an event can actually cause it to occur.

Referent Power: A person's unique personal characteristics.

Reward Power: A person's ability to provide rewards.

Trait Theory: Leadership theory that concentrates on identifying the common traits that effective leaders have.

Transactional leader: One who bargains with their employees and provides rewards if performance criteria are met.

Transformational leader: One who cultivates the acceptance of the group mission.

Practical Concepts in Management

Management Is an Art

Most of the activity of managing is an *art*. The artistic part of management is how one uses his or her acquired knowledge of the subject and job experience. It is the application of the sum total of all this knowledge and experience to a given situation to bring about the desired results. The emphasis is on "how" or the "way" you do something.

Management styles and techniques are as varied as the number of managers. Given the same decision to implement, ten different managers will cause ten different results. This is because of the "way" managers do things—the *art*.

Every practicing manager is an artist who performs every day in front of employees, bosses, peers, vendors, customers, etc. Yet, every manager is so different in background, experience, education, perception, training and knowledge that each will manage differently. This adds to the need for managers to be judged on results. Any individual manager should be free to perform in his or her own way as long as there is no violation of company policies and the philosophy of higher management is maintained. The bottom line is results not method!

Education, IQ, and Success in Management

Advanced education and having a high IQ are not requirements for success in management. If you possess a college degree and if you have a high IQ, congratulations! But, neither of these things guarantees success in dealing with people, making sound decisions, being creative, planning properly, etc. Most of managing is an "art" which cannot be taught in school. Being bright or having a high native intelligence does not necessarily produce stability, high motivation, or the human skills needed to work with and through people. In fact, the highest IQ in an organization may belong to a secretary or a shop worker, not a top manager.

Management is so complex that it is hard to isolate any single characteristic as a true key to success. You need to be smart enough to get the job done and know enough to minimize mistakes. No one is handicapped in management by lack of an extensive education or an IQ in the genius range. Willingness to learn, hard work, dedication to profesional goals, and good common sense are qualities that lead to success in management.

References and Chapter Notes:

[1] Gary Yukl, *Leadership in Organizations*, Third Edition (Englewood Cliffs, NJ: Prentice-Hall, 1994) pp. 438-439.

[2] Robert Turknett, "New workplace to require leadership qualities in all," *The Atlanta Journal/Constitution*, March 12, 1995, p. B3. Mr. Turknett is president of Turknett Associates Leadership Group, executive leadership consultants.

[3] George R. Terry, *Principles of Management*, Third Edition (Homewood, IL: Richard D. Irwin, 1960), p. 493.

[4] James A. F. Stoner, *Management*, Second Edition (Englewood Cliffs, NJ: Prentice-Hall, Inc., 1982), p. 468.

[5] Leslie W. Rue and Lloyd L. Byars, *Management*, Seventh Edition (Chicago, IL: Irwin, 1995), p. 375.

[6] Robert M. Fulmer, *The New Management* (New York: Macmillan, 1974), p. 336.

[7] Andrew D. Szilagyi, Jr., and Marc J. Wallace, Jr., *Organizational Behavior and Performance* (Glenview, IL; Scott, Foreman and Company, 1990), p. 384.

[8] Keith Davis, *Human Relations at Work* (New York: McGraw-Hill, 1967), pp. 96-97.

[9] Abraham Zaleznik, "Managers and Leaders: Are They Different?", *Harvard Busines Review*, May-June, 1977, p. 70.

[10] Zaleznik, "Managers and Leaders:", pp. 74-75.

[11] Paul Hersey and Kenneth H. Blanchard, *Management of Organizational Behavior* (Englewood Cliffs, NJ: Prentice-Hall, 1993), p. 5.

[12] Yukl, *Leadership in Organizations*, p. 195.

[13] Eugene E. Jennings, "The Anatomy of Leadership," *Management of Personnel Quarterly*, I, No. 1 (Autumn, 1961).

[14] Gary A. Yukl, *Leadership in Organizations*, Second Edition (Englewood Cliffs, NJ: Prentice-Hall, 1989), p. 176.

[15] J. Sterling Livingston, "Pygmalion in Management," *Harvard Business Review*, July-August, 1969, pp. 81-89.

[16] Rensis Likert, *New Patterns of Management* (New York: McGraw-Hill, 1961).

[17] Hersey and Blanchard, *Management of Organizational Behavior*, p. 109.

[18] Fred E. Fiedler, *A Theory of Leadership Effectiveness* (New York: McGraw-Hill, 1967), p. 371.

[19] Robert J. House, "A Path-Goal Theory of Leader Effectiveness," *Administrative Science Quarterly*, 16, No. 5 (September 1971), pp. 321-328.

[20] See Martin G. Evans, "Leadership and Motivation: A Core Concept," *Academy of Management Journal*, 13, No. 1 (March 1970), pp. 91-102.

[21] Yukl, *Leadership in Organizations*, Third Edition, p. 351.

[22] Yukl, p. 352.

[23] Fulmer, *Management*, p. 336.

[24] John H. Melchinger, "Leadership Essentials," *Minding Your Own Business* (Tampa, FL: John H. Melchinger Company, 1990), based on a study conducted at the Labor and Management Center at Yale and reported in *Psychology Today*.

CHAPTER 13

THE COMMUNICATIONS PROCESS

After studying this chapter, you will know:

- The importance of communication
- The definition of communication
- Steps in the communication process
- Barriers to effective interpersonal communication
- How to overcome barriers in interpersonal communication
- General principles of good communication
- About communication in the formal organization
- Why the "grapevine" can be a communication asset or liability
- The value of external communication
- More about electronic communication and its advantages and disadvantages

Introduction

This chapter provides a basic understanding of the importance of communication for managers in any type of organization. Sport managers are no different from managers in other industries who desire to implement plans and programs effectively and must transmit information, ideas and feelings accurately to other parties. Of particular value to students are sections in this chapter on steps in the communication process, barriers to effective communication, and general principles of good communication. Also included is a discussion of the informal communication system within the formal organization, called the *grapevine*, which can be an asset or a liability to managers.

Communication is an integral part of managing, and generally the success and efficiency of an organization reflect the effectiveness of its communications.

Communication is central to human activity and interaction. All people communicate whether they are managers, employees, committees, customers, fans, stakeholders, students or the general public. Management personnel communicate with all of these groups and types of publics in the process of performing their daily jobs.

While the fundamentals of communicating effectively have stood the test of time and are presented in this chapter, students should be aware of some dramatic changes in the communications field. The advent of electronic communication has revolutionized the transfer of information from person to person, group to group, and/or person to group. Note the section on electronic communication at the end of this chapter.

The Importance of Communication

In earlier chapters we have seen that without managers chaos and confusion would reign, and there would be no organized effort. With managers in place we know that the world is better; individuals have jobs and higher standards of living; and society in general benefits. To be an **effective** manager one must have knowledge of the job and environment, possess a variety of skills, and be totally dedicated to achieving organizational objectives. Perhaps the most important skill a manager needs is the ability to communicate effectively.

Effective communication refers to the receiver understanding the message as intended by the sender.

Here are a few of the major jobs of managers. Note how important communication skills are to the successful performance of each:

Planning. All managers plan for the purpose of attaining the objectives in the proper period of time, with a minimum of problems, and in the most efficient and effective way. Planning often involves more than one person. Plans have to be approved by higher management; plans are implemented through others; and plans usually impact employees and other individuals and groups both inside and outside the organization. Would you say communication skills are needed to implement plans successfully? The answer is yes. A manager may be a master planner on paper, but he or she can fail miserably in the implementation stage because of poor communication skills.

Decision-making. Managerial decisions flow downward in the organization and generate "actions" which in turn cause "change" in the organization. Managers must effectively communicate the need for action and change if decisions are to be accepted and not resisted by those affected.

Coordinating. A major responsibility of managers is to combine the needed resources, human and otherwise, in the right quantity, of the right quality, at the right place and at the right time to generate efficiency as the goal is reached. Doing this requires effective communication skills as the manager must explain, educate, visualize and harmonize to attain coordination among the employees involved.

Leading. For leaders to have followers they must communicate the objectives of the effort in such a way that followers become enthused, excited and stimulated. If they cannot do this, there will be no followers. Effective leaders must be good communicators whether they are managers or not. Historic leaders such as Franklin D. Roosevelt, Winston Churchill, Adolph Hitler and Martin Luther King, Jr. were master communicators.

Delegating. Assigning work to others is an essential part of management. The job of the manager is not to "do" the work but rather to "get it done" working through others. Can you think of any other management activity that requires greater communication know-how? If delegatees do not understand exactly what is expected, why it is important, and when the work is to be completed, then the anticipated result must be unsatisfactory performance and failure. Managers are judged on these results.

Controlling. This managerial function appears in all aspects of running an organization. Standards must be established, and the employees affected by them must understand what is expected. Employee performance is measured against the standard, and corrective action is taken if standards are not met. Control programs are essential and work well if employees and departments affected understand the importance of control; if they believe the standards are fair; and if the evaluation and corrective action taken are positive and help both the individual and the organization. None of the desired results occur unless managers communicate effectively in the administration of control programs.

Organizing. Sound organization requires placing qualified employees in the right jobs and balancing the output of work between human resources and physical ones. This generates efficiency of effort. Structuring an organization refers to a clear definition of position authority, responsibility, accountability and communication channels. Lines on an organization chart represent the formal lines of communication. Defects in the organization, especially in the area of communication, are the number one source of daily management problems. To organize soundly requires managers to inform, educate, visualize, train and review employees on a regular basis—all of which demand good communication skills.

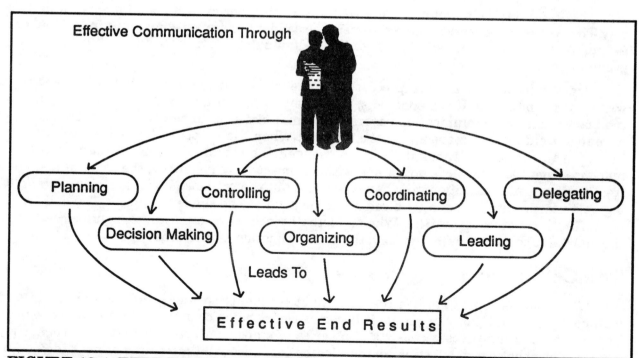

FIGURE 13-1: EFFECTIVE COMMUNICATION LEADS TO EFFECTIVE END
　　　RESULTS

In summary, every aspect of a manager's job requires good communication skills, and a considerable amount of a manager's time is spent communicating. American organizations are learning to appreciate the value of effective communication.

D. M. Kersey reports in a study of 1,700 members of the International Association of Business Communicators that effective communication in an organization means higher profits and improved employee relations. He states that communication professionals are becoming instrumental in areas such as customer relations, employee training, benefits delivery and investor relations. Also, communication departments are now more involved in business planning and strategy development.[1]

A second important study which emphasizes the role of effective management communication was conducted by Posner, Kouzes and Schmidt. Their study relates to organizational values shared between managers and employees and the impact such shared values have on job satisfaction, efficiency and employee commitment to organization goals. Their findings indicate that a similarity between organizational values and employees' value systems strengthens both the individuals and the organization as a whole. They recommend that managers use these findings and develop programs to communicate organizational values; then, recruit and train personnel who best fit within the corporate value system.[2]

Interpersonal Communication

Communication can be defined as the act or action of imparting or transmitting ideas, information, facts or feelings to a second party.

There are dozens of definitions of communication; however, all communication is two-way. There must be a sender and a receiver. The sender or receiver may be an individual or a group. Communication takes place between individuals; individuals and groups; and from group to group.

Communication is a joint process. If someone speaks, someone listens. If someone writes, someone reads. If someone acts, someone watches. If a second party does not listen, read or watch, no communication occurs. For communication to be **effective** there must be an understanding and response by the receiver. When the response from the receiver is in line with the message transmitted by the sender, the communication is **effective**. If the response from the receiver is not in line with the message transmitted, the communication if **ineffective**. Communication may have occurred, but the response indicates misunderstanding, misinterpretation or simply a refusal to respond as the sender requests. The end result is **ineffective communication**. When a football coach sends a play in to a quarterback, but the quarterback calls a different play; the communication is ineffective.

The Communication Process

When one seriously studies the activity of transmitting ideas, information, facts and feelings to a second party or group, it becomes clear that a communication **process** exists. The communication process consists of a series of steps that are in sequential order. They are the steps that every effective communicator goes through (knowingly or not): idea origination; the message; channel selecting and encoding; transmission; receiving; decoding, and feedback.

Idea Origination. Ideas are the source of planned communications. If a manager has some ideas about the cause of low employee morale, he or she may wish to communicate these ideas to the supervisors at a group meeting. If an athlete has ideas about improving team performance, he or she may want to convey these ideas to the coach or team's manager. If a fan has an idea about improving a team's performance or an individual athlete's effort, he or she may wish to transmit this idea to the team's manager or to the athlete. It is important that the sender consider ideas carefully before developing a message. Ideas should have legitimate value and warrant the time and effort it takes to communicate them effectively to a second party. If it passes this test, a decision will be made to communicate.

The Message. The message is the formalization of the ideas which the sender wishes to convey. The message in its physical form may be transmitted by words, written or spoken, or by body language of the sender (nonverbal). Messages must be framed carefully to minimize misunderstanding by the receiver.

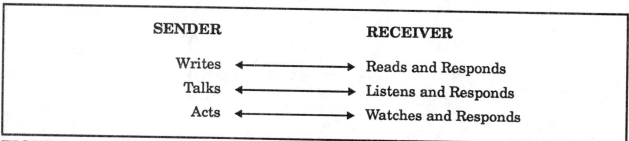

FIGURE 13-2: COMMUNICATION IS A JOINT PROCESS

Channel Selection and Encoding. Selecting the right channel for transmitting a message is a key to effective communication. Common channels are writing, speaking, electronic media equipment, and nonverbal physical actions. In the old West, Indians used smoke signals to communicate danger, tribe movements and warnings. The channel selected also must be compatible with symbols selected for encoding. Specific channels used to transmit messages might be face-to-face meetings, written letters, fax messages, computer printouts, telephone calls and many others.

Encoding refers to the symbols or gestures a sender selects to transmit a message through the desired channel so that the receiver decodes it properly. Forms of expression may be charts, tables, facial looks, purposeful anger, words and written summaries.

Transmission. Transmission of the message through the selected channel is the next step in the communication process. This is the physical activity that takes the encoded ideas to the receiver. Occasionally problems occur in transmitting messages, such as a memo being lost in the delivery of interoffice mail; however, transmission tends to be the easiest of steps in the communication process because no interpretation is required.

Receiver. The receiver or receivers are the persons to whom the message is directed. If the message does not get to the intended receiver, no communication takes place.

Decoding. Decoding is the step in the communication process where the receiver translates the sender's symbols and gestures into meaningful thought. If the sender and receiver have similar values, experiences and word interpretations, there is less chance of a communication breakdown. Effective communication occurs when a receiver interprets the message from the sender in the same way as the sender intended.

Feedback. Feedback is a response by the receiver to the sender's message. It may be an acknowledgment that the message has been received, or the receiver may take the action desired by the sender. Feedback reverses the steps in the communication process. The receiver becomes the sender and the sender, the receiver. All steps in the communication process are followed by the receiver, now the sender, to transmit response to the original sender's message.

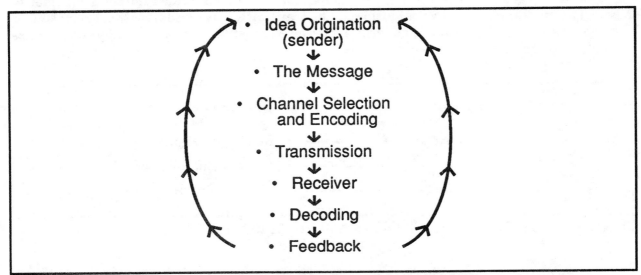

FIGURE 13-3: STEPS IN THE COMMUNICATION PROCESS

Barriers to Effective Interpersonal Communication

Studies about causes of communication breakdown list dozens of reasons. Each of these reasons can be a barrier to effective communication. Reasons run the gamut from the receiver not trusting the sender to prejudice and physical conditions. Figure 15-4 shows some typical barriers to effective interpersonal communication.

For our purposes six of the most common barriers to effective interpersonal communication will be discussed. They pertain to semantics, resistance to change, perception differences, listening, credibility and noise.

The Semantics Barrier. Semantics problems occur because people may have a different meaning or understanding of the words used in written or verbal communications. *Semantics is the science or study of word meanings.* When a sender uses a word with one meaning in mind and the receiver interprets the word differently, the intended message becomes distorted. The word "table" for example has over 100 meanings in the English language. Additionally, words may take on a different meaning depending on how they are expressed by the sender to the receiver in person.

A sender should carefully choose the words that go into a message to minimize the risk of misinterpretation by the receiver.

The Resistance to Change Barrier. It is almost a natural phenomenon for people to resist new ideas, new ways of doing things, or anything that might change the status quo of an organization. Frequently resistance to change by an individual or group becomes a barrier to effective communication. If the receiver does not like the ideas in the message, he or she may reject it totally, only accept the parts of the message they like, or interpret and apply the ideas in a way that will not upset the existing environment. Careful planning, educating and selling new ideas or changes to the parties involved helps to break down resistance to change. **Empathizing** with the receiver while you plan your communication is important. Putting yourself in the receiver's place or imagining you will be the receiver of the message helps a sender plan the communication better. Often this will remove the resistance to change as a significant barrier.

The Perception Difference Barrier. Often a message is communicated to a receiver who interprets the message in a totally different way from that intended by the sender. The receiver's perception of the information is quite different from that of the sender. Differing perceptions occur because individuals have different values, experiences, education, expectations and personalities. Often receivers perceive only information that matches their expectations. Also, they see and hear only what they want to see and hear.

A group of managers may brainstorm an overall organization problem and individually recommend action that mostly benefits their own functional areas. They do not perceive the importance of problems in other areas. Notice that in court several witnesses may be brought in to testify about what they have all observed. Each one's perception of what occurred may be quite different.

The Listening Barrier. Listening is the responsibility of a receiver in the communication process. This requires a receiver to be alert, attentive and to concentrate totally on the message being directed toward him or her. The responsibility of the sender is to make sure the receiver is really listening, not just appearing to be listening. In the process of delegating work to employees managers must make sure that employees correctly understand what they are being asked to do. Sometimes managers have employees repeat back what they have been told to check the receiver's interpretation and make sure the message was heard and understood as sent. Failure of a receiver to listen to a sender is a common barrier to effective interpersonal communications.

The old story is God made us with two ears and one mouth so that we could listen twice as much as we talk! How many of your friends talk twice as much as they listen?

Some receivers fail to listen effectively because they may be day dreaming, not interested in the subject, do not really understand the message, are bored, or are planning after-work activities. It is important to be certain you have the receiver's attention.

Good listening habits can be developed if one wants to improve. Several suggestions are give the speaker your undivided attention; be patient and let the speaker finish before you say anything; make sure your questions and comments are on the subject; do not be on the defensive; and repeat back or summarize what the speaker has said.

The Credibility Barrier. Problems of credibility arise when the sender is not trusted. If receivers doubt the knowledge base, the integrity, or the past performance record of the sender, credibility diminishes. It is difficult for subordinates to respond enthusiastically to messages received if the sender's credibility is in doubt.

A major case involving institutional credibility is reported by D. A. Safer. He reported that the American automobile industry in 1985 had every reason to believe that national public opinion would support their position on Japanese auto imports. The industry's statements and subsequent contradictory actions, however, encouraged the public to question the accuracy and sincerity of its statements, creating a credibility gap.[3]

Perceived credibility by receivers is based primarily on the sender's honesty, competence, enthusiasm and objectivity.[4] The sender may or may not possess these characteristics. It is how the receiver perceives the sender that matters.

The Noise Barrier. Noise is a word used in the communication field that denotes any factor that causes confusion, distortion, or disturbs communication. Examples of "noise" are poor lighting, lack of privacy for conversations, hand written (hard to read) memos, noisy equipment, the drone of ringing telephones, or emotionally upset employees. Most "noise" or interference occurs during the encoding and decoding stages of the communication process.

Overcoming Barriers in Interpersonal Communication

A manager's effectiveness depends significantly on his or her ability to communicate. The transfer of information whether by word or actions is effective if the receiver understands the message just as the sender intended and if the desired action is initiated.

Managers will be better communicators if they are aware of all the barriers that can hamper the communication process. They will be better communicators if they know how to overcome these barriers. Organizations have a responsibility to train their managers to be more effective communicators. For example, Xerox Learning Systems has developed a training program to help people prepare persuasive talks. Their program suggests that the most important rule for a speaker is to know the audience. They teach six steps that can enable a speaker to prepare a presentation that will meet audience needs:

1. Setting objectives
2. Analyzing audience needs
3. Developing benefits that address the needs identified
4. Analyzing audience attitudes
5. Rehearsing and adding special touches
6. Following the basic principles of good delivery.[5]

Figure 13-4 lists some of the barriers to effective interpersonal communications. Perhaps the best way to overcome many of these barriers is for a manager to develop a set of communication values. *Values may be referred to as standards or principles to influence personal conduct.* If a manager keeps his or her communication values, standards or principles in mind when planning to communicate, many of the barriers will be overcome.

Years ago, John F. Mee, a well-known management professor and author at Indiana University, developed a set of communication principles. These principles, reproduced in Figure 13-5, are as valid today as they were then. Managers can benefit by reviewing all these principles. Here we will elaborate on several of the most significant principles.

No One Communication Technique Will Meet All Needs. Creative communicators know that to insure effectiveness they may need to transmit information in a variety of ways. A manager who delegates a work assignment to a subordinate may do so both verbally and in writing to minimize the possibility of any misunderstanding. Students in a classroom will listen to a professor lecture and take notes on the key points while also tape recording the lecture to review later. In these examples the receivers are using more than one channel to insure communication effectiveness. Perhaps no company is more famous for the effectiveness of its advertising than Coca Cola, the most widely recognized corporate name in the world. Notice how many channels of communication Coca Cola uses to advertise (transmit its message) products.

Action Speaks Louder Than Words in Communication. Managers communicate as much by their actions as they do by their words. Can you imagine a department head strongly enforcing the fifteen minute coffeebreak rule for employees, but personally enjoying a twenty or thirty minute "break?" It helps to overcome barriers to effective communication if verbal or written communications are reinforced by managerial action. If a manager says one thing but does another, employees eventually ignore the verbal communication and imitate the action. Furthermore, management loses credibility.

```
                        Sender Lacks Credibility
                    Poor Listening Habits of Receiver(s)
              Semantics Problems — Differences in Word Meanings
            Predisposition of Receiver (The Closed Mind Syndrome)
             Status Differences Between Sender and Receiver(s)
                   Noise — All Disruptive Physical Factors
                        Climate in the Work Place
             Prejudice and Deep-Rooted Feelings and Emotions
            Perceptual Differences Between Sender and Receiver(s)
        Information Overload — Too Much Information At One Time
                           Resistance to Change
```

FIGURE 13-4: BARRIERS TO EFFECTIVE INTERPERSONAL
                      COMMUNICATION

Know Your Subject. A person's ability to communicate tends to vary directly with the person's understanding of the subject being communicated. This principle is a **truism.** Before transmitting information to a second party a manager should do his or her homework. Always research the subject fully before developing your message and before determining the channel for transmitting it. Knowledge about a subject allows a manager to communicate with enthusiasm, confidence and clarity. Receivers such as listeners quickly catch a speaker who does not seem to know what he or she is discussing. Lack of detail, incomplete information, or unclear information become major barriers to effective communication. Knowing your subject is a form of technical skill which supervisory managers need. Can you imagine a tennis coach as a football coach or a soccer coach as a baseball coach if neither coach understands much about football or baseball?

Plan Your Communication. Planning with regard to any major managerial decision should include planning for communicating it to those who will execute the decision and those who will be affected by it. As we learned in earlier chapters, planning is an activity of today that pertains to the future. Communication, like planning, is initiated to achieve certain end results. Planning your communication requires a determination, in advance, of the ideal end result. A manager then reviews alternative ways to communicate to reach the ideal. Involved in the planning effort is a review of facts, options, risks (barriers), and knowledge of the intended receivers. Communicating too hastily without thinking or planning carefully can lead to disappointing end results. Empathizing with your intended receiver is a valuable step in the communication planning process.

1. No one communication technique will meet all needs. A communication program uses many techniques, methods and channels.

2. Confidence is a basic principle of communication. An employee who suspects that he or she is being sold a "bill of goods" will resent the communicator's intrusion and will not be receptive to the message.

3. Action speaks louder than words in communication.

4. Each communication program needs to be tailored to fit the needs and wants of the individual human organization.

5. Planning with regard to any major managerial decision should include planning for communicating it to those who will carry it out and those who will be affected by it.

6. Generalized of "canned" communications cannot form the core of a communication program. Communications which are directed to everyone will probably fail to meet the specific need of anyone. "Canned" communication should be used only when it is complementary to the central theme.

7. Establish good daily communication. If employers communicate solely as a defense against attack, then employees may turn elsewhere for information. Or even worse, they may create in their own imagination answers which will be worse than the truth.

8. A person's ability to communicate tends to vary directly with his or her own understanding of the subject to be communicated.

9. Management's effectiveness with communication tends to vary directly with its belief in the importance and value of adequate communication.

10. Respect for downward communication channels tends to be in direct proportion to the extent to which the supervisor receives and transmits information before the subordinate gets it elsewhere.

11. Development of good communication relationships takes time. They cannot be built in a day — or a year — but they can be improved regularly.

FIGURE 13-5: CARDINAL PRINCIPLES OF EFFECTIVE COMMUNICATION

Source: *Personnel Handbook*, edited by John F. Mee (NY: The Ronald Press Company, 1951)

Communication and the Formal Organization

Communication within the framework of the formal organization is as important as communication between individuals. The effectiveness of communication in the formal organization relates to the philosophy of higher management, the culture, whether the organization is highly centralized or decentralized, the communication networks, and much more.

Philosophy of Higher Management. Higher management controls and influences everything in an organization. If the general attitude of top management is to support openness; to practice and encourage participative management; decry rigid rules; follow an "open door" policy; and encourage a team spirit in approaching problems, then communications will flow freely. This is often the practice in relatively small organizations. Also, this philosophy may be apparent in research organizations, some colleges and universities, and where individual employees are viewed as professional type workers. Usually this type of organization is decentralized in structure, and communications flow upward, downward, and laterally without worry about violating the chain of command (scalar principle).

In other types of organizations, the philosophy of top management may be to maintain tight control over all aspects of the organization. If so, the communication process likely will be more formalized according to the networks depicted on the organization chart. Organizations like this are usually highly centralized in structure, more bureaucratic in practice, and follow strict adherence to the chain of command. The branches of the United States military would be prime examples.

Culture. Organizational culture has a direct impact on communication within the formal organization. Several meanings of culture are included here:

1. Observed behavioral regularities when people interact, such as the language used and the rituals around deference and demeanor
2. The norms that evolve in working groups
3. The dominant values espoused by an organization
4. The philosophy that guides an organization's policy toward employees and/or customers
5. The rules of the game for getting along in the organization
6. The feeling or climate that is conveyed in an organization by the physical layout and the way in which members of the organization interact with customers or other outsiders.[6]

Notice that the meanings of culture include the words behavior, norms, interactions, rituals, values, rules, feelings, and climate. All of these words or subjects can be part of or have an effect on the communication process.

Centralized and Decentralized Organizations. A centralized organization refers to the decision-making, authority, responsibility, and control being held closely by top management. This would be a vertical organization with relatively smaller spans of control under lower level managers. Communication would follow prescribed channels upward and downward and sometimes laterally if approved first by higher level managers.

In contrast, the decentralized organization pushes decision-making, authority, responsibility and control downward as much as possible. Lower level managers assume much more of the responsibility and have more authority to decide and control their parts of the organization. This would be a horizontal type structure. Communication tends to flow more freely upward, downward and laterally in this framework. Part of the openness is due to the improved status of lower level managers who have more responsibility and feel more important to the organization. Lower level managers make more decisions and must communicate more often to larger numbers of subordinates.

DOWNWARD	UPWARD
Reprimanding Employee	Submitting Ideas—Suggestion Box
Company-wide Meeting	Quality Circle Report
Benefits Change in Pay Envelope	Committee Recommendation
Announcement Over Public Address System	Response During Employee Appraisal Session
Employee Handbood	Survey Feedback
Delegating Work	Filing a Grievance
Training a New Employee	Exit Interviews
Scheduling Production	Accident Report
Laying Off Employees	Informal Meeting with Boss
Distribution of Bonus	Signing a Petition

FIGURE 13-6: EXAMPLES OF VERTICAL COMMUNICATION

Communication Networks. Communication networks refer to the flow of information. Networks can also be called communication systems. The most common networks or systems are downward, upward and lateral. Downward and upward communication combined is called vertical communication. The simplest example of vertical communication would be between a supervisor and one employee. The supervisor tells the employee what to do (downward communication) and the employee acknowledges understanding what to do (upward communication.

Downward communication originates from higher levels of management and flows downward to lower levels. Downward communication can be an announcement to all employees over the public address system or the posting of important information on the bulletin board. Normally downward communication follows the chain of command (i.e., flows downward one level at a time without skipping any level) unless information is transmitted to all employees at one time. Downward communication tends to be faster than upward communication because of the status and authority associated with the sender. Downward communication is most effective when information is transmitted directly and personally to individuals, small groups and departments. It is least effective when the channel selected for transmission is indirect and impersonal. Examples of this are notices in the paycheck envelope, employee handbooks, and any form of "canned" communications directed to employees at lower levels.

Upward communication becomes effective if higher level managers encourage employees to communicate with them. Upward communication can be suggestions; ideas; responses to questions; reports on work completed, sales made and job problems encountered; and much more. Two major problems hinder the effectiveness of upward communication. One is the fear of employees that higher managers will not welcome their comments, suggestions or ideas, or that they will be misinterpreted in a negative sense. The second problem is that employees are not eager to communicate problems or bad news upward to higher managers.

Upward communication can be valuable to higher management in the following ways:

1. It can demonstrate the effectiveness of downward communication.
2. It can provide information on the progress and achievements of employees below.
3. It can transmit employee suggestions and ideas for improvement.
4. It can send signals to management above concerning employee morale and job satisfaction.

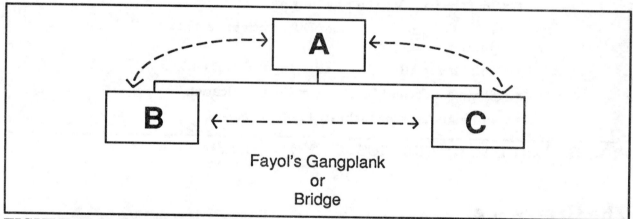

FIGURE 13-7: COMMUNICATION: UPWARD, DOWNWARD, AND LATERAL

Lateral communication traditionally was not acceptable because it violated the scalar principle (chain of command). If "A" is the boss and has two employees, "B" and "C" reporting to him or her (see Figure 13-7), would you allow "B" to communicate formally with "C" without going through "A?" The answer is no since "A" should give permission to "B" to communicate with "C" and since "A" is going to be held totally responsible for what happens under his or her jurisdiction (including actions taken by "B" and "C").

It took the publication of Henri Fayol's famous book, *Industrial and General Administration*, in 1916 in France for managers to look at the value of lateral communication. Fayol advocated allowing "B" and "C" to communicate directly to save time, paperwork and for convenience. This direct communication link between "B" and "C" has been called **Fayol's bridge or gangplank**.

Lateral communication works effectively and can be justified if the parties involved have been instructed by higher management to do so; if such a responsibility is in the employees' job descriptions; or if it has become a traditional and expected work practice for employee "B" to communicate directly with employee "C." A second justification is that employee "B" or "C" or both keep manager "A" above informed about the direct communication between them.

Lateral communication probably is more common between managers than between nonmanagers. The advantages involve more than savings in time, paperwork and convenience. Lateral communication is vital to coordinating efforts and resources between mutually dependent departments. Also, lateral communication is necessary for a matrix organization structure to function effectively.

- Cannot Be Seen on Organization Chart
- Communication Network Changes Daily/Hourly
- All Employees Are Part of the System
- "Chief Grapes" Are the Key Players
- Has No Conscience! Cannot Differentiate Facts or Truth from Rumors and Lies
- Available for All to Use — Give Input & Get Output
- Follows No Formal Channels of Communication
- Can Be an Asset or Liability to Management

FIGURE 13-8: CHARACTERISTICS OF THE GRAPEVINE

The Grapevine

The grapevine is not a formal communication system; however, it does overlap and intertwine with the formal system. The grapevine is the communication system of the informal organization. Neither the informal organization or the informal communications system (grapevine) are seen on the formal organization chart.

The mystery of the grapevine is that it is invisible yet real; that it is permanent yet elusive; and that it is remarkably efficient in transmitting information even though its communication network changes often—perhaps many times each day. Anyone who has worked full time in the same organization for a few months is well aware that there are "chief grapes" in the grapevine who thrive on moving information around the organization.

How important is the grapevine to managers? It is extremely important because it is a communication system that should be made into an asset instead of a liability. Managers should realize that every employee is part of the grapevine whether they wish to be or not. Managers should understand that the grapevine is accessible to everyone in the organization for input or output. Further, managers should realize that the grapevine has no conscience: It cannot separate the truth from lies nor can the grapevine identify rumors (as different from facts).

Information transmitted via the grapevine follows no formal channel of communication. Plotting information along the grapevine on an organization chart would show a zigzag pattern of lines and crossovers before you traced the origin of the information.

From a management standpoint, the grapevine can be an asset if you wish certain information circulated quickly throughout the organizaton. For example, mention to one employee that raises next year will be around five percent! Also, the grapevine can be a managerial asset if managers tune into it once in a while and listen to what employees are saying and doing. Often this can be a good source of information for evaluating job satisfaction or morale of the employees. In addition, information may be obtained that foretells of employee unrest or dissatisfaction with a situation or issue. This applies especially to sport management/administration. Rumors abound among team members when the sport season is not going well; fans and the general public grumble and generate information about professional teams when there are obvious signs of dissatisfaction among team members (such as a fight in the locker room); personnel within the department create various scenarios when a problem arises. Sport managers must be aware of the grapevine and employ it to their advantage just as much as any other manager.

External Communication

Some mention should be made of the importance of an organization's external communication. We have discussed interpersonal communications, formal communications within the organization and the grapevine. Management must view external communication and its effectiveness as equally important.

In the sport world external communication is common through the use of direct mailings, radio, television and newspapers. Major sport firms often relate externally to the public through public relations departments or agencies. The purpose of the public relations firm or department is to create the proper public image of the organization, a team, an athlete, a sport or a product line. It has been a point of contention for many years about how much this type of external publicity affects the selection of various special athletic award recipients, such as those chosen to receive the Heisman Trophy, the Cy Young Awards, the Naismith Awards and many others. A general opinion has emerged that without an effective external communications campaign, a particular athlete is not given due consideration for the honor. Providing information to the public can generate more fan support, more demand for a product or service, more spectators, more donors and more customers.

In collegiate athletics, sport information departments are created to perform services like those of a public relations department or firm. A sports information department or its director (often called a Sports Information Director) is the communications connection between the media, students, alumni and followers. Sport information departments publish media guides, statistical data, athletic yearbooks and sport releases. Through effective communication methods, the sports information department hopes to create a favorable image of the college's athletic program with those whose support and patronage it needs.

If a sport organization has no staff specialist or public relations firm to provide external communications to its constituents, then line managers must perform this function. Examples of this are high school coaches, owners of sporting goods stores, spa managers and teaching professionals at clubs and sports centers who generate their own external publicity.

Another classic example of this is the star athlete or popular coach/manager of a professional team who supplements the team's professional communications staff with public appearances and various promotional efforts.

Organizations should develop strategy for externally communicating effectively in light of their communication objectives. This means a concerted, planned effort at getting the right message to the right public at the appropriate time. Planning and organization are required, and a goal or objective must be firmly established and communicated effectively within the organization.

It appears that more organizations will face scrutiny in the future because of a demanding and well-educated public. Such a climate makes the effectiveness of any organization's external communication programs more crucial. Planned external communication programs can provide a major "payoff" for organizations that provide quality information in an effective manner.

Electronic Communication

Subject matter presented on preceding pages is extremely important because the fundamentals of communicating effectively have stood the test of time. Students who begin their careers in the 1990s, however, will note a dramatic difference in the way communication occurs. The advent of electronic communication has revolutionized the transfer of information from person to person, group to group and/or person to group. Communication technology has brought about the popularity and widespread use of facsimile (fax) machines, cellular telephones, teleconferencing, voice mail and E-mail via the computer. Additionally, services on the information superhighway, such as Internet, are revolutionizing the communications world.

According to Mike Toner, Internet:

- is the global network of computer networks that has become the world's fastest-growing communications medium
- processes 30 million messages daily and is growing
- allows individuals to interact, share, argue, plead, preach, court, annoy or harvest information in a way the world is only beginning to explore
- allows a user to use E-mail and contact individuals or groups in any one of 147 countries in six/tenths of a second
- promises to be one of those technologies that inevitably reshapes society in unpredictable ways.[7]

Internet was developed by the Department of Defense during the "Cold War" period about 25 years ago. In the late 1980s, the National Science Foundation took over; and in 1991, Congress approved $2 billion to expand the network. Also in 1991, the government ended restrictions on the use of the Internet for business.

Internet's popularity is unrestrained and essentially unregulated. The official name of the network is the *National Research and Education Network*. It is more popularly known by the unofficial name, the "information superhighway."

Problems can occur when managers rely too heavily on electronic communications. There is an absence of personal contact; communications are sterile; there is a loss of camaraderie; senders and receivers miss the informal relationships and the face-to-face meetings; and it may be more difficult to project the desired organization image. Also, conceivably managers may receive so much information electronically in a short period of time that they cannot digest or process it properly. This can lead to frustration, greater stress and management "burnout."

Summary

Perhaps the most important skill a manager should possess is the ability to communicate effectively. Some of the major jobs of managers that require effective communication skills are planning, decision-making, coordinating, leading, delegating, controlling and organizing.

Communication is defined as the act or action of imparting or transmitting ideas, information, facts or feelings to a second party. Communication is always two-way. There must be a sender and a receiver. Communication is a joint process: If someone writes, someone reads; if someone speaks, someone listens; if someone acts, someone watches.

For communication to be effective there must be an understanding and response by the second party. When the response of the second party is in line with the message transmitted by the sender, the communication is **effective**.

The communication process consists of a series of steps that are in sequential order. They are idea origination, the message, channel selection and encoding, transmission, receiving, decoding and feedback.

Typical barriers to effective interpersonal communication are lack of sender credibility; poor listening habits of the receiver; semantics problems; predisposition of the receiver; status differences between sender and receiver; noise; prejudices and more. There are ways to overcome communication barriers. One is for a manager to have a philosophy of communication which consists of standards, values or principles which guide the manager when planning to communicate. One important principle is that a person's ability to communicate tends to vary directly with his or her own knowledge of the subject to be communicated.

Communication within the framework of the formal organization is as important as communication between individuals. The effectiveness of communication in the formal organization relates to the philosophy of higher manager; the culture; whether the organization is highly centralized or decentralized; and the communication networks.

Communication networks refer to the flow of information. The most common networks or systems are downward, upward and lateral. Downward and upward communication combined is called **vertical** communication.

The grapevine is the communication system of the informal organization. Neither the informal organization nor the grapevine appear on the formal organization chart. The mystery of the grapevine is that it is invisible yet real; permanent yet elusive; and that its communication networks change often but it is efficient in transmitting information.

Every employee is part of the grapevine. Managers should view the grapevine as an asset and use it for the good of the organization.

Now, American organizations face a challenge to identify themselves to the public they serve. Therefore, external communication has become more important, and organizations must develop strategies for effective external communication.

Electronic communication is the result of new technology which has produced facsimile (fax) machines, cellular telephones, teleconferencing, voice mail, E-mail and more. *Internet*, called the information superhighway, is revolutionizing the communications world and transfers millions of messages daily, via computer, to all parts of the world in fractions of a second.

Review Questions

1. What is the importance of communication to the management function of planning? To organizing? To implementing? To controlling?

2. Name the steps in the communication process. Where do most of the communication problems occur in the process? Why?

3. Why is the semantics problem such a barrier to effective communication?

4. There are many other barriers to effective communication. Name and explain at least five more.

5. A number of communication principles are mentioned in this chapter. Which one do you think is of greatest importance to a practicing manager? Justify.

6. The "grapevine" is the communication system of the informal organization. Are you familiar with five or six characteristics of the grapevine? Do you know how managers can make the grapevine an asset instead of its being a liability?

7. Why do you think an organization should have a formalized external communication program that relates to its strategic objectives?

8. Give examples of electronic communication and some advantages and disadvantages of such.

Assignments for Personal Development

1. Identify the sport organization in your geographic area that appears to be most effective in carrying out its planned external communication program. Outline why you think this is so. Include examples of advertising, brochures, written releases, personal appearances, etc. Examples can be found in your daily newspaper.

2. Review some written publications produced by your school for the benefit of the students. How many of these publications are examples of "effective" communication? How might they be improved significantly?

Incident

WHICH WAY TO GO?

Harry Smith was a charter member of a new, prestigious suburban athletic club. The Club was open to the public but had a limit on its membership. Owner/investors poured several million dollars into the creation of physical facilities that provided many sporting opportunities for its members with the exception of golf. Harry enjoys the use of the facilities but notices that confusion exists in the administration of programs. None of the employees, including the managers, seem able to make a decision without checking with someone higher up.

Last week two of the major owners asked Harry to take leave from his job as a vice president at a large urban bank to become Executive Director of the Club for at least a year. If he liked the job, he could keep it permanently; and if not, he could go back to the bank at the end of the year. They told him they had enough clout to get him the "leave," and they needed help badly. The major problem they described to him was a lousy organization with everyone doing their own thing without anyone knowing what anybody else was doing.

Harry promised to consider the offer seriously if they would let him study operations for a few days. They readily agreed.

After three days of observation and interviewing, Harry concluded many things were wrong with the administration of the Club. There was no leadership; poor or nonexistent planning, and the organization was chaotic. The most immediate problem Harry found, however, was the lack of an effective communication system which could provide pertinent information to and from all employees. Improving the formal communication program would be his first priority after he accepted the job.

Questions:

1. If you were Harry Smith, new Executive Director of the Club, which communication system would you advocate and try to implement? Why? (See **Notes on Communication**.)

2. Give an example of another type of sport organization where you might advocate the opposite approach and explain why.

NOTES ON COMMUNICATION:

Traditional American managers believe in the value of formal communication channels that follow the lines on the organization chart. The communication channels or networks would be upward, downward (together called vertical) and lateral. These managers understand the virtue of organization principles such as unity of command; the scalar principle, and the principle of delegation. To some degree they may practice participative management and even the "open door" policy, but never at the expense of "stabbing" the formal communication channels.

Other American managers find that in the 1990s the old communication systems don't work very well. Following the principles mentioned above and never violating the chain of command, for example, stifles quick action, problem solving, and organization flexibility. These new management thinkers consider communication "openness" vital to dynamic organizations. They believe that today's environment requires organizations to adjust to change quickly and to view employees as growing valuable resources. Such managers also believe in a team approach to solving problems. Traditional communication networks are viewed as obsolete. There is merit to both these approaches.

Glossary of Key Terms

Communication: Defined as the act or action of imparting or transmitting ideas, information, facts or feelings to a second party or parties.

Communication networks: Also called communication systems, refers to the flow of information in a formal organization.

Communication process: Consists of a series of steps that are in sequential order. They are idea origination; the message; channel selecting; encoding; transmission; receiving; decoding; and feedback.

Effective communication: The goal of communication, it occurs when the response from the receiver is in line with the message transmitted by the sender.

Fayol's Gangplank or Bridge: Refers to the direct communication between parallel persons or departments (cross communication).

Grapevine: The communication system of the informal organization.

Internet: Global network of computer networks that has become the world's fastest growing communication medium.

Semantics: The science or study of word meanings.

Values: Standards or principles to influence personal conduct.

Practical Concepts in Management
How to be an Effective Communicator

Developing good communication skills requires practice. You are not interested in just passing along information, ideas or facts to another person. You are interested in communicating **effectively!**

Effective communication means that the receiver (usually your employees) understands the message as you have intended; and the receiver responds, if necessary, as you desire.

Becoming an effective communicator suggests that you plan your communication and the techniques you will use before you act. Hasty communication is rarely effective. Professional managers also use empathy.

Empathy is putting yourself in the receiver's place. This is an important psychological technique which helps you better understand how to communicate effectively with another person or a group of employees.

Consider these suggestions for increasing your effectiveness as a communicator:

1. Know your subject thoroughly.
2. Plan your communication
3. Empathize with the receiver before you act
4. Develop a multifaceted communication approach.
5. Follow-up on your communication
6. Learn from communication mistakes.

In addition, do not forget that communication is a two-way street. Listen to your employees, as well as your peers, bosses and colleagues, give them your attention just as you expect them to do for you

Make a Friend of the Grapevine

The informal communication system of the informal organization is called the "grapevine." Every organization of any size has a grapevine. Too many managers try to eliminate this informal communication system to no avail. Instead, managers should convert the grapevine into an asst.

To convert the grapevine, you use it. For example, tune into the grapevine. Listen to what is being communicated. Identify the "chief grape," that person who is always in the middle of the communication. This is an inexpensive way of evaluating morale, of finding out what is of real interest to the employees, and of keeping up with what is going on. The danger is that the grapevine has no conscience and communicates the untruths as readily as the truths.

Some managers have used the grapevine to distribute company information rather than calling meetings or sending out memos. The only problem with this is the risk that the information will be distorted as it is passed along. The grapevine is fast, follows no formal lines of communication, and is available for all employees—management and nonmanagement alike—to use at no cost.

Accept the fact that the grapevine is here to stay, but learn to use it to your advantage as a manager when possible.

References and Chapter Note

[1] D. M. Kersey, "Faith, Hope, and Clarity," *Management Focus*, Vol. 31, No. 4, July/August, 1984, pp. 4-5

[2] B. Z. Posner, J. M. Kouzes, and W. H. Schmidst, "Shared Values Make a Difference: An Empirical Test of Corporate Culture," *Human Resource Management*, Vol. 24, Fall, 1985, pp. 293-309.

[3] D. A. Safer, "Institutional Body Language," *Public Relations Journal*, Vol.41, No. 3, March 1985, pp. 26- 30.

[4] Jack L. Whitehead, Jr., "Factors of Source Credibility," *Quarterly Journal of Speech*, 54 (February 1968), 59-63.

[5] J. J. Franco, "Speaker, Know Thy Audience," *Training and Development Journal*, Vol. 39, No. 6, June, 1985, pp. 20-21.

[6] E. H. Schein, *Organizational Culture and Leadership* (San Francisco: Jossey-Bass, 1985), p. 6

[7] Mike Toner, "Surfing on the Internet," *Atlanta Journal-Constitution*, July 24, 1994, p. F1, F4

Additional Readings

Goldhaber, Gerald M. *Organizational Communication*, 4th ed. Dubuque, Iowa: William C. Brown, 1983

Lesikar, Raymond. *Business Communication*. Homewood, IL: Richard D. Irwin, 1972.

Lucas, Stephen E. *The Art of Public Speaking*, 4th ed. New York: McGraw-Hill, Inc., 1992.

CHAPTER 14

MANAGING CHANGE, CONFLICT AND STRESS

After studying this chapter, **you will know:**

- Under what conditions organization change occurs
- How organization change is classified
- Most common reasons employees resist change
- Commonsense suggestions to offset employee resistance to change
- Meaning of Organization Development (OD)
- Why managing conflict is so important
- Causes and consequences of conflict
- Major types of conflict
- Conflict resolution methods available to managers
- Definition and importance of managing stress
- Meaning of employee burnout
- Why Employee Assistance Programs (EAPs) exist
- Purpose of wellness programs

Organization Change

Chapter 3 presents information on the environment of management that influences and affects organizational activities and managerial decision-making. Significant changes in the external environment often affect internal operations and in turn impact employees, the organizational strategy and the use of resources.

Organization change occurs when there is a modification of an existing policy, practice, procedure, method, strategy or technology that employees are accustomed to following. Change may affect customers as well as other groups of people.

Changes occur often in the world of sport. See Figure 14-1 for examples.

➭ CHANGES IN FINANCIAL AID PRACTICES FOR STUDENT-ATHLETES ON COLLEGIATE ATHLETIC SCHOLARSHIPS

➭ RESTRUCTURING OF A GOVERNANCE ORGANIZATION

➭ NEW CONTRACTS BETWEEN UNIONS AND MANAGEMENT IN PROFESSIONAL SPORTS

➭ RELOCATION OR NEW OWNERSHIP/MANAGEMENT OF A TEAM

➭ CHANGE IN ACADEMIC ELIGIBILITY RULES FOR HIGH SCHOOL AND/OR COLLEGE STUDENT-ATHLETES

➭ BEING PLACED ON PROBATION BY A GOVERNANCE AUTHORITY

➭ DEATH/SERIOUS INJURY TO A PLAYER OR COACH

➭ CHANGES RELATED TO COMPLIANCE WITH TITLE IX (GENDER EQUITY)

➭ SUSPENSION/BANISHMENT BY A LEAGUE FOR A STAR PLAYER

➭ CHANGE IN THE PUBLIC'S ATTITUDE TOWARD SPORTS

➭ CHANGE IN SOURCE OF SPORTING GOODS PRODUCTS, I.E., FOREIGN-PRODUCED REPLACING MADE IN THE U.S.A.

➭ CHANGES SUCH AS OLYMPIC PARTICIPATION BY PROFESSIONALS

FIGURE 14-1: EXAMPLES OF CHANGE IN THE SPORT WORLD

According to Hersey and Blanchard:

> In the dynamic society surrounding today's organization, the question of whether change will occur is no longer relevant. Instead, the issue is how do managers and leaders cope with the inevitable barrage of change that confronts them daily in attempting to keep their organizations viable and current? Although change is a fact of life, if managers are to be effective, they can no longer be content to let change occur as it will. They must be able to develop strategies to plan, direct, and control change.[1]

Change occurs in society in general at a ever-increasing rate. An example that illustrates this point is found in a speech given over 35 years ago by J. Lewis Powell:

> ...If the whole history of mankind [50,000 years] had happened in 50 years, what would have happened and when would it have happened? If all mankind's history had happened in your lifetime, what would have happened and when? Well, this is it: ten years ago you would have stopped being a cave man; five years ago

the smartest man here might have invented some kind
of pictorial writing; two years ago Christianity would
have appeared on the scene; fifteen months ago you
would have had the printing press; twenty days ago,
electricity; eighteen days ago, the airplane; ten days
ago, radio; and four days ago, TV.[2]

Now, back up 35 years and review what has changed since then: the advent of the computer and its many applications; space exploration and people landing on the moon; the demise of the Soviet Union; the worldwide competition in automotive production, and college textbooks which now cost $60.00 instead of $10.00 or $15.00. And these are just a few of the developments!

Managers must respond effectively to changes rather than resist them. The failure to adapt to change can create havoc, be expensive for the organization, or even threaten the survival of the organization.

Types of Change

Organizational changes can be classified as *technological, environmental and internal. Technological changes involve new equipment, new processes, robots, automation, computer-aided activities and much more. Environmental changes are changes that originate outside the organization but affect operations such as new federal legislation, evolving social trends, alterations in demographics, the internationalization of markets and new competitors. Internal changes are those that occur within the organization such as downsizing of the labor force; unionization of employees; the introduction of a new pay scale, new work methods and procedures and more.*

Managers face all types of changes. How they react to change and handle the implementation of it present formidable challenges.

Relatively minor changes within the organization may be handled by individual managers who identify associated problems and take action to correct them. This is management performing in a *reactive* way. Managers also identify situations that require change and initiate action to achieve the change with a minimum of problems. This is *proactive* management behavior.

Ideally when organizations decide on a major internal change, a *program of planned change* should be developed. According to Thomas and Bennis, a program of planned change is "the deliberate design and implementation of a structural innovation, a new policy or goal, or a change in operating philosophy, climate or style."[3]

Resistance to Change

Most people resist something that is new and different if it means changing the *status quo*. This is not abnormal behavior, but a natural reaction to change. Employee resistance to change might take the form of a work slow-down, or it can be a subtle resistance like silent disgust or diffidence. Whatever the form employee resistance takes, managers should be aware that change does generate resistance, and a program of planned change should incorporate ways to modify, lessen or eliminate this resistance as much as possible.

Barriers to Change. The most common reasons employees resist change are the following:

1. **Job security and income.** Whether real or imagined, employees are likely to view change as a threat to their employment status even though the changes may increase efficiency and streamline the organization. Employees suspect jobs may be eliminated in implementing the change.

2. **Uncertainty.** Employees have a fear of the unknown when the purpose of a change is not explained in advance. Such uncertainty about the impact or outcome of a change may generate considerable resistance. When a well-liked boss is replaced by an unfamiliar manager, employees become suspicious. When outside consultants start observing employee work performance, employees may start worrying. Misunderstandings often occur when change creates uncertainty.

3. **Personal inconvenience.** Employees may perceive any change in work location site, working hours or shifts as a personal inconveniece or a change requiring personal sacrifice; thus, they will resist.

4. **Loss of status and power.** Restructuring an organization may cause some employees and managers to be relocated to new jobs in different departments. The result of losing the familiar setting and co-workers may be a reduction in power and status that has been achieved over time, causing the affected employee or manager to resist the change.

5. **Change in personal relationships.** Many employees enjoy their work-related friendships and associations. These interpersonal relationships often carry over beyond the work environment and become social relationships. Any change that threatens these relationships can cause strong resistance. Friends at work often eat lunch together, go out after work, and support each other on the job. These friendships are part of the informal organization which exists in every formal organization.

Implementing Change

Introducing any change requires managers to plan why, where, how and when to implement the change. First, there must be a justifiable reason to introduce change; second, there must be a determined location where the change will occur; third, a carefully planned sequence of steps to follow must be in place to guide managers when implementing change; and finally, there must be a time table established to tell managers when to implement change.

Substantial resistance to change can be eliminated or reduced if sound planning is practiced and good common sense applied in implementing change.

Offsetting Resistance to Change. Managers are the primary initiators of change. Much employee resistance to change can be eliminated or reduced if employees know in advance why the change is occurring; where it will take place; how it will be implemented, and when it takes effect. Some sound common sense suggestions to follow in achieving this include these:

1. **Develop empathy.** Managers should put themselves in the place of the employees and try to anticipate their questions, moods, reactions, etc. once they are informed of the proposed change. This should help in planning for the implementation of the change.

2. **Open communication channels.** Discussing the proposed change with employees and eliciting their feedback helps lessen the fear of the unknown.

3. **Introduce employee participation.** Involve the employees throughout the change process. Invite their input and suggestions. When employees participate in an activity that directly affects them, they are less likely to resist change because they have been part of the decision-making process.

4. **Build trust.** It is important to employees to know that management is honest, forthright and sincere. Management must be truthful in explaining the change, its value to the organization and its impact on employees if the employees are to have trust and confidence in management.

5. *Explain the time and place of change.* Carefully explain to employees when change will occur and where. Timing the change requires careful consideration as does selecting the logical place for implementation. For example, it is not good to make a major change right before a holiday period, nor is it wise to introduce change that benefits one department or area over another that has a greater need.

6. **Accentuate the positive.** Organization change happens because the change is best for the whole enterprise. Any improvement in the organization passes benefits on to the employees. Managers should educate employees on the long-term benefits of change and, in effect, honestly sell them on the positive nature of the change (even though some of the short-term consequences may be negative). Any change should be reasonable, and coercing or threatening employees to accept change guarantees their resistance.

Organization Development and Change

Over the last two decades, an approach aimed at improving overall organization effectiveness has emerged called *Organization Development (OD)*. OD is a collection of ideas and techniques which can help organizations deal with changes.[4] Rue and Byars state that "OD is an organizationwide, planned effort managed from the top, with a goal of increasing organizational performance through planned interventions in the organization. In particular, OD looks at the human side of organizations."[5]

OD is not an approach designed to solve isolated problems. Rather, it is a long-term, broad approach, instigated in numerous ways, to achieve change in attitudes and values of employees so that both the organization and its employees benefit.

OD arises from a lack of cooperation between departments or divisions; from ambiguous lines of responsibility; because of labor-management disputes; due to poor problem-solving relationships in project teams; or from technological change that redirects company objectives.[6] Other problem areas may be identified as well through diagnosis.

Diagnosis is the analysis of information obtained from employees via questionnaires, surveys, personal interviews, direct observation and a review of records. Diagnosis is a first step when implementing an OD program.

Conducting a diagnosis and analyzing the information received reveals areas that need improvement within the organization. After this step, management must carefully develop a plan, with measureable criteria, to achieve the desired organizational change and improvement. The third step in an OD program is to decide how to inform employees of the need for change and prepare them through an education program to accept and make the change.

Finally, management should evaluate the OD program to determine if the process produced the desired results.

Organization Development as a formal program varies considerably in definition and implementation. The primary objective, however, is to change employees and the nature and quality of their working relationships.[7] Such a result should improve overall organization effectiveness and performance.

Managing Conflict

Conflict is a clash of opposing ideas and interests which leads to disagreement. The parties involved are in opposition and differ in opinions.

Organizationally, conflict can occur when one or both parties express hostility and interfere with each other's efforts to accomplish objectives.[8] Historically, the term conflict has had a negative connotation and was to be avoided if at all possible. Conflict occurs in all organizational settings, however, and is a natural outgrowth of social interactions.

Since conflict is inevitable in organizations, managers should strive to minimize the damage from harmful conflict and maximize the beneficial aspects of conflict.

Stoner has said that "conflict is inherently neither functional nor dysfunctional but simply has the potential for improving or impairing organizational performance, depending on how it is managed."[9] This clearly puts the onus of making conflict work for the organization instead of against it on management.

Causes and Consequences of Conflict. Many factors can cause conflict: competition between individuals vying for a promotion; departments dividing scarce resources; communication breakdowns; assignment of unreasonable work goals; personality clashes; managerial favoritism; disparate pay increases and many other things.

The negative consequences of conflict can lead to employee turnover, low morale, a decrease in employee performance, a lack of cooperation between the parties involved plus hostile feelings. The potential positive effects of conflict are renewed motivation to achieve objectives; creative approaches to solving problems; innovative methods of communication; a healthy outlet for expressing repressed feelings; and the identification of problem areas of which management was not aware. In addition, participating in a conflict situation can be an educational process where one or both parties acquire information and gain previously unknown insights.

Types of Conflict. There are four major types of conflict: *interpersonal, intergroup, interdepartmental and organizational.*

Interpersonal conflict occurs between two or more persons. The causes of interpersonal conflict include these:

- Two employees working closely who have opposite type personalities;

- Veteran employees and new employees receiving the same pay;

- Union workers working side-by-side with nonunion workers;

- Employees with prejudices toward other employees about age, sex, race, religion, marital status, etc.;

- Employees working together who have widely different education backgrounds and levels.

Intergroup conflict occurs when two or more groups within the same department are antagonistic toward each other. Frequently, line and staff personnel have conflicts over who has authority over whom and what. Internal auditors may question the work and procedures of accounting supervisors when both work in the finance department, resulting in conflict. Informal groups within a department may generate conflict, too. One group could be favoring flex-time hours while the other is pushing for a four-day work week.

Interdepartmental conflict involves departments rather than individuals or groups and usually occurs when there are signs of some type of favoritism. In business organizations, the sales, production and finance functions are directly related to the attainment of the profit objective. Each would appear to have equal importance; however, when higher management places more emphasis on sales and marketing than on the value of quality production, conditions are right for conflict and hostility between the two departments. Sales managers may make commitments to customers that strain the capability of the production department. Arguments ensue and conflicts abound. Other potential conflict areas include budgeting, especially when budget requests are arbitrarily honored and favoritism is suspected. Head coaches of varsity sports may become upset over the denial of budget requests especially if they think another sport is getting favored treatment.

Organizational conflicts are usually viewed as an inherent characteristic of the American economic system if competition between firms is the cause. Competitiveness leads to the creation of new products and services, lower prices and more efficient utilization of resources. Society benefits from this type of conflict. When conflict between competing organizations becomes harmful or dysfunctional to society, such as might be the case when a bribe or deliberate misrepresentation is involved, government laws and regulations can be applied to manage the resulting conflicts. The Federal Trade Commission (FTC) and The Food and Drug Administration (FDA) are examples of federal agencies that often manage conflict between competing organizations.

Organizational conflicts are rampant in the professional sport world. A major conflict situation occurs when a team threatens to move to another city. This upsets league alignment, television coverage, revenue sharing, traditional rivalries and fans, city officials, players and those who work at games in supporting services (concessionaires, maintenance, etc.). A recent example of a conflict situation in professional sports occurred when a basketball player refused to observe the National Basketball Association's requirement to stand at attention during the national anthem. His team's management exhausted its efforts to affect his behavior, and the league suspended him. Several days and reams of bad publicity later, an acceptable compromise was reached.

Resolving Conflicts

No one patented method of resolving conficts exists which guarantees success. Each conflict situation is unique and requires special attention by management before introducing a means to resolve the conflict. Much like the contingency approach in leadership situations, selecting the right conflict resolution method depends on the circumstances of the situation.

If the conflict situation is organizational, there may be little management can do except improve its own competitive position or report unfair trade practices or illegal activities of competitors to the appropriate governing agency.

When interdepartmental conflicts occur, higher management may restructure an organization; redesign the work flow; relocate centers of authority; transfer functional managers; conduct required training for the parties involved; get the parties together to work out their differences; create a joint committee to study the conflict and make recommendations; or arbitrarily announce that "this is what will be done."

Where intergroup and interpersonal conflicts exist, managers have several conflict resolution methods as options.

Conciliate the conflict. This requires a third party to work with both groups to try to appease each group. A conciliator attempts to defuse the hostility or antagonism and generate goodwill among the parties involved. This is often called *smoothing over* the conflict. If conciliators are selected from each of the conflicting groups, they may be called *linking pins* because they can present the views of their group and hear the views of the other group or groups. Sometimes the results of such conciliation is compromise.

Mediate the conflict. Mediation requires a third party who talks with both individuals or groups and attempts to bring the two together to resolve their differences. This is also called *confrontation*, but it is an effective method if the two parties can jointly solve their problems.

Arbitrate the conflict. Arbitration is a method of settling disputes between persons or groups by an agreement on both sides to accept the findings of an independent third party. Both parties must trust in the arbitrator to be fair and objective, to listen to all points of view, and to render an impartial decision. Arbitration is a common conflict resolution method in union—management situations, but it is rarely used internally to resolve conflicts between individuals. Management can require the conflicting parties to present their case; however, and, after hearing from both, make a decision that is binding without regard for the agreement of the parties involved. This is arbitrary decision-making, but it does force the conflict to a conclusion.

Negotiate the conflict. Managers are often placed in the position of settling disputes between their employees. Here, the manager is a mediator and conciliator trying to reach an acceptable compromise that will alleviate the problems and return the workers to productivity. The manager's role is to keep each side calm and focused on the specific conflict subject while satisfying as much of each party's complaint as possible.

Too many factors must be considered in choosing the proper conflict resolution method to state that there is one right or best method to use. Conflicts which negatively affect the economic performance of the organization demand immediate attention and resolution efforts. Other conflicts, if left alone, may benefit the organization. Management must make decisions about resolving conflicts based on each situation and its ramifications.

Managing Stress

Change and conflict are normal expectations in the working lives of Americans. Stress, too, abounds in the organization as well as in every other aspect of our daily lives.

Dr. Hans Selye was the first to define the term stress and to do stress research. He describes *stress as a nonspecific physiological response to anything that challenges the body.*[10]

Stress affects people's lives either positively or negatively, depending on the individual's reaction to it. Positively used stress can contribute to personal growth, development and mental health. Dr. Selye's research demonstrated that people respond to stress by showing increases in the heart rate, muscle tension, blood pressure, blood sugar and much more. Today's researchers believe that many physical ailments are associated with stress including coronary heart disease, hypertension, obesity, diabetes, tension headaches, migraine headaches, ulcers, cancer and greater susceptability to infectious diseases.

Stress can serve as a positive force in a person's life. This point is presented in Dr. Selye's book, *Stress Without Distress* (1974). He identifies three types of stress: *negative stress or distress; normal stress; and positive stress or eustress.* Whether stress is positive or negative depends on the individual's assessment and perception of it.[11] Thus, the most effective way to change *distress* into *eustress* is to work on changing the *mind-set* of an individual.[12]

Excessive stress among employees can cause both physical and emotional problems. These problems can then lead to increased absenteeism, job turnover, lower productivity, poor quality of work, low morale, an increase in conflicts and mistakes in decision-making. Helping employees manage stress is important to management because of the staggering costs associated with poor mental and physical health of workers.

Both management and employees should be aware of *stressors. A stressor is any physical, psychological or environmental event or condition that initiates the stress response.*[13] The problem is that the factors which cause stress vary with the employees. A department head may ask an employee to verbally summarize the work of a committee at the departmental meeting today not realizing that the employee is terrified of speaking in front of a group (major stressor). Another employee may enjoy such an assignment. Many students suffer "test anxiety" when taking an exam or especially a standardized test; while others breeze through both.

According to Anspaugh, Hamrick and Rosato, stress response is not a genetic trait; and because it is a response to external conditions, it is subject to personal control.[14] If the effects of stress are subject to personal control, then people should learn ways to lessen the effects of stress. To lessen the effects of stress, a person must be able to identify their personal sources of stress. Some of the sources of stress within an organization setting come from the examples listed in Figure 14-2.

- Work is delegated without the needed authority to complete it.

- A requirement of continuous overtime work.

- Having a boss who is a perfectionist and/or who has little empathy with employees.

- Being placed in a job without proper training.

- Managing employees who were your peers and friends.

- Working for an organization experiencing merger, consolidation or downsizing.

- Reporting to two different bosses who each demand your full time and talent.

FIGURE 14-2: TYPICAL SITUATIONS THAT INDUCE STRESS

Employees have limited control over many of the stressors generated on the job. Experts suggest that when you cannot change the situation, you try to change your outlook. Even so, changing your outlook does not change bad management practices that cause stress. Of greater importance is knowing how to cope with distress once the warning signs appear (see Figure 14-3).

•Chronic fatigue•	Irritability
•Back pain•	Depression
•Difficulty Sleeping•	Anxiety
•Overspending•	Overeating
•Apathy•	Unable to eat
•Unable to concentrate•	Physical weakness
•Excessive crying•	Profuse perspiration

FIGURE 14-3: WARNING SIGNS INDICATING EXCESSIVE DISTRESS

Coping with Stress

Coping is the effort made to manage or deal with stress. Coping does not mean that stress is eliminated, only that an effort is made to handle it and not allow stress to ruin your life. Some organizational situations are so bad and create such employee distress, the only way to cope is to quit the job. Many other situations generating stress can be managed and handled so that the negative effects of the stress are reduced or controlled. A number of relaxation techniques have proved beneficial but should be used selectively by individuals. The most common relaxation techniques are shown in Figure 14-4. There are many more options, such as gardening, fishing, woodworking, or other crafts. The choice is strictly an individual preference, but any technique used should bring more relaxation, less distress, more personal time and a happier, healthier life.

```
• Deep breathing exercises
• Massage therapy
• Autogenics
• Meditation
• Visualization
• Biofeedback
• Music
• Humor
• Effective   time   manage-
  ment
```

FIGURE 14-4: EFFECTIVE STRESS-CONTROL AND RELAXATION TECHNIQUES

Burnout

One of the results of stress is *burnout. Burnout occurs when work is no longer meaningful to an employee.* Burnout results from stress or from other causes, such as job-related problems or a combination of family, social and personal factors. Many executives, hourly employees, professional athletes, students, coaches and homemakers just "walk away" from their lives each year due to burnout. Their particular activity adds to their stress to such a degree that it is no longer possible for them to perform. They have burnout!

```
• Public school teacher
• Long-haul truck driver
• Waitress
• Air traffic controller
• Combat pilot
• Surgeon
• Police detective
• Basketball coach
• Probation officer
```

FIGURE 14-5: STRESSFUL JOBS LIKELY TO PRODUCE BURNOUT

From a management point of view, jobs that have the highest potential for burnout should be identified (see Figure 14-5). Once these jobs are identified, managers can set up a program of action to minimize employee burnout. Such a program might include job rotation so that no one holds that job longer than six months; job simplification to eliminate some of the strenuous demands on the employee; shorter work hours; job enrichment; and perhaps improved training provided the employee on the job.

Employee Assistance Programs (EAPs)

Employee assistance programs (EAPs) are created by large and small organizations to help employees with stress, burnout, substance abuse and many other personal, medical and psychiatric problems. The purpose of EAPs is two-fold: provide help to employees and save costs to the organization.

Professor David Chenoweth has studied the impact of substance abuse at the worksite. His conclusions are as follows:

- The cost to American business of substance abuse is $30 billion annually in lost productivity and quality defects.

- Each substance abuser costs the employer over $7,500 annually in lost productivity, increased medical care and property damage.

- At least 10 percent of America's health care costs can be attributed to substance abuse.

- Approximately 15 percent of American workers abuse alcohol and/or other drugs.

- Of all industrial accidents, 47 percent involve alcohol.

- Forty (40) percent of all worksite deaths involve alcohol abuse.[15]

Substance abuse is only one of many personal problems that can have a direct effect on the productivity, accidents, insurance costs, absenteeism, tardiness, morale and more of an organization's employees. Management's traditional approach to handling these problems was a "hands off" policy. The view was that if you aided one troubled employee, you would have to provide the same assistance to all employees. If the employee's problem interfered significantly with his or her job performance, the employee was dismissed.

This view prevails in many organizations, but more firms are realizing that it is to their advantage and more cost effective to help employees when their personal problems start affecting job performance. Union pressures and government legislation have influenced this change in approach.

EAPs vary in type and scope. Delta Air Lines, Inc., is an example of a large organization that changed its approach. In 1994, Delta announced a new health plan for its 60,000 nonpilot employees and their dependents in the Atlanta, Georgia metropolitan area. The plan is a new style benefits concept that is becoming popular nationwide called a "point of service" plan. The plan seeks to slow down health care costs for the employer while allowing employees choice and flexibility. In a "point of service plan," members pick primary-care doctors from a network list. The doctor chosen directs the patient's care, including referring them to specialists as necessary. If patients use network doctors, the out-of-pocket costs to them are minimal; if they use doctors outside the network, they pay more. But the choice is the patient/employee's.[16]

While health care plans provide assistance to employees, many types of personal problems of employees must be addressed separately through the formalized EAPs. Professor Chenoweth estimates that EAPs have grown from around 50 in the early 1970s to over 10,000 in place today.[17]

One type of EAP includes help and treatment provided directly by the organization. The organization hires a qualified person to listen to employees and diagnose their problems; then, the employee is referred to the proper source for treatment. Another type of EAP within an organization has a coordinator who listens to employees' problems minimally and refers them to the proper agency or clinic for further evaluation and treatment.

EAPs can be established on-site or off-site. Both choices have particular advantages and disadvantages. One factor to consider is privacy: many employees do not want others to know of their problems and prefer an off-site location.

Small organizations have special problems when recognizing the need for an EAP. The major problem is cost. One remedy for this problem is to form an affiliation with other small companies to jointly fund and administer an EAP whose services become available to all employees (and their dependents) of the affiliated companies.

Trends in Employee Assistance Programs

Professor Chenoweth identifies the following trends in today's EAPs:

- EAPs are focusing more on early identification and encouraging self-referral.
- A growing number of EAP providers are becoming "Mental Health HMOs" by expanding traditional EAP services (evaluations, referral services and counseling) and becoming the outpatient mental health plan for some companies.
- EAPs are broadening their scope from alcoholism-only treatment to the areas of mental health, financial management, stress management and preretirement planning.
- EAPs are merging with other health promotion and health care programs to streamline administrative procedures and increase participation rates.
- Companies are moving EAPs off-site and hiring more consultants to ensure greater confidentiality.
- More program directors are trying to determine EAP impact on absenteeism, health care usage, productivity, turnoer and other botton-line indicators.[18]

There are conditions that must exist for an EAP to be successful. Upper management must totally support the program and adequately fund it. The EAP must be professionally staffed. The employees must understand the services provided by the EAP and not be afraid to use it.

Wellness Programs

Beyond EAPs, many organizations, such as banks, insurance companies and hospitals, have established *wellness programs. Wellness programs are designed to improve the health and well-being of employees and prevent both physical and mental problems.* This preventive approach to health care may include periodic medical exams; stop-smoking clinics; hypertension detection and control; seminars on dietary practices, weight control and stress management; immunizations; and exercise and fitness facilities.

Organizations which sponsor wellness centers believe the benefits outweigh the costs. Results shown have included employees' using fewer sick days, maintaining better overall health and reducing major medical costs. Employees involved in the exercise and fitness programs tend to be highly productive with a positive outlook toward work. Numerous studies report that regular exercise improves self-esteem, reduces anxiety and hostility, and can even lift clinical depression.[19] Results from wellness programs are difficult to quantify and express in bottom line results, but employees who participate consider such programs an excellent fringe benefit.

Summary

Significant changes in the external environment often affect internal operations and, in turn, impact on workers, the organization strategy and the utilization of resources.

Organization change needs to be managed whenever there is a modification of an existing policy, practice, procedure, method, strategy or technology that employees are accustomed to following. Change occurs in society at an ever-increasing rate.

Organization change is classified as technological, environmental and internal. Technological change might involve new equipment; environmental change might relate to new federal legislation; and internal change might refer to downsizing the labor force.

Ideally when organizations decide on a major internal change, managers should develop a program of planned change.

Resistance to change occurs when something is new and different that alters the *status quo*. The most common reasons that employees resist change are concern about job security and income; uncertainty about the outcome; personal inconvenience; loss of status and power; and change in personal relationships.

Management can offset employee resistance to change by developing empathy; opening communication channels; introducing employee participation; building trust; explaining time and place of change; and accentuating the positive aspects of the change.

Organization Development (OD) is an approach aimed at improving overall organizational effectiveness. OD is a collection of ideas and techniques which can help organizations deal with changes. The primary objective of OD is to change employees and the nature and quality of their working relationships to improve overall organization effectiveness.

Conflict is defined as a clash of opposing ideas and interests which leads to disagreement. Conflict occurs in all organizations and is a natural outgrowth of social interaction. Managers should strive to minimize the damage from harmful conflict and maximize the benefits of conflict. Negative consequences of conflict can lead to turnover, low morale, low productivity and a lack of cooperation. The potential positive effects of conflict can lead to improved motivation, creative approaches to solving problems, better communications and more. Four main types of conflict are interpersonal, intergroup, interdepartmental and organizational.

Resolving conflicts may prove difficult, and there is no one patented method to follow. Where intergroup and interpersonal conflicts exist, managers may try to resolve conflicts through conciliation, mediation, arbitration or negotiation.

Managing stress is an important subject to managers and to individuals. Stress is a nonspecific physiological response to anything that challenges the body. Stress affects people's lives either positively or negatively depending on the way they react to it. Positively used stress can contribute to personal growth, development and better mental health. The three types of stress are negative (distress), normal and positive (eustress). Whether stress is positive or negative depends on the individual's assessment and perception of it.

One of the results of stress is burnout. Burnout occurs when work is no longer meaningful to an employee. Management attempts to identify which jobs are more likely to cause burnout and establish a program to minimize employee burnout. Options include job rotation, job simplification, shorter work hours and job enrichment.

Employee Assistance Programs (EAPs) are created by both large and small organizations to help employees with stress, burnout, substance abuse and many other personal, medical and psychiatric problems. EAPs can be established on-site or off-site; however, many employees prefer off-site locations to protect their personal privacy. A growing number of EAP providers are becoming "mental-health HMOs" by expanding traditional EAP services. Organizations which establish EAPs do so to help employees and to reduce costs and improve employee performance.

In addition to EAPs many organizations have established wellness programs. These programs are designed to improve the health and well-being of employees and prevent physical and mental problems from occurring. This preventive approach to health problems may include periodic medical exams, seminars on dietary practices and weight control, exercise and fitness facilities and much more.

Review Questions

1. When does organization change take place?

2. Describe three types of organizational change.

3. Why is resistance to change considered a natural reaction?

4. Name the most common reasons employees resist change.

5. What common sense suggestions can managers introduce to offset employee resistance to change?

6. Describe Organization Development (OD) and its primary purpose.

7. Define conflict.

8. Outline major causes and consequences of conflict.

9. List and briefly discuss four major types of conflict.

10. What are possible conflict resolution methods which managers can use if the conflicts are intergroup or interpersonal?

11. Define stress and explain the positive and negative aspects of stress.

12. Identify three kinds of stress.

13. What is burnout?

14. Describe Employee Assistance Programs (EAPs).

15. What is the purpose of a wellness program?

Assignments for Personal Development

1. Talk to anyone in your family or to a friend who is employed and ask this question: Is there anything about your job or place of work that upsets you? After hearing the response, ask them what management is doing to resolve the conflict. If you want to pursue the question further, ask your subject what they recommend management do to resolve the conflict. Will the resolution benefit both the organization and the employee?

2. Wellness programs are enthusiastically endorsed by employees when the organization foots the entire bill for equipment, maintenance, administration and special programs. Survey your classmates and ask how many would participate in a company wellness program if a fee of $35.00 was deducted from their paycheck each month to cover their membership in the program.

Incident

STRESS AND BURNOUT

Patricia Flannagan is the Women's Basketball Coach at a small midwestern college. In addition to these duties in intercollegiate athletics, Pat is a full time professor in physical education and serves on several important college committees. Pat also is married and the mother of two teenage children. Her husband, who is very supportive of her career, is in industrial sales and travels much of each week.

After five years of coaching, traveling, teaching, being a mother, serving on committees and more, Pat is "burned out!" Although it is the middle of the basketball season, Pat knows she must do something before she has a complete breakdown. Her problems extend beyond the job. She is exhausted every night, has difficulty sleeping, suffers frequent headaches and does not look forward to going to work each day.

Pat decides to discuss her problems with her boss who is Chair of the Physical Education Department and an understanding older woman. Her boss listened carefully until she finished; then replied, "Pat, I empathize with you. I understand your problems and would like to do something to help you. But I do not know what to do. Why don't you make some recommendations to me? If they sound reasonable, I'll recommend them to the Vice President. Remember though, we're on a tight budget and we can't spend any large sums of money to alleviate your problems."

Questions:

1. Was it smart for Patricia to identify herself as an employee with problems? Explain.

2. Can you make any suggestions to Patricia to improve her job situation?

Glossary of Key Terms

Arbitration: Method of settling disputes between persons or groups by an agreement on both sides to accept the findings of a third party.

Burnout: Occurs when work is no longer meaningful to an employee.

Conciliation: When a third party attempts to appease both parties in a conflict situation.

Conflict: A clash of opposing ideas and interests which leads to disagreement.

Coping: Effort made to manage or deal with stress.

Distress: Negative stress.

Employee Assistance Programs (EAPs): Created by organizations to help employees with personal, medical and psychiatric problems.

Environmental changes: Changes from outside the organization that impact the organization, such as new federal legislation.

Eustress: Positive stress.

Interdepartmental conflict: Conflict between two or more departments in the same organization.

Intergroup conflict: When two or more groups within the same department are antagonistic toward one another.

Internal change: Change from within the organization such as downsizing the labor force.

Interpersonal conflict: Conflict between two or more persons in the same department.

Mediation: A third party in a conflict situation attempts to bring both sides together to work our their differences.

Negotiation: A conflict resolution method in which the third party (negotiator) attempts to resolve differences by having the parties calmly exchange view points and determine common points of agreement.

Organization change: Occurs whenever there is a modification of an existing policy, practice, procedure, method, strategy or technology that employees are accustomed to using.

Organization Development (OD): An approach introduced to improve overall organization effectiveness. Relies on a collection of ideas and techniques which can help organizatons deal with changes.

Organizational conflict: Conflict between two or more firms.

Stress: Nonspecific physiological response to anything that challenges the body.

Stressor: Any physical, psychological or environmental event or condition that initiates the stress response.

Technological changes: Changes such as new equipment, new processes or the addition of robotics.

Wellness programs: A type of fringe benefit designed to improve the health and well-being of employees and prevent physical and mental problems.

Practical Management Concepts
The Mysteries of Change

Nothing is more important to an organization than innovation or change. It makes the difference in competition for survival. But there are two facts about change that complicate its use for management.

Change in an organization refers to doing things differently from before. If change is to have a lasting effect, it will be authorized by top management and flow downward throughout the organization. Change is never lasting when introduced from below. Higher management must instigate it or approve it, and then introduce and endorse change for anything new and different to happen in the organization.

Bringing about change in the organization which improves work activity, the work environment, the morale of employees or anything else is a responsibility of all managers. The problem is that employees generally resist change of any type.

A managerial decision designed to benefit employees will be subject to resistance just as much as if it benefitted customers, stockholders, and the general public at the expense of employees. Prepare the introduction of any change carefully to minimize this resistance. It is a true test of managerial effectiveness to institute change with a minimum of employee resistance.

Employees must be made aware of the value of the change. They must understand the importance of change and that it makes the organization grow and compete better.

You as a manager have the responsibility to prepare and educate your employees so well that they accept change and grow with the organization and with you.

Learn the Value of Empathy

Empathy is defined as putting yourself in the other person's place. Having empathy is a positive characteristic of managers who really care about communicating effectively. Psychologically the manager who can consider the feelings and attitudes of employees before he or she talks or writes to them will do a better job of getting a particular message across. Trying to understand how people feel and think before praising, criticising or delegating work to them allows a manager an opportunity to select a method of communication and a form of communication that should be more effective.

Putting yourself in the employee's place tells him or her that you place a high value on employee's needs and feelings. It tells your employees you are concerned with doing whatever is necessary to communicate more effectively and get along more smoothly with them. It gains their support for all you try to accomplish when you begin your tenure with them in this manner. You find your employees more cooperative, supportive and productive when they believe you genuinely take their feelings into consideration in your day to day management decisions.

References and Chapter Notes:

[1] Paul Hersey and Kenneth H. Blanchard, *Management of Organizational Behavior*, sixth edition (Englewood Cliffs, NJ: Prentice-Hall, Inc., 1993), p. 363.

[2] Excerpt from a speech by J. Lewis Powell entitled "The Collapse of Time," June, 1958.

[3] John M. Thomas and Warren G. Bennis, editors, *The Management of Change and Conflict* (New York: Penguin Books, 1972), p. 109.

[4] Robert Mathis and John H. Jackson, *Personnel*, 3rd edition (St. Paul, Minnesota: West Publishing Co., 1982), p. 37.

[5] Leslie W. Rue and Lloyd L. Byars, *Management, Skills and Application*, 7th ed. (Chicago, IL: Richard D. Irwin, Inc., 1995), p. 427.

[6] Donald P. Crane, Personnel, *The Management of Human Resources*, 4th ed. (Boston, Ma: Kent Publishing Company, 1986), p. 318.

[7] James A. F. Stoner, *Management*, 2nd ed. (Englewood Cliffs, NJ: Prentice Hall, Inc., 1982), p. 392.

[8] Gary Yukl, *Leadership in Organizations*, 3rd ed. (Englewood Cliffs, NJ: Prentice-Hall, Inc., 1994), p. 137.

[9] Stoner, *Management*, p. 408.

[10] Hans Selye, *Stress Without Distress* (New York: New American Library, 1975).

[11] Selye, *Stress Without Distress*.

[12] *Health, Annual Additions*, 95/96 (Guilford, CT: Dushkin Publishing Group and Benchmark Publishers, 1995), pp. 70-71.

[13] David J. Anspaugh, Michael H. Hamrick and Frank D. Rosato, *Wellness, Concepts and Applications*, 2nd ed. (St. Louis, MO: Mosby Year Book, Inc., 1994), p. 233.

[14] Anspaugh et al, *Wellness*, p. 233.

[15] David Chenoweth, *Planning Health Promotion at the Worksite* (Dubuque, Iowa: William C. Brown, Publishers, 1991), pp. 117-118.

[16] Andy Miller, "Delta's Health Plan Charts a New Course," *The Atlanta Journal/Constitution*, February 11, 1994, p. D1.

[17] Chenoweth, *Planning Health*, p. 117.

[18] Chenoweth, *Planning Health*, p. 124.

[19] Kathleen McAucliffe, "Out of the Blues," *Walking*, March/April, 1994, pp. 42-44.

SECTION V

THE CONTROLLING PROCESS

CHAPTER 15

THE CONTROL FUNCTION

After studying this chapter, you will know:

- The meaning of control
- Steps in the control process
- The need for control
- How much control organizations should have
- The relationship between planning and control
- The types of controls
- Characteristics of effective control
- Why employees resist control
- Methods to overcome employees resistance to control
- How to control (minimize) control
- Financial control methods
- The benefits from zero-base budgeting

Introduction

Theoretically, control is the only management function you could eliminate. If managers were perfect at planning, organizing and implementing, there would be no reason for them to follow-up activities with control programs. We know that this is impossible; so, the control function exists in some degree throughout every organization.

It would be difficult to over stress the importance of the control function in the sport management profession. Any time customers, fans, students, clients, members, employees or personnel of any kind are involved in organizational activity, control to some degree becomes necessary. There are dozens of situations in the sport world where control programs are needed. We talk about "noise control" at football games; "fan control" at basketball games; and "player control" during contests just to mention a few examples. Many organizations require employees to adhere to a dress code when working, and most colleges and some professional teams have certain dress requirements when teams travel. The dress code becomes a control program.

Controlling financial expenditures and maintaining desired quality of performance are other major areas saturated with control programs. All "red tape" or organizational guidelines are introduced to influence (control) the behavior of employees or personnel for whom management has responsibility. Employee handbooks tend to put in writing some of the most important standards of personnel behavior. Much of what is in a handbook is part of a control program. In summary, most control programs are centered around financial, physical, human and information resources.

You should read the chapter carefully. It is possible to over control. That is, the benefit from the control program does not exceed the cost of implementing the control program. Costs may be measured in dollars, but costs also include low morale, personnel turnover and lagging performance. As this chapter indicates, you need some control activities to insure conformity of activities, output and behavior; but managers must guard against imposing excessive controls.

A control activity is not a substitute for sound management. In a way a control activity is a result of sound planning that attempts to prevent or avoid negative outcomes before they occur. Failure to plan and control all organizational activity properly is a major cause of management turnover.

Origin and Meaning of Control

Control is a management activity that originates from need. Managers need to insure that work is performed properly; that a quoted price is correct; that the quality of an end product is guaranteed and consistent. The control function also provides managers with information they need for making decisions. And control activities originate from the need organizations have to provide satisfactory services and products to customers at reasonable prices. Without the function of control, the managers of an organization would, in effect, be "flying blind."

The essence of control is to adjust work activity to predetermined standards which are based on data obtained from that same work activity.

It is important to note that managers who develop sound strategy, viable objectives, achievable mission statements, clear organization charts, reasonable schedules, etc., are vulnerable to serious consequences if they confuse these activities with **control**. Control is the step added to assure that desired objectives are met in an efficient manner.

Control should not be viewed as a negative activity which is introduced to punish, restrain or confine individuality or creativity within or outside the organization. Control programs have a positive purpose: to insure conformity of activities, output and behavior.

The control function generally pays for itself many times over unless the program is so complex and cumbersome that costs of implementation override the benefits.

Athletics department employees typically are required to keep receipts of all expenditures when traveling. This ensures proper allocation of expenses against budget categories and provides the basis for reimbursement of out of pocket moneys spent. There is a positive purpose to this control activity.

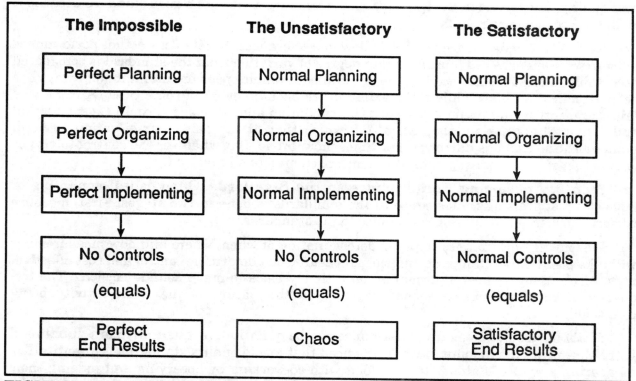

FIGURE 15-1: APPROACHES TO CONTROL

The Control Process

Any control process involves these three steps:

1. Setting standards
2. Appraising conformance to the standards
3. Taking appropriate corrective or remedial action if the standards are not met or are exceeded.

Step 1. Setting Standards. Standards originate from managerial planning and are based on the goals and objectives of the organization. Standards may pertain to everything from the quality of products to the number of days of employee sick leave; from sales quotas and inventory levels to the length and number of breaks an employee gets during the working day. For standards to have value, they must be expressed in measurable and understandable terms that are accepted by the people affected. For example, if American motorists do not accept 55 miles per hour as the standard speed limit on highways, this standard has little value. If employees routinely take thirty minute breaks rather than the allowed fifteen, the standard is meaningless. Standards should be objective, easily measured and relevant to the goals of the organization. Managerial subjectivity and judgment should be limited in the implementation of standards, and standards should be expressed in quantifiable terms whenever feasible. An organization's philosophic ideal, such as "We're going to provide the best quality and service in the industry," is a noble target, but not a good standard because it is difficult to measure results.

Normally standards are set with allowable tolerances. Rarely does actual performance meet exact standards or plans. A certain degree of variation from the standard is considered acceptable in most cases. Recently, the minimum allowable speed on interstate highways has been 40 miles per hour while the maximum has been 55 or 65 in some cases. Anyone who failed to meet the minimum or exceded the maximum allowable speed could expect a ticket and a fine. Managers set the *control tolerances* that fit the particular situation or need. Sometimes the range is narrow; other times more broad. But whatever the control tolerance is, it is best if put in writing, formalized and circulated to all involved.

Step 2. Appraising Conformance to the Standards. Often called monitoring or inspecting, appraising conformance to the standards is done in two stages. First, measure performance; then, compare performance to the standards.

Measuring performance requires determination of when, where and how measurement will take place. How often performance is measured can determine control and cost effectiveness. Also managers need information on a timely basis to make sound decisions. The frequency of repetitive measurement depends on the nature of the work activity being controlled.

Methods used to measure performance can be quantitative, qualitative or a mixture of both. Measuring the amount of work produced that meets quality standards is quantitative. Measuring a worker's ability to get along with co-workers by observing and judging their interactions is solely qualitative. A manager's performance over a year may be measured by how well he or she stays within budget in his or her area of responsibility and by improvement in employee morale in the work area. This evaluation combines quantitative and qualitative methods.

Comparing performance to standards is the second stage of appraising conformance. Performance may match the standard, fail to meet it, or it may exceed the standard. The need for corrective action depends on the allowable deviation from the standard. When the organization allows employees six days of sick leave per year without a doctor's explanation, no action is necessary until an employee misses that seventh day.

Step 3. Taking Corrective or Remedial Action. If the standard is satisfied by performance measured in Step 2, there is no need for Step 3. But is the performance does not meet the standard, some type of corrective or remedial action should be taken. When a driver fails to meet the 55 mile per hour speed limit by driving 70 and being stopped and ticketed, corrective action has identified the problem (failure to match the maximum standard) and issued a remedy. A manufactured part that fails to meet the quality standards may be thrown out or reworked until it does conform to the standard. Correcting a deviation from the standard requires an evaluation by the manager in charge. The manager focuses on the planning (Was it faulty?); on the standard itself (Was it unrealistic?); or perhaps on the personnel involved (Were they trained and qualified to perform the task?). Whatever the source of the problem, it will continue to occur unless appropriate corrective action resolves the underlying problem.

The case study in Figure 15-2 concerns one of the critical problems that faced the United States in the 1980s, widespread insolvency in the savings and loan industry. The case shows the consequences of an activity getting out of control. The same sort of impact, on a smaller scale, could adversely affect the operations of any organization. Without question, control is an essential function of management.

Controls Fail in Thrifts

A major problem in the United States today, one that affects everyone, is the scandal about insolvent thrifts. How did such a problem occur when these financial institutions are audited regularly and governed heavily by legislation and the Federal Home Loan Bank Board? And how can this crisis be solved so that similar problems do not arise in the future?

Banning K. Lary[1] reports that, by the end of 1988, nearly 1,000 of the 3,400 thrifts in the U.S. were losing money. His figures come from a U.S. House of Representatives Government Operations Committee Report. What went wrong? Some people blame the deregulatory reforms of the early 1980's which allowed the savings and loan industry to diversify, reduced its restrictions and made competition fairer. Many experts say this deregulation has backfired. Others say the causes are high inflation, new competition for home loans, and fraud and mismanagement by officers of the insolvent thrifts. Regional economic problems, such as the real estate and oil busts in the Southwest during the 1980's, have also been cited.

Without question corrective action had to be taken. On Friday, August 4, 1989, Congress passed the most far-reaching restructuring of the nation's financial institution industry since the Great Depression of the 1930's. The thrift bill is designed to bolster thrifts and remedy the insolvency problems in the savings and loan industry caused by poor—and in some cases fraudulent—loan practices. The bill will pump $50 billion in cash into the ailing thrift insurance fund. The total cost to taxpayers starts with a minimum of $159 billion over the next ten years. The bill requires thrifts to concentrate more on traditional business; requires more of the owners or investors cash as part of capital requirements; and mandates that at least seventy (70) percent of their loans must be housing-related.[2]

[1]Banning K. Lary, "Insolvent Thrifts: A National Crisis," Management Review, March, 1989, Vol. 78, No. 3.
[2]James A. Mallory, "S & L Bill Considered Important First Step," Atlanta Journal and Constitution, August 6, 1989, p. 1E.

FIGURE 15-2: CASE STUDY

The Need for Control

The need for control depends on answering this question: How expensive would operations be without controls? In very small organizations the control activities may be informal and largely unplanned. The managers react when a problem appears. But in well-managed organizations, control activities are planned, implemented, regularly reviewed and changed when conditions warrant.

These major factors affect the need for controls:

- The way organizations are structured
- Types of employees and the nature of their work
- Changes in the internal and external environment

Organization Structure. Organizations that are highly centralized (tall structures)[1] concentrate authority, responsibility, decision-making and control near the top of the hierarchy. These organizations are more bureaucratic, with more "red tape," than decentralized firms (flat structures). More rigid control programs exist in highly centralized organizations, such as banks, to assure that all employees conform to the same standards, procedures, rules and policies. When we say managers make decisions "by the book," we acknowledge they operate in a tightly controlled, highly centralized organization that allows little room for individual initiative or creativity. The control function in these organizations becomes extremely important due to the sensitive nature of the work activities. Examples of highly centralized organizations with many rigid control programs are commercial banks, government agencies, the military and most educational institutions.

While most educational institutions qualify as bureaucracies, the employees are viewed as professionals. Professors, as an example, are not subjected to tight controls on a daily basis; however, the results of their endeavors are compared to expectations on an annual basis.

Organizations that are highly decentralized (flat structures) are relatively less controlled at the top of the hierarchy. The control function is pushed downward to lower level managers. Examples of major control programs at lower management levels are conformance to budgets and achieving desired objectives (such as projected anticipated sales) over the set period of time.

Types of Employees and Their Work. Employees who are relatively unskilled and those in the process of acquiring more skills normally must be more controlled until they have achieved the level of competency which matches the desired quality and quantity standards. Thereafter, minimum control programs may be implemented to insure their conformance to standards. Highly professional employees such as researchers in a pharmaceutical laboratory may need little control over their activities whereas those who produce the pharmaceutical product need strict quality control programs. Obviously the nature of the work has as much effect on control activities as the type of employees. Getting the space shuttle ready to launch or preparing a new public stock offering dictate tight control programs. A creative team working on a new advertising campaign may require few controls (perhaps only a time deadline) until they present their work. Building a house in a residential neighborhood may require strict controls in selecting the craftsmen hired for the project; then, little control as they work except for observation of physical progress and conformance to the plans each day. Other factors that influence the need for control programs are age of employees; educational background; certified skills possessed; complexity of the work; dollars invested in work activities; geographic spread of the workers; time constraints for completion of work; and budget restrictions.

Changes in Environment. Change is inevitable. Managers must be alert to changing internal and external factors that precede a change in the way activities are controlled. Examples of internal changes are unionization of the work force; budget cutbacks; an expansion of the services offered; introducing new equipment; or a change in ownership or top management which brings a new philosophy or different techniques to the job. External environmental changes can include new legislation or rules and regulations; a slumping economy; higher than expected inflation; unusual weather conditions; a change in the prime rate or a gasoline shortage.

Sometimes information generated by current control programs influences managers to change the way activities are controlled. A new need arises which can only be met by changing the control program. An example of this is the professional sports leagues' responses to the growing problem of drug and alcohol abuse within their industry over the past decade.

How Much Control?

Control programs must have a "pay off." There is no need to control an activity if the cost is greater than the benefit. Economic considerations play an important role in deciding the amount of control. For example, no organization can afford to inspect the quality individually of thousands of items as they are received or shipped. Instead sampling based on probability theory is used to monitor the items. Inspectors of the U.S. Department of Agriculture use this approach when inspecting products under their jurisdiction.

How much control should an organization have over its activities? Like the old question, how long should a person's legs be; the answer is just enough (whether to reach the ground or to accomplish the desired results)! Anything beyond "just enough" is pure waste. Organizations should have just enough control to meet desired objectives. Control programs should be audited regularly to make certain that they are current and not obsolete, and to determine that they are functioning as designed.

Additionally, organizations should consider the impact of control programs on employees. If employees resent tight control programs and their productivity and morale are affected, the cost of control may be greater than the value. Many organizations today involve their employees in the design and implementation of control programs which affect them. One technique which allows this participation is Quality Control Circles.

Quality Control Circles originated in the United States; then became popular in Japan. In a Quality Control Circle (QCC) a small group of individuals meet to discuss and resolve quality control issues. The concept of allowing employees input in decisions affecting them is a form of participative management. As already discussed, participating in the problem-solving and decision-making process tends to make employees identify with the outcome and lessens their resistance to any change.

In collegiate athletics, team members who violate team rules often are meted out punishment based on standards set by graduating seniors at the beginning of the sport's season. This, too, is a form of participative management.

Planning and Control

The purpose of planning is to reach objectives in the proper period of time, as efficiently and effectively as possible, with a minimum of problems. It is highly unlikely that this can occur without introducing a planned control program. Managers plan, organize, implement and then control. Sound control programs alert managers to time delays, quality defects, poor employee performance, schedule problems, and much more. The opposite is also true. Good performance, being ahead of schedule and other positive indicators are valuable to managers, and such data results from using controls.

Planning involves the determination of necessary control programs. Since planning is future-oriented, and the future involves risks and uncertainties; controlling becomes an essential activity. There is a balanced dependency between planning and controlling as shown in Figure 15-3.

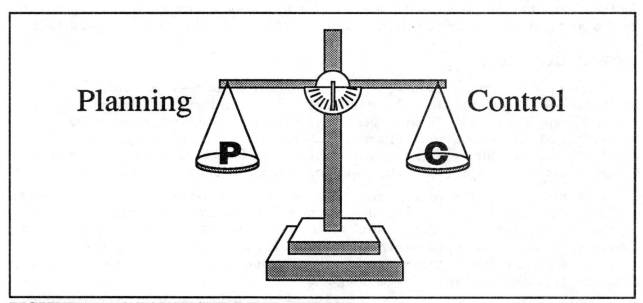

FIGURE 15-3: A BALANCED DEPENDENCY

Some common athletic activities that require formal control programs which must be anticipated and planned are shown in Figure 15-4.

Types of Controls

Managers can introduce control anywhere along the continuum of work activity: at the beginning, during the process, or at the end. The placement of control relates to the timing of work activity and the importance of each phase of the work. Figure 15-5 illustrates the three types of control commonly used in manufacturing organizations such as those which manufacture sporting goods.

> ⇨ Salary Caps (Professional Teams)
>
> ⇨ Eligibility Compliance Programs
>
> ⇨ Allowable Athletic Scholarships Per Sport
>
> ⇨ Allowed Recruiting Trips and Expenditures
>
> ⇨ Team Travel Dress Codes
>
> ⇨ Player Behavior During Athletic Contests
>
> ⇨ Coaches' Behavior (During Contests and Otherwise)
>
> ⇨ Substance Abuse Testing
>
> ⇨ Monitoring Academic Standing/Progress
>
> ⇨ Expenses/Activities of Recruits During Visits

FIGURE 15-4: ATHLETIC ACTIVITIES REQUIRING FORMAL CONTROL PROGRAMS

Incoming or Screening Control. If control is introduced at the beginning, it is called incoming or screening control. The purpose of control at this stage is to prevent problems from occurring. This is a positive approach to control. Checking everything about a new car before you purchase it is one example. Commercial airline pilots who checklist the equipment and its systems before takeoff are another example. Incoming control also is called *preliminary control.*

In-process Control. When manufactured goods are subjected to quality checks (against standards of excellence) during the manufacturing process, the manager is using **in-process control.** This type of control also uncovers problems with time delays, quantity output, and employee performance before the end of the work cycle. In-process control does not prevent problems, but it does spot deviations from the standard before work activity is completed. In-process control provides an opportunity to adjust performance to the standard prior to incurring major problems. For example, if in-process control checks prove production is not meeting quantity standards, the production line can be accelerated. If a quality control check in-process reveals that two parts do not fit together as they should, it can be fixed before the integrity of a whole unit is threatened. If a baseball pitcher with a one run lead walks two batters and throws three straight balls to the third he faces in the fifth inning, he may be removed from the game before it gets out of hand. These are examples of in-process controls which also are called *concurrent controls.*

Final-stage Control or Postaction Control. This is the type of control that reviews the results of the final product or service. Information obtained about deviations from the standard or plans can be used in controlling and improving performance in the future. Final-stage control also can provide information to support major management decisions such as to cancel offering advertised services; to scrub a shuttle lift-off; to add or discontinue a product; or to approve continuing past work practices.

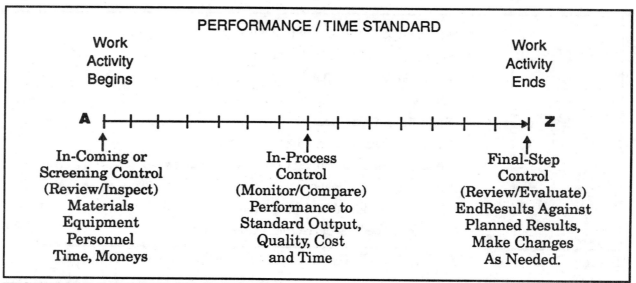

FIGURE 15-5: TYPES OF CONTROL

Characteristics of Effective Control

The control function is essential to insure that work performance matches the standards and to uncover the reasons for any deviations. Also, we know there is a balanced dependency between planning and control. Without sound planning and effectively designed control programs, the control function is ineffective.

Certain points must be remembered when designing control programs. These points may be considered the characteristics of effective control.

1. **The details of each control program should be tailored to fit the needs of individual organizations.** Every organization's products and services, work environment, types of employees and objectives are different from every other's. Establishing the control function must include consideration of all the variables which make that organization unique.

2. **The establishment of controls must have the complete support of top management.** Without such support it will be difficult to convince either managers or employees that controls are essential.

3. **Control programs must be cost-effective.** There is little cost justification to introduce controls if the cost, either in dollar value or in employee upheaval, is greater than the benefit.

4. **Control activities should possess enough flexibility to adapt to change.** When new standards are needed, it is better to modify the existing control program than to create an entirely new system.

5. **Control programs should provide information in a timely way.** Through a carefully designed system of communication pertinent information generated by the control function must be available to managers as needed. Sometimes data must be reviewed hourly; or it can be needed daily, weekly, quarterly or yearly. Generally information is

needed less often when the work setting is stable, but needed more often when the work situation is subject to unpredictable changes and uncertainty. Timeliness means providing usable information exactly when needed.

6. **Objective information is the essence of sound control.** Often employees complain of management's showing favoritism: that one employee gets better treatment or a better evaluation than another without justification. Management's objectivity comes under question. Objective information is a must if control programs are to function properly. This is true whether the source of information is employees at work stations, computers, sales representatives in the field, or from managers evaluating personnel. It can become a legal issue if the information gained in a control program is not as objective as possible. Even cybernetic controls that are self-regulating must be designed to provide useful and objective information.

Employee Resistance to Control

It is common for the introduction of a control program to upset employees. After all these programs represent change, which most people resist by nature. Employees may resent implementing a new procedure or system, changing long-established work patterns; or they may balk at closer supervision, with each move questioned, and their performance measured against a nebulous standard. The result of too much control is to suppress and stifle individual flexibility, creativity and originality. This may be a purpose of the control program, but overcontrolling quickly generates a cost greater than the value of the control.

According to Jaeger and Baliga the Japanese have been able to introduce bureaucratic and cultural controls effectively which have enabled them to produce quality products at reasonable prices. Much of the credit is given to the use of their cultural control systems and the technology with which they are working.[2] Japanese managers consider the "total" employee as an integral link in successfully implementing a control program. They minimize employee resistance to controls and involve employees in the planning and implementation of control. This practice is becoming common in large American organization today.

Overcoming Employee Resistance to Control

There are four recommendations to overcome or prevent employee resistance to control. Consider each recommendation a step to take to overcome or prevent resistance.

Step 1: Sound Planning

Ideally well planned control will avoid any employee resistance to control. Managers need to establish the objectives of the control program; then create a program that possesses all of the characteristics of effective control.

Step 2: Employee Involvement

Allowing employees to participate in the development of a control program through ideas, suggestions and feedback eliminates a lot of resistance once a control program is introduced. Their input can be valuable throughout the planning stage. Since they are the ones to be directly affected by the control and often they are more knowledgeable about the situation needing control, their views and suggestions must be encouraged, reviewed and recognized in all cases.

Step 3: Careful Implementation

This step deals with the actual introduction of the control program. Careful implementation is a three phase process: First, employees must be **educated** about the control program. The employees directly affected by the control understand how the program works, its purpose, and the impact of it on them and the whole organization. More importantly they must be **sold** on the control program. This requires stressing the value of the control program to them, the benefits which will accrue, and the cost-effectiveness of the control. Finally, the control program should be **demonstrated**. A live demonstration presents a point more effectively than any other method. After the demonstration, questions should be encouraged and answered, once again involving employees in the control program.

Step 4: Follow-Up

Once a control is introduced, all employees involved should be encouraged to report their reaction to it. Each verbal or written comment should be recognized by management positively. Sometimes a follow-up group meeting is helpful in providing a forum for evaluating control. Some organizations use quality circles as a forum for continuous follow-up. When management identifies problems with the control which prevent achieving desired objectives, corrective action should not be delayed.

If these four steps are followed, management should be able to minimize or prevent employee resistance to control.

Organization and Control

Top management has the ultimate responsibility for the control function. In small organizations each employee may be assigned the duty to control his or her own work activities according to management's instructions. As organizations grow larger, staff persons and positions emerge, created by higher line management, to assist all employees in performing their duties. Often the new staff personnel are directly involved in control activities such as internal audits, safety, quality and scheduling. As growth continues and more complex organization structures evolve (such as organization by divisions, geographic regions or product lines), control departments may be created to function as specialized staff units. The most common of these deal with quality, inventory, budgets, production, forecasting, maintenance and safety. Staff control personnel are advisory to line managers but are delegated limited line authority in some specialized areas such as inspectors in quality control. Staff control specialists or departments, as shown in Figure 15-6, are located in the area where they advise line managers, but the placement of the staff, position or department on the organization chart does not indicate the relative importance of the work.

The fact that staff departments are created to assist and advise line managers about control does not decrease the line manager's responsibility to control.

The larger organizations usually have a position entitled controller. The controller is a manager whose full time job is to control activities throughout the organization. The controller assists all line managers with their control activities and gathers and interprets data for the benefit of higher line management. Recently other job titles have been coined which reflect similar duties and responsibilities as that of a controller. In the healthcare industry the job title of Quality Assurance Director is popular. A quality assurance director in a large hospital deals with facts, data, trends, costs, etc., that are relevant to the control of services provided and their costs. This information is measured against the projected standards.

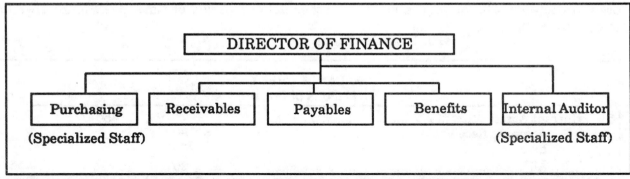

FIGURE 15-6: LOCATION OF SPECIALIZED STAFF CONTROL FUNCTIONS

Controlling Controls

As essential as the control function is, organizations can become overcontrolled. Control programs are a form of red tape and are expensive to administer. Control should be a result of a formulated control strategy developed by top management and should not be introduced out of crisis. Periodically management should audit all control programs to make sure they are still useful, current, and continue to possess all of the characteristics of effective control. Excessive control contributes to inefficiency which reflects directly on top management.

Financial Control Methods

There are many methods and techniques to help managers more effectively control programs centered on financial, physical, human and information resources.

Activities in any organization are so varied and numerous that a single control system cannot be implemented that encompasses all areas that need attention. Instead, managers introduce specific control programs aimed at specific functional activities in order to make the control programs effective and efficient.

One such functional area is finance. Financial control methods and techniques are among the most common forms of control implemented in most organizations; and the most widely used are financial statements, ratios, break-even analysis, budgets and audits. Some sport management graduates will work in the finance areas of sport organizations. Familiarity with financial control methods is recommended for all managers in any industry. All managers should know how to read financial statements, understand how to develop budgets, and be able to calculate the ratios which pertain to their specialty. Such knowledge will help these managers to determine ways to maximize use of the money allocated to them and to determine if it is advisable to continue certain activities.

Financial Statements. There are a group of financial statements which use various numerical formats to show the *liquidity*, the *financial condition* and the *profitability* status of an organization over a certain period of time. Such statements become focal points for controlling plans and decisions regarding the output of goods and services. One example is a *balance sheet*, which shows an organization's assets, liabilities and net worth at a particular point in time. An *income statement* or *profit and loss statement* shows profit or loss for the organization for a fiscal year, a month or other defined period of time. See Figure 15-7 for examples of these.

BALANCE SHEET (In Millions of Dollars)		
Current Assets		350
Accounts Receivable	$ 80	
Inventory...	250	
All Other	20	
Fixed Assets (Net)...		800
Total Assets...		1,150
Current Liabilities..		250
Long-term Debt		400
Stockholders' Equity...		500
Common Stock [20,000 shares outstanding].....	100	
Retained Earnings...................................	400	
Total Liabilities and Equity		1,150
INCOME STATEMENT		
Sales...		800
Expenses		700
Interest...	50	
Depreciation..	80	
All Other	570	
Operating Profit..		100
Taxes		40
Net Income...		60

FIGURE 15-7: BALANCE SHEET AND INCOME STATEMENT EXAMPLES

Managers use these same financial statements developed on a pro forma basis to gain better control and make wiser decisions. A *pro forma is a projection*, usually involving expected profits or losses on a proposal, new venture or some kind of organizational enterprise. Data from past operations is projected into the future, and certain precautions must be taken: make the assumptions upon which the projection is based completely clear; be wary of projections submitted by the (sometimes overly optimistic) proponent of whatever you are considering; and always be aware that projections into the future are likely to be wrong, sometimes by a wide margin. The pro forma is a useful and sometimes essential device largely because it requires objective, quantitative analysis of a proposal. If new managers are required to develop a pro forma for a new product or venture, they must remember the qualifications as well as be fully prepared to defend their projections. This can lead to better control and decision-making.[3]

Ratios. The most common financial ratios helpful to managers in the control process pertain to profit, liquidity, debt and operations. Profit ratios include the calculation of gross and net profit margins as well as the *return on investment* (ROI). *ROI* is always an important question for any organization. Managers must decide how to invest capital by choosing among several alternatives such as new equipment, new plant, additional personnel, acquiring another firm and other considerations. Calculations must be made to show the return on investment on each option so that the one which provides the organization with the greatest benefit over time can be determined. Another important ratio to most businesses is the *return on net worth or equity* or the measure of net earnings divided by stockholders equity. It is considered a critical measure of organization and management performance; and management can improve the return on equity by increased efficiency, better productivity, larger market share and greater financial leverage.

Current assets divided by current debt is called the *current ratio*. The current ratio determines a firm's ability to pay its short term debts and indicates the firm's liquidity, measures that are of primary concern to creditors. Another important ratio is *debt to equity*, determined by dividing long-term debt by stock-holders equity. This shows the organization's debt load and long-term security to investors and long-term lenders. Increasing debt or *financial leverage* can be a highly desirable and profitable action for an organization, but it comes with the drawback of greater risk. Management must determine the amount of risk it wishes to entertain when developing plans and programs; and calculation of these particular ratios, current ratio, debt to equity and leverage ratio (total assets divided by stockholders equity), can guide management toward prudent decisions by highlighting opportunities for increasing leverage or spotting overextension and liquidity problems. All these factors untimately reflect on the quality of an organization's management.

Operating ratios are identified by functions such as sales or manufacturing. Calculating the cost of sales as a percent of total sales provides information for comparison with previous years. Operating ratios become standards of comparison that are important in the control process to assess improvement in performance over time.

The ratios described in Figure 15-8 give management an idea of the relative strength of the organization. All managers at every level should learn how to read and calculate these vital organizational signs.

In professional sports franchises, managers can modify these ratios and determine the effect of a player on attendance to judge the value of the player to the team. For example, a baseball team can measure attendance and/or ticket sales on days when certain pitchers play and gain some insight into that player's effect on team revenues. This is especially helpful when salary negotiations take place or when trading players is discussed.

Break-Even Analysis. The break-even analysis is a financial control technique that determines the relationship between cost and revenue at various levels of sales and production. It shows that point at which it is profitable to produce and sell a product. The break-even chart (see Figure 15-9) presents a visual image of this information. Professional sports franchises can use break-even analysis to determine how many season tickets they need to sell to meet revenue requirements. A spa, club or county recreation program can use break-even analysis to measure how many members or participants they need to justify funding a program or opening a facility.

Profits ratios:

Profit margin on sales:	net income + total sales
Return on net worth:	net income + stockholders' equity
Return on assets:	net income + total assets

Liquidity ratios:

Current ratio:	current assets + current liabilities
Quick ratio:	current assets/inventory + current liabilities

Debt ratios:

Debt to equity:	long-term debt + stockholders' equity
Leverage:	total assets + stockholders' equity
Debt to total assets:	long-term debt + total assets
Debt to total capitalization:	long-term debt + long-term debt + stockholders' equity
Fixed charges coverage:	income available to meet fixed charges + fixed charges
Times interest earned:	before tax income + interest + interest charges

Operations ratios:

Inventory turnover:	total sales + value of inventory
Average collection period:	total accounts receivable + sales per day
Sales to fixed assets:	total sales + fixed assts
Total asset turnover:	total sales + total assets
Direct selling costs (%):	total sales salaries + gross sales
Sales per hour:	gross sales + total hours worked by salespeople
Sales per salesperson (#):	number of sales + number of full-time or equivalent full-time salespeople
Sales per salesperson ($):	gross sales + number of full-time or equivalent sales staff
Average sales per transaction ($):	gross sales + number of sales transactions
Cost of sales to total sales (%):	total cost of sales + total sales revenue

FIGURE 15-8: FINANCIAL RATIOS EVERY MANAGER SHOULD KNOW HOW TO USE

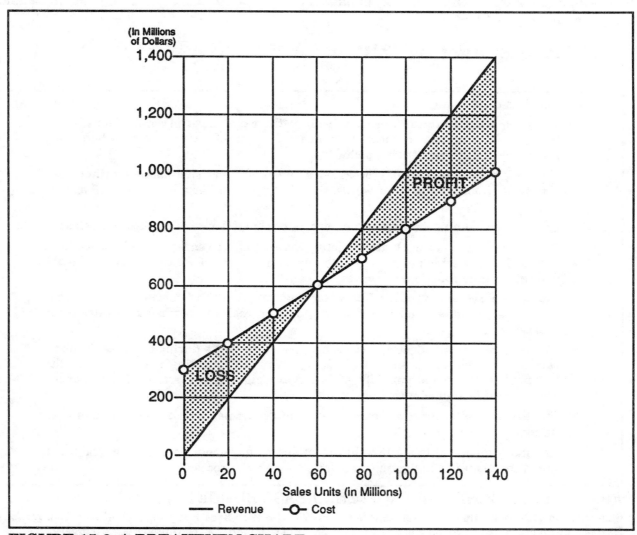

FIGURE 15-9: A BREAKEVEN CHART

Budgets

A budget is a financial forecast or plan that projects expected income and expenditures over a given period of time.

Budgets influence many managerial decisions such as the size of the labor force, wages, funds available for supplies and equipment, operating expenditures and much more. The most common budgets are operating budgets, capital budgets and financial budgets. Operating budgets are used to relate projected revenues to projected expenditures to determine adequate cash flow, the break-even point, and to project a net profit or loss. Operating budgets normally are for a one year time period. Capital budgets project the sources and uses of capital. Financial budgets are used to determine the cash flow and balance sheet items. Managers would be most interested in operating budgets and on occasion capital budgets when, for example, a new facility is being planned. Budgets, as a tool to aid planning/decision-making, become a major aid to managers as they address problems and formulate and implement decisions.

Zero-Base Budgeting (ZBB)

Former President Jimmy Carter:

From my experience in government as well as the experiences of corporations in the business world, a number of clear-cut benefits from an effective zero-base budgeting effort can be cited. These benefits include:

♦ Focusing the management process on analysis and decision-making rather than simply on numbers—in other words, the what, why, and how issues as well as how much.

♦ Combining planning, budgeting, and operational decision-making into one process.

♦ Forcing managers to evaluate in detail the cost-effectiveness of their operations. This includes specific programs—both new and old—all of which are clearly identified rather than functionally buried.

♦ Providing a system to trade off between long-term and short-term needs during the budgeting period, as well as a follow-up tool on cost and performance during the year.

♦ Allowing for quick budget adjustments or resource shifts during the year. If necessary when revenue falls short. In so doing, zero-base budgeting offers the capability to quickly and rationally modify goals and expectations to correspond to a realistic and affordable plan of operation.

♦ Identifying similar functions among different departments for comparison and evaluation.

♦ And most important to me, broadly expanding management participation and training in the planning, budgeting, and decision-making process.

FIGURE 15-10: BENEFITS FROM ZERO-BASE BUDGETING

Source: Jimmy Carrter, "Jimmy Carter Tells Why He Will Use Zero-Base Budgeting," reprinted from *Nation's Business* 65 (January 1977): 26, published by the Chamber of Commerce of the United States, January 1977.

This approach to budgeting is nothing more than common sense but has received much attention since former President Jimmy Carter popularized it while Governor of Georgia and then President of the United States (see Figure 15-10).

Zero-base budgeting was conceived by Peter A. Pyhrr in the late 1960s when he was employed by Texas Instruments. Then-Governor Carter, impressed with the concept, recruited Pyhrr to help install zero-base budgeting throughout state government in Georgia. Zero-base budgeting is an operating, planning and budgeting process which requires each manager to begin each budget period at zero expenditures and justify every budget request in detail. The pressure to support spending any money on any item rests with the manager/ preparer. Budget requests are reviewed by higher managers, and through a participatory process, funds are allocated for those expenditures that are acceptable and judged appropriate. ZBB originates at the lower level of management and moves upward unlike MBO which begins at top management and spreads downward throughout the organization.

ZBB is especially useful in nonprofit organizations such as collegiate athletics associations where funds are frequently scarce and must be budgeted among alternative uses carefully. In many organizations funds are limited and the supply of additional moneys to supplement or cover budget overruns is nonexistent. Nearly all nonprofit organizations or service oriented firms could use ZBB, but large organizations such as manufacturers would find it difficult to implement.

Audits. *A review or investigation of an organization's activities is called an audit.* Although usually associated with a firm's financial practices, audits can be of any activity of the organization. When the audit concerns nonfinancial activity in the organization, it is called a *management audit.* An evaluation of the firm's policies and procedures is an example of a management audit.

Audits can be performed by the organization's own personnel or by outside consultants/specialists. Internal audits using the firm's own personnel are used to examine the accuracy and honesty of financial information. A public accounting firm is usually called upon to perform an external audit in which they compare the financial practices and reports of the organization to professional accounting standards. External auditors note any variations and make recommendations to management for improvements. Specialists, such as management consultants or behavioral scientists, conduct external management audits to improve practices and procedures, determine the attitude and quality of management and nonmanagement employees, increase productivity, improve quality control, and identify and remedy any problem areas of the organization's overall performance.

Managers at every level in any type of organization need to know how to read and interpret vital financial data. First-level managers are involved in budgeting, costing and other financial calculations even if their expertise or job area has nothing directly to do with the organization's financial operations.

Total Quality Control (TQC)

Total Quality Control (TQC) is not a method, but rather a practical and philosophical approach to the control of quality with all parts of the organization involved. Quality control departmentally works with managers, designers, maintenance personnel, vendors and the line employees to implement quality control programs for each function in the organization. This approach is different from some historical programs such as "zero defects" which attempted to improve quality by changing the attitude of workers. One of the pioneers of TQC was A. V. Feigenbaum, formerly with General Electric.

A. V. Feigenbaum says of TQC

> Total quality control is an effective system for integrating the quality development, quality maintenance, and quality improvement efforts of various groups in an organization so as to enable marketing, engineering, production and service at the most economical levels which allow for full customer satisfaction.[4]

Today, Total Quality Management (TQM) is the most widely known movement in the U.S. designed to control quality and improve all aspects of an organization's activities. While many dismiss the movement as faddish and even destructive, others describe it as a continuous process that will lead to improved quality, greater efficiency and higher employee morale. All these features are contributors to increased productivity in American organizations which is the key to economic growth without inflation and to international competitiveness.

The four key points of TQM are a continuous process in which an organization does the following:

1. Statistically analyzes how jobs are done.

2. Disposes of procedures that do not work.

3. Uses all employees' broadest expertise and rewards it meaningfully.

4. Purges itself of stereotypical thinking.[5]

TQM has its origins in the work of George Edwards, Walter Shewhart, W. Edwards Deming and A. V. Feigenbaum. These men advocated the concept of quality control in every functional area of an organization from design to sales. They stressed a preventive (proactive) approach to control of quality rather than relying on corrective (reactive) activities.

W. Edwards Deming is the most well-known of this group. Dr. Deming gained fame for influencing Japanese industrialists after World War II. His ideas and methods, which had not been accepted well in America at the time, appealed to the Japanese, who used Deming's methods to improve the quality of their products to become the best in the world. Today, Deming's ideas have gained new attention and acceptance and are spreading throughout the U.S. The philosophical basis of most TQM programs today can be found in Deming's management philosophy which stresses constancy of purpose toward improvement of products and services; using modern training and supervision methods; a vigorous program of education and training; an attitude of teamwork and pride in workmanship (for a complete discussion of Deming's management philosophy, see Gitlow and Gitlow, *The Deming Guide*, pp. 29-31).

Some educational institutions have introduced TQM in a modified way. Many major medical centers, banks, businesses and government agencies as well as other types of organizations have TQM programs. Sport managers should become familiar with the philosophical approach of TQM because it fits many aspects of a sport manager's job: service to customers without defects or delays; teamwork and pride in results; stress on education and training; constant improvement to ultimately reduce costs; and loyalty and trust based on eliminating fear within an organization.

Summary

Control is a managerial activity that originates from need. The need to insure that work is performed correctly; the need to assure that quoted prices are accurate; the need to guarantee the quality of goods and services and much more.

The essence of control is to adjust work activity to preset standards based on information obtained from monitoring work activity.

Theoretically control is the only function of management that could be eliminated, but only if planning, organizing and implementing were performed perfectly. Such is never the case.

Control activities originate from the need organizations have to provide customers with satisfactory products and services at reasonable prices.

The control process has three steps: setting standards; appraising conformance to the standards; and taking corrective or remedial action if the standards are exceeded.

Major factors affecting the need for control are these: the way organizations are structured; the types of employees and the nature of their work; and changes in the internal and external environments.

Quality Control Circles (QCCs) are widely used by Japanese firms and are popular in the U.S. QCCs are small groups of individuals who meet to discuss and solve quality control issues. The idea of QCCs originated in the U.S., but the value of having employees participate in solving control problems was not fully appreciated nor practiced much in the U.S. until the past decade.

Sound planning includes the determination of needed control after objectives have been formulated. There is a balanced dependency between planning and control.

Three types of control are incoming or screening; in-process; and final-stage. These are also called preliminary, concurrent and postaction controls.

Characteristics of effective control are these:

1. The details of each control program should be tailored to meet the needs of individual organizations.
2. The establishment of controls must have the complete support of top management.
3. Control programs must be cost effective.
4. Control programs should possess enough flexibility to adapt to change.
5. Control programs should provide information in a timely way.
6. Objective information is the essence of sound control.

Employees often resist new control programs. Four recommendations to overcome or prevent employee resistance are through sound planning; employee involvement; careful implementation, and managerial follow-up.

Top management has the ultimate responsibility for the control function. It is an essential activity, yet organizational activities can be overcontrolled. Management should audit all control programs periodically to make certain they are still useful and current and that they continue to possess all the characteristics of effective control. Excessive control contributes to inefficiency and reflects on top management.

Financial control methods and techniques are common is most organizations and include financial statements, ratios, break-even analysis, budgets and audits. All managers at every level in the organization need to know about financial analysis.

Total Quality Control (TQC) and Total Quality Management (TQM) are practical and philosophical approaches to improving products and services which include all parts of an organization in their implementation.

Review Questions

1. Under what conditions could an organization do without the control function?

2. What are the essential steps in the control process? Explain each.

3. Discuss the balanced dependency between planning and control.

4. There are three types of controls. Each type serves a unique purpose. Clarify the purpose of each.

5. List and briefly discuss the characteristics of effective control.

6. Review options management has to overcome or prevent employee resistance to new control.

7. Why must control programs have a "pay off?"

8. Discuss the purpose of Quality Control Circles (QCCs).

9. Describe financial control methods that are common to most organizations.

Assignments for Personal Development

1. Gain access to a high school or collegiate athletics program. Talk with a principal, athletics director or head coach to ascertain how many different control programs exist in the administration of an athletics program. For example, most institutions require anyone who is going to purchase supplies or equipment to go through a purchasing requisition procedure with final approval from above before an order can be placed. Find out how these programs control participants' eligibility, monitor coaches' behavior, insure compliance with governance rules and regulations, etc.

2. The typical college student is saturated by control programs. There are deadlines for registration, for withdrawing from a class, for turning in papers and projects; every professor has a standard for passing the course -- both for grades and class participation; classes begin at a specified time and attendance is generally mandatory, etc. All these examples involve all the steps in the control process: a standard is set, conformance appraised, and corrective or remedial action taken as necessary. If 70 is a passing grade and you make 75 on the exam, you relax; but if you make 60, you take corrective action. That action can be to study harder for the next exam or to drop the course before you fail it!

   Apply the principles of control to your student life and keep a record of your performance. See if you can meet your predetermined standards. Set your areas of desired improvement or control; then, establish some standards (reasonable but excellent); use some type of system to monitor your progress (the appraisal phase); and at the proper time, make adjustments (take corrective/remedial action) to keep yourself on target.

   Following simple controls can make a world of difference in the life and regimen of any student. Try it!

Incident

A SMOKING GUN!

Ms. Fitzgerald, recently promoted manager, directly supervises five women in the administrative services area of a fundraising and development office of a major university. At the time of her promotion her immediate superior, who was an Associate Director, told her she had a real challenge on her hands. The women employees were accustomed to a boss who had a laidback style of management because she was about to retire and was congenial and friendly to everyone. The former boss was extremely popular with her employees who all considered her a friend.

Her boss told Ms. Fitzgerald that the time had finally come when change was necessary to improve productivity and efficiency. Furthermore, he told her the socializing throughout the day had to stop. All employees had to realize they were there from 8 to 5 to work; and coffee breaks morning and afternoon as well as the lunch period were to be kept to their strict time limit. Ms. Fitzgerald was cautioned to expect trouble from these employees when she tried to straighten them out, but her job was to control their behavior enough to produce a sharp improvement in productivity and performance.

Questions:

1. Recommend ways to control employee work behavior in this situation so that employee productivity and efficiency will improve.

2. What advice would you give to Ms. Fitzgerald to overcome or prevent employee resistance to new controls?

Glossary of Key Terms

Audit: Review of an organization's activities or practices in the financial or managerial areas.

Break-Even Analysis: Financial control technique that determines the relationship between cost and revenue at various sales levels. Shows point at which it is profitable to produce and sell a product or service.

Budget: Financial forecast or plan that projects expected income and expenses over a given period of time.

Control: Essence of control is to adjust work activity to predetermined standards which are based on data obtained from that same work activity.

Control Process: Involves three steps: setting standards; appraising conformance to the standards; taking corrective or remedial action if the standards are exceeded.

Financial Control Methods and Techniques: Include financial statements, ratios, break-even analysis, budgets, audits and other financial measures of an organization's overall welll-being.

Final-Stage Control: Also called postaction control, review the results of the final product or service.

Incoming Control: Also called screening or preliminary control, designed to prevent problems from occurring.

Income Statement: A profit and loss statement that shows the profit or loss of an organization during the fiscal year. A pro forma income statement shows projected profit and loss for the fiscal year.

In-process Control: Also called concurrent control, a program to spot deviations from standards while work is in process.

Quality Control Circles (QCCs): Small groups of employees meet to discuss and resolve quality control issues.

Return on Investment: The central question for each organization about how to invest its capital; often decisions are based on expected return or payback analysis.

Return on Net Worth (Equity): Ratio of net income (earnings) to stockholders equity.

Zero-Base Budgeting: Operating, planning and budgeting process which requires each manager to begin each budget period at "zero" expenditures and justify every budget request in detail.

Practical Concepts in Management

The Span of Control Principle

Every new manager should recognize there is a limit to the number of employees you or any other manager can manage effectively. This is not a predetermined number. There is no magic number of employees to manage which minimizes conflict and problems. On the contrary, some individual managers may be able to supervise 25 employees effectively while others may have their hands full with three.

Factors which affect this span of control have been identified, though, and you must consider them as a manager:

1. The type of work being performed;

2. The type of workers performing the jobs;

3. The individual talent and skill of the manager, and

4. Physical factors such as noise, geographical distance, barriers, temperature, lighting, etc.

When a proven manager begins to have employee problems with turnover, overtime, low productivity and complaints, it is a good idea to check the span of control of that manager. It may be that the limit of the number of employees the manager can supervise *effectively* has been exceeded.

As a new manager, be aware that there is a limit to how many employees any manager can supervise well. Know the factors that influence the limit for any individual, and learn to recognize the "people problems" that indicate you may be near or at your personal limit.

Number One Economic Waste

When you get into management, be careful not to fall into one of the major traps that characterize average (synonym of mediocre) managers. That trap is doing part of the work your employees should perform. When twenty-five dollar per hour managers do the work of eight dollar an hour employees, there is a waste of seventeen dollars per hour. Multiply that by real wages and you can see the scope of the economic waste.

Your job, by definition, is to achieve the objectives of the organization by working **through** others, not **for** others. Your job is to see that the work is done properly and on schedule, not to do the work yourself.

Emergency situations and crises will occur occasionally which demand everyone's efforts to complete a job or accomplish the desired results. This sort of involvement by a manager should be an exception and not the rule. And proper planning should all but eliminate these situations.

Think about the purest management situation: the football coach. He will incur a strong penalty if he loses control and runs out on the field to make a tackle. Instead, he develops eleven others (players) who can and will execute the plays while he stands on the sidelines. This is the real job of the manager.

References and Chapter Notes:

[1] For a complete discussion of organization structures, see Chapter 8.

[2] A. M. Jaeger and B. R. Baliga, "Control Systems and Strategic Adaptation: Lessons from Japanese Experience," *Strategic Management Journal*, April/June 1985, Vol. 6, No. 2, pp. 115-134.

[3] Alan S. Donnahoe, *What Every Manager Should Know About Financial Analysis* (New York: Fireside Book, Simon & Schuster, Inc., 1989), pp. 80-81.

[4] Armand V. Feigenbaum, *Total Quality Control*, Third Edition (New York: McGraw-Hill Book Company, 1986), p. 6.

[5] Susan Harte, "Total Quality," *The Atlanta Journal/Constitution*, October 11, 1992, p. R1.

Additional Readings:

Gitlow, Howard S. and Shelly J. Gitlow. *The Deming Guide to Quality and Competitive Position*. Englewood Cliffs, NJ: Prentice-Hall, Inc., 1987.

Hutchins, David. *Quality Circles Handbook*. New York: Nichols Publishing, 1985.

Mockler, Robert J., ed., *Readings in Management Control*. New York: Appleton-Century-Crofts, 1970.

Rhodes, David and Mike Wright. "Management Control for Effective Corporate Planning." *Long-Range Planning* 17 (August 1984): 115-121.

Shetty, Y. K. "Product Quality and Competitive Strategy." *Business Horizons* (May/June 1987): 46-52.

CHAPTER 16

PERFORMANCE APPRAISAL AND REWARDS

After studying this chapter, **you will know:**
- The definition of performance appraisal
- Management's uses of performance appraisal
- The value of performance appraisal to employees
- Personal and environmental factors affecting job performance
- Traditional steps in the appraisal process
- Twelve methods of performance appraisal
- Why job descriptions are crucial to the appraisal process
- Common rating errors made when conducting employee performance appraisal
- How to conduct an appraisal interview
- Kinds of organizational rewards related to employee work performance

Introduction

The overall control of employee work activity is just as important as the control of inventories, production output, quality of products and expenditures of moneys. The mechanism used to control employee performance is called the *performance appraisal system. Performance appraisal is a process that involves determining and communicating to employees how they are performing their jobs and establishing a plan for improvement.*[1]

Performance appraisal has also been called performance rating, employee evaluation, employee performance review and merit rating.

The primary reason for appraising performance is to recognize outstanding employee effort and to encourage the continuation of such effort toward the achievement of organizational goals. Other uses of performance appraisal relate to making decisions about promotion, transfers, layoffs, firings and merit pay increases.

Overview

In the sport industry, a plethora of performance appraisal methods are employed including the use of no method at all. Firms involved in sport marketing and promotions; those industrial manufacturers of sporting goods and equipment; public relations firms; arena management organizations; professional franchises and many more are profit-seeking organizations. They, like any other business firm, utilize performance appraisal results to make decisions regarding promotions, layoffs, firings, pay increases and more. Management of organizations that are classed as nonprofits may be more restricted in their use of performance appraisal results.

Nonprofit organizations include elementary and secondary schools; colleges and universities; YMCAs and YWCAs; community and county recreation programs, and other similar organizations. These organizations tend to be more bureaucratic in nature which often limits the flexibility of managers, directors and administrators. For example, the performance appraisal method preferred by a manager in this group may never be used because of traditional methods introduced by higher management previously. This would be true in a public school system where Boards of Education or Superintendents determine the standard methods for evaluating performance. Colleges and universities also tend to have a set way of evaluating employee performance which is handed down to Deans, department heads and administrative personnel, including athletics administrators. Other factors which limit performance appraisal decisions in the educational field pertain to a ratee's seniority, tenure status, rank and area of work specialization.

In high school, college and university coaching ranks an employee's performance may be rated good or bad based on the won-loss record. This is not the case in many situations, however, where the purpose of sponsoring team sports is something other than producing winning teams.

To many colleges, maintaining an image of sponsoring an athletics program that stays within the rules and regulations of its governance organization is of primary importance. In these institutions, coaches are required to sign an agreement that acknowledges they will be dismissed if they knowingly violate any of these rules.

The material in this chapter is important to sport management students. Graduates who move into management/administrative positions should be familiar with the purposes and methods of performance appraisal. All those in the sport industry should understand the value of being appraised and learn how to use the appraisal system to develop and grow as professionals.

Uses of Performance Appraisal

Mathis and Jackson suggest that information provided by performance appraisal is useful in three major areas: compensation, placement and training.[2]

Compensation. Rewarding employees who perform above expected levels reinforces their behavior to continue that level of performance. Using performance appraisal information as a basis for pay increases is their most common use.

Placement. Performance appraisal information often is the reason for promoting an effective employee to a higher-level job. Also, the information obtained may be used to transfer laterally or demote an employee. Information from performance appraisals cannot acurately predict employee performance in another job; but it provides useful information about work habits, capacity to learn, dedication to the organization and the ability to mix well with bosses and peers.

Training and Development. When appraisal forms are completed, they should point out the areas where employees show strengths as well as weaknesses on the job. The areas of weakness indicate specific needs for training and development which, when improved or corrected, will lead to improved job performance.

Richard I. Henderson, a renowned author of books and researcher in compensation management, states that performance appraisal data is used for making decisions in the following major areas:

1. Organizational and human resource planning

2. Employee training and development

3. Compensation administration

4. Employee movement (lateral transfers, demotions, promotions, layoffs and terminations)

5. Validation of the selection procedure[3]

Other expert studies of the applications of performance appraisals have shown them useful for one or more of the following purposes:

1. To provide feedback to employees on their individual performance.

2. To serve as a basis for modifying behavior toward more effective performance.

3. To provide data to management for judging future job assignments, promotions and compensation.

4. To identify promotable employees.

5. To force managers to relate employee behavior to actual results.

6. To eliminate marginal and low-performing managers.

7. To provide data showing both the need for and the effectiveness of training programs.

8. To receive feedback from employees on the effectiveness of the reward structure.

9. To provide the basis for validation of predictors used in the selection and placement process.

10. To tie human resource functions to the organization's long-range plans.[4]

Without question, information obtained in performance appraisals has many valuable uses for management.

How often should performance appraisals be conducted? There is no definitive answer to this question. Many organizations rely on one formal employee appraisal annually; others conduct quarterly appraisals. It would appear that management should conduct enough appraisals each year to keep both themselves and employees informed about each employee's work performance on a current basis. It is easier and more advantageous to both management and the employee to remedy employee performance as soon as possible rather than months after the fact. While it is true that supervisors informally appraise employee performance daily, the opportunity for open discussion about strengths and weaknesses of the job performance is missing. More frequent appraisals than once annually can also pinpoint the need for additional training more quickly to overcome any employee work deficiencies.

Implementation Concerns

Determining a valid method for appraising performance is a challenge to most organizations. Many have eliminated formal appraisal programs altogether and others continue to search for the "right " program. Organized labor, in general, has opposed formal appraisal programs because they do not believe such methods are a valid way of appraising job performance. Unions prefer to use "seniority" as a criteria for rewards. Seniority of employees is determined objectively rather than subjectively which removes the rater's potential bias. Seniority is a system all employees understand, but it has flaws. A worker's number of years on a job is no true indication of how well he or she performs the work. An old adage says, "A person can have 20 years of seniority on a job (with the growth and development that implies), or a person can have one year of seniority and experience repeated 20 times (with the stagnation that implies)."

If a major purpose of performance appraisal is to justify employee rewards and improve employee work behavior, there must be a direct correlation between the two.

Frederick W. Taylor's Differential Piece Rate Plan was an incentive plan that rewarded employee behavior when the work standard was met or exceeded (see Chapter 11). This is an example of a direct correlation between work performance appraisal and rewards. Today, the work place is much more complicated than in the time of Taylor, and identification of individuality of effort is difficult in many instances.

The appraisal process should promote successful goal attainment. This means that the value of having a formal appraisal program should be far greater than the cost of implementing one in terms of time and effort expended. A poorly administered appraisal program can lead to employee hostility, low morale, decreased productivity, high turnover and increased costs of operation.

Beyond these considerations, management must be aware of government regulations that directly influence the complexity of implementing appraisal programs.

Government Regulations Affecting Appraisal Programs

Most employees want to know where they stand with their supervisors, and workers often pressure compensation managers to relate pay and job performance equably. In addition to these concerns within the organization, federal legislation and court rulings make management's job of appraising performance even more complex and difficult to achieve.

Title VII of the Civil Rights Act of 1964 and Equal Employment Opportunity Commission (EEOC) guidelines state that

1. Employers must take affirmative action not to discriminate because of race, color, religion, sex, or national origin when making employment decisions.

2. Employment decisions include those involved in the selection, training, transfer, retention, promotion, and compensation processes.

3. Any paper-and-pencil or performance measure used in making employment decisions is a test.

4. A test must be fairly administered and empirically validated.

Most formal performance appraisal techniques involve paper-and-pencil methods to identify demonstrated employee work behaviors. The information gained by these techniques helps management make employment decisions. The EEOC and the courts recognize the impact that the appraisal process has on employment opportunities as well as the possibility of inherent bias in many parts of any appraisal process. The EEOC and the courts have played and will continue to play a major role in developing and fine-tuning the process of performance appraisal.[5]

Factors Affecting Employee Performance

The factors that affect employee job performance fall into two categories: *personal factors and environmental factors.*

Personal Factors Affecting Performance. Performance appraisal concentrates on determining how well an employee is doing his or her job. It attempts to answer such questions as these: Are the demands of the job being met? Did the employee achieve the desired results? To what degree is the employee meeting the requirements of the job? This does not measure the effort the employee expends. *Effort is the result of motivation and refers to the energy used to perform a job.* High effort does not automatically mean job success. A student may work tremendously hard on a term project, but for some reason receive a "C" grade. Performance is low although effort is high. This same situation can occur on the job.

Job performance is also affected by personal abilities and by the worker's perception of the job itself. *Abilities include the talent and skill of an employee plus other personal characteristics. Role or job perception relates to the view and understanding an employee has about the requirements of the job.* This perception influences the employee's effort when performing the job.

To perform satisfactorily any employee should have a clear and accurate perception of the job, use all his or her abilities well, and put forth the effort needed to achieve the desired end results.

Environmental Factors Affecting Performance. Personal factors discussed above are within the control of the employee. Outside the control of the employee are environmental factors which can hamper job performance and for which the employee should not be held accountable.

Detrimental environmental factors include such items as poor working conditions (excessive heat or cold), inadequate lighting, noisy work conditions, old and unreliable equipment, and direct management practices. Harmful management practices include unclear work procedures, delegating responsibility without giving the employee enough authority to perform the job properly, making conflicting demands on the employee's time, and failing to properly train employees so they can fully utilize their abilities.

Performance appraisal results are most meaningful when management provides employees with proper training for the job, satisfactory working conditions, and positive managerial support.

Personal Factors (Under employee's control)

Effort expended — The energy used to perform a job

Abilities — Individual talent, skills and other personal characteristics

Role perception — The view and understanding an employee has about the requirements of the job

Environmental Factors (Not under employee's control)

Excellent working conditions — Modern equipment, proper lighting, clean work areas

Poor working conditions — Excessive heat or cold, inadequate lighting, old equipment

Direct management practices — Positive and supportive or negative and threatening to the employees

Training opportunity — Employees are properly trained by management or they learn on the job

---

FIGURE 16-1: EXAMPLES OF FACTORS THAT AFFECT EMPLOYEE PERFORMANCE

Appraisal Standards

Formalized work standards are central to the development and administration of performance appraisals. One cannot assess performance on the job without comparing actual performance to output expectations. This objective approach relies on the comparison of quantitative results with known work standards (job expectations). Work standards can be developed using time and motion studies; through the averaging of past output of previous workers who held the same positions; through the output of equipment which sets the work pace of employees, or simply by the boss's estimate of the amount of work that should be done in a certain period of time. Regardless of the approach used to set work standards, employees must be informed of the standard which will be the basis of their performance appraisals.

Managers who are committed to objective performance appraisals know that *job descriptions* are crucial to the appraisal process. Often in larger companies the personnel department will perform *job analyses* and then prepare *job descriptions*. Job descriptions, which detail all the duties and responsibilities of a worker doing a certain job, are the foundation of the appraisal process.

Beyond the objective evaluation of measured work performance, employees are often rated subjectively. Raters may evaluate how cooperative an employee is; how well he or she gets along with others; how loyal one is to the organization; how well an employee accepts criticism and so forth. Subjective evaluations are open to much criticism, but many organizations deem them important.

With the complexity of business activity today, many jobs have aspects of work that are difficult to measure. Job duties of one employee may overlap with others, and much of the work performed may not be visible to the rater. Computer programmers, researchers and some engineering work would qualify as difficult to evaluate objectively. All of these points indicate why some organizations have dropped performance appraisal programs; instead, preferring to evaluate annual results of a department or a group of employees rather than appraise individual performance.

The Appraisal Process

Once an organization decides which performance appraisal system is best to use, an appraisal process is developed. This includes the steps to be followed when implementing the program, whether the evaluation is done annually or more often. In larger organizations the personnel or human resources department distributes forms to be used in evaluating employees to the appropriate rater or supervising manager. The manager appraises the employee; then, the manager and employee meet and review the evaluation with open discussion. The manager discusses the appraisal with his or her superior manager and this manager reviews the appraisal. This is a traditional process which can be modified if the supervising manager is not the rater.

Sometimes subordinates rate superiors and peers rate each other. In other instances there is a combination of raters. The most popular approach is to have the superior rate the subordinate. Regardless of who rates the employee, the ratee must have feedback to understand how others view their job performance and to understand how they can improve performance to maximize the benefits of the appraisal program and receive performance-associated rewards. Figure 16-2 outlines the important steps in the performance appraisal process.

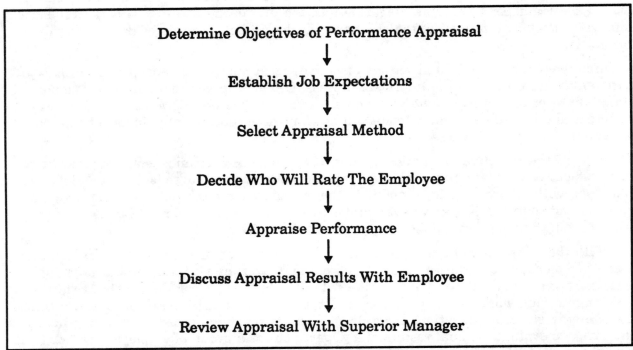

FIGURE 16-2: STEPS IN A PERFORMANCE APPRAISAL PROCESS

Methods of Appraisal

There are numerous performance appraisal methods in use. The most informal method used is when someone asks a supervising manager: "What kind of worker is employee X?" The routine answer, "X is not that bad; in fact, X is pretty good!", does not provide much information to anyone; but this is an evaluation of employee X—a weak example of performance appraisal.

Organizations that take performance appraisal seriously employ more sophisticated approaches. Some of the better known methods are the Checklist, the Graphic Rating Scale, Forced Choice, Ranking, Paired Comparison, Forced Distribution, Essays, Critical Incidents, Field Review, Peer Ratings, Management By Objectives (MBO) and Assessment Centers. Each is briefly discribed.

Checklist. *The checklist is a simple rating method wherein a manager answers yes or no to a series of statements about an employee's behavior on the job.* Here is an example :

Question	Yes	No
Does the employee cooperate fully with others?	( )	( )
Does the employee have a positive attitude toward the organization?	( )	( )

A series of statements such as these can be weighted and the results quantified. Usually the rater does not know the weights of the individual questions and someone else, ideally a personnel specialist, calculates the results. Among the disadvantages to this method are the rater does not assign the weights nor know them; the statements may be interpreted differently by various raters; and it is difficult to conduct a positive performance appraisal interview with limited knowledge available.

Graphic Rating Scale. This is a common method employed to evaluate the work performance and behavior of employees. Factors such as attendance, accuracy, quality of work, knowledge of the job and others are assessed. Not only are employees numerically rated, usually from one to five, but a written explanation of the numerical rating is required. The rater circles the appropriate numerical category and writes a brief explanation, such as the following:

Category: Quality of Work

1	2	3	4	5
Unsatisfactory Performance	Meets minimum work standards	Satisfactory quality work	Above average/ few defects	Outstanding quality record

Explanation: _____

_____

The major weaknesses of this method are that managers may interpret written descriptions differently and may explain the numerical rating checked in words not accurately understood by others. Also, the categories listed for employee evaluation may have little to do with daily job performance.

Forced Choice. This is a more complicated version of the checklist appraisal method. The rater is required to check two of four statements as "most like" or "least like" an employee; or the rater is asked to rank the statements as 1 (most descriptive) to 4 (least descriptive) of the employee (see Figure 16-3 for an example). Weights are normally attached to statements and the resulting score is calculated by someone other than the rater. Again, the weakness of this method is that managers who evaluate their employees are at a disadvantage during performance appraisal reviews without complete information about the weighted scores. One objective of using the Forced Choice method is to eliminate managerial bias.

Choose the statements which most accurately and least accurately describe the ratee. Place a "1" by the statement to indicate "most accurate" and place a "4" to indicate the statement "least accurate."

_____ A. Conscientious and hard working

_____ B. Refuses to accept blame for mistakes

_____ C. Cooperates well with other employees

_____ D. Cannot wait for the work day to end

FIGURE 16-3: EXAMPLE OF FORCED CHOICE RATING

Ranking. *Ranking is a comparative method that rates individuals in terms of a specific characteristic or of overall job performance from highest to lowest.* The weakness of this method is that the differences between individuals are not clearly defined; plus, there is potential for rater bias. The negative aspect of the ranking method is that some employees are rated last or near the bottom in some category when, in fact, they may be excellent employees when overall performance is considered.

Paired Comparison. This is another ranking method which formally compares each employee with every other employee one at a time. Each rating factor used requires the rater to make a large number of comparisons. This is the major drawback of this method. If overall performance is the main rating factor, the supervisor indicates which employee is best when compared to every other employee. A scoring system will then determine which employee is most frequently selected as the better. All employees can be ranked from highest to lowest.

Forced Distribution. In this method of appraisal, the supervising manager or rater must place a certain percent or number of employees in each category: the lowest, the highest and the average performance categories. This method is based on the "Bell-Shaped Curve," which assumes that normal performance of individuals will be distributed according to the shape of the curve (see Figure 16-4).

Employees placed in the lowest category can get hostile when the rater tries to explain the decision which put them there. Many raters resist placing employees in a low category as well because it is so difficult to justify the decision. Students do not appreciate instructor's who use a forced distribution of grades. Such a method creates much hostility and is not a fair method if half of a class scores As on an exam. This approach is used in many classrooms, however, just as it is used in many performance appraisal programs.

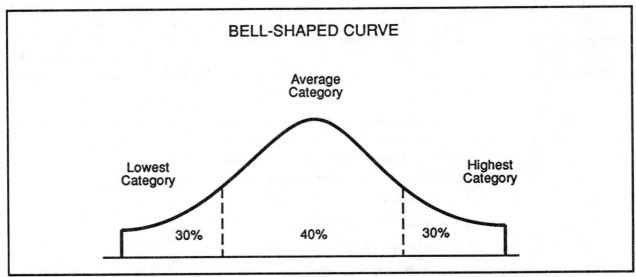

FIGURE 16-4: EXAMPLE OF A FORCED DISTRIBUTION RANKING OF EMPLOYEES

Essays. Several written methods of performance appraisal are in use. *The essay or free form method, one of the oldest forms of appraisal, allows the rater to write a description of the ratee's performance during the rating period.* This description would include the strengths and weaknesses of the worker and perhaps some comment about the worker's potential for advancement. The method is considered free-form because the rater is not restricted to specific categories or considerations when writing comments.

The weakness of this method involves the ability of the supervising manager or rater as an effective writer. Writing skills affect the quality of the rating, and this method is time consuming for the rater.

Critical Incident. The critical incident method of performance appraisal takes the form of written observations of employee performance that are either very favorable or very unfavorable. This method is time consuming, but becomes a form of documentation that has value beyond just performance appraisal. Written incidents become the focal point of discussion during the evaluation meeting between the rater and the worker/ratee. Review of unfavorable incidents can be the basis for suggesting change which should lead to overall improvement in worker performance. The drawbacks to this method are that not all supervisors interpret incidents the same way, and some supervisors may overlook situations which the employee thinks are favorable incidents.

Field Review. *The Field Review is a written method of performance appraisal that is not done by the immediate supervisor.* Someone, such as a personnel specialist, discusses each employee's performance with the supervisor, compiles the information and rates each employee. Then, the personnel specialist and immediate supervisor discuss each employee's rating; and, after a give-and-take exchange, agree on the employee's rating. The supervisor signs the rating once the two agree it presents a fair description of the employee's performance.

Peer Ratings. *Peer Rating or Buddy Rating is a method of assessing personnel through co-workers's evaluations.* In this process each group member rates every other group member on one or more identifiable qualities, such as "cooperativeness." Each group member then assigns each of the others a score, such as 1 through 10, or they place them in a category, such as "high" or "low." The results rank an individual's status within the group on certain identifiable qualities.

Management By Objectives (MBO). MBO has been discussed in Chapter 5. It is a valuable approach to use in planning; but it also is a method of performance appraisal when written annual objectives of employees, managers and units of the organization become work standards or expectations. Annual performance (results) are compared to formalized objectives; then corrections, solutions or other changes are made if objectives have not been achieved. For MBO to be an effective performance appraisal method, objectives should be quantifiable and measurable as well as clear, concise and written.

Assessment Centers. *Assessment Centers are a special kind of program designed to evaluate managerial potential of experienced and new managers.* As mentioned in Chapter 10, Assessment Centers are an outgrowth of World War II when the approach was used to select agents for the Office of Strategic Services (OSS, the forerunner of today's Central Intelligence Agency). Many large organizations in the United States now have assessment centers. It is estimated that over 500 organizations run assessment centers, and the number is growing steadily.

Assessment Centers can be used for initial management selection or for purposes of promotion. In the Assessment Center, the candidates are asked to participate in a wide range of simulation exercises while trained observers note and assess the candidates's actions. The procedure also includes personal interviews, management games, leaderless group discussions, individual presentations, in-basket exercises, mock interviews, pencil-and-paper tests and more.

Upon the conclusion of the assessment program, which typically lasts several days, specially trained management evaluators spend several days estimating the managerial potential of each participant. The evaluation report generally summarizes the strengths and weaknesses of each candidate and makes recommendations on a candidate's suitability for employment or promotion.[6]

Selecting a Performance Appraisal Method

The performance appraisal method selected must relate to the job itself. This emphasizes the importance of the job description to the appraisal process. Job descriptions are developed after conducting a *job analysis. A job analysis is written information abtained about a job through observation, interviews and study.* Every effort is made to include all the pertinent information about a job in developing a job analysis, which could be called a "fact-finding" mission to learn everything possible about the nature of the job, the skills required of a worker in performing the job, the problems encountered when doing the job, and more. From a review of this information, a job description is developed. *Job descriptions include a listing of all the duties and responsibilities of a person holding a particular job.* It may also include performance expectations, general areas of responsibility and formal lines of accountability.

Once the job description is developed and written, a performance appraisal method can be selected which suits the job.

Common Rating Errors

A major cause of ineffective performance appraisal programs involves the errors made by raters. In Figure 16-5, Richard I. Henderson lists the most common rater errors. Notice the number of rater errors that relate to personal preferences, biases and prejudices. Because of these factors, organizations should provide supervising managers or raters with professional training in conducting performance appraisals. Many rater errors in performance appraisals could be eliminated with such training.

The Appraisal Interview

The results of the employee performance appraisal should be communicated to the employee. If the interview is not properly conducted, the employee and the manager will have a negative experience which could affect future job performance. Here are several suggestions to create an appraisal interview that benefits both the employee and the supervisor.

- Make certain the interview is held in pleasant surroundings. This may be the supervisor's office or in a conference room; however, the environment must be nonthreatening for the employee. Perhaps some type of refreshments should be offered.

HALO EFFECT:	Rating an employee "excellent" in one quality which influences the rater to give higher than deserved scores on other qualities.
HORN EFFECT:	Rating an employee "unsatisfactory" in one quality; then lowering the rating on other qualities as a result.
CENTRAL TENDENCY:	Tending to grade employees "average" on all qualities.
STRICT RATING:	Rating lower than the normal or average; being consistently overly harsh in rating performance qualities.
LENIENT RATING:	Rating higher than the normal or average; being consistently loose in rating performance qualities.
LATEST BEHAVIOR:	Rating influenced by most recent behavior; overlooking most commonly demonstrated behaviors of entire appraisal period.
FIRST IMPRESSION:	Basing rating on initial impression; overlooking most consistently demonstrated behaviors of entire appraisal period.
SPILLOVER EFFECT:	Allowing previous performance rating to improperly influence current ratings.
STATUS EFFECT:	Overrating employees in higher-level jobs or jobs held in high regard while underrating employees in lower-level or less well-regarded jobs.
SAME AS ME:	Rating employee higher than deserved because he or she possesses qualities similar to the rater (or highly-regarded qualities).
DIFFERENT FROM ME:	Rating the employee lower than deserved because he or she exhibits less desirable qualities or qualities different from the rater.

FIGURE 16-5: COMMON APPRAISAL RATING ERRORS

Source: Richard I. Henderson, *Compensation Management*, pp. 428-429.

- The supervisor or rater should always recognize and praise good performance before turning attention to other subjects. Use a positive approach; be constructive with criticism.

- Allow the employee to speak freely about problems on the job. Show genuine empathy and mutually discuss how these problems might be overcome or modified.

- When discussing improving job performance, let the employee make suggestions followed by constructive comments by the supervisor. Employees want management's support and understanding.

- Discuss organizational rewards that relate to job performance. Identify realistic incentives that can be reached by the employee through continued good performance or by even better performance.

Performance Appraisal and Rewards

The sole purpose of having a performance appraisal program is to maintain and improve employee performance toward the achievement of organizational goals. This purpose will not be achieved without having a reward system that positively motivates employees to maintain high levels of job performance.

Organizational rewards can be described as *intrinsic or extrinsic. Intrinsic rewards are internal to the individual and stem from the work itself.* Examples would be pride from a sense of accomplishment, job satisfaction, feeling of growth on the job and the status associated with the position held. *Extrinsic rewards are distributed by higher management and are not under the control of the employee.* Examples are pay raises, promotions, fringe benefits and some form of formal recognition.

Another way of viewing rewards is to denote the three kinds of income employees receive. These types of income are *monetary, real income* and *psychic income.*

Monetary income is the total wages and benefits paid to the employee for work performed. Real income is what the employee can purchase in goods and services with his or her money. Psychic income are the psychological benefits received on the job.

Management cannot control real income, which involves the prices employees have to pay for goods and services in the marketplace. But management directly controls monetary and psychic incomes that employees receive on the job. As many motivational researchers have discovered, pay itself is not a motivating factor unless directly related to job performance. Receiving an annual pay increase for outstanding work performance can boost the job satisfaction of an employee, but the reward is more psychological than monetary. Other forms of psychic income which management can distribute as it sees fit are complimentary memos for a job well done; "thank you's," "attaboys," or statements such as "I wouldn't trade you for any other employee in the world!" Managers can also reward employees by creating a positive work environment and by assuring them of job security as long as acceptable job performance is maintained

If rewards are to have real meaning and produce the desired effect, they should be distributed to employees as soon as they are earned. Waiting for days to tell an employee he or she did a good job is ineffectual. Holding off for weeks on pay increases tarnishes the positive impact.

The famous Lincoln Electric Company in Cleveland, Ohio, distributes the employees' share of the profit sharing plan annually rather than at the time of retirement. No employee has ever received less than 55% of his or her annual salary as profit sharing, and all 2500 employees qualify to be part of the annual distribution through a merit rating program.

Determining the reward system to associate with a performance appraisal program is just as important as the selection of the proper performance appraisal method.

Summary

Controlling employee behavior is as important as controlling inventories, quality and expenditures. The mechanism used is called performance appraisal. Performance appraisal is a process that involves determining and communicating to employees how they are performing their jobs and establishing a plan for improvement. Other uses of performance appraisal relate to making decisions about promotions, transfers, layoffs, firings, merit pay increases, training and rewards.

Performance appraisals may be conducted annually, quarterly or as often as the organization sees fit. However, evaluating employee performance and discussing the results with the employee weeks after the appraisal is not recommended. Also, rewards associated with performance appraisal programs should be distributed to those who earn them shortly after performance appraisal if the reward system is designed to increase or maintain high motivation.

Governmental regulations affect performance appraisal programs. Title VII of the Civil Rights Act of 1964 and the EEOC guidelines state that

1. Employers must take affirmative action not to discriminate because of race, color, religion, sex or national origin when making employment decisions.

2. Employment decisions include those involved in the selection, training, transfer, retention, promotion and compensation processes.

3. Any paper-and-pencil or performance measure used in making employment decisions is a test.

4. A test must be fairly administered and empirically validated.

Personal factors that affect an employee's performance include their talents and skills (called abilities), the effort they put into a job, and the role perception they have about the job. Environmental factors which also affect employee performance are usually beyond the control of the employee and include conditions of the work area, state of the equipment, attitude of other employees and quality of supervision.

The appraisal process consists of the steps to be followed when implementing an appraisal program. These are the steps in a traditional appraisal program: determine the objectives of performance appraisal, establish job expectations, select an appraisal method, decide who will rate the employee and discuss the appraisal results with the employee.

Among the numerous methods of performance appraisal in use are Checklist, Graphic Rating Scale, Forced Choice, Ranking, Paired Comparison, Forced Distribution, Essays, Critical Incident Method, Field Review, Peer Ratings, MBO and Assessment Centers.

The performance appraisal method chosen must relate to the job itself. Basic to the appraisal process is the job description which is formally developed after conducting job analysis.

Individuals selected to rate employees should be trained to conduct professional performance appraisals and to avoid common rater errors. These common errors include the Halo Effect, Horn Effect, Central Tendency, Strict Rating, Lenient Rating, Latest Behavior, First Impression, Spillover Effect, Status Effect, Same As Me and Different From Me Effects. All of these errors lead to some type of assumption that reduces the value of the performance appraisal.

The appraisal interview involves the rater and the ratee. If the interview is not properly conducted, the employee/ratee and the manager/rater will have a negative experience. The rater should insure that the interview takes place in pleasant surroundings; that the employee is recognized and praised for good performance; and that the employee is allowed to speak freely about problems on the job.

Organizational rewards related to job performance are either intrinsic or extrinsic. Intrinsic rewards, which are internal to the individual and stem from the work itself, include a sense of accomplishment, job satisfaction and the status associated with the job held. Extrinsic rewards are distributed by higher management and include pay raises, promotions, fringe benefits and other forms of formal recognition.

Review Questions

1. Define performance appraisal.

2. What are some of the major uses of performance appraisal information?

3. Explain the value of performance appraisal to the employee.

4. Define performance and discuss three personal factors that influence employee performance.

5. List and clarify the traditional steps in the appraisal process.

6. Support the statement that job descriptions are crucial to the appraisal process.

7. Describe these performance appraisal methods: Checklist, Forced Choice, Graphic Rating Scale, Ranking, Force Distribution, Essay, Critical Incident and Peer Ratings.

8. Identify four common rating errors which can occur in appraising employee performance.

9. List suggestions for making an appraisal interview a positive experience.

10. Distinguish between intrinsic and extrinsic rewards

Assignments for Personal Development

1. Imagine that a few years after graduation you become the general manager of a successful professional sports franchise. You wish to share some of the success with the employees in the office who work behind the scenes and do not share in the financial benefits of winning a championship, but you want to make their reward meaningful. Recalling your introductory course in management, you remember that a performance appraisal program tied to a reward system is a positive way to improve and maintain a high level of motivation on the job. Decide: (1) Which method of employee performance appraisal you will use and justify your decision; and (2) what kind of reward system you will introduce to accompany the performance appraisal program. Explain your decisions fully.

2. One of the major problems with county recreation programs in the U.S. is the high turnover of personnel. Arrange to meet with a manager of a local recreation program and find out what kind of performance appraisal method is used and what kind of reward system is in place. After hearing the manager's remarks, contemplate whether you could do a better job of reducing employee turnover if you were in his or her position. Outline a plan of appraisal and reward.

Incident

THE DILEMMA

Sonny Hamilton had just begun his new job as an assistant coach in a major college basketball program. His success as a junior college coach had earned him this job at a very young age, and he knew his future in coaching at the top level would depend on his success here.

One of Sonny's first assignments before the start of the basketball season is in recruiting prospective players. He picks up a player at his home out of state and drives him to visit the campus. The distance is more than 100 miles; and after the visit is over, the athletics director reviews a recruiting trip report and calls Sonny's attention to a rule that limits such trips to fewer than 100 miles. Once the violation is discovered, it is reported to the governance organization which penalizes the school by reducing their basketball scholarships for the next school year by two.

Once the season starts, Sonny is involved in the coaching and team strategy for games. His knowledge and skill as a coach prove to be a great asset to the veteran head coach, and the team has great success beating nationally-ranked opponents and participating in the national championship tournament.

Now the season is over, and the entire coaching staff is making plans for next year. A nervous Sonny is on his way to the athletics director's office for his first performance appraisal.

Questions:

1. Which performance appraisal method would you use to evaluate Sonny's first year on this job? What factors could influence the rater to make errors?

2. How should Sonny use the evaluation for his personal benefit?

Glossary of Key Terms

Abilities: Includes the talent and skills of an employee plus other personal characteristics.

Appraisal Process: Consists of the steps to be followed when implementing a performance appraisal program.

Assessment Centers: Special kind of program designed to evaluate managerial potential of experienced and new managers. Specially trained evaluators assess the qualities of candidates over a several-day period.

Checklist: Simple rating method wherein a manager answers yes or no to a series of statements about an employee's behavior on the job.

Effort: The energy used to perform a job.

Essays: Free-form method of employee appraisal which allows raters to write a description of employee performance during the rating period.

Extrinsic Rewards: Those distributed by higher management and not under the control of the employee. Examples are pay increases and promotions.

Field Review: Method of rating employees by someone other than the immediate supervisor after discussing employee performance with the immediate supervisor.

Forced Choice: Rating method that forces the rater to check two of four statements as "most like" or "least like" the employee with statements weighted. A number of statements comprise the method.

Forced Distribution: Rating method uses the Bell-Shaped Curve and assumes normal performance of individuals will e distributed according to the shape of the curve.

Graphic Rating Scale: Rating method where the rater evaluates employee performance and behavior on subjects usually using a 1 to 5 scale accompanied by a written explanation.

Halo Effect: Rating an employee excellent in one quality, which in turn influences the rater to give the employee a rating higher than deserved on other qualities.

Intrinsic Rewards: Rewards which are internal to the individual; the source of the reward is the work itself.

Job Analysis: Study and observation of a job to gather pertinent information about the nature of the job.

Job Description: Written description of all the duties and responsibilities of a specific job.

Paired Comparison: Rating method that formally compares each employee with every other employee one at a time on each rating factor.

Peer Ratings: Rating method which allows co-workers to evaluate each other on identifiable qualities; also known as "buddy ratings."

Performance: Refers to how well an employee meets the demands of the job.

Performance Appraisal: A process that involves determining and communicating to employees how they are performing their jobs and establishing a plan for improvement.

Ranking: Comparative method that rates individuals in terms of specific characteristics or of overall job performance from highest to lowest.

Role Perception: The view and understanding an employee has about the requirements of the job.

Practical Concepts in Management
Discriminate Your Way to Competency

The word **discriminate** has taken a beating over the last thirty years. Laws tell us what discrimination can lead to in society, and the punishment for breaking antidiscrimination laws has much of the business community on edge all the time. There is, however, a positive side to this word, and every professional manager must know it.

If you are a manager, it is good to discriminate between good employees and bad, between sound decisions and risky ones, and between what actions are good for the organization and those that are wrong. All managers should be discriminating. What is bad about discrimination, and the part that gets you into trouble, is when you let biases prejudice the decisions. This can occur when the subject pertains to employment, promotion or reward of employees on the basis of sex, age, race, religion or national origin. This is really not a problem, however, if you adopt competency as the standard for making these kinds of decisions.

The most qualified applicant should be employed and the most productive employee should be promoted and rewarded. Forget the questions of sex, race, religion and national origin. Go with the employees who are overall the most highly qualified to do a particular job and who, by their performance, deserve promotion and recognition.

Remember, your decisions should be made in view of what is best for the organization. This should override individual prejudices and biases at all times.

Managers Are Judged on Results

Managers are judged on results (performance). If not, managers would be judged on years of sevice, personality, how hard they try, how many hours they spend in the office, how well liked they are, and on and on. None of these criteria mean anything unless they are combined with the successful completion of the assigned objectives.

Although there are exceptions to all concepts, the majority of organizations do attempt to judge managers on performance. This is sound and fair as long as

1. All managers know clearly what their objectives are, and

2. Higher managers making the judgments are fair-minded and objective in their evaluations.

Many decisions made today cannot be judged fairly until enough time has elapsed to know the results.

References and Chapter Notes:

[1] Leslie W. Rue and Lloyd L. Byars, *Management, Skills and Application*, seventh edition (Chicago, IL: Richard D. Irwin, 1995), p. 482.

[2] Robert L. Mathis and John H. Jackson, *Personnel*, third edition (St. Paul, MN: West Publishing Co., 1982), p. 283.

[3] Richard I. Henderson, *Compensation Management* (Englewood Cliffs, NJ: Prentice-Hall, Inc., 1994), p. 412.

[4] Charles J. Fonbrun and Robert L. Laud, "Strategic Issues in Performance Appraisal: Theory and Practice," *Personnel*, November-December, 1983, pp. 23-31.

[5] Henderson, *Compensation Management*, pp. 413-414.

[6] Donald P. Crane, *Personnel, The Management of Human Resources*, 4th ed. (Boston, MA: Kent Publishing Company, 1986), pp. 213-214.

CHAPTER 17

MANAGEMENT INFORMATION SYSTEMS

After studying this chapter, you will know:

- The meaning of Information Technology (IT)
- Something about information overload
- What describes useful information
- A definition of a Management Information System (MIS)
- The distinction between data processing and MIS
- The Purpose of Decision Support Systems (DSS)
- Who uses Executive Information Systems (EIS)
- Why Information Centers are created
- The meaning and purpose of *outsourcing*
- Why the Internet is the prototype of the global information infrastructure
- Trends in global telecommunications

Introduction

Organizations today desire managers and staff personnel that are computer literate and well-versed on *Information Technology (IT)*. *Information Technology is defined as computer and communications technology and its applications*. Most economists believe that IT will have a significant impact on the economy's growth in the future. New channels of communication, such as the Internet, will provide organizations new means to reach customers and vendors quickly and efficiently. Any reduction in costs associated with communication technology can be used to improve services provided.

Robert B. Cohen, an Adjunct Fellow with the Economic Strategy Institute in Washington, D. C., summarizes the benefits of IT:

> While the benefits of IT have been debated, it is now more evident that businesses obtain important benefits from the use of advanced communications and computing. In addition, substantial improvements have been made in business operations and product development through the use of IT. Consumers are also likely to be beneficiaries of the movement to higher bandwidth communications, because it will provide better services from many of the institutions, such as hospitals and HMOs, that consumers depend upon for the delivery of serivces. In the future, the expansion of the availability of on-line services is likely to offer further improvements for consumers by reducing the time to obtain services and goods.[1]

In Chapter 1 academic areas of study required of sport management majors was discussed. One such area is communication (refer to Chapter 13).

In 1994, Professors Kelley, Beitel, De Sensi and Blanton of the University of Tennessee conducted research designed to present undergraduate and graduate sport management curricular models for sport management professionals to use when implementing accreditation guidelines. They noted six areas in which all sport managers need to be knowledgeable. The first of these areas is *communication*. The fundamentals of communications presented in Chapter 13 are important, but information technology is rapidly altering the way people communicate. No doubt future majors in sport management will be required to take an academic course entitled: Information Technology or Communications Technology and Its Applications.

This chapter provides information on management information systems (MIS) which are part of information technology (IT). Use material in this chapter to guide you toward further study. Electronic communication is here to stay although the traditional methods of communicating will continue to play an important role in everyday lives.

Information and Management

Managers have always desired pertinent information to plan, organize, implement, control and make decisions better. Hardly anyone realized 35 years ago that the advent of the computer could lead to *information overload* in many cases today. *Information overload implies that managers have more information than they can digest.* Sources include not only information from electronic computers but also from print and sound, such as facsimile, voice mail, E-mail, newspapers, trade journals, memos, conversations, meetings, reports and much more. Prior to this era, managers acquired information the hard and slow way. Researchers would scan reports, review library materials, read newspapers, conduct surveys and do interviews. Often the gathered information would not be the most current, but it could be digested.

When a manager faces information overload today, the problem may not be with the quality of the information but with the method or system used to prioritize its value. The value of information is subjective and is determined by the user/manager. The user may identify information as useful or not useful.

Useful Information

Useful information can generally be described as that which is accurate, timely, complete and relevant.[2]

Accurate information is valid and correct.

Timely information means that managers have facts, data, figures and such available for review before they must make decisions.

Complete information provides the manager all of the facts and information about a particular subject.

Relevant information refers to a manager's having the kind of information he or she needs in particular circumstances.

Management Information Systems (MIS)

To succeed as planners, organizers, implementors, controllers and decision-makers, managers must have adequate information. The information must be timely and pertinent to the situation confronting the manager. Before computers were widely used, gathering such information was tedious and laborious. Much of the necessary information was out of date or inaccurate. Managers depended on staff personnel to do research in newspapers, trade publications, by interviews and so forth. Such information gathering efforts took time. Today managers have readily available more information than they can digest, and the focus is on determining what information to use and on managing the timely flow of the information. The key to a manager's success rests with determining what information to rely on and what to discard.

Professor James A. Senn wrote the following:

> If the aviation industry had developed at the same rate as electronic data processing, we would have landed people on the moon less than six months after the Wright brothers made their first flight at Kitty Hawk. If the cost of a 1955 Cadillac (introduced about the same time as computers were introduced in business) had been reduced as much as that of computer memories while efficiencies were raised to an equal degree, the Cadillac would now cost $5 and go 20,000 mph.[3]

MIS are not new in organizations, but technological progress in the evolution of electronic computer applications has magnified the importance of MIS.

Today, a Management Information System (MIS) is a computer-based network that integrates the collection, processing, storing and transmission of information.[4] This information is made available to managers who must make decisions. The computers do not make decisions! Experts view information as a resource available to managers to use as they see fit. One view of information as a resource is presented by John J. Connell:

> Information is not a resource in the same sense as people, money, materials and facilities. Information has no intrinsic worth as people do; its worth is entirely subjective. Information does not vary in value because of external factors, as money does; its value is in the mind of the user. Information is not consumed in its use as are materials. Information is not physical in nature, as are facilities. The mediums for recording and moving information

may be physical, but the information carried is intangible and only useful to thinking human beings.

If not a resource on its own, then, what is information? It is brain food. It is the feedstock used in the intellectual process of managing other resources.[5]

One should not confuse MIS with data processing. *Data processing is the capture, processing and storage of data* whereas MIS uses that data to produce information for management.[6] Data processing provides the database of the MIS. Data is composed of facts about places, things, people, events that have not been interpreted. Data, once interpreted for the benefit of managers, is called information.

Computers are the centerpiece of MIS. Computers have evolved from bulky pieces of equipment in the 1950s to the **mainframe** of the 1960s, to the **minicomputers** of the 1970s and on to the **microcomputers** (personal computers—PCs) of today. The personal computer, costing only a few hundred dollars, is capable of processing vast amounts of data and is no larger than a typewriter. They are widely available and versatile.

The most important components of MIS are hardware and software. **Hardware** includes the physical components such as the computer, printer, monitor (screen), keyboard and so forth. **Software** refers to the various programs which can run on the hardware and which include the instructions to a computer to perform certain tasks. Software can be standard or customized. Standard software can be purchased in any computer store. Customized software is written by consultants or computer specialists specifically for an organization to perform a special task. **Programmers** are the people who write instructional programs that tell the computer what to do. **System analysts** are people who investigate potential computer applications and determine the types of programs needed.

Decision Support Systems

A special kind of information system is known as a *Decision Support System (DSS)*. This system takes time to develop and is complex. The purpose of DSS is to support managerial decision-making when problems are semistructured and specific decisions are required. Normally DSS supports a relatively small group of managers working as a problem-solving team.[7] A major distinction between MIS and DSS concerns the value of each. MIS provides information; DSS is directly involved in the decision-making provess. DSS decisions may involve subjects such as estimating profit potential for new products, selecting new site locations, and the acquisition of other companies.

Executive Information Systems. The newest form of information system is the *Executive Information System (EIS)*. These systems are designed to meet the specific information-processing needs of top managers. Executives do not need to have basic computer skills to use such systems which can provide highly specialized information. EIS are developed to be user-friendly and require little skill to acquire information. Typical information from EIS would show trends and patterns that influence strategic planning and decision-making. EIS summarizes information and excludes specific details.[8] Such systems are complex to develop, but easier to use. They become powerful aids to executives in strategic management positions.

Information Centers. Information centers are becoming more common in large American organizations today. Much like a public library, they are designed to help managers gain direct access to information when the managers lack the time or the skills (or both) to proceed on their own. Information Centers are staffed with skilled specialists who assist and train people who are not computer literate to access data and use available software.[9]

Outsourcing. Many organizations do not want to invest large sums of money in equipment and personnel to create internal information systems. Instead, these firms subcontract with independent outside sources to provide information systems work. While the work of the information system is not on the organization's premises, there is the advantage of low capital expenditures. Also, independent outside sources are full-time specialists in information systems.

Information System Realities. Companies install information systems to increase effectiveness and efficiency. Often, this is the end result; however, information systems have limitations. They can be costly to develop and administer; some systems are poorly designed and do not meet the needs of the managers who use them; many employees feel that MIS and the computerization of work dehumanizes their activities and threatens them with a loss of individuality; and managers can rely too heavily on information systems and lose touch with the real world. Regardless of the technological progress in the computer field and MIS, managers still must make the final decisions. Information systems can be of tremendous value to decision-makers, but nothing replaces a manager's human judgment when faced with complex human problems.

Global Information Infrastructure

Today's managers as well as those preparing for future management jobs must be prepared for electronic commerce and its effect on business practices and strategy. The Internet is the key to global communications as well as a valuable resource to use for research and other purposes.

The Internet is the prototype of the global information infrastructure. Internet and new low cost data communications infrastructures specifically impact four business processes: innovation, production, exchange and service.

The Internet is a collection of computer networks that interconnect computers all over the world. Users of computers on the Internet have access to a variety of electronic communication, information, retrieval and interaction capabilities.

Wide-area information services including the World Wide Web (WWW) are available on the Internet. These services allow users to navigate and browse multimedia documents, interact socially or undertake commercial transactions.[10]

A new survey of Internet access by the Associated Press shows 3.7 percent of American adults are online. While 5.8 million Americans had direct access to Internet, another 3.9 million subscribed to online services such as CompuServe and Prodigy. It is estimated that these figures will grow by another six million adults over the next year.[11]

Corporate use of the Internet is growing rapidly. Internet provides the largest common interactive data communications infrastructure in the world. Given the declining costs of using the Internet, firms have used it primarily to reduce communication and publishing costs and to improve the innovation, production, sales and service processes of their organizations.

Global Telecommunications

Global telecommunications goes beyond the discussion of transmitting and using global information on the computer and the Internet. The transmission of voice and data is both pleasurable and profitable. Everyone has or wants a telephone. Experts predict that the majority of individuals and organizations will see evolutionary changes in their telecommunications. The shift will be from basic to enhanced services; from analog to digital networks; from wireline to wireless equipment; from regulation to liberalization; and from monopolies to a wide array of competition.[12]

Telecommunication enhanced services include voice mail, electronic mail (E-mail), facsimile transmission, data capture and storage, and online database access. All management information services have a direct relationship to telecommunications.

As more and more firms become international or global in operations, it is significant to note that the global market for telecommunications equipment is growing as the rate of 9.2 percent per year, with the fastest growth in Southeast Asian markets (see Figure 17-1).

Region	1987	1992	1997	2002	% Ann. Incr. 2002/1992
Equipment					
North America	24.0	28.2	43.7	62.0	8.2%
Latin America	4.2	6.5	12.4	20.5	12.2
Western Europe	24.7	43.7	66.2	95.7	8.1
Eastern Europe	7.0	9.9	18.0	32.3	12.5
Africa-Mideast	2.5	4.3	7.5	12.7	11.4
Asia-Oceania	13.3	27.6	48.1	79.4	9.7
World-total	75.7	120.1	195.9	302.6	9.7
Services					
North America	141.0	193.1	282.5	403.0	7.7%
Latin America	9.9	18.1	35.9	65.0	13.6
Western Europe	97.7	137.5	211.1	314.3	8.6
Eastern Europe	17.8	21.0	33.2	60.7	11.2
Africa-Mideast	8.9	15.6	26.0	42.5	10.5
Asia-Oceania	48.3	82.9	141.7	232.1	10.8
World-total	323.6	468.2	730.4	1117.6	9.1
Grand Total World					
Equipment & Services	399.3	588.3	926.3	1420.2	9.2

FIGURE 17-1: THE GLOBAL TELECOMMUNICATIONS MARKET BY REGION
(Sales in Billions of Current Dollars)

Source: E. D. Hester, *World Telecommunications*, Study #519. Cleveland, Ohio: The Freedonia Group, August 1993, pp 17-19, updated.

Summary

Organizations today want managers and staff personnel who are computer literate and well-versed on Information Technology (IT). IT is computer and communications technology and its applications.

Managers have always needed pertinent information to plan, organize, implement control and make decisions better. When managers have more information than they can digest, it is called information overload. The value of information is subjective and is determined by the user. If the information is useful, it can be described as assurate, timely, complete and relevant.

Management Information Systems (MIS) are a computer-based network that integrates the collection, processing, storing and transmission of information. MIS is different from data processing, which is the capture, processing and storage of data. MIS uses such data to produce information for management.

A special kind of information system is called a Decision Support System (DSS). The purpose of DSS is to support managerial decision-making when problems are semistructured and specific decisions are required. The newest form of information system is Executive Information Systems (EIS). EIS are designed to meet the special information processing needs of top managers. EIS are user-friendly and require little skill to acquire information used in strategic planning and decision-making.

Outsourcing refers to organizations who subcontract information systems work to independent outside sources whose personnel are full-time information systems specialists.

The Internet is the prototype of the global information infrastructure. Managers today and in the future must be prepared for electronic commerce and the effect on business practices and strategy. The Internet is a collection of computer networks that interconnect computers all over the world. The Internet provides users the opportunity to do research, interact socially or undertake commercial transactions.

In the field of global telecommunications, many changes are taking place. There is an evolutionary shift from basic to enhanced services; from analog to digital networks; from wireline to wireless equipment; from regulation to liberalization; and from monopolies to a wide array of competition. Telecommunications enhanced services include voice mail, E-mail, facsimile transmissions, data capture and storage, and online database access.

Review Questions

1. Why do you think organizations today desire managers and staff personnel who are computer literate?

2. Discuss the meaning of information overload.

3. Explain four things that make information useful.

4. Define MIS.

5. Elaborate on the difference between MIS and data processing.

6. Distinguish between Decision Support Systems (DSS) and Executive Information Systems (EIS).

7. What are the advantages to an organization when they get involved in outsourcing?

8. What is the Internet?

9. Discuss the purpose of using information services such as the World Wide Web (WWW) on the Internet.

10. Identify some enhanced services available in the telecommunications industry which benefit business organizations.

Assignments for Personal Development

1. Visit your campus' athletics office and record the type of information system its uses. If a computer is part of the system, list the purposes for which it is used. Can you think of some additional uses for the computer in an athletics program?

2. What precautions or safeguards can you list that any type of sport organization should initiate to prevent misuse of a computer-based information system? To prevent fraud or alteration of stored information?

Incident

SURFING THE NET

Three female employees from the ticket office of a national football league franchise had just left the office of the ticket manager. They complained to the manager that other employees in the department were using the Internet for purposes other than tracking ticket information and keeping records. Specifically, they complained that their male colleagues occasionally used the team's Internet account to watch sexually explicit material which is degrading to women. They threatened to file a sexual harassment charge with the nearest EEOC office if something was not done about this immediately. The manager realized something would have to be done right away.

Questions:

1. How is it possible that employees can surf the Internet using a corporate or organizational account? What kind of costs are involved?

2. What recommendations can you give the manager to control more effectively employees' use of the Internet?

Glossary of Key Terms

Data processing: The capture, processing and storage of data.

Decision Support Systems (DSS): A special kind of information system to support managerial decision-making when the problems are semistructured and specific decisions are required.

Executive Information Systems (EIS): Designed to meet special information processing needs of top managers; systems are user-friendly and require little skill to use.

Hardware: The physical components such as the computer, printer, monitor, keyboard etc.

Information Centers: Organizational locations where a skilled staff assist and train personnel who are not computer literate to access data and use available software.

Information overload: When managers have more information than they can digest.

Information Technology (IT): The computer and communications technology and its applications.

The Internet: A collection of computer networks that interconnect computers all over the world.

Management Information Systems (MIS): A computer-based network that integrates the collection, processing, storing and transmision of information.

Outsourcing: Occurs when an organization subcontracts independent outside sources to provide information systems work.

Programmers: People who write instructional programs that tell a computer what to do.

Software: Refers to the various programs which can run on the computer hardware; provides instructions to a computer to perform certain tasks.

System Analysts: People who investigate potential computer applications and determine the types of programs needed.

Telecommunications: The transmission of voice and data through the telephone, voice mail, E-mail, facsimile and such.

Useful information: Information that is accurate, timely, complete and relevant.

Practical Concepts in Management

Put It in Writing

One of the true pearls of wisdom in management today says, "Put things of importance in writing."

In this world of legal relief for virtually everything, it is essential to document in writing every event, reprimand, commendation, accident, etc. because organizations have many laws and legal regulations with which they must abide in the conduct of business. Nowhere is this more true than in the area of personnel, dealing with your employees, and when dealing with customers and clients.

With the advent of voice mail, E-mail, faxes and other advances in telecommunications, it may appear to be difficult to follow this advice. Think again; set up an information control program that makes a permanent record of important communication.

Principle of Simplicity

Despite the simplicity of it and the obviousness of it, this principle is one of the most important in organization. To a manager it means keep everything just as simple as possible. The value of simplicity cannot be overstressed.

For example, a manager should concentrate on the really important things when supervising people, not on trivia. Work processes should be streamlined around the essential activities. Red tape should be kept to a minimum. Employee talents should not be wasted. Control programs should be adequate but not excessive.

Unnecessary complexity in work activity is a waste of time, effort and money. It is your responsibility as a manager to pare activities continuously and operate just as efficiently as possible. Consider using the Internet for communications, research and a variety of other purposes. Costs of electronic mail are substantially less than the cost of paper mail. Streamline the organization in this age of electronic commerce.

References and Chapter Notes:

[1] Robert B. Cohen, "The Economic Impact of Information," *Business Economics*, October 1995, Vol. XXX, No. 4, p. 21.

[2] Charles A. O'Reilly, "Variations in Decision Makers Use of Information Sources: the Impact of Quality and Accessibility of Information." *Academy of Management Journal*, December 1982, pp. 756-771.

[3] James A. Senn, *Information Systems in Management*, 2nd ed. (Belmont, CA: Wadsworth, 1982), p. 83.

[4] Robert Kreitner, *Management*, 2nd ed. (Boston: Houghton Mifflin Company, 1983), p. 495.

[5] John J. Connell, "The Fallacy of Information Resource Management," *Infrosystems* 28 (May 1981), 81-82.

[6] "Using MIS Strategically," *Management Review*, April 1984, p. 5.

[7] Raymond McLeod, Jr., *Management Information Systems*, 4th ed. (New York: Macmillan, 1990), p. 340.

[8] Jeremy Main, "At Last, Software CEO's Can Use," *Fortune*, March 13, 1989, pp. 78-83.

[9] William Clarke, "How Managers with Little DP Know-How Learn to Go Online with the Company Database," *Management Review*, June, 1983, pp. 9-11.

[10] Ajit Kambil, "Electronic Commerce: Implications of the Internet for Business Practice and Strategy," *Business Economics*, October, 1995, Vol. XXX, No. 4, pp. 27-28.

[11] As reprinted in *The Atlanta Journal/Constitution*, October 1, 1995, p. R5.

[12] Andrew C. Gross, Edward D. Hester and Rajsnekhar G. Javalgi, "Global Telecommunications: The Market and the Industry," *Business Economics*, October 1995, Vo. XXX, no. 4, p. 55.

INDEX

Gilbreth, Frank 11, **190, 199, 231**
Gilbreth, Lillian **11**
Ginzberg, Eli **259**
Glaxo PLC **159**
Global Information Infrastructure **409**
Goal of motivation **278**
Gordon, William J. J. **191**
Gore, W. L. **233**
Graicunas, V. A. **217**
Graicunas' Theorem **218**
Grand or Corporate strategies **159**
Graphic Rating Scale **393**
Griehs, Leonard **64**
Group action **198**
Group Behavior **242**
Group cohesiveness **244**
Group conformity **244**
Group Decision-Making **188**
Group norms **244**

H

Hamilton, Ian **217**
Hardware **408**
Hawthorne Studies **202, 280, 301**
Henderson, Richard I. **387, 396**
Hersey **278, 300**
Herzberg, Frederick **284**
Higher Management
    Philosophy of **327**
House, Robert J. **307**
Human Relations Movement **280**
Human Resource Planning (HRP) **253**
Human Resources **257**
    Selection Process **259**
Hunger, J. David **159**

I

Illumination **190**
Immigration Reform and Control Act of 1986 **255**
Implementing **32**
    defined **277**
Implementing and control functions **199**
Incubation **190**
Independent contractor **100**
Ineffective communication **320**
Influence
    Sources of **300**
Informal organization **202**
Information Centers **409**
Information overload **406**
Information System Realities **409**

Information Technology (IT) **405**
Initiating Structure **304**
Injunctive Relief **92**
Innovation **189**
Interdepartmental conflict **345**
Intergroup conflict **345**
Internal Constraints **51**
Internet **332, 409**
Intrinsic rewards **398**
Intuition
    defined **185**
Intuitive Approach **185**
Invasion of privacy **103**

J

Jefferson, Thomas **199**
Job
    analysis **234**
    description **234, 391**
    engineering **231**
    enlargement **290**
    enrichment **232, 290**
    Performance **290**
    rotation **231, 290**
    Satisfaction **290**
    specification **234**
Job Depth **229**
Job Design
    defined **228**
    Economic Restrictions **230**
    Enlargement **232**
    Implementing **233**
    Organization Philosophy **230**
    role clarity **234**
    Sociotechnical Approach **232**
    Time and Motion Analysis **231**
    Types of Employees **229**
    Union Limitations **230**
Job Scope **229**
Judicial Review **90**

K

Kanouse **264**
Kennedy, John F. **63**
Kersey, D. M. **320**
Kossen, Stan **278**

L

Labor Law **116**
Labor-Management Relations Act of 1947 (Taft-Hartley Act) **254**
Lao-tsu **299**